THE FORT LANGLEY JOURNALS,
1827-30

Chief Factor John McLoughlin
Though he had serious reservations about the suitability of the Fraser
as a transport route from New Caledonia, Chief Factor John McLoughlin
obeyed orders and sent the expedition to found Fort Langley.

EDITED BY MORAG MACLACHLAN

THE FORT LANGLEY JOURNALS, 1827-30

WITH CONTRIBUTIONS BY WAYNE SUTTLES

UBC PRESS / VANCOUVER

Printed in Canada on acid-free paper ∞

ISBN 0-7748-0665-6 (paperback)

Canadian Cataloguing in Publication Data

Main entry under title:
The Fort Langley journals, 1827-30

(The pioneers of British Columbia, ISSN 0847-0537)
Includes bibliographical references and index.
ISBN 0-7748-0664-8 (bound); ISBN 0-7748-0665-6 (pbk.)

1. Fur traders – British Columbia – Fort Langley – Diaries. 2. Fur trade –
British Columbia – Fort Langley – History. 3. Langley (B.C.) – History.
4. Hudson's Bay Company – History. I. Maclachlan, Morag. II. Suttles, Wayne,
1918- III. Series.

FC3849.F64A23 1998   971.1'33   C98-910406-0
F1089.5.F64F64 1998

This book was published with the generous support of
the Vancouver Historical Society.

UBC Press gratefully acknowledges the ongoing support
to its publishing program from the Canada Council for the Arts,
the British Columbia Arts Council,
and the Department of Canadian Heritage of the Government of Canada.

Set in Palatino by Artegraphica Design Co.
Printed and bound in Canada by Friesens
Copy editor: John Eerkes
Proofreader: Edward Wagstaff
Indexer: Danielle Bugeaud
Cartographers: Eric Leinberger, Cameron Suttles

UBC Press
University of British Columbia
2029 West Mall
Vancouver, BC V6T 1Z2
(604) 822-5959
Fax: (604) 822-6083
E-mail: info@ubcpress.ubc.ca
www.ubcpress.ubc.ca

CONTENTS

ILLUSTRATIONS AND MAPS

ILLUSTRATIONS

MAPS

Acknowledgments

The Leon and Thea Koerner Foundation provided a grant to facilitate research on this project. My sense of indebtedness has helped me persist in seeing the project completed in spite of setbacks and delays. I am also grateful for the support of the Vancouver Historical Society.

I wish to thank Randy Bouchard and Dorothy Kennedy for providing a number of leads, and Jamie Morton for reading the manuscript and making several useful suggestions.

I have been fortunate to meet family members of the three fur trade journal keepers, all of whom have provided information, shown great interest, and in the process have become friends. Meg Dunlop Johns is a great-granddaughter of George and Helen (Matthews) Barnston, Hugh MacMillan is a direct descendant of James McMillan's uncle and the MacMillan family chronicler, and Jean Murray Cole is a great-great-granddaughter of Archibald and Jane (Klyne) McDonald, and biographer of Archibald whose love of writing she obviously shares.

I wish to thank the helpful people in Special Collections at the University of British Columbia, the British Columbia Archives, the Provincial Archives of Ontario, the National Archives of Canada, and a special thanks for the help received at the Hudson's Bay Company Archives.

Last but not least, my thanks to Wayne Suttles, whose participation in this project went far beyond his discussion of the ethnographic significance of the journals. His interest, his helpful suggestions, and his pertinent questions have all made a significant contribution to the publication of these documents.

Morag Maclachlan

THE FORT LANGLEY JOURNALS, 1827-30

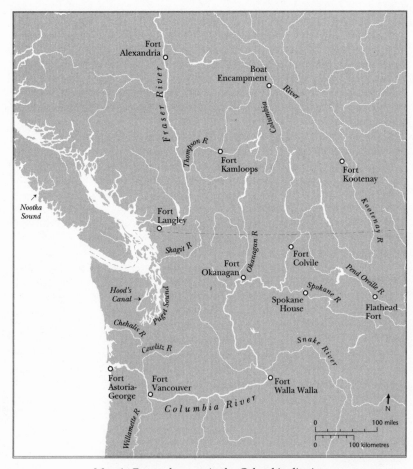

Map 1. Fur trade posts in the Columbia district

Introduction

The Establishment of Fort Langley

The first Europeans to exploit the fur resources of North America's north Pacific coast were the Russians, who extended their land empire to the area. When the Spanish became aware of Russian activity in territory they claimed as their own, expeditions were sent as far north as the Queen Charlotte Islands in 1774 and 1775. The British exploratory and scientific expedition led by Captain James Cook entered the area in 1778, laid the basis for challenging Spain's claim to sovereignty, and carried back news of the rich furs on the Pacific coast and the ready market for pelts in Canton.

Among the traders lured to the coast in search of sea otter pelts was Charles Barkley, who discovered Juan de Fuca Strait in 1787. Further exploration of the inland sea was begun in 1790 by Manuel Quimper and continued in 1791 by Francisco Eliza. Meanwhile, the Spanish seizure of British ships at Nootka Sound precipitated a crisis and, in order to avoid war, the Spanish were forced to sign the Nootka Convention of 1790, which revoked their claim to sole trading rights in the area.

An expedition led by Captain George Vancouver was sent to confirm the British rights gained and to chart the north Pacific coast. Immediately on his arrival in 1792, he began exploring the inland sea, which he named the Gulf of Georgia in honour of his king. When he met Cayetano Valdés and Dionisio Alcalá-Galiano, who were completing the Spanish survey that year, he invited them to join forces. His negotiations over the treaty with Juan Francisco de la Bodega y Quadra were equally amiable. In spite of this knowledge of the inland waters, most ships traded along the outer coast, and there are no records of ships entering Juan de Fuca Strait for more than thirty years.[1]

British imperial policy was implemented here, as in other parts of the vast empire, by granting exclusive trading rights to selected agents. It was Americans, very recently freed from this mercantile system, who quickly dominated the maritime fur trade. Ships, mainly from Boston, carried trading goods around Cape Horn to the north Pacific to be traded for furs, which were sold in Canton. Goods from the Orient were carried back to New England.

The land-based fur trade reached the Pacific in 1793 with the expedition led by Alexander Mackenzie. He represented the North West Company, an amalgamation of smaller trading ventures that sprang up after the British conquest of New France. Using access to British markets, employing skilled Canadien voyageurs, and taking advantage of routes established by the French, these aggressive entrepreneurs, once united, became a serious rival to the Hudson's Bay Company, which had been established in 1670 and granted a huge area of North America by Charles II of England.

More than a decade passed before the North West Company took advantage of Mackenzie's exploration by establishing posts in New Caledonia – a rich source of furs. Between 1805 and 1808 Simon Fraser established a post at Rocky Mountain Portage, and bases which became Fort McLeod, Fort St. James, Fort Fraser, and Fort George. In 1808, having assumed that Mackenzie had been on the upper reaches of the Columbia, Fraser travelled to the sea only to discover that he had reached the mouth of the river later named after him.

The first overland expedition to reach the mouth of the Columbia was led by Americans – Meriwether Lewis and William Clark – following the Louisiana purchase of 1803. This opened the way for the establishment of John Jacob Astor's Pacific Fur Company, organized to take advantage of the furs and the Canton market. Astor drew heavily on former personnel of the North West Company to man his expeditions. His ship, the *Tonquin,* arrived at the mouth of the Columbia in 1811, and Fort Astoria was founded while an overland expedition followed the land route pioneered by Lewis and Clark. When David Thompson completed his exploration of the Columbia for the North West Company, he arrived at the mouth shortly after Fort Astoria had been established.

The North West Company faced enormous problems with the extension of their fur trade empire west of the Rockies. Though it had pioneered the exploration of the Pacific Slope, it did not gain official recognition from the British government and failed to gain access to the Canton market, to which the East India Company had been granted exclusive trading rights. The supply line from the Montreal headquarters was too long, and overtures to use the Hudson's Bay Company route were rebuffed.

Astor was also beginning to have difficulties with the long supply line, but during the War of 1812, his interests were sold to the North West Company by the men in charge of the posts (former Nor'Westers). This move gave the Canadian company a firmer hold on the Pacific slope, but intense competition over a dwindling supply of furs east of the Rockies and the unresolved problems on the Pacific forced the North West Company into union with the Hudson's Bay Company in 1821. In 1818 the boundary between the United States and British North America was accepted as the 49th parallel from Lake Superior to the Rockies, but on the western slope the area between 54° 40' N. latitude, the boundary of Russian control, and 42° N., the limit of Spanish territory, was to be held in joint occupancy for ten years. The British government granted exclusive British trading rights to the Hudson's Bay Company. Boston traders continued to dominate the maritime trade, but few American settlers arrived overland until the 1840s, and the boundary was not settled until 1846.

George Simpson, made governor of the Northern Department of the Hudson's Bay Company in 1821,[2] immediately began implementing policies designed to increase efficiency and to deal with Russian and American competition. Inventories made at the various forts after the union of the companies revealed a heavy dependence on imports and an extravagance that appalled Simpson. Under Governor Simpson, living was to become much plainer and the posts made more self-sufficient. Some

Governor George Simpson.
Simpson has been described by biographers as very energetic and innovative, as a man who simply followed orders, as cold and harsh, and as a "man of feeling."

employees of the Hudson's Bay Company were sent to the Pacific and many of the most useful of the North West Company men were retained, but the workforce was drastically reduced.

Both companies had constantly attempted to inhibit settlement in fur country. It had been customary to return employees leaving the service to the place they had signed their contract. This continued to be the policy on the Pacific coast throughout the 1820s, but it could be applied only to those hired elsewhere. Those who were not retained and who chose to stay in the country were considered a threat to the trade. In order to direct their activities in the best interests of the company, trapping expeditions were organized under the command of a company officer. The free men who joined were equipped and guaranteed a market for their furs.

These expeditions fanned out into the Snake River Valley and as far south as the California boundary, which, on occasion, they crossed. This policy of creating a "fur desert" far from the best fur country would, it was hoped, discourage American traders arriving overland and thus delay settlement. The delay that occurred, however, probably had as much to do with the difficulties experienced by American traders as with Hudson's Bay Company strategy. But the annual expeditions continued to use free men for a number of years, and the furs purchased from them added to the company's profits and maintained a British presence.

Company control of the north Pacific coast became more effective in 1824 with the arrival of Chief Factor John McLoughlin,[3] a former partner in the North West Company who had been put in charge of the districts of New Caledonia and Columbia. A second expedition, led by George Simpson, set out from York Factory and caught up to the first party. On 8 November both parties reached Fort George, the post at the mouth of the Columbia founded as Astoria and renamed by the North West Company. Convinced that the Columbia River, the most southerly boundary they could hope for, would probably be lost, the governor and council of the Hudson's Bay Company were interested in establishing a headquarters north of the 49th parallel to link New Caledonia, the source of the best furs, with the Pacific. Almost immediately, Simpson sent an expedition to the lower Fraser to assess it for that purpose.

The North West Company had made few contacts with the coastal Native peoples to the north, using the Chinook at the mouth of the Columbia as intermediaries in the trade. Many stories were told of ferocious northern tribes, and their destruction of the *Tonquin*[4] in 1811 was a memory that refused to die. During the tenure of the North West Company the Cowlitz people had been savagely attacked to avenge the death of an Iroquois[5] trapper, and no reconciliation had been effected (Spaulding 1956:129-30; Merk 1968:113). Safe transport on the Cowlitz River was desirable for communication between the Columbia and the lower Fraser.

A large party consisting mostly of experienced people was sent on this hazardous venture. James McMillan,[6] the leader, was supported by Michel Laframboise[7] as interpreter and three clerks – Thomas McKay,[8] John Work,[9] and Francis Annance.[10] Of the thirty-six men sent, there were nine Iroquois, three Hawaiians,[11] two Abenaki, twenty Canadiens, one American, and one Englishman. Some were free men whose names appear on lists of those engaged in the Snake River expeditions. The party left in three boats[12] and travelled up the coast to the mouth of the Chehalis, which they followed to its junction with the Black River. Because of his skill as a hunter, Pierre Charles,[13] who was living with Chehalis Natives, was persuaded to join the party. Eight miles up the Black River they began the portage to Puget Sound. They went through the sound, and assisted by Snohomish guides, travelled up the Nicomekl River, then portaged to the Salmon River, which took them to the Fraser. They went upstream as far as Hatzic Slough and then followed the river west to its mouth. McKay and Annance returned the way they had come, but McMillan and Work ventured home through the Cowlitz Valley and returned to Fort George safely. All the clerks made maps and kept journals of the expedition.[14]

McMillan reported that the Natives described the upper part of the Fraser as far as Kamloops navigable but with a strong current (McMillan 1824; Merk 1968:248-9). Simpson, initially cautious about making a final decision to establish a headquarters on the Fraser, seized on this information. After arriving at Fort George he had heard that the area drained by the Fraser had a dense, friendly population, fertile soil, a salubrious climate, and rich resources of fish and animals. "In regard to the navigation it is sufficient to say," he wrote, "that those Gentlemen [Fraser and Stuart] went down and returned safe" (Merk 1968:74-5). Proveau, one of the men with McMillan, had been on the famous voyage of 1808. Simpson's cavalier attitude toward danger and the proverbial bravado of the voyageur may explain Simpson's failure to obtain from Proveau the graphic description the Fraser Canyon deserves. Simpson recommended that a headquarters should be established on the lower Fraser to which New Caledonia furs would be sent using the river for transport. The overland route between Fort Alexandria and Kamloops would be abandoned, eliminating the necessity for pack horses.

During the winter of 1824-5 the decision was made to establish a fort on the north bank of the Columbia, ninety miles upstream, where farming operations could reduce dependence on food imports. Eventually food production at various forts provided surpluses for export and for concluding an advantageous treaty with the Russian American Fur Company. By mid-March, the new post was completed and the move made. Alexander McKenzie[15] was left at Fort George with a small group of men, and the transfer of all the property was completed by June. On his way east, Simpson named the new post Fort Vancouver "to identify our claim to the Soil and Trade with his [Vancouver's] discovery of the River and Coast on behalf of Gt. Britain" (Merk 1968:124). McMillan accompanied Simpson east, winning the governor's approval for his ability to maintain the maniacal pace set by his superior. During a stop at the Okanagan post, Simpson had a long interview with the principal chief of the Thompson's River whom he

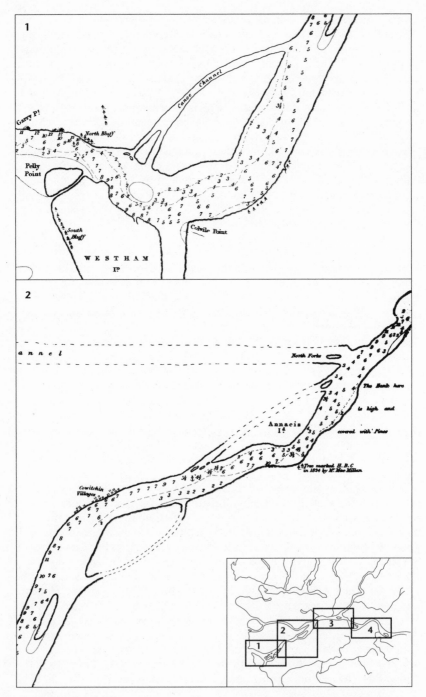

Map 2. Captain Aemilius Simpson's chart (adapted by Eric Leinberger)

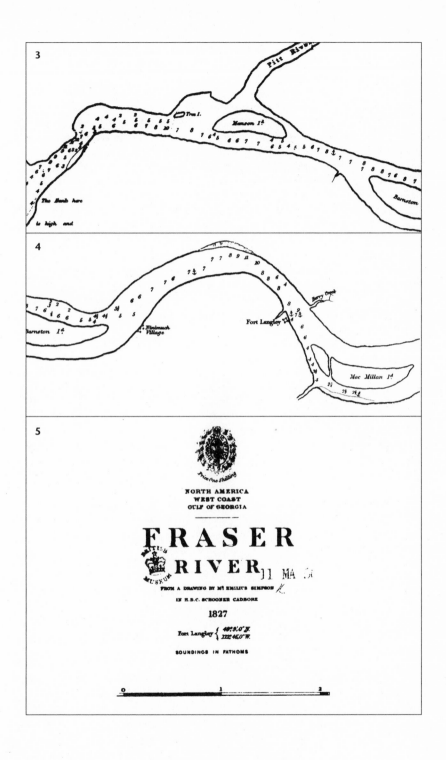

3

Pitt River

Tree I.

Manson I.d

The Bank here

to high and

Barnston

4

Barnston I.d

Ninimuch Village

Berry Creek

Fort Langley

Mac Millan I.d

5

NORTH AMERICA
WEST COAST
GULF OF GEORGIA

—

FRASER
RIVER

Price One Shilling

FROM A DRAWING BY M.R EMILIUS SIMPSON

IN H.B.C. SCHOONER CADBORO

1827

Fort Langley { 49°9.0" N.
122° 46.0" W.

SOUNDINGS IN FATHOMS

0   1   2

described as "the most respectable manly looking Indian I ever saw." He felt that the friendship established would do much to ensure the future good conduct of the Indians (Merk 1968:124).

A three-hour stop was made at Fort Carlton, where John Stuart was in charge. He had been with Fraser in 1808, had spent years in New Caledonia, and was one of those who pioneered the brigade route between New Caledonia and the Columbia through Kamloops. Stuart encouraged the establishment of a fort on the lower Fraser, obviously downplaying the treachery of the Fraser Canyon. Simpson appears to have had some doubts. In a report to Addington on 5 January 1826, he gave a vivid description of the rapids and falls, which rendered the river "nearly impassable" (Merk 1968:265). Nevertheless, the committee ordered that the post be built (Merk 1968:267), and Simpson relayed instructions, apparently dismissing his doubts. McMillan took charge of Fort Assiniboine on the Athabasca River and from there explored the Yellowhead Pass looking for a route to the headwaters of the Fraser. Francis Annance went to the Okanagan post for the summer, but John McLoughlin sent a replacement and moved him to Fort Vancouver where, as he said, "he would assist us from his knowledge of the Country hereabouts more than any other that could be sent" (Rich 1941:304).

In the summer of 1825 the brig *William and Ann*,[16] under the command of Captain Henry Hanwell, was sent north from Fort Vancouver to obtain information about the coast. McLoughlin sent Alexander McKenzie to trade with the Natives. McKenzie kept a journal[17] in which he voiced his frustration that Hanwell appeared "to be Much alarmed No less with the Coast than its inhabitants." The voyage was considered a failure because so little information was obtained as a result of Hanwell's reluctance to go into harbours or to anchor close to Native villages. The brig went as far north as Observatory Inlet, and on its return entered Juan de Fuca Strait. During the passage from Cape Flattery to the mouth of the Fraser River, it encountered many of the Natives who were later to trade at Fort Langley. McKenzie promised each group that traders would return the next year.

At Clallam Bay the ship was surrounded by more than a hundred Natives. The Clallam chief, Lochquelum, was away, but his son, Auicactin,[18] described by McKenzie as "a fine looking Indian," attempted to have the vessel approach the village. Hanwell, as usual, refused, but trade was carried on, and McKenzie had an opportunity to note goods among the Clallam that had been obtained from Chief Tla-Kow-ak of Chee-hee-lees (Chehalis) or Whitby Harbour (Gray's Harbour) and Scanewah,[19] the Cowlitz chief, both of whom had been regular traders at Fort George. The Clallam tried very hard to prevent the vessel from continuing to the Fraser River to visit their enemies the Cowichan and "Yokletas" (Lekwiltok) whom, according to McKenzie, "they painted in the blackest colours."

Near New Dungeness, more Clallam were encountered. They were led by Squastin, "a chief of as great authority as any we saw in the Straits," wrote McKenzie. Here the trade was even brisker, showing that the Native peoples had little communication with the trading vessels along the coast.

McKenzie met several Natives who had "a perfect recollection of Vancouver's voyage," and he surmised that no vessel had come this far since. A Native with whom McKenzie could converse visited and discussed the expedition of the winter before. He declared that the party had reached, not the Cowichan, but the Quotlin (Kwantlen) River. McKenzie subsequently discovered that both names applied to the river the traders called Fraser's. The ship remained near New Dungeness for three days. Squastin supplied the visitors with an abundance of fish and berries and proposed to bestow his thirteen-year-old daughter on either Hanwell or McKenzie. The offer was tactfully refused.

Just past Protection Island, a Snohomish chief called Waskelatchee[20] by McKenzie, came aboard and agreed to travel with McKenzie as interpreter. At Lummi Island, Chief Sawhaomcan and a number of his people welcomed the visitors and brought skins to trade. He also exhibited animosity toward the Cowichans and Lekwiltok.

While anchored near a Saanich village at Point Roberts, a number of Natives approached with great caution. Among those in the first canoe was a man dressed in the red stroud, capote, and wool hat presented to the Kwantlen chief by McMillan the previous winter.[21] He refused to come aboard until he was reassured by Waskelatchee, with whom he was obviously well acquainted. There was little evidence of European goods among the Natives, most of whom wore dog's-hair blankets.[22]

When the ship was within seven or eight miles of the entrance to the Fraser River, a party of Cowichan came alongside. In describing their chief, McKenzie stated, "This Indian had Certainly the appearance of a Chief and his manly Countenance Would Command respect any where, his name is Chaseaw. As usual with all Indians who have little intercourse with the Whites this one Showed a good deal of diffidence and required No small Solicitation to Entice him on board."[23]

Waskelatchee became uneasy and disappeared, but McKenzie insisted that he play his part as interpreter. Soon the two Natives were on friendly terms. The next day Chaseaw cemented his relations with the visitors by informing them of a plot to attack the vessel and massacre everyone on board. For averting this plan and disclosing it, he was rewarded with a hawkbell, a dozen rings, half a pint of applejack, and a promise of future visits and trade.

A search began for the best channel, and boat crews were sent to sound the waters. When, after several tries, they located the south arm, Hanwell refused to enter it. McKenzie was chagrined because he had promised Chaseaw that the ship would visit his summer village, which was close to the entrance. McKenzie wrote a hasty message addressed to the chief factors, traders, and clerks of the Hudson's Bay Company announcing that the *William and Ann* was at the entrance to the Fraser River on its return from the north, and at the insistence of Captain Hanwell, he reported that a channel had been found to enter the river. This letter was entrusted to Chaseaw to be sent to the Columbia through the interior. He was also supplied with a "Certificate of his Character." The Natives at the mouth of the

Fraser were promised not only that the traders would return, but that a trading post would be built on their lands.

The *William and Ann* prepared to return to Fort Vancouver. Among a number of Saanich Indians alongside was Chief Whotleakenum, who, McKenzie was told, had been presented with a chief's clothing by the McMillan party though he did not have the outfit with him.[24] McKenzie described him as "a good Natured old man." He gave Whotleakenum a note that described him and was intended as a letter of introduction to any of the Hudson's Bay Company people. Whotleakenum wished to be considered distinct from the Cowichan, who, he said, "had no business with the Quotlin River."[25] On its return through Juan de Fuca Strait, the ship stopped at Lummi Island, where the Natives were preparing to abandon the site. Waskelatchee, after being rewarded for his services, was returned to his relations. No stop was made at New Dungeness, but a few Natives came alongside the ship. Among them was one of the Nitinaht chiefs who had not appeared before. The vessel continued to the mouth of the Columbia River and had with no further contact with Natives.

The Snake River expedition of 1825, led by Peter Skene Ogden, had difficulties because many of his men deserted, selling their furs to an American trader. This led to the realization that the free traders were not being fairly compensated. These desertions and the fact that the supplies did not arrive in 1826 made it impossible for McLoughlin to make up a party for the Fraser expedition that year as planned. He was still not convinced that the project was feasible. The men had a "Dread of Frasers River," and he feared they might desert, particularly those who had families (Rich 1941:32).

Archibald McDonald took charge of Kamloops very early in 1826. William Connolly instructed him to explore the Thompson River to its junction with the Fraser and sent James Yale to travel the Fraser from Fort Alexandria to Kamloops. As a result of their reports McLoughlin concluded that the Fraser was not navigable with loaded boats (McLouglin 1827:51d).

In the fall of 1826, McKenzie was sent on a trading excursion to Puget Sound and proceeded from there to the Fraser River (McLoughlin 1827:53d). No account of this expedition has survived, but it seems reasonable to assume that he contacted and traded with the Natives he had met on the 1825 voyage.

By the summer of 1827, McLoughlin had assembled a party to establish Fort Langley. He intended to send the 161-ton brig *William and Ann* to carry supplies and to protect and assist the founding expedition, but Captain Hanwell refused to comply (McLouglin 1827:51d). The *Cadboro*, a 70-ton schooner built at Rye, England, in 1826, was sent instead though it was feared it ran the risk of being boarded by the large Native canoes (Rich 1939:84). It was under the command of Lieutenant Aemilius Simpson[26] (later promoted to captain), one of the only naval officers on whom McLoughlin could depend.

The Fort Langley Journals reveal much about the decade of the 1820s. American maritime traders were beginning to look for new areas to exploit; the "Boston ships" were a formidable opposition mainly because of the difficulties that faced the British traders. Most of the captains hired by the Hudson's Bay Company were incompetent or had problems with alcohol abuse, and McLoughlin's frustration was intensified because they defied his jurisdiction.[27] The company policy of sending supplies sufficient for only one year, compounded by numerous shipwrecks, left the traders unable to meet the competition adequately.

This was a period of transition from North West Company to Hudson's Bay Company control, and tension remained between some of the employees who had formerly competed so bitterly.[28] The differences between the first two men in charge of Fort Langley reflect some of the changes that affected the lives of many people. James McMillan, a "Caesar of the Wilderness," was well suited to lead an expedition into unknown and potentially hostile country, and to establish and maintain a post where his small company was vastly outnumbered. Archibald McDonald understood the importance of widening the company's economic base and possessed the skills to manage a post where food production became an important part of the operation. The structured society became even more structured and authoritarian, and the number of levels increased as different skills were required. Interpreters, guides, and *bouts* (bowsmen and steersmen) had always outranked the *milieux* (middlemen or paddlers), but now many who had been valued for their skills as canoeists became common labourers at reduced rates of pay, and the need for tradesmen put pressure on some to perform in unfamiliar capacities.

A measure of the change is evident in the fact that, while McMillan was in charge, the men were referred to by name. McDonald, however, began to record the activities of the carpenter, the blacksmith, and the cooper, and he was frequently frustrated by their lack of skill. The usual pay rate for *milieux* had been £17 per annum with food and clothes supplied, which continued to be the basic rate for labourers, with increases for those with special skills. The gradation depended not only on specialized skills, but also on race. Simpson planned to bring in more Sandwich Islanders, who could be paid less than other servants,[29] and gradually Natives were hired to unload cargo and perform other menial tasks. The Canadiens, who made up the majority in the workforce, could not expect to become officers. Few were educated, and the ability to read and write was considered a minimum requirement for a clerk. Michel Laframboise, an invaluable servant, was not allowed clerk status but was kept at £40 a year as interpreter.[30] The office of postmaster was usually the highest level most Canadiens and certainly any mixed-blood men could achieve.

Partners in the North West Company had made fortunes. Hudson's Bay Company officers had been employees, but after amalgamation 40 percent of company shares were reserved for officers,[31] referred to as "gentlemen," as distinct from the "men" or the "people" who made up the bulk of the workforce. Those who aspired to commissions began their service as clerks at pay that ranged from £50 to £100 per annum. The union of the two companies and the decline of the fur trade created a surplus workforce at all levels. During this period of retrenchment the ambitious, educated young men who had joined the company as clerks[32] found advancement discouragingly slow and the amassing of wealth impossible. Life in fur trade country was hard. The main hope for a comfortable retirement was to obtain promotion.[33] Simpson commented on the problem of having so many "Young Gentlemen of higher expectations who can never be provided for by shares in the concern and to whom the business cannot afford such Salys [salaries] as their qualifications and respectability might appear to entitle them and who consequently become dissatisfied and disaffected."[34]

Qualifications included physical endurance, the ability to lead men and deal with Natives, and managerial skills. Undoubtedly the clerks who achieved promotion had these qualities, but the proviso that "respectability" was a requirement indicates that a rigid social system was being strengthened and fiercely maintained in fur trade country. Many of the men had disadvantages of birth that were handicaps at home, but on the fur frontier simply being British became an important requisite for promotion. A 1696 act of the Scottish parliament ordering a school in every parish, although never fully implemented, resulted in Scotland having more schools and better educational standards than any other European country. This system gave a decided advantage to the many young Scotsmen who sought to enter the trade. Even in parts of the Highlands where school standards were low, Gaelic-speaking children learned to read and write English, a necessity for employment with the Hudson's Bay Company.

An employee such as Francis Annance, however, found that a white man's education did not bring him the privileges he desired. The Native strain in his mixed blood prevented him from rising above the role of Indian trader[35] or postmaster. Such prejudices were not confined to those in command. The insistence of the men that Sandwich Islanders be paid less than *milieux*, and the jealousy of Thomas Dears and Francis Ermatinger over Alexander Roderick McLeod's dependence on Michel Laframboise on the expedition against the Clallam, indicate that these values were endemic in fur trade society after the amalgamation of the companies.

Before amalgamation, many men in both fur trade companies had formed alliances with Indian women according to "the custom of the country." Some of these marriages were permanent, and the men, particularly Hudson's Bay Company men, retired with their country families to the Red River settlement. Others arranged for another man to take over their responsibilities. Some women returned to their Native families, but for most this was impossible. Inevitably there were husbandless women and fatherless children dependent on the fort.

For Governor Simpson, this was an expensive burden on the trade. In 1824 a regulation stated

That no Officer or Servant in the company's service be hereafter allowed to take a woman without binding himself down to such reasonable provision for the maintenance of the women and children as on a fair and equitable principle may be considered necessary not only during their residence in the country but after their departure hence – and that

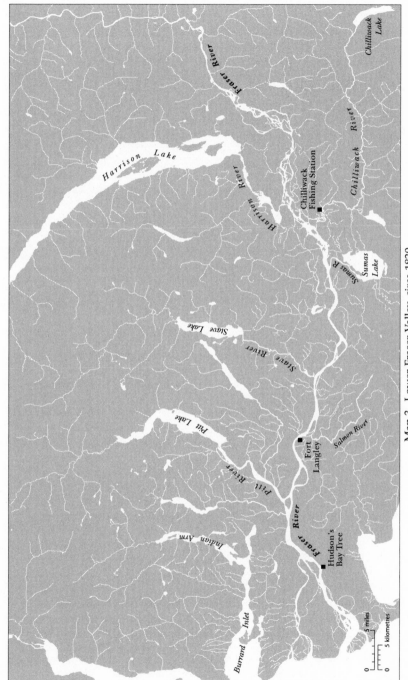

Map 3. Lower Fraser Valley, circa 1830

all those whose engagements expire and who retire from the service leaving children in the country be required to make such provision for the same as circumstances call for and their means permit.[36]

The regulation was reiterated and strengthened at the council meeting at York Factory in 1828, which Archibald McDonald attended, and this probably explains the firm control he took in arranging marriages. By permitting single men to take wives, he was clearly identifying the person responsible for their support. According to James McMillan, most of the men were unhappy at Fort Langley and wished to leave. By providing them with family ties and with "good cheer" at the year's end, McDonald was able to persuade them all to renew their contracts. Though marriage with Native women was discouraged at this time in order to provide husbands for the mixed-blood daughters of traders, McDonald bent this rule because no such girls were available at Fort Langley. He used these unions to build his trading network, a strategy easier to implement because it was customary for the Coast Salish to create alliances by arranging marriages between villages (see Suttles 1963:513-4).

During this transition period, some of the highest-ranking men in the company began to look for white brides. McMillan, the old Nor'Wester, had more than one fur trade family, but while on furlough in 1829-30 he married a Scottish woman, Eleanor McKinley. In doing so he was following a trend established by Governor Simpson and Chief Factor John George McTavish, who also found white brides that year. As a Nor'Wester, McMillan expected to achieve prosperity. Promoted to a position as superintendent of the agricultural operation at Red River, he chose a partner he considered suitable to his new position. Ironically he came to dislike intensely the mean-spirited, gossipy society, with its growing prejudice against mixed-blood families that evolved there with the introduction of white women.[37]

Archibald McDonald, who joined the fur trade much later, was still working hard to impress his employers and gain promotion. His life was more settled than McMillan's had been, and, in overseeing trade and farming operations, his very capable wife was of great assistance. Jane Klyne had only one Native grandparent, a fact that probably made the transition to a more settled life at Fort Colvile and retirement at St. Andrew's, Lower Canada, much easier than it would have been for most fur trade wives.

There appears to have been a sense of camaraderie between James McMillan and the men that is less evident under McDonald, whose management style ranged from heavy-handed authoritarianism to the implementation of schemes to keep the men content. As well as controlling their relations with local women, McDonald controlled the women, who, once admitted to the fort, were considered "property," and, on occasion, became part of the workforce. Liquor was strictly controlled and used as a bribe or reward. Company policy, when adhered to, maintained a peaceful though dull society, best suited to the business of maximizing profits.

It is ironic that these changes, which produced a more highly structured and authoritarian society, should occur at a time when the intrusion of the settlement frontier into fur country was imminent. The large numbers of American settlers, with their egalitarian ideas and concepts of self-government, did not arrive for over a decade, but the first farms were established in the Willamette Valley in 1829, and John McLoughlin had to deal with the incursion of American traders arriving overland. His manner of doing so led to conflicts with Governor Simpson which, though in part personal disputes, were essentially differences between a chief factor making pragmatic decisions on a frontier to which Americans had equal access and a governor dictating policy from headquarters.[38]

Because fur traders were necessarily dependent on the Native peoples, relations with the Natives were much less hostile than those on a settlement frontier. It has been argued that during the fur trade period the Natives remained in control of their culture and of the trade.[39] There is considerable evidence in the journals that good relations with the Native peoples was of paramount importance to the traders, but there is also evidence that white dominance was rapidly and firmly established.

The futile efforts of the Clallam and the Cowlitz to prevent the establishment of Fort Langley, and McLoughlin's insistence that Scanewah trade at Fort Langley are clear indications that the white man was in control. In 1827, the men at Fort Langley were dependent on the Natives for a food supply of fish; by 1830, the fish stock was being exploited for export and Natives were being introduced into the workforce at the lowest level.

The traders' lack of understanding of Coast Salish social structure must have created considerable strain between the cultures. Their assumption that control over the inhabitants could be maintained through a leader must surely have created problems for the person chosen and had the effect of distorting native society. Shashia, who, according to Alexander McKenzie, had never seen a white man until 1825, was courted by the traders and was able to trade to his own advantage. He worked to establish a good relationship with the people at the fort, and undoubtedly those links enabled him to build the large trading network that he eventually controlled. As the traders became more secure, however, his position became less influential. The deterioration of his name from Shashia, the Great Chief, to "Old Joe" reflects the changing attitude of the traders. McDonald's reaction to the disappearance of Maniso indicates that by 1830 Shashia had little reason to trust the fort people.

The culture clash can be seen in such incidents as the refusal of food to a Native who visited the fort and in McDonald's indignation that the daughter of the Kwantlen chief should present her father with a blanket when he arrived at the fort. In both cases the white man's values prevailed over Coast Salish custom.

Plans to use the Fraser River as a transport route were abandoned when Governor Simpson came down the river in 1828, but Fort Langley was maintained because of the rich salmon resource and the possibilities for agriculture. J.M. Yale was put in charge when McDonald left, and he continued there until he retired after the gold rush of 1858.

THE JOURNALS

The British Columbia Archives has in its holdings the Fort Langley Journal kept from 27 June 1827, when the founding party left Fort Vancouver to establish the new post, until 30 July 1830. Each year a copy of the journal entries was made and sent to headquarters with the spring express. The Hudson's Bay Company Archives in the Provincial Archives of Manitoba has the copies made by George Barnston for 1827-8, copies made by Archibald McDonald for 1828-9 and 1829-30, and a letter book containing an extract from a post journal covering the period from 27 August 1830 to October 1830. In this publication we have made use of all these sources – the original post journal, the annual copies, and the letter book – to record daily occurrences at Fort Langley in its earliest years.

There is no record in the BC Archives to explain how the post journal came to be there, but it appears to be the original. It is the standard Hudson's Bay Company issue with a marbled-paper cover, and the handwriting can be identified as that of Barnston, McMillan, and McDonald. Why did it survive, when so many Fort Langley documents were destroyed in the fire of 1840? In 1832, there were plans afoot to build Fort Nisqually as a replacement for Fort Langley. It may be that McDonald, who was asked to assess the site, took the completed post journal with him to Fort Vancouver. Fort Nisqually was established in 1833, but the decision to abandon Fort Langley was reversed. The journal was probably removed to Fort Victoria when it became the Pacific headquarters of the Hudson's Bay Company. We know that Hubert Bancroft thanked Chief Factor Charles of Fort Victoria for the copy that was given to him – a slightly abridged version of the original (Bancroft 1884:478). We also know from the post journal that the three annual copies were sent to Fort Vancouver. How or why they survived when others did not it is impossible even to guess, but they found a home in the Hudson's Bay Company Archives when it was started by R.H.G. Leveson-Gower in 1927.

Men in charge of a Hudson's Bay Company fur trade post were required to keep a daily journal or assign that responsibility to a clerk. They were to record the weather, the trading done, visitors to the fort, and the work accomplished by the men. Even though this chore was narrowly prescribed to the needs of the trade, the journals contain a great deal of valuable information. In terms of fur trade history, Fort Langley was not of great significance, but the contribution the journals make to our knowledge of local history, geography, and ethnology is substantial. We are grateful to the men who were responsible for preserving these documents, to the Hudson's Bay Company for establishing an archive and preserving its records, and to the British Columbia Archives for caring for the post journal.

In editing these journals, it has been necessary to deal differently with journals kept by three different men, but an effort has been made to remain as faithful as possible to the originals. Two general rules have been followed throughout. Obvious slips have been corrected without comment, and names have been retained as deciphered. {Braces} are used to indicate information contained in one journal but missing from the version being presented. Since there is an occasional use of (parentheses) in the journals, [brackets] are used to indicate editorial comment within the context of the journals. Where older and modern Native tribal names are markedly different, the modern term appears in [brackets] after the first occurrence, as do place names. Modern names for tribes are given in Appendix E. Materials in the Hudson's Bay Company Archives are numbered only on recto pages; verso pages carry the same number but with the addition of a "d." These folio numbers are used for page references in all HBCA material.

All the journal writers used capital letters freely and inconsistently. These have been largely retained, but less elaborate forms have been printed in lower case except when a capital letter is clearly required, and initial letters written in lower case are transcribed as such. The use of the possessive form for places named after people was in transition. McMillan retained the "s," but omitted the apostrophe, as did Barnston on occasion. McDonald retained the correct form for possessive adjectives but omitted apostrophes elsewhere. In all cases, apostrophes have been supplied where missing. Colons used for abbreviations have been replaced with periods in the McMillan and McDonald journals. Words and phrases originally underlined for emphasis in the journals are italicized in the printed journals, and the names of sailing vessels also are italicized. In punctuating their copy, all the writers adhered to the breath-pause theory of pointing in common use at the time.[40] This has been retained in their journals. The method of dating has been made consistent, following the pattern established by Barnston.

There is evidence in the journals that the writers were familiar with languages other than English. Barnston's spelling of Canadien names suggests that he was familiar with European French. He used the acute accent and the circumflex in writing French names, giving even Annance, who always signed himself Francis, the French version. Since the Canadiens, most of whom were illiterate, anglicized their names after settlement, it is only in the journal kept by Barnston for 1827-8 that the acute accent and the circumflex have been retained. Both McMillan and McDonald were Gaelic speakers. The highland lilt can be heard in their doubling of the "s" in words such as busy, positive, and position and in their difficulty with "d" and "t" as final consonants, a distinction not found in Gaelic.

JOURNAL KEPT BY
GEORGE BARNSTON, 1827-8

GEORGE BARNSTON

George Barnston, who kept this journal, was born in Edinburgh about 1800. He joined the North West Company in 1820 and was retained by the Hudson's Bay Company after the union. A.C. Anderson described him "as a man of great energy of character, of high education, and universally esteemed" (Anderson 1878:33). Probably because of his training as a surveyor and army engineer, Barnston was sent to the Columbia District to assist Aemilius Simpson with survey work on the Pacific coast. No doubt his skills were also useful in laying out the establishment at Fort Langley.

At the time of Barnston's death in Montreal in 1883, many tributes of love and respect were paid, not only to his fine character, but also to his work as a naturalist. During his twenty-year retirement, Barnston was an active member of the Natural History Society of Canada and served as its president in 1872–3. This interest had been roused when he set off as a clerk with the Fort Langley expedition. He arrived at Fort Vancouver in 1826 and during the winter made friends with David Douglas, the renowned Scottish botanist, who was on the first of his two exploratory trips to northwestern North America. Douglas travelled extensively throughout the Columbia District and along the Pacific coast. He spent the early part of 1827 consolidating his collection before leaving for Britain on 20 March 1827 (Davies 1980:16-7). Barnston began collecting insects and keeping records for the Royal Geographic Society of London and the Smithsonian Institution in Washington. He wrote many articles, among them a sketch of Douglas's travels. His eldest son, James, shared his interest and became a professor of botany at McGill University.

While at Fort Langley, Barnston went through a difficult period in his life. An intelligent man, better educated than most of his peers, he was so frustrated over low pay and lack of advancement that he became of "a gloomy disponding turn of mind," which Governor Simpson reported had led people to "have frequently been apprehensive that he would commit suicide in one of those fits" (HBCA A.34/2). Barnston was ill when he left Fort Langley and reached Fort Vancouver suffering "from the old complaint"

George Barnston
"A man of great energy of character, of high education
and universally esteemed."

(Work 1829). Within the next year he took as his wife Helen Matthews, the daughter of William Matthews, one of John Jacob Astor's men, and Kilakotah, the daughter of Coboway, a Clatsop chief.[1] In 1831 Barnston resigned as a result of a sharp dispute with Governor Simpson and travelled east to Montreal. He never returned to the Pacific slope, but the quarrel was made up and he rejoined the Hudson's Bay Company. His happy marriage and the large family of six sons and five daughters, constant sources of comfort and interest, were important factors in enabling George Barnston to reconcile himself to life in the fur trade.[2]

Barnston started the post journal, kept it until 17 February 1828, and made the copy presented in this volume. He had a clear hand, and though his writing did deteriorate over time, probably because of ill health, it was always legible. He made no substantial changes, merely polishing the rough copy, which contained few errors.

1827

Wednesday 27th June

Left Fort Vancouver in two Boats early in the morning, and encamped at ½ past 6 in the evening, 15 miles up the Cowlitz River.

Thursday 28th We were off, at Sunrise – passed the Forks Fork at 6 A. M. and arrived at the Cowlitz Portage at 2 P. M. – Mr Annance was immediately dispatched to find Horses, and returned in the evening with two: he says we will get more on the morrow

Friday 29th. After the two Horses were laden the men had still 80 lb each to carry. Halted to breakfast, close to the Tents of several Indians, and met Scanawa with Horses about One O'Clock near the Quinze Sous River. – Encamped soon afterwards that the men might have time to come up with their loads, and that we might settle with the Indians about the hire of their Horses

Saturday 30th Started before Sunrise – Breakfasted close to Scanawa's Tent, passed Vassals River at midday, and encamped near the north End of the Big Plain.

Sunday 1st July.. We were on the move at Sun[rise] Breakfasted beyond the last Hill on the [road] and got to Puget Sound about 2 P. M. [   ] arrived in the evening with his family.

Monday 2d The Indians not bringing Canoes in the morning as they had promised, Messrs Manson & Annance went to find them, and succeeded in [buying] One Canoe and bringing another along : with them which was also paid for at a reasonable rate. An Indian in the evening arrived with another which was purchased. This will enable us to [   ] in the morning, every thing else being ready

Page from the post journal in George Barnston's hand.

Journal of the Voyage of the party destined to form an Establishment at the Entrance of Fraser's River; and of their Proceedings and other Occurrences at Fort Langley, the whole commencing with the 27th June 1827 and carried up to the 16th February 1828.

The persons appointed twenty five in number[3] were

James MacMillan Esq.	in charge
Donald Manson	clerk[4]
François Noel Annance	Do
George Barnston	Do
Amable Arquoitte	Do
James Baker	Orkneyman
Louis Boisvert	Canadian
Oliver Bouchard	Do
Pierre Charles	Abenaquois Indian
Como	Sandwich Islander
Joseph Cornoyer	Canadian
Jean Bte. Dubois	Do
Jean Bte. Ettue	Do
Dominque Faron	Do
John Kennedy	Irishman
Anawiskum alias Macdonald	York Factory Indian
Peopeoh	Sandwich Islander
Antoine Pierrault	Canadian Half Breed
Jacques Pierrault	Canadian
François Piette dit Faniant	Canadian
Simon Plomondeau	Do
Louis Satakarata dit Rabaska	Iroquois
Laurent Sauvé dit Laplante	Canadian
François Xavier Tarihonga	Iroquois
Abraham Vincent	Canadian

[June 1827]

Wednesday 27th. Our Party left Fort Vancouver early in the morning in two Boats, and encamped at ½ past six in the evening, about 15 miles up the Cowlitz River.

Thursday 28th. We were on the water at Sunrise, passed the Toutle Fork at 6 A.M. and arrived at the Cowlitz Portage [near present site of Toledo, Washington] at 2 P.M. Mr. Annance was immediately dispatched to find Horses and returned in the evening with two: he says we will get more from the Indians on the morrow.[5]

Friday 29th. After the two Nags were laden, our men had each about 80 lbs.[6] weight of Luggage & Provisions still to carry. We halted to breakfast, close to the Tents of several Cowlitz Indians, and met Scanawa with Horses about One O'clock not far from the River Quinze Sous [Newaukum]. Soon afterwards we encamped that the People might have time to come up with their loads, and that we might settle with the Indians about the hire of their horses.[7]

Saturday 30th. We started before Sunrise, breakfasted near to Scanawa's Lodge, passed Vassal's River [Skookumchuck] at midday, and encamped within a short Distance of the North End of the Grande Prairie [Violet Prairie].

Sunday 1st July. At Sunrise we were on the move; we breakfasted beyond the last hill of any consequence in the Portage, and arrived at Puget Sound about 2 P.M. Scanawa with his family joined us in the evening.

Monday 2d. The Indians of the Sound not accommodating us with Canoes this morning as they had promised, Messrs. Manson & Annance went to their village, and contrived to purchase one, and fetch another to our Encampment, which was also paid for at a tolerably reasonable rate. In the evening an Indian arrived with a third, which he disposed of to us at the same price as the others. This will enable us to depart in the morning, every thing else being ready for us to pursue our voyage.

Tuesday 3d. As soon as the Tide permitted we embarked in three Canoes, one of which being very round and narrow, and likely to upset in rough weather, we put on shore at a few Indian Tents and exchanged it for another. Scanawa with his family kept in company with us all day, and encamped with us at night on the west side of the Sound opposite the South End of Vashan's Island.

Wednesday 4th. We embarked at Daybreak, at 7 A.M. reached Port Orchard, which had been agreed upon as the place of Rendezvous with the *Cadboro*. After having breakfasted and visited the Soquam [Suquamish] Village, the chief of which we honoured with a trifling present, we proceeded a little farther & encamped, Mount Baker appearing on a line with the entrance to Possession Bay. Here we intend to await the *Cadboro*. The Soquam chief came to our encampment and went away again in the evening. Scanawa is still in Company.

Thursday 5th. Mr. Annance this morning killed a Red Deer[elk], the meat of which was brought to the Camp; Pierre Charles & Rabaska also went out to hunt but returned unsuccessful. No appearance of the *Cadboro*, tho' she left Fort Vancouver on the 24th of last month.

Friday 6th. The old Soquam Chief with about 30 of his tribe paid us a visit, and brought the meat of four Chevreux[8] or small Deer which we purchased. Eight Sinahomes [Snohomish] were also at our Encampment. We were on the alert all day to prevent them from pilfering, and felt considerable relief when they withdrew in the evening.

Saturday 7th. Scanawa who appears uneasy in the vicinity of Soquams & Sinahomes went off early this morning with all his family. We followed and proceeded leisurely from 8 A.M. till midday, when we encamped opposite the South end of Whidbey Island, about three miles from the mouth of Hood's Canal. Pierre Charles was immediately sent off to hunt, and he returned in the course of a few hours, having succeeded in killing three Red Deer – a Doe and two young.

Sunday 8th. Eight men were dispatched to fetch the meat of the animals killed yesterday to the camp. They were back before 9 A.M. We traded some salmon from the natives for knives. The day passed very quietly, but still no *Cadboro*.

Monday 9th. We were visited by two Sinahomes chiefs Washkaladga & Sinoktin[9] who gave us some small Salmon. They were each presented with a few fine Beads, a little Tobacco, & a Looking Glass, and they then took their leave of us apparently well pleased with their entertainment. There is a Breeze from the North west, but it brings no Schooner.

Tuesday 10th. The Breeze still continues. Nothing particular occurred during the day,[10] but the wind fell with the ebb tide of the evening, and about 8 P.M. the Sound of a Great Gun was heard at our encampment, which we conclude of course to have been fired by the *Cadboro*.

Wednesday 11th. We set off with the ebb tide, and crossed to Whidbey Island, keeping down Admiralty Inlet. We heard another Gun very distinctly,[11] and soon afterwards descried the Schooner off Protection Island making straight for the Inlet. Mr. McMillan attended by Mr. Manson went on board, and she immediately came to an anchor not far from where the Land Party had put on Shore. Mr. McMillan slept on board, but the rest of us encamped not far from Point Partridge on Whidbey Island.

Thursday 12th. The Schooner's Boat was on shore early to take in water. Washkaladga & Sinoktin again came to our encampment, smoked a little and received a trifling present. After Breakfast we all embarked on board the *Cadboro*, and at 10 A.M. she weighed anchor and set sail, but as the wind failed at 2 P.M. and the flood tide began to set strongly in up the Inlet, it was with some difficulty she regained her anchorage of last night. Stackeinum a Tlalam [Clallam] Chief was on board for a short time during the course of the day.

Friday 13th. At 8 A.M. we got under weigh [way], the ebb tide being favorable, but the wind against us; the latter however soon changed to the Westward, and we were enabled to double Point Partridge, and make a straight course for the Gulf of Georgia. We passed Strawberry Island at 3 P.M. and Fish [Lummi] Island at 4, with the wind fair aft, & came to anchor in Point Robert's Bay about 10 at night.[12]

Saturday 14th. Early this morning a number of Indians were assembled in Groups upon the Beach, and in Canoes round the vessel. To check the first advances that their curiosity prompted them to make, required a little firmness & severity on our part, but upon the whole we could not complain much of their forwardness or obtrusion.[13] About 11 A.M. Mr. McMillan went on shore with a party of 12 to look out for a suitable situation for an establishment, but he returned without having been able to satisfy himself in that Particular.[14]

Sunday 15th. Shashia a Cowitchen Chief was taken on board and was received in such a way that he went off to all appearances highly pleased.

We got under weigh today for Fraser's River, but the wind being from the north west, and the ebb tide setting strongly against us, we made little or no progress, and were obliged to come to an anchorage not far from the one of Friday night.

Monday 16th. The wind still unfavorable; with the morning flood we weighed Anchor & stood out into the Gulf & with change of Tide again anchored on the edge of Sturgeon Shoal. In the afternoon the same process was repeated, but we made little or nothing out of it. Shashia came on board, was received as before, and slept upon deck perfectly at ease with his new acquaintance. Scanawa who has contrived to follow us thus far was also on board, but went away in the evening.

Tuesday 17th. Another attempt was made this morning to beat up to the entrance of the Channel into Fraser's River,[15] but without advancing any distance, for the wind fell, and about 7 A.M. the anchor was again cast on the edge of the South Sturgeon Shoal. Captain Simpson & Mr. Annance were off twice in the Boat during the day to sound for a Channel, but returned after 9 O'clock at night without having discovered one.

Wednesday 18th. Mr. Sinclair[16] the first mate was sent off to sound, and upon his return reported that there was a good channel into the River, in the fair way of which two Fathoms were the least Soundings that he had.[17]

Thursday 19th. This morning we stood across the mouth of the Channel, and anchored on the edge of the north Shoal.[18] About 11 at night the vessel was discovered to be drifting, her anchor having lost hold of the steep bank on which it had been cast. The Cable was let loose with an idea that the depth of the water was still not great, and that the anchor would again catch – this however did not happen – the cable was dragged out its full length 80 or 90 Fathoms, and with difficulty checked at the end. All Hands were then called, Canadians as well as the Ship's Company to heave upon the windlass.

Friday 20th. By two O'clock in the morning the Cable was got in, and all sail was set to beat up again for the entrance of the Channel. At Break of Day it was perceived that we had drifted considerably to the North-west. During the early part of the day we had a fresh breeze against us from the South East, but in the afternoon the wind shifted to the southward, and we succeeded before night in again anchoring near the entrance of the Channel.

Saturday 21st. We weighed anchor early, made across to the Southward till we had on the proper Bearings for entering the River; and then stood in. At 7 A.M. we got aground upon the Shoal which forms the South Side of the Channel, but luckily no damage was done. We were afloat again at Half tide about 2 in the afternoon, and as it blew a light air from the South East we anchored at 3 O'clock close to a remarkable clump of Pines[19] a mile up in the River on its North Bank.

Sunday 22d. Captain Simpson went down at 12 O'clock, to the north Point of Entry which he named Point Garry, and by a meridian observation[20] made the Latitude about 49° 5' 30". This observation however was but an indifferent one on account of the Shoals that extended themselves to a great distance along the horizon. Mr. Sinclair was sent up the River in a boat to sound, and returned in the evening saying that he had found deep water as far as he had gone which was a considerable way up. During the afternoon the *Cadboro* was got under weigh, but as it was still uncertain how the Channel led, and the wrong side of the River being unluckily taken, we got into Shoal Water, and were obliged to return to our anchorage to await the arrival of the Sounding Party.

Monday 23d. This morning all hands were employed towing across to the other side of the River. At 3 P.M. sail was set on a Breeze springing up from the South west, and we passed the Cowitchen Villages Saumause [Somenos] Pinellahutz [Penelakuts] & Quomitzen [Quamichan][21] about 6 O'clock, and anchored about a mile above them, two hundred yds. from the north Bank. Scanawa was on board all day, but went on shore at night. The Population of the Cowitchen Villages may be at a rough guess nearly 1500 Souls.

Tuesday 24th. At Half past ten in the forenoon there arose a light Breeze from the South west, and we got under weigh. At noon we passed a small village on the south side where there are two trees marked HBC, which was done by the Party under Mr. McMillan in 1824–25. The neck of Land between Birch Bay {or rather Sanch [Saanich] Bay [Boundary Bay]} and this part of the River is not above a League across. At 1/2 past one we were abreast of the north Channel or Fork which runs into the Gulf not far from Point Grey, and at 2 passed a very small village on the south side. We were opposite the Quoitle [Kwantlen] or Pitt's River[22] about 5 P.M. and at ½ past 7 P.M. anchored close to the north Bank Half a mile above Pine Island.[23]

Wednesday 25th. Whittlakainum[24] a Quoitle chief was on board this morning, and was kindly received. He traded a few Beaver Skins for Knives and then went away. The wind being extremely light, it was 11 o'Clock before the anchor weighed, after which we proceeded at a very slow rate against the current which was running pretty strong. At 2 P.M. we passed the Nanaimooch village, which at a moderate computation may contain 400 Souls. The Houses are small, but appear cleaner and more neatly constructed than those of the Cowitchen Tribe. Here a number of Canoes came off to us, containing upwards of 150 Indians, & not one woman amongst them. They occasioned us some annoyance by repeatedly and obstinately attempting to come on board, and it was not till all were under arms that they desisted from their purpose. They were urged forward by an elderly man [Punnis: see journal entry for 23 August 1827] who gave out his orders with a loud Voice, and in a very determined tone. Finding their efforts of no avail they went quietly away, and soon afterwards the vessel came to anchor.

Thursday 26th. Many natives were alongside this morning, but all were quiet & orderly. At midday we weighed anchor and hoisted sail, but as there was scarcely any wind, and a strong current in the River to stem, we made scarcely a mile in advance when we were obliged to anchor to keep what little we had gained. On the South Side at this point there is a tolerably good situation for a Fort, but we still entertain hopes of finding a better.

Friday 27th. Mr. MacMillan[25] accompanied by Messrs. MacLeod[26] and Annance, and Shashia went off up the River to look out for a more eligible site for an Establishment & on their return Orders were given out to have all ready for warping the Schooner farther up in the morning.

Saturday 28th. By midday the Crew with the assistance of our Canadians had succeeded in warping up opposite to the Place that the Gentlemen had in view for building upon,[27] but it was found that the vessel could not approach within 2 or 300 Yds. of the Shore on account of the Shoalness of the water – indeed we were fast aground for some time in the middle of the Stream. As it was desirable to have the vessel close to the Landing Place to cover the operations of the Land Party as well as to effect the easy and safe discharge of her cargo, and the present situation not admitting of such facility, it was determined upon to drop down to the berth of last night, where we have 6 or 7 Fathoms within a few Yards from shore. A Theft was committed today by some Indians who had been allowed to come on board. Shashia when spoken to on the subject undertook to recover the Property. A few Beaver Skins were traded today.

Sunday 29th. Early this morning Shashia went off to recover what had been stolen yesterday. During the day we dropt down to our anchorage below. Shashia in the evening returned with most of the articles that had been stolen, and had some remuneration allowed him for his trouble. He reports badly of the Indians, who, he tells us, threaten our annihilation should we persist in settling. We ourselves do not feel much alarmed at this, tho' it appears to make a serious impression on our friendly Cowitchen who after having traded for 15 Beaver Skins, and been presented with a Blanket and a few fine Beads in consideration of his services, suddenly took his departure – promising however to return, as soon as we should be firmly established.

Monday 30th. This morning the Schooner was brought close to the Shore, and the Horses were landed by slinging them off to the Bank. The Poor animals appeared to rejoice heartily in their liberation. At noon our men were all busily employed in clearing ground for an Establishment, and in the evening they came on board to sleep, a precaution considered very necessary until we are better assured of the friendly disposition of the natives. A few Indians & Indian women were alongside, and were very quiet and peacable. One of the Ship's company, a man of the name of Lackey,[28] was put in irons for making use of Language calculated to promote discontent and create disorder among the crew.

Tuesday 31st. At 5 in the morning the Fort Langley men were put on Shore to go on with their operations, which are of a very laborious description, the Timber being strong [dense] and the ground completely covered with thick underwood, which is closely interwoven with Brambles

This drawing of Natives sturgeon fishing illustrates the process described in the journal entry for 31 July 1827. The sketch was made by John Keast Lord and appeared in his book *The Naturalist in Vancouver Island and British Columbia.*

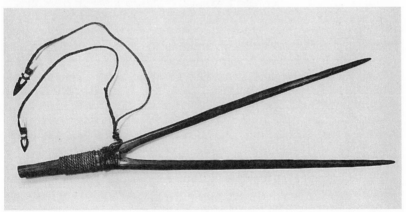

Sturgeon harpoon. Shown here is the end of the shaft, which may have been several metres long, two foreshafts that are attached to the end of the shaft, and two heads, each composed of a pair of spurs or "valves," probably of antler, and (in this example) an iron blade. The lanyards attached to the heads (and attached to the bases of the foreshafts in this example) were probably originally simply joined to a line longer than the shaft.

& Briars. We procured from the Indians today for the first time a supply
of fresh sturgeon, which are as large here as in the Columbia. The Spears
made use of in killing them are sometimes fifty feet long, running into a
fork at the end, on the two claws of which, are fixed Barbs pointed occasionally with iron, but oftener with a piece of shell. When the Fish is
struck the Barbs are unshipped, and being attached in the middle by a
cord which is carried along the spear and held by the Fisherman, they
are drawn across the wound in the same manner as a Whale Harpoon,
and the Fish when exhausted is drawn up and killed.[29] Everyone as
usual slept on board.

Wednesday 1st August. The Canadians all at work as yesterday. An axe
was stolen this morning by an old Nanaimooch Indian, but upon application being made for its restoration, it was soon delivered up. Forty
to Fifty of the Tribe assembled on the occasion, and long harangues
were made by their chiefs, the purport of which as we afterwards heard,
was upon the whole of a friendly nature. They retired very quietly, and
the remainder of the day passed smoothly away. All came on board to
sleep.

Thursday 2d. Some of the men began to prepare wood for a Bastion and
the others are still employed in clearing the ground. Two Hundred
weight of Sturgeon was traded for, with Red Baize [coarse felt-type
wool,] Axes, Knives and Buttons which, with the exception of Blankets
& ammunition, are articles in greatest request with the Indians here. Six
fresh salmon were also purchased being the first we have seen since
entering the River. The arrival of this fish is hailed by the natives with
joy & festivity. At this time they are excellent, but only to be had at the
Rapids above,[30] where in the course of the season great quantities of
them are taken by the natives and dried for winter provisions. All slept
on board.

Friday 3d. Bouchard, Ant. Pierrault, Ettue, Tarihonga, Rabaska, Jacques
Pierrault, Plomondeau & Pierre Charles are squaring Logs for the Bastion. Faniant & Peopeoh sharpening Pitsaws,[31] and the remainder felling Timber and burning & clearing away the Underwood & Rubbish. A
Party of twenty Nanaimoochs visited us on shore for the purpose of
satisfying their curiosity in observing the various operations of the People at work. A little Sturgeon was purchased from Canoes alongside,
and the day closed quietly, all coming on board as usual to sleep.

Saturday 4th. Work going forward as yesterday. The Fires which were kindled to consume the Branches & Cuttings of the felled Timber, commu-
nicating with the surrounding woods occasioned us much inconvenience
& trouble; at one time we were completely enveloped in Flame & clouds
of smoke, and it was with great difficulty that the People succeeded in
getting the conflagration checked. Squatches a Nanaimooch chief was
taken on board today and shewn the vessel, with which attention he
appeared to be particularly well pleased. This evening Seven or Eight
of our men remained on shore to sleep, and Mr. Annance along with
them.

Sunday 5th. This forenoon a number of Indian women were alongside the *Cadboro*, trying to dispose of Berries for trifling articles such as rings, buttons, etc. etc. It is amusing to observe the spirit of Rivalry & opposition that in this species of trade pervades the bosom of our fair visitors. By a meridian observation of the Sun taken this day Fort Langley appears to be in north Latitude 49° 11' 38". This night many of the People slept on Shore.

Monday 6th. All Hands busily employed – Como & Peopeoh erecting a Saw Pit. Of the rest – some are felling & squaring Timber others burning and clearing away the Chips, Branches and Underwood. Vincent is confined to his bed with Venereal.[32] A meridian observation of the Sun this day gives the Latitude 49° 11' 30". A little Sturgeon was procured from passing Canoes. At night most of the people remained on Shore.

Tuesday 7th. Vincent confined and likely to be so for months to come. All the others at work – The two Sandwich Islanders sawing; Sauvé & Cornoyer also attempting the same, but theirs can be called only an attempt for they make preciously little progress. Bouchard, Ettue, Plomondeau & Jacques Pierrault preparing the wood that has been cut for the Bastion. A few occupied in clearing the Ground and the rest cutting Pickets.[33] Meridian observation of the Sun today makes the Latitude 49° 11' 0". A considerable number of Indians visited us, from whom a little Sturgeon was procured. Most of the People slept on Shore.

Wednesday 8th. The men employed cutting Pickets were obliged to abandon their work on account of a fire in the woods, which we have every reason to suppose was kindled by Indians with the malicious intention of forcing us to relinquish our purpose of establishing. A few Beaver Skins were traded today.

Thursday 9th. The Fire which had raged with so much violence Yesterday, broke out again today with redoubled fury on the setting in of the Breeze from Sea. It swept part of the little open meadow on our flank, and was arrested in its progress on that side only by the intervention of the small Rivulet that runs through the plain. The Blaze communicated with the woods directly behind us, but luckily at a considerable distance off. In consequence of this we expect much annoyance should the wind come to blow from that quarter. The work notwithstanding is going forward as rapidly as possible.

Friday 10th. The Clerks keep regular watch at night on shore that the services of none of the men may be lost during the day. Bouchard & five others working at the Bastion, Como & Peopeoh, Sauvé & Jacques Pierrault sawing & Eight men supplying them with Logs, which is very weighty work, but the ground is as yet too rough and the Horses too weak to haul heavy timber. Faniant however has commenced making traces & harness to be ready for Service when required. About midnight Scanawa arrived with a few Scadgat [Skagit] Indians, & took up his quarters close to our camp.

Saturday 11th. A number of Indians both from above and below were on the ground today and many long and pithy orations were given by the

leading men, who seemed to vie with each other in talking with vociferation, and noise. The Scadgats traded some furs which they have
brought with them, a business which was luckily managed without
much jarring as to prices. The fire this forenoon approaching very near
our camp occasioned us much trouble and anxiety before its progress
was stopped, and took most of the People from their regular occupations. In other respects our operations advanced as usual. The Bastion is
nearly at its height, and appears to command respect with the Indians,
who begin shrewdly enough to conjecture for what purpose the Ports &
Loop Holes are intended. In the afternoon the Company who had visited us retired quietly to their respective houses; and our Scadgat Friends
also went away as soon as they had finished trading. They are intent at
present on the recovery by ransom, of some females of their nation who
have been carried off into captivity by the Yucletaws [Lekwiltok] a powerful Tribe to the northward.

Sunday 12th. Few Indians looked near us. The fire hitherto our most
dreaded foe has sunk to rest, the dried wood, Branches and other
Combustibles around being at length entirely consumed. We had consequently a day of rest, a day of calm & undisturbed tranquility throughout. The scarcity of fish among the natives is the only circumstance now
which gives us any cause for regret or inquietude, as it prevents us from
provisioning the People as we could wish, or as they during the present
laborious duty would require.

Monday 13th. The Bastion has now only to be covered, and Pierre Charles
& Cornoyer are busy raising Cedar Bark for that purpose. Jacques
Pierrault commenced hauling Pickets with one of the Horses from a
distance of a quarter mile. The other men are employed as during last
week.

Tuesday 14th. Faniant and others squaring wood for a Store – Jacques
Pierrault & Kennedy carters – Como & Peopeoh sawing Pickets, and
eight or nine men cutting and carrying Logs to the Sawpit. A small supply of fresh sturgeon was got from the Indians as also a few dried salmon.
The few Natives that we have seen today were very quietly disposed &
report that the Salmon are becoming plentiful in the River.[34]

Wednesday 15th. Work as yesterday. Some half dried Salmon were procured from Canoes passing down from the Rapids.

Thursday 16th. No change in the work of the People. A little dried Salmon
was again purchased from Canoes alongside. We had a few Indians on
shore, and from these few the best of behaviour. Since leaving Fort Vancouver up to the present date we have experienced as fine weather as
one could wish for. Clear & unclouded Skies and a pure Atmosphere,
and the heats, generally so prevalent at this season, agreeably tempered
by the Breezes and Airs from Sea.

Friday 17th. Some of the men felling timber close to the camp preparatory
to erecting the Fort Picketing & others still squaring Wood for the Buildings – Como & Peopeoh sawing – Jacques Pierrault & Kennedy Carting
with the three Horses. During the night we had heavy showers of Rain,

and this morning the weather still appeared lowering and unsettled nor did it clear up during the course of the day. From the Indians who were alongside of the *Cadboro* we succeeded in getting twenty small salmon. On Shore we had no visits whatever, of course every thing went on smoothly & quietly. Heavy rain again at 7 O'clock in the evening.

Saturday 18th. Work the same as yesterday. Indians bringing a few Salmon, and a little Sturgeon, besides Bark for covering our Buildings which is received from them in exchange for Buttons, Rings and other trifling articles of Trade.

Sunday 19th. More Cedar Bark was procured today from the Indians of the Quoitlan Village above – excepting this business nothing else stirring.

Monday 20th. Sauvé & Pierre Charles sick, & Vincent under a course of mercury.[35] So stands the Sick List. Most of the wood required for Picketing is now cut and hauled to the site of the Establishment, and preparations for the Storehouse get on apace. Some of the men are employed in burning and rolling into the River the useless Logs, and dried Trunks of Trees that are lying promiscuously through the Camp, and which with the exception of the Standing Stumps, are the greatest impediments to be removed in the process of levelling the Ground which is to be occupied by the Buildings. Six or Seven Sinahomes Indians made their appearance this forenoon, from whom nine Beaver Skins were traded, a business which was accomplished with infinite trouble, and after long and earnest expostulation on their part as to prices. This arises from their having had communication with the American Vessel[36] that visited the Straits of De Fuca last Spring, and supplied them with clothing & other articles at a cheaper rate than our Tariff will admit of. Fifteen to Twenty Chomes [Squamish] & Misqueam [Musqueam] Indians arrived from above, who having parted with 2 or 300 Dried Salmon continued their route down to the Nanaimooch Village where they are to sleep. The Sinahomes also withdrew in the evening to visit some of their neighbours. Soon after their departure a number of Cowitchens passed with their families and moveables on their way up to kill Salmon at the Rapids, where they are to remain some time collecting a Stock of Dried Provisions for the winter.

Tuesday 21st. This morning four men commenced opening a trench three feet deep in which to sink the Pickets. The Ground is a hard Gravel composed of round Stones of Granite mixed with Sand, with a very thin vegetable mould on the surface. Como & Peopeoh are still sawing and Jacques Pierrault & Kennedy carting. Boisvert is burning waste wood and the rest are squaring and preparing Timber for a Storehouse, and another Bastion etc. etc. Our troublesome friends the Sinahomes visited us again today, and after a great deal of talk and palaver traded ten Beaver Skins – the last they have. They left us in the evening to sleep at the Nanaimooch Village. The two Canoes of Chomes and Misquiams that went down yesterday – passed on their return to their villages above. Bark for covering the Houses is still occasionally traded from the Quoitlans, and is paid for at as low a rate as possible.

Wednesday 22d. Work continues the same as yesterday, except that a few hands have been set to smooth the edge of the rough Pickets in order that when put up they may come close together. Some Bark was purchased today from Scanawa as well as from other Indians. The Sinahomes went up to visit the Quoitlan Village. There is a report current that eight Misqueams have been cut off by a nation high up the River, whom the Indians here call Chilcocooks [Chilliwacks].

Thursday 23d. Employment of the People continues as yesterday. Plomondeau one of our best men is unable to work, on account of a swelling in his hand and arm, which have been severely injured in the use of the axe. Towards the close of the afternoon we procured about one day's Rations of fresh Salmon for the men, and during the course of the day a considerable quantity of Bark was traded from the Quoitlans. The Sinahomes have at last left the River to return to their houses. Punnis an old chief of the Nanaimooch, the same who made himself so conspicuous when we passed their Village, was allowed to go on board the *Cadboro*, and was shewn the Cabin, with which treatment he appeared to be highly gratified. Cowitchens are passing now in numbers with their families to the Rapids.

Friday 24th. Bouchard & three others employed at the South east Bastion, of which the four corner posts were planted, and the sides partly filled up before night. The rest of the people are engaged at the same work as Yesterday. The Sick List stands as follows – Vincent under mercury, Plomondeau's Hand and Arm worse, and Pierre Charles complaining sadly of Rheumatism, but still contriving to work a little. Few or no Indians on the ground today but many passing to the fishery above.

Saturday 25th. All Hands employed as yesterday, sick list the same. Quaskainum an old Scadgat chief with about a dozen followers arrived to trade and having asked permission to encamp on our premises was allowed to do so, tho it is an indulgence not granted to Indians generally. Families from the Sanch Village at Point Roberts have been passing in continued succession during the day all bound for the Salmon fishery. Their Luggage as well as that of the other tribes is transported up and down the River on Rafts, which are formed by laying Boards across two or more Canoes Kept 8, 10 or 12 feet asunder. They have also among them large War canoes procured from Indians to the northward, which are used by them as Luggage Boats, and which contain a great Bulk of Furniture & Baggage. The Size of some of these craft is fully 50 feet in length and 6 to 7 ft. across the middle. On the Top of the Stern which is flattish there is in general carved out the resemblance of the face of a human Being, and the Stern [bow] rises to the height of at least 7 feet from the water. Whether this latter be intended merely for ornament or not it is impossible to say, but it gives the Canoe an imposing appearance, and must afford to the crew a tolerable defence against arrows when they are advancing straight against an enemy. The Sides of the Bow and Stern are very fancifully ornamented with circles and other regular figures which are laid on with various coloured Paints or Clay.

Sunday 26th. The Scadgats who arrived yesterday having traded their Furs took their departure, and there was no stir for the remainder of the day.

Monday 27th. Operations going forward the same as on Saturday last, and the Sick list as it then was. Bouchard, Ettue, Antoine Pierrault and another are the men employed in getting up the second Bastion. Tarihonga, Dubois, Cornoyer, and Arquoitte are preparing Pickets, Jacques Pierrault Carting & Como & Peopeoh at the Saw. The rest of the hands are kept busy in supplying the Saw Pit with wood and in doing other little Jobs about the Place. Shashia the Cowitchen chief shewed himself today, and took up his quarters alongside of the camp. More Indians still removing to the Rapids.

Tuesday 28th. No change whatever from the Work of yesterday. Shashia traded 15 Beaver Skins, and then went off to the Quoitle River, where the Chief of the Quoitlans, Whittlakainum has his residence. Swarms of Indians with their families proceeding to the Fishery above.

Wednesday 29th. All Hands employed as yesterday and the day before. Fewer Indians passing.

Thursday 30th. Baker has got himself severely hurt in carrying Logs. An attempt was made to bleed him,[37] but he sickened on the touch of the Lancet, and the vein in consequence would not run. We will lose his services for some time to come. Work as Yesterday.

Friday 31st. The second Bastion is up and roofed in, and it only remains now to finish the flooring to complete it. Faniant, with Cornoyer, Dubois, and Arquoitte began to erect Pickets on the side of the Fort facing the River. All the other men at their occupations of yesterday. The few Indians who were with us today were very quiet and orderly in their behaviour.

Saturday 1st September. Eight men employed at the Picketing. Ettue & Antoine Pierrault finishing the flooring of the South East Bastion. Jacques Pierrault carting; Como & Peopeoh sawing, the rest digging the Trench for the Pickets, and supplying the Sawyers with wood. An Indian this morning stole a Crow Bar, which had been left out by the men while they were at Breakfast. Every exertion was made to recover it, but without success. All natives were in consequence prohibited from landing for the remainder of the day in order to evince to them our disapprobation of so knavish a behaviour.

Sunday 2d. It being a most desirable object to have an inclosure up as quickly as possible, all hands with the exception of the sick & maimed are at work. No Indians were allowed to land on account of the Theft committed yesterday, but the want of fresh provisions will soon compel us to concede a little in regard to this restriction, and indulge them with the same familiarity & freedom of intercourse that they before enjoyed. As it is they appear already to feel the deprivation of our good will and friendly disposition towards them as severely as we had any reason to expect they would, which is so far satisfactory. Shashia the Cowitchen chief arrrived this evening, and was allowed to encamp on the ground with all his Family.

Monday 3d. Bouchard, Ettue, Antoine Pierrault, Tarihonga, Faniant, Cornoyer, Arquoitte, Dubois, Faron, & Sauvé employed in getting up the picketing: Anawiskum & Boisvert rooting out Stumps, Como & Peopeoh sawing, & Kennedy, Jacques Pierrault and Rabaska carrying Logs. Pierre Charles is attacked so severely with Rheumatic pains, that he makes one more upon our Sick List. Plomondeau's Hand is no better, Vincent is salivating[38] and Baker has his side blistered. A considerable quantity of fresh and dried Salmon was procured today, and 15 Beaver Skins were traded from the Nanaimoochs.

Tuesday 4th. Every thing going forward as yesterday, & the Indians continuing to bring us fresh and dried Salmon which they part with at a moderate price.

Wednesday 5th. Operations continued as yesterday. Sick List the same. The Weather is to all appearance breaking up, for we have now frequent Rains, a damp climate, & foggy atmosphere.

Thursday 6th. Two Sandwich Islanders from the *Cadboro* were on shore assisting in rooting out the Stumps of the felled timber. Kennedy and Jacques Pierrault carting, the others at the same occupations at which they were engaged yesterday. Pierre Charles is recovering & we have him again actively employed, but Dubois is *hors de service* in his stead, his thumb having been cut in such a manner that he cannot without danger make any use of it.

Friday 7th. Since Sunday last we have had very gloomy weather, and almost incessant rain. It has however cleared up this afternoon, and we entertain hopes of a favorable change which we certainly much require both for the sake of advance with our business and for the health of the people, who have not yet had time to put up for themselves any thing like comfortable Lodgings, and consequently suffer greatly from their constant exposure to so wet a climate. Sickness at present prevails among them to an alarming extent, and we can ascribe it only to this, and the late change in their diet; for they are now living entirely upon Salmon, whereas their Rations before consisted chiefly of Grain – say Indian Corn, Pease etc.[39] Antoine Pierrault has taken to his Bed, complaining of Headaches & Pain in his Breast and Shoulders. He is labouring besides under a violent Gonorhoea, and has several ugly and obstinate sores about his lower extremities. A Tlalam Woman Sister in Law of Scanawa has been restored by the Yucleltaws who had taken her prisoner during their last plundering incursion down the Gulf of Georgia. Her ransom has cost Scanawa seven or eight Blankets, and some trifling articles of trade besides, but the old Rogue intends to indemnify himself for this expense by appropriating to himself the person of the fair captive, who is now considered as a member of the Haram [harem]. The negotiator with the Yucletaws was a Woman of that tribe, who is married to an Indian that lives up this River, and is very well known here by the name of the Doctor.

Saturday 8th. The Picketing of the Fort was completed, and the gates hung. The Rectangle inside is 40 yards by 45, and the two Bastions are 12 ft.

square each, built of 8 inch Logs, and having a lower and upper flooring, the latter of which is to be occupied by our artillery. The *Tout ensem-
ble* must make a formidable enough appearance in the eyes of Indians
especially those here who have seen nothing of the kind before. Sick
List the same as yesterday. Antoine Pierrault & Baker were both bled.
We have just been informed of the murder of the Yucletaw woman who
made herself so serviceable in ransoming the Tlalam & Scadgat Captives. It seems that a brutal Indian of this place performed the *meritori-
ous* deed because the poor creature had not been equally successful in
recovering some women of his own tribe, which arose probably from
the ransom offered not being sufficiently valuable.

Sunday 9th. Our People all very busy removing the Bark Shed which they
have for Shelter to one side of the Fort, in order to make room for the
Building of the Houses. Indians still supply us with fish in the greatest
abundance.

Monday 10th. Part of the men commenced building the Store-house, and
the others are employed in preparing wood for its completion. The two
Owyhees are making another Sawpit. Dubois now works a little, as his
thumb is getting better.

Tuesday 11th. Como & Peopeoh sawing, the others employed as yesterday. Nothing of moment occurring, I may only remark that the Indians
now bring us more fresh Salmon than we choose to accept of, and they
dispose of their dried fish willingly at as low a rate as the Kootoomins
[Thompson] at the Fork of Thom[p]son's River.

Wednesday 12th. All going on smoothly and no change from the work of
Yesterday.

Thursday 13th. Peopeoh is this morning on the sick list – he complains of
acute pain in his loins, and violent cholic. Cornoyer takes his place at
the saw. Every thing else the same as during the preceding part of the
week.

Friday 14th. The Storehouse is now finished with the exception of the roof
which is to be put on tomorrow. The Sick List is lessening. Peopeoh at
his own request had a blister applied to his side. Vincent is still under
mercury, and Plomondeau's Hand is not much better, but Baker is recovering, and Ant. Pierrault is on his legs again – both of them are working a little.

Saturday 15th. The Storehouse was roofed in with an excellent Bark covering, and our Outfit was landed from the *Cadboro*, and stowed away,
every thing in the best possible order and condition.

Sunday 16th. The *Cadboro* taking in Ballast and preparing for Sea.

Monday 17th. Captain Simpson on shore. Bills Lading clearance etc. signed
& delivered – fine weather.

Tuesday 18th. Work going forward as usual – Peopeoh feels considerably
relieved in consequence of having been blistered yesterday. The *Cadboro*
left us early this morning under a Salute of three Guns which she returned. Scanawa who has been encamped here since the 10th August,
took his departure at the same time,[40] but he leaves with us about 50

Beaver Skins, which will put him under the necessity of returning again, whether it should be to trade them or take them away. We learnt in the evening from Indians that the Schooner had got safely out of the River.

Wednesday 19th. The people are collecting and preparing Timber for a Dwelling House to be built near the Front Gate. Peopeoh is now recovering.

Thursday 20th. Three Canoes of Tlalam Indians arrived last night. They bring furs for trade and report the Schooner has steered to the northward towards the Yuculta Country. Work as yesterday. Our dwelling house is rising rapidly.

Friday 21st. The Tlalams went away after having traded upwards of sixty Beaver Skins, which were paid for wholly in Blankets. These Indians make great difficulty in bartering at our prices, in consequence of having been visited by the Americans last Spring by whom they were supplied with Goods much more cheaply than we can afford to do.

Saturday 22d. The Carpenters finished the outside shell of our dwelling House, and gave a good Cedar Bark covering. In the afternoon the Young chief of the Scadgats arrived with a few followers and some furs to trade. Heavy rain.

Sunday 23d. Another Scadgat Indian arrived, and soon afterwards the band disposed of their few furs and went off. The men now are partly occupied in preparing a Wintering House for themselves.

Monday 24th. This forenoon a number of Cowitchens and Nanaimoochs landed at the wharf giving out that they were so far on their way to avenge on the Chilcocooks the murders which they have committed among the Misquiams. Shashia & Stackeinum the Tlalam Chief and others harangued the party on the occasion. Our men were called from their work in the woods into the Fort, in case of quarrels and to prevent mischief. Whatever had been the intention of this Band of warriors, instead of pursuing their journey, they retired in the afternoon very quietly to their own homes. Peopeoh resumed his work at the Saw today.

Tuesday 25th. The Tlalams who arrived on the 21st and who have been visiting the different Indian villages in the River, took their leave for this season, Stackeinum their chief alone remaining in the neighbourhood. A few Nanaimoochs, whom we saw today declare their intention of leaving their village below very soon, to go to their own Lands on Vancouver's Island, where they always pass the winter.

Wednesday 26th. The Cowitchens, who went up some time ago to the Fishery above, begin now to drop down the River; some of them do not look near us, while others again visit our wharf, and dispose of a part of their store of Provisions. This Trade costs us very little, as vermilion [a bright red pigment of mercuric sulphide used as a cosmetic or paint], Rings, and other trifles are the only articles we allow them for dried Salmon. A little fresh Sturgeon and Salmon we still procure, but the latter fish are getting scarce and bad, and the natives do not look so much after the other as formerly, being mostly all on the eve of quitting the River for their lands, and of course occupied in making preparations for that movement. Our Wintering House gets on apace, and promises to make snug and comfortable quarters. It is 30 ft. long by 15 in Breadth, and is divided into two apartments each of which is provided with a fireplace and two windows.

Thursday 27th. Indian Canoes and Rafts are continually dropping down the Stream, and the Provision trade might be carried on briskly, for they are all extremely anxious, poor creatures, to part with their Salmon. Work going on as usual.

Friday 28th. Nearly One Hundred Canoes and Rafts of the Homes [Squamish] Tribe passed today on their way down the River, & their Chief is expected tomorrow accompanied by the remainder of his people. Some of them encamped opposite to the Fort.

Saturday 29th. Indians with their families are still passing in crowds down the River. At night it was discovered that a theft had been committed by them through an opening in one of the Bastions, and our old acquaintance Shashia was employed to recover the articles. The men occupied as yesterday.

Sunday 30th. This morning Shashia could give us no account or throw any light upon the Theft that was committed, he was accordingly again dispatched to extend his enquiries, and he at length returned, after having made out that the Pilferers were of the Homes tribe. Whapplakainum their chief who is now here, and who has just traded for 20 Beaver Skins undertakes to go in quest of the Rascals tomorrow morning, and to bring us back all of the Property that he can lay hold of.

Monday 1st October. The Misquiams are now removing from above to the Quoitle River, and the Sanch Indians are also leaving our neighbourhood to make the best of their way to their winter quarters. This afternoon Washkaladga, Sinoktin and 7 other Sinahomes arrived with Beaver Skins. Three of them were received in the Fort, were presented with something to eat, and had wherewith to smoke – they slept however outside with their countrymen. Work goes forward as usual.

Tuesday 2d. Indians of the Sanch Village are still passing down the River. Wapplakainum the Homes chief who had gone in search of the stolen property came back to day with a Part of it, and received two axes as a recompense for the trouble he had taken, and the expenses he had incurred in its recovery. The nine Sinahomes who arrived yesterday, started to visit the Nanaimooch Village, but on second and better thoughts they returned, and merely went across the River to see a few Misquiams who are encamped opposite to us. Stackainum the Tlalam chief still makes his appearance occasionally but without being attended by any of his people.

Wednesday 3d. The Sinahomes bartered their Furs, and as usual gave much trouble in trying to beat down our Prices. One Hundred and Sixty Beaver and Otter Skins, large and small is the amount of what they have brought, and Blanketing the only article of which they have accepted in exchange. These fellows are at present somewhat alarmed at a report that the Cowitchens intend cutting them off, and we have some difficulty in dispelling their fears, as they were not long ago at variance with that people. Three or four men are employed in making a Shed in which to hang up our dried Salmon, the Storehouse being so damp that every thing in it of the meat kind becomes mouldy in a very short space of time. The House work is carried on as expeditiously as possible.

Thursday 4th. Early this morning our Sinahomes friends took their departure. They do not go by the River, but cross on foot the neck of Land between this & Birch Bay [Boundary Bay], and then take canoe to their own country. Our Dwelling House is now nearly completed, and the men are beginning to put up one for themselves, for which there is great part of the timber requisite, already prepared and hauled to the fort.

Friday 5th. Shashia made a move this morning and left the place with all his family which consists of four wives and three or four children. He is to remain for some time at the Quoitle River, whither Stackainum the Tlalam chief accompanies him. During the remainder of the day, we saw but few Indians only two families of Quoitlans having passed being on their way to join their Relations at the Forks below. We hear that a mass of Indians are collected there, and that their women are busied in gathering Wappatoes [wapatos] a root of which they are particularly fond, and which is found under water in Pools and Marshes. The Indians here call it Skous, tho' I have given it the name by which it is known on the Columbia.[41] When they have made a harvest of this and what little else they can contrive to collect on this side of the Gulf, the greatest part of them clear out of the River for their own lands, and do not return again till the ensuing summer.

Saturday 6th. A little Deer's meat was purchased today from Sanch Indians who have their Lodges not far distant up the little Portage River [Salmon River]. The People are getting well forward with their wintering House, which occupies one side of the square of the Fort, and cuts a very respectable appearance being [blank] feet in length by [blank] in breadth,[42] and having 3 Apartments with a fireplace in each. The Salmon Shed is now finished and half our Stock of dried Salmon hung up in it. Constant Fires are kept burning under it to dry the air, and prevent the Provisions above from being spoilt by getting damp and mouldy.

Sunday 7th. Six Cowitchens were alongside of the wharf this forenoon their Canoes laden with fish, and a supply of fresh sturgeon was procured from them at a very reasonable rate: a few Nanaimoochs also visited us, by whom we were informed that their countrymen were still at the Forks below. Towards Night fall there arrived two loaded Rafts from above, upon which were two Indians with their families from the Forks of Thom[p]son's River, one of whom delivered a letter that had been entrusted to his care October 1826 by Mr. Archibald Macdonald[43] who it would appear must have entertained an idea that there was a possibility of this Post being established that same Season – These Indians crossed with their Rafts to the mouth of the small creek opposite, where they encamped for the night. Today Pierre Charles and Antoine Pierrault went off to set Traps for Beaver, and remained out all night, &

Tarihonga & Kennedy took a small canoe that has been traded from the natives, and crossed the River to visit the little creek, with the intention also of setting Traps, in case they should find traces of Beaver. They returned however at night to sleep at the Fort.

Monday 8th. We got comfortably housed in our new lodgings, and the men are now all occupied in rendering their own dwellings habitable, with the exception of a few hands who are kept constantly employed in rooting out & burning the Stumps within and without the Fort, which is a work of no small toil and trouble. Tarihonga & Kennedy got us Beaver from their traps this morning, and Pierre Charles and Kennedy were equally unfortunate for they returned towards the close of the day without having met with any success. More Nanaimoochs made their appearance today, and the Indians who brought the Letter yesterday again came to see us before their departure to join their friends at the Forks below. In the afternoon arrived the Eldest Son of the old Soquam chief with a slender retinue, for the purpose of trade. It would seem that he is under the protection of the Cowitchens, for Shashia has sent his eldest Boy[44] along with him. Weather uncommonly fine.

Tuesday 9th. The Soquams traded upwards of twenty Beaver Skins, and then took their departure. Work going on as yesterday.

Wednesday 10th. Weather remarkably fine for the Season. We hear from passing Indians that the Cowitchens are still bent upon punishing the Chilcoyooks, and that a war party will pass tomorrow to carry their purposes of revenge into effect.

Thursday 11th. Eighty Six Cowitchens & Misquiams passed this forenoon on their way up to *make war* upon the Chilcoycooks, tho' certainly their marauding excursions scarcely deserve to be so entitled. Their canoes contained generally 3 or 4 men each, but we observed one half sized one in which there were eight or nine persons. Work as yesterday.

Friday 12th. We are occasionally visited by straggling Indians, who still bring us fresh fish and a little venison. There are a few of the Sanch Village Indians encamped not far from us upon the little Portage River, where they take a quantity of Salmon on wears [weirs] by barring up part of the River. They also kill a few Beaver in wooden Traps constructed in the same manner as those for Martens, and contrive to secure a Red Deer now and then in a Pitfall. Como & Peopeoh constantly at the saw; one or two hands busied in rooting out the Stumps close to the Fort, others in the woods squaring Timber, and the rest occupied in getting up their own houses.

Saturday 13th. The Indians who went up the River on Thursday returned today without having performed any feat worthy of notice. One of them has been wounded by an arrow. The men's houses are up and covered, and there are already some of the apartments occupied.

Sunday 14th. We were visited today by two or three Indians who as usual brought us a little fresh Sturgeon. Every thing very quiet.

Monday 15th. Pierre Charles returned from hunting. His traps have produced Six Beaver, and he has had the good fortune besides to kill a Red

Deer; which comes very acceptably to us at the present moment, after we have been living so long upon fish. All the men except the two Sawyers are employed in Building the Chimneys of their Houses.

Tuesday 16th. Work as yesterday. Few or no Indians.

Wednesday 17th. Weather remarkably fine. All employed as yesterday.

Thursday 18th. Another War Party of Cowitchens and Misquiams went up the River again today to repeat their attack upon the Chilcoyooks. Shashia the Cowitchen chief leads them, and their number is about 70 in all, which would lead us to imply that their Enemies are not very powerful.

Friday 19th. The Houses of the men are nearly completed, and some of the hands are again in the woods felling and squaring Timber for various purposes. The war Party of Cowitchens returned this afternoon from their expedition, in which they have managed to murder one man and a woman. The head of one of their Victims was pendant at the Bow of the largest Canoe, presenting a spectacle as dismal and disgusting as can well be imagined – a spectacle, the most shocking to humanity, that this land of Barbarism can well produce.[45] Several Women and children have been taken prisoners, who as a matter of course become Slaves,[46] and the greater number of the Canoes are laden with dried and fresh provisions, Baskets, Mats, and other Furniture, the Spoils of the Camp of the unhappy creatures that they surprized.

Saturday 20th. A Poor Indian from above was on shore here for some time, trying to dispose of a few Beaver Skins, but not feeling satisfied with what was offered him, he continued his voyage down the River, intending as he told us to ransom one of the women who was taken by the Cowitchens. The Chilcoyooks it appears are not the people who have suffered, but a small and weak tribe called Maes [Sumas] who are not very far distant.

Sunday 21st. An Old Sanch Indian of the name of Yokum visited us today, and purchased a Blanket for four Otters and a Beaver Skin. Our Sanch neighbour from the Portage River who is named Chaheinook was also at the wharf for a short time, but had nothing to trade. François Tarihonga the Iroquois visited his traps and returned with two Beaver.

Monday 22d. The Maes Indian whom we saw on Saturday last passed up on his way home with his wife and other females, whom he has ransomed from the Cowitchens. To accomplish this he has parted with all his little property, for his canoe is emptied of every thing which he took down. We had a long conversation at the Wharf today with two Indians from below, who said they were going to apprize our neighbours at the Quoitlan Village, of the Yucletaws having formed a determination to punish them for the murder of the Yucletaw woman at their village last September. They informed us besides that the *Cadboro* had been seen on her way back to the Southward, and mentioned that there was a report current among the Indians, that four of her crew when on shore for water, had been massacred by the natives near the Entrance to the narrows at the northern extremity of the Gulf of Georgia.[47] We do not however put much credit in this last piece of intelligence. Three or four men are employed in rubbing the dried Salmon, and hanging them up in their houses, where it is supposed they will be less liable to turn mouldy on account of the warmth of the fires. Faniant, Rabaska, and Faron are constructing a Gallery at the South east corner of the Fort, Como & Peopeoh sawing, Pierrault still carting, Pierre Charles out hunting, and the rest busy in the woods felling and squaring timber for different purposes.

Tuesday 23d. Three or four men at the Salmon as yesterday. Faniant & three more at the South east Gallery, Como & Peopeoh sawing, Pierrault carting, Sauvé & Anawiskum Cooks – the others in the Woods felling and squaring timber. François' Traps produced one Beaver and one Otter. An Indian of the Quoitlan Village passed down the River today with his family, on his way to Vancouver Island to pass the winter. This fellow repeats the report that we heard yesterday that four of the *Cadboro*'s Crew have been murdered by the Yucletaws. Pierre Charles still out. Weather remarkably fine.

Wednesday 24th. Faniant and his men erecting a Gallery at the North West corner of the Fort. Baker, Arquoitte and two others drying, rubbing & dusting Beaver Skins,[48] which have become mouldy by remaining in the Store. The rest of our men employed as yesterday. Pierre Charles is not yet returned. A few Indians were with us today, from whom fresh Sturgeon was procured in sufficient quantity for one day's rations.

Thursday 25th. Bouchard, Plomondeau, Ettue, & Kennedy are at Timber in the woods, Faniant, Faron, Rabaska & Cornoyer are at the North West Gallery, Como & Peopeoh are sawing; Pierrault carter, Baker levelling the Ground within the Fort, Boisvert burning and rooting out Stumps, and Pierre Charles and Ant. Pierrault not yet returned from hunting. Dubois was taken ill this afternoon with fits to which he is subject, and he had repeated relapses during the course of the night. A number of Quoitles from above were on the Ground today, and traded twenty five Beaver Skins.

Friday 26th. Dubois is still badly, and five men are frequently required to hold him during the recurrence of the fits. Pierre Charles and Antoine Pierrault returned from hunting. They have taken two Beaver and killed five Red Deer. The rest of the People with the exception of those who attend on Dubois are occupied with the same Work as yesterday.

Saturday 27th. Nine men were sent off to bring home the meat that was killed by the Hunters. Kennedy is now cutting firewood and attending to the Traps set in the little River opposite. The others employed as yesterday. Vincent is recovering from the effects of the course of mercury which he has undergone, but Dubois is still subject yet to returns of the Fits which began to attack him on Thursday – It seems to be ordained that we shall have at least one Individual always on the Sick List.

Sunday 28th. All without Doors quiet. Dubois does not recover, on the contrary tho' very weak in the intervals of recollection, he is so strongly convulsed during the recurrence of the malady that the same number of men as at first are still required to hold him.

Monday 29th. The men returned with the meat that they had been sent for. Dubois still badly, and getting very low, so much so that he despairs of his recovery. Torrents of Rain all day.

Tuesday 30th. Faniant and four men are finishing the Gallery. Bouchard, Plomondeau, François and several others are in the woods preparing Timber for a large House which it is in contemplation to build. Como and Peopeoh are sawing, Jacques Pierrault carting, Kennedy chopping firewood, and visiting his Traps – Sauvé and Macdonald are cooks. Pierre Charles & Antoine Pierrault went off on another hunting excursion. Vincent is recovering fast, but Dubois is no better.

Wednesday 31st. Men employed as yesterday except that those who were working at the Galleries are now busied in the woods. Vincent begins to go about a little and is now occupied in drying & rubbing mouldy Salmon. Dubois tho' still very weak is recovering from his complaint.

Thursday 1st November. This being All Saints' day,[49] no work was exacted from the people. A number of the Quoitlans were on the ground today, but without doing any business in the way of the Fur Trade. Two large Sturgeon were purchased from them.

Friday 2d. Faniant employed as a Carpenter, Faron as a Tailor. Arquoitte & Baker are clearing the Bank of the River opposite the gate of the Fort, and the rest are at the same occupations which they had on Wednesday. One of our Horses got into a quagmire last night and died in consequence during the day. Weather still rainy.

Saturday 3d. All Hands employed as yesterday. Dubois is recovering slowly, tho' the quantity of Blood that was drawn from him during his illness renders him still very weak. Rain as yesterday.

Sunday 4th. Pierre Charles and Antoine Pierrault returned from hunting. They have killed three Red Deer, and their Traps have given them one Beaver and one Otter. We are informed by them that the small Rivers and Lakes have been much swollen by the late rains.

Monday 5th. Four men with the two hunters were sent off for the meat, and returned with it in the evening. Faniant employed as a Carpenter at various little jobs. Jacques Pierrault constructing a Shed for the two remaining Horses, the two Owyhees sawing, and the rest of the people engaged at the same occupations as last week. Dubois is now recovered, and Vincent is perfectly well. One or two Indians passed here today on their way up the River to fish.

Tuesday 6th. One of our Horses was found dead this morning, being drowned or rather smothered in the swampy creek that runs through the little prairie close to the Fort. Ten or twelve Cowitchens and Misquiams were at the wharf this day Eight of them going up the River to fish Sturgeon. All our men employed as they were yesterday, except that the four who were fetching meat to the fort are working in the Woods. Kennedy was taken ill this evening with a violent pain in his Stomach and Bowels.

Wednesday 7th. Pierre Charles and Antoine Pierrault were sent off again to hunt. Arquoitte, Baker, and Dubois are employed in clearing away the trees and shrubs that obstruct the view down the River. Faniant and another are facing the front of the two Galleries lately constructed, with thick Boards, so as to render them more secure from Shot. All the rest are occupied as they were yesterday. Kennedy is still complaining.

Thursday 8th. Como & Peopeoh were taken from the Saw and sent to assist Baker & Arquoitte in clearing the Bank of the River; all the others employed as yesterday.

Friday 9th. All Hands at the same work as yesterday. Sauvé has exchanged his situation as Cook with Dominque Faron, who is allowed to take the place. Two Nanaimoochs passed down the River; they still hold true to the report of some of the *Cadboro's* crew having been killed to the northward. Kennedy still sick; he was bled this afternoon.

Saturday 10th. All employed as yesterday, Kennedy not recovering. Our only remaining horse has died.

Sunday 11th. All very quiet.

Monday 12th. Kennedy still confined. The Two Sandwich Islanders with Baker and Dubois are clearing the Bank in front of the Fort, Cornoyer cutting firewood, the rest of the men preparing timber for the Big House.

Tuesday 13th. Every thing going forward as yesterday.

Wednesday 14th. Clear weather & frost this morning. Faniant & Como strengthening the two Galleries with a Breastwork of Plank two inches thick. Peopeoh, Baker, Arquoitte and Dubois are rooting out Stumps and levelling the Ground outside the Fort. Vincent & Boisvert employed as yesterday. Pierre Charles and Pierrault cleaning the arms in the Bastions and making ready for another hunting excursion. Faron & Macdonald in the Kitchen, Cornoyer chopping firewood, and the rest in the woods squaring Timber. Kennedy is getting a little better, but he is still very weak. Chaheinook the Indian who has been so long encamped in our neighbourhood paid us his last visit; he says he goes off tomorrow to join his countrymen.

Thursday 15th. Pierre Charles & Pierrault went off to visit their Traps and returned in the evening with two small Beaver and one Raccoon. The rest of the men are employed as yesterday. In the afternoon Scanawa arrived bearing a Letter from Doctor McLoughlin dated Fort Vancouver 18th October. It mentions the arrival of Mr. Ogden[50] and Party from the Snake Country, and their subsequent departure on another expedition. The Furs they had brought were shipped on board the *William & Ann* which had not at that time left the River. The *Cadboro* had not then made her appearance, but we have news of her from Scanawa who says that she left the Tlalam country which is on the south side of De Fuca's Straights twelve or fourteen days ago. The Letter Bearer took up his quarters close to the Fort.

Friday, 16th. The frost still continues and work still goes forward as yesterday. Shashia the Cowitchen Chief made his appearance with part of his family, and took up his quarters alongside of Scanawa's Tent. One of his wives was sent up to the Quoitlan Village to trade Dried Salmon, which is the object of his present visit.

Saturday 17th. Every one employed as yesterday. Kennedy still very weak. Shashia took his departure late in the afternoon, after his wife had arrived from above with a Canoe load of Dried Salmon. Before he went away, he was invited into the Fort, and presented with something to eat: a little ammunition was also given him, which appeared to be most acceptable.

Sunday 18th. Every thing quiet. Very fine weather.

Monday 19th. Peopeoh, Arquoitte, Baker, and Dubois putting up a chimney in Mr. Annance's House, the one which was first built having fallen down.[51] Boisvert and Como burning Stumps. Vincent[52] occupied as usual at the stock of dried Provisions. Faniant employed as a Carpenter, Cornoyer chopping firewood, Pierre Charles and Pierrault visiting traps and hunting. Anawiskum cook, and Faron servant. Kennedy confined, & Bouchard not at work, his hand having been badly bruised. The rest squaring timber for building. A few Indians from the Quoitlan Village were here with some Furs. They disposed of five Beaver Skins for Blue Strouds [cheap blankets or blanket cloth made from woollen rags], and paid Scanawa ten Skins for a debt which they owed him. Soon afterwards they went away.

Tuesday 20th. Work going forward as yesterday only that Peopeoh is assisting Como & Boisvert. At Dusk Pierrault returned alone with all the traps which Pierre Charles and he had set. Pierre left him to take a turn in the woods thinking to fall in with animals. Weather very fine for the Season.

Wednesday 21st. All busied as yesterday. The Kitchen chimney was repaired today. Pierre Charles returned, but without having killed any thing.

Thursday 22d. All employed as yesterday, except that the Hands who were occupied in mending Chimneys are today clearing away the Stumps, and breaking down the inequalities of ground in front of the Fort. Pierrault not on duty, he complains of a pain in his wrist, which he sprained a few days ago. Kennedy is recovering but slowly.

Friday 23d. Last night a noise was heard by some of the People resembling the sound of Distant cannon. The Houses were shaken at the time, which makes us suppose it to have been a slight shock of Earthquake, as a tree falling would not have been so sensibly felt.

Saturday 24th. Four men employed covering part of the Fort with Gravel, which is dug out from below the Storehouse. Most of the others squaring timber for building. Pierrault and Kennedy not on duty as yesterday.

Sunday 25th. Two Quoitlans were here with a few furs; they traded one small Beaver Skin and one small Otter Skin for Brass Collarwire[53] and then went away. It blew hard all day from the SSE, but at night the wind fell. The tide rose higher this forenoon than we have yet seen it, the effect probably of the Gale at Sea.

Monday 26th. Men still employed strewing gravel over the Fort; others of them are working in the woods squaring timber, chopping firewood etc. This morning a Flag Staff was cut in the woods, and prepared, and in the afternoon erected in the South east corner of the Fort. The usual forms were gone through – Mr. Annance officiated in baptizing the Establishment, and the men were regaled in celebration of the event.[54] The Firing which took place on the occasion was heard by our hunters who were not far distant and they came home very much alarmed.

Tuesday 27th. The people squaring timber, and burning and rooting out Stumps – Our Hunters went off again. Kennedy still keeps to the House.

Wednesday 28th. Work as Yesterday.

Thursday 29th. All who are at the fort engaged as Yesterday. Pierre Charles & Rabaska returned with three Beaver. A Band of Scadgats made their appearance today with a few Furs.

Friday 30th. The Scadgats traded their furs and went off. Their trade amounts to 109 Beaver Skins and 31 Otters. Work going forward as yesterday.

Saturday 1st December. Every thing going on as during the preceding part of the week.

Sunday 2d. Quiet times and frosty weather. Ice drifting in the River.

Monday 3d. Work as during the last week.

Tuesday 4th. No change in either work or weather.

Wednesday 5th. Scanawa traded One hundred Beaver Skins. Cold severe, and the Ice in the River increasing.

Thursday 6th. Pierre Charles & Rabaska came in with the meat of a Black Bear.

Friday 7th. Work as it has been for the last fortnight. Weather cold and clear.

Saturday 8th. Dull and monotonous times, Every thing bearing a wintery appearance.

Sunday 9th. Pierre Charles brought in four Beaver, which he killed not far from the fort.

Monday 10th. All Hands employed hauling the wood, which they have been lately squaring to the fort. The weather is favorable for this work. Snow on the ground and sharp cold.

Tuesday 11th. Work going forward as yesterday.

Wednesday 12th. All Hauling wood as yesterday. Weather very cold. Kennedy still complaining.

Thursday 13th. Work the same as yesterday.

Friday 14th. Every thing going forward as during the week.

Saturday 15th. All Hands employed in hauling squared timber to the Fort. Snow all day. Wind westerly.

Sunday 16th. Weather mild. Wind East. Pierre Charles and Plomondeau arrived with two Beaver late in the evening.

Monday 17th. Weather extremely cold. The men at the same work as last week. Pierre Charles was fitted out for a hunting excursion.

Tuesday 18th. Pierre Charles went off early. All the men occupied as yesterday. The cold is increasing, and the River is frozen across so solidly that the tide does not as usually, break it up.

Wednesday 19th. Severe cold. The ice is so strong that the River may be crossed. The men today finished hauling wood for the mess House.

Thursday 20th. Mild Weather. Snowing all day. Men employed hauling Logs to the Saw Pit, and at sundry little jobs besides. Pierre Charles arrived with Ettue; he has killed four Red Deer.

Friday 21st. Weather dark and cloudy. Sixteen men were sent off to fetch the meat killed yesterday by the hunter: three returned in the evening with the meat of the two animals that lay nearest the Fort. The Hands at the Establishment employed at various little jobs.

Saturday 22d. Weather as Yesterday. Strong thaw. All the Party which had been sent for meat were back by noon. Pierre Charles has cut his hand severely with an axe.

Sunday 23d. Weather still the same. Nothing stirring.

Monday 24th. Weather changed. Clear and cold. In the morning two Indians from the Musqueam camp near the Quoitle River arrived with a note from Mr. A. McKenzie, the purport of which was that he was disagreeably situated with only four men amongst a formidable Band of Indians, and was doubtful whether he would be able to extricate himself without our assistance. Messrs. Manson and Annance with nine men went off immediately to his relief, but they had not proceeded far, before they met him and his party all uninjured. The Indians have stolen a little property from them, but it will be very easily recovered. Mr. M. is a welcome visitor – he is the bearer of our Home Letters and news from Vancouver.

Tuesday 25th. Christmas Day.[55]

Wednesday 26th. Mr. Annance with Six men was dispatched to fetch Mr. McKenzie's Canoe on the Ice to the Fort, and to recover what had been stolen from that Gentleman at the Misquiam Camp. In the Latter Business they succeeded nobly, but the Canoe they found it impracticable to bring up, as the Ice was too weak to bear them, and at the same time too strong for them to break their way through it for any distance with the canoe. Pierre Charles was sent off to try and kill animals, and 6 men accompanied him in order to fetch home the meat.

Thursday 27th. Weather clear and cold. Men chopping firewood, clearing the Fort of snow, and doing sundry other little jobs.

Friday 28th. Weather the same as yesterday. In the evening the Hunter arrived, and informed us that he had killed seven Red Deer, and a Black Bear, the meat of which the men who had been sent with him were securing.

Saturday 29th. Eight more of the people were started with Pierre Charles to assist in bringing home the meat. Weather mild with snow.

Sunday 30th. Light wind from the South west. Weather mild. Pierre Charles and his men arrived with Sixteen hundred Pounds of meat.

Monday 31st. Weather a little cold: nothing of moment occurring.

Tuesday 1st January 1828. New Year's Day.[56] Every one in high glee, Jean Bte. considerably elevated, and as a matter of course displaying his manhood.

Wednesday 2d. The men still enjoying themselves, tho' the effervescence of Spirits has in a great measure subsided. Mr. McMillan preparing for a trip to Fort Vancouver. We had heavy Snow last night, and this morning the weather is still very cloudy.

Thursday 3d. Two of the men from Vancouver, Louis Ossin[57] and Etienne Pepin[58] are to remain here, and two of our Hands Antoine Pierrault and François Tarihonga return with Mr. McKenzie in their stead. Early in the forenoon Mr. McMillan with Messrs. McKenzie and Annance left us for Fort Vancouver with every prospect of fine weather and a speedy voyage.

Friday 4th. All Hands employed putting the Snow out of the Fort.

Saturday 5th. Men employed as yesterday. Weather getting cold again.

Sunday 6th. Clear Frost and blowing fresh.

Monday 7th. Weather Boisterous and cold. Three men cutting alder for charcoal.[59] The two Owyhees sawing Logs for the Big House – the rest cutting firewood, and felling trees that are still standing too near the Fort.

Tuesday 8th. Work and weather the same as yesterday.

Wednesday 9th. Blowing hard with continued snow. Some of the People clearing it out of the Fort – Others employed in the woods as on Monday and yesterday.

Thursday 10th. Cloudy weather and snow. Pierre Charles and Faniant making Snow Shoes, which are required by the People to bring to the Fort the meat which was left out. They will be wanted again if the winter holds on as severely as the present weather seems to indicate.

Friday 11th. Two men were sent out to procure Birch wood for Sledges. Clear cold weather.

Saturday 12th. Weather milder a little with appearances of more snow. The Charcoal Kiln [pit] is finished, and Ettue watches it while burning. The men are getting on with the Snow Shoes and Sledges, and the Snow is nearly all out of the Fort.

Sunday 13th. Mr. McMillan and Annance arrived with the men from this place who had composed their party. They were detained a week at Point Roberts by uncommonly boisterous weather. Perceiving that after such detention and with such a change in the season he could not accomplish the Voyage except at the expense of a longer absence than he could afford, Mr. McMillan considered it advisable to return, and accordingly left Mr. McKenzie to pursue his route himself, having first seen him provided with Guides, and well supplied with Provisions.

Monday 14th. Some of the Hands cutting firewood; others making Sledges, and a few shovelling Snow out of the Fort.

Tuesday 15th. Work as yesterday – Soft weather.

Wednesday 16th. Every thing going on as during the two preceding days – Rain.

Thursday 17th. Pierre Charles was sent off to hunt and twelve men accompanied him to bring home the meat should he chance to kill animals. Of this we have every hope, as numbers of Red Deer were seen by Mr. McMillan's Party as they were coming up the River.[60] Men at the fort cutting firewood and overhauling Beaver Skins which are very apt to take damp and become mouldy. Soft weather.

Friday 18th. Very mild morning – Work as usual.

Saturday 19th. Sleet and Snow.

Sunday 20th. All quiet – Weather continues mild.

Monday 21st. Two men arrived with a load of meat each. The Thaw continues.

Tuesday 22d. The men at the Fort employed in the woods.

Wednesday 23d. Work going on at the Fort as usual.

Thursday 24th. Men arrived with meat from the Hunters. 360 lbs. weight.

Friday 25th. Several men were again sent off to Pierre Charles the Hunter, to remain out until they get another supply of meat for the Fort. Two Okinagan Indians who have been here for some time back took their departure for the Interior – They undertake to deliver Letters at Kamloops, and are accordingly entrusted with two by Mr. McMillan. Clear but mild weather.

Saturday 26th. We had a heavy fall of snow last night, and have still the appearance of more.

Sunday 27th. Nothing stirring.

Monday 28th. The men in the Fort employed in clearing away the Snow and working in the woods.

Tuesday 29th.	Nothing particular
Wednesday 30th.	occurring and
Thursday 31st.	work going
Friday 1st February	forward as on
Saturday 2d.	Monday.

Sunday 3d. All quiet. Pierrault Jacques and Ossin arrived from the Hunters' Camp. They come for Beaver Traps, Pierre having discovered several Lodges.

Monday 4th. Pierrault and Ossin were sent off with Traps for Pierre Charles. Men employed cutting Logs, and blasting them with Gunpowder, that being the easiest method of breaking them up.

Tuesday 5th. Every thing going forward as Yesterday.

Wednesday 6th. The Hunter's men with the exception of two arrived with meat. 320 lbs.

Thursday 7th. Faniant smoothing Boards and the two Owyhees sawing. The rest of the men employed as on Tuesday and yesterday.

Friday 8th. Work the same as yesterday.

Saturday 9th. Work as during the week. Weather mild.

Sunday 10th. All quiet.

Monday 11th. Annance went to a small Village above to inquire about a Canoe for sending the Party with the Spring Express to Fort Vancouver.[61] He returned with an Indian who is to accompany him tomorrow to a Village Below, where it is expected that a suitable one will be easily procured. Work at the Fort going forward as during last week. Faniant preparing Boards for the Big House. The Two Owyhees sawing, and the others cutting firewood, blasting Logs etc.

Tuesday 12th. Messrs. Manson and Annance with four men went off early to try and procure a Canoe in which to send the Express to Puget Sound. In the evening they returned and informed us that they arrived very opportunely at a camp of Kijis [Katzies], and succeeded in purchasing a Canoe which was ready to leave the Village, the Indians being about to proceed farther up the Quoitle River. The cause of their removal they alleged to be their dread of being cut off by the Yucletaws who, they believe are in the neighbourhood with the avowed intention of paying a Plundering visit to the River, as soon as the navigation opens. Three men were sent off to fetch home the meat of an animal which the Hunter has killed. The work at the Fort going on as usual.

Wednesday 13th. Work the same as Yesterday. Weather a little milder than usual and the thaw of course increasing. In the afternoon Shashia the Cowitchen Chief with two other Indians arrived, bringing a few Beaver Skins with them of which they disposed to Scanawa, in whose tent they took up their quarters for the night. We are told by Shashia that he heard a Report in the Holumma [Lummi] Country that Mr. McKenzie with his party of four men were murdered by the Tlalams somewhere in the vicinity of Whidbey Island. Such a Rumour vague as we at present take it to be, tends still to inspire us with serious alarm, and if confirmed the event will cause much sorrow, and be attended with very important consequences.[62]

Thursday 14th. Shashia and his companions went away and Annance with eight men soon followed them in order to look after the Canoe which has been traded from the Kijis, and lay it up in a place of greater security than where it at present is. Pierre Charles arrived with all the people who were out. The meat which they bring is 220 lbs. weight. Mr. Annance returned with his party after having succeeded in bringing the Canoe a mile nearer the House.

Friday 15th. Three men were employed in cutting wood and squaring Posts for a Gallery which it is intended to carry round the Fort inside of the Pickets. Faniant preparing Boards for the Big House, the two Owyhees sawing, and the rest of the men cutting firewood and blasting Large Timber: Weather becoming mild. The thaw is now strong.

Saturday 16th. Work the same as yesterday. Weather very mild. Mr. Manson making Preparations to start with a party for Fort Vancouver. Several Quoitlans were seen fishing in an opening of the River at the Point above.

Sunday 17th. It is proposed that Mr. Manson with 7 Men[63] shall leave this place tomorrow with the Packet,[64] which of course brings this Journal to a close –

Journal Kept by James McMillan and Archibald McDonald, 1828-9

James McMillan

James McMillan, born in Scotland about 1783, joined the North West Company around the turn of the century. He worked in the Saskatchewan department, accompanied David Thompson on his first expedition west of the Rockies, and spent almost a decade in the Columbia District before the union of the fur trade companies. In 1813 he was at the mouth of the Columbia River, where he was one of the Nor'Westers who signed the agreement to buy out the interests of the Pacific Fur Company. At that time he made a will that named Ewan on the Saskatchewan and Helen[1] and Margaret on the Columbia as his heirs (McMillan 1821).

In 1821 he was retained by the Hudson's Bay Company as a chief trader, and the same year a daughter, Victoria McMillan, was born to Kilakotah,[2] one of McMillan's country wives. Two years later he went to Upper Canada because of the death of his father.[3] He took with him two children – Margaret, born 16 September 1813, and Allan, born 1 January 1816 – who were baptized at St. Andrew's Presbyterian Church, Williamstown.[4] While he was at Fort Langley, two of his children were with John McLeod and his wife, Charlotte, at Norway House.[5]

In his mid-forties, McMillan had a formidable reputation as an Indian trader, an intrepid explorer, and a man of great physical stamina and courage. The speed with which the post on the Fraser was built, in spite of the many problems, is a tribute to his abilities. Barnston declared him to be "without exception ... the most valuable man on the Columbia" (Barnston 1829:158). His promotion to chief factor was obviously well deserved. But McMillan's career had peaked. Throughout 1827 he suffered from a complaint he feared would cost the use of his leg (McMillan 1827b:17), and his days as an explorer were behind him. He wanted to get medical attention in Scotland but had "pretensions" to consider. "I hope you did the needful for the poor girl before you gave her as it would be less trouble for the man that took her," he wrote to McLeod, who had arranged to have a step-daughter married (McMillan 1828b:104). It seems safe to assume that McMillan did "the needful" for his "concerns."

On his return from his furlough of 1829-30, he was made responsible for establishing and administering an experimental farm at Red River, but he was much less suited for this work than for the more dangerous and demanding tasks he had performed on the Pacific slope. Eleanor McKinley became his wife while he was on furlough, and over the next few years they had a number of children. They retired to Scotland. After McMillan's death in 1858, his widow was in such financial difficulty that the company decided to give her a grant from the pension fund.[6]

Governor George Simpson described McMillan as "a very steady plain blunt man ... fit for any Service requiring physical strength firmness of mind and good management provided he has no occasion to meddle with Pen & Ink in the use of which he is deficient his Education having been neglected."[7] As George Barnston prepared to leave for Fort Vancouver, McMillan "meddled with pen and ink"; he kept the post journal until he left in October 1828. Archibald McDonald prepared the 1828-9 journal to be sent to London. In copying McMillan's entries, he eliminated some errors, but also made considerable change, imposing his own style. In order to let the "plain blunt man" speak for himself, entries from 18 February to 8 October 1828 have been taken from the original journal kept at Fort Langley.

McMillan's punctuation followed no logical system, and his spelling was most inconsistent, but he was more careless in keeping the journal than he was in his correspondence. If he had made the annual copy, he would undoubtedly have corrected many of the errors himself. In order to make the documents more readable but still remain as true to the original as possible, spelling errors are considered slips and are corrected without comment where the correct form appears at least half the time. Where an incorrect form has been used consistently, it is shown initially and subsequently corrected. Forms correct at the time have been retained (e.g.,

Excerpt from the post journal in James McMillan's hand.

employ'd). Most of McMillan's dashes have been retained, but punctuation has been added where necessary to make the meaning clear, and removed where obtrusive. Where McDonald's copy contains additional interesting information or where his version provides an interpretation that makes McMillan's meaning clear, McDonald's excerpts have been included within {braces}. These excerpts reveal the great differences in the styles and personalities of the two men.

～

Journal of Occurrences at Fort Langley
February 18, 1828 to February 17, 1829

[February 1828]

Monday 18th. Mr. Manson with a party of Seven men Started for Vancouver with the accounts, Provisioned for Eight days. Sent two men to Car[r]y their things as far as the Canoe {which is at the mouth of the river}. The men at work as follows, Kennedy Cleaning and put[t]ing the arms in order. Bouchard and two men Squaring wood. The two Owhyhees Sawying [sawing] plank. Boisvert dusting the few Furs. The two men that accompanied Mr. Manson Came back. They Saw Some Indians fishing Sturgeon. A few Straggling Quaitlands [Kwantlen] about.

Tuesday 19th. Frosty weather. The men employed as yesterday. Sent Ossin fir [for] Traps Pieer [Pierre] Charles Sett [set] a few days before he went off.

Wednesday 20th. The weather Cold and Clear. The men dragging home posts for a Gallery. An Indian who passed the winter in Scaniwa's lodge was drowned Coming from the Kutche [Katzie] Camp where he had gone two days ago, to buy a Slave. The Ice brock [broke] under him. He had 3 Blankets and a Steel Trap when he fell in the water. Several Indians going about fishing. Ice floating in the river.

Thursday 21st. Soft weather. The men at work as yesterday. Indians about fishing.

Friday 22nd. The weather as yesterday – Ice floating in the river. The men employed as usual.

Saturday 23rd. Fine Clear frosty morning. The men Still employed Squaring wood etc. Indians about fishing Sturgeon but don't like to part with any.

Sunday 24th. The weather as yesterday – Sent two men for the meat of a red deer. Whitlakenum the Chief of the Quaitlands, Came to the Fort. He brought 2 Beaver Skins and made them a present to the widow of the Indian that was drowned. Scaniwa and Rabaska went down to the Cowitchen village for a Canoe.

Monday 25th. Hard frost. The widow of the Okinukun [Okanagan] that was drowned a few days ago, left this [day] to go to her own lands. She goes up the river and Crosses over near the foot of Mount Baker, to the Scadget and Sinihooms Country, from thence to the Sinuwames [Duwamish] {South end of Puget Sound} where She Considers her home. A Shissal [Sechelt] from beyond Burrard's Canal Came to the fort. He informs us that the Yewkeltas are preparing to Come and take our Blankets from us *Sans Ceremonee* – As this is rather a Cheap way of getting goods, we will not likely Come to terms amicably. In that Case our Iron Interpretters [interpreters] will have to Settle the dispute – Ossin & Perrault making a *net* to try and Catch Sturgeon – The Others bussy [busy] as yesterday.

Tuesday 26th. The weather foggy and Soft. The men employ'd as yesterday.

Wednesday 27th. Clear frosty morning – Bouchard with four men working at the Gallery – two men dragging home Small picketts [pickets] to line the fort inside – The two Owhyhees Sawing plank – Sauve and Boisvert Cutting fire wood. Ossin & Perreault busy at the net – which was Set in 12 fms. water.

Thursday 28th. Soft with a thick fog – The men as yesterday employ'd. Visited the net but got nothing.

Friday 29th. Thick Fog in the morning. Showers of rain all day. The men busy as yesterday. Indians about and Seem much afraid of the Yeukeltas.

Saturday 1st March. Soft rainy weather. The men at their usual work. The Quaitlands about fishing.

Sunday 2nd. Rain all day. Nothing else particular.

Monday 3rd. The weather etc. as yesterday.

Tuesday 4th. Showers of rain all day. Arquoitte and four men making a new Chimney in the Kitchen. Faignant, Bouchard, Suave, and Rabaska Squaring wood for the Saw pit. Ossin making Floats for the net. Three Indians from the upper part of the river Came here this morning, brought nothing.

Wednesday 5th. Rain and fog. The men employed much the Same as yesterday. A Sturgeon went through our net. The twine is too weak.

Thursday 6th. After a night of incessant rain, the morning became fair with a thick fog – A Sturgeon made his way through our net by breaking three mashes [meshes] – The men Squaring & Sawing – Three Indians from the Kutche Camp paid us a visit, brought nothing in the way [of] a trade.

Friday 7th. Rain all day. The men doing little Jobs indoors – Whitlekenum with a few others passed up. He Says that Jashia is Coming Soon. He also Confirms the report of Mr. McKenzie being Cut off by the Clalams. A Quatland Indian that Came, Says his tribe are gone to war on the Chiliquiyouks [Chilliwacks].

Saturday 8th. Heavy rain during the night, but Cleared up towards morning. The men Squaring and getting Logs to the Saw pit. Indians about fishing.

Sunday 9th. A fine dry day. The men etc. at the work of yesterday.

Monday 10th. Heavy rain. Fagnaint & Bouchard planing boards. The two
   Owhyhees Sawing plank. The rest of the men Clearing ground for
   potatoes.
Tuesday 11th. Incessant rain all day. Sheinten a Masquiam [Musqueam]
   Chief paid us a visit from Vancouver's Island, with a Canoe load of
   Shell fish. Nothing Strange from that quarter. He Says the Chief of the
   Clalams [Clallams] Saved one of Mr. McK.'s party, and Sent him off to
   Vancouver. He also Says the Yeukeltas are Coming to See us soon.
Wednesday 12th. A fine day. The men at work as Yesterday.
Thursday 13th. This morning a war party of Cawitchens Headed by
   Lammus passed up. They Say they are going to kill the Chiliquiyouks a
   tribe that lives on a Small river that Come[s] in from Mount Baker. The
   man that Stood watch last night observed a large Canoe full of Indians
   Coming on Slily till they were opposite to the Bastion but perceiving
   they were discovered they about Ship at once. We Suppose it was those
   vagabonds on the look out if every thing was quiet in the Fort, and take
   us for Chiliqueyoukes. They are 150 men in ten Canoes, and ugly looking Devils they are – {painted to their very ears.} A Slave from the
   Sockwans [Suquamish] told that Mr. Manson was Safe passed, and
   Waskuladget a Sinihome Chief went along with him. A little after the
   war party left this they met Shientin the Musqueam Chief with his wife
   and two of his daughters. The war Chief took the eldest from him, menacing if he did not keep very quiet he would kill him & make Slaves of
   his family – two very fine looking girls.
Friday 14th. Showers of rain. The men Cutting away Stumps.
Saturday 15th. Thick fog this morning. Kennedy & Sauve who Stood the
   Second watch Saw Indians Skulking about the Fort, but seeing we keep
   a Strick [strict] guard they did not venture too near. They threw a Couple of Stones at the men who were walking on the Gallery, but from the
   darkness of the night they Could not See to fire at them. This is the first
   [thing] of this kind we experienced Since we are among them. They
   generrally [generally] left very quiet during the nights. Should they try
   Such pranks in a Clear night Some of them will repent it, as the watch
   has orders to fire at once if the least insulted. I Suppose it to be the war
   party on their return home.
Sunday 16th. Fog and Drizily [drizzly] rain during the first part of the day.
   Cleared up in the afternoon. [A] few Straggling Indians about.
Monday 17th. Cloudy with Showers of rain. A few Indians from the little
   river were about fishing – The men employ'd as on Saturday.
Tuesday 18th. The weather much the same as yesterday. The men piling
   the wood and brush, ready to burn. Two men dusting and rubbing the
   few furs. Faynaint Sick.
Wednesday 19th. Clear frosty morning. Three Indians from the Kutche
   Camp up *Pit[t]'s River* informed us that the Cowitchen war party were
   passed, that they killed 10 of the Penault [Pilalt] tribe and had taken a
   number of their women & Children Slaves. They must have passed here
   at night. This tribe lives about a day's march up. This warfare keeps the

Indians of this vicinity in Such Continual alarm, that they Can[n]ot turn their attention to any thing but the care of their family and that they do but poorely [poorly]. While the powerful tribes from Vancouver's Island harass them in this manner, little hunts Can be expected from them and unless the Company Supports them against those lawless villains little exertions Can be expected from them.

Thursday 20th. Cloudy morning. The men at their usual work. Indians about fishing. Heavy rain in the Evening.

Friday 21st. Incessant rain till noon. The men Still Clearing ground Squaring, Sawing etc. A little after dark Skaniwa gave us the alarm by Calling out the Yeukeltas were Coming. All hands called to arm themselves, with a view to meet these fellows as well as our means would admit us. But on getting up upon the Gallery we observed the noise was from abouve [above], and was [were] agreeably dissappointed [disappointed] by the arrival of a large Canoe full of Coutoomuns from the forks of Thompson's River, going down to the Kutchu Camp to See LaPetchun a Chief from that quarter that passed the winter up Pitt's River {& is himself occasionally backwards and forwards to that Country.}

Saturday 22nd. Thick fog in the morning with rain. Our visitors of last night went off to Pitt's River. They traded one Beaver and 1 Otter, for which they wanted amm. They told me the river from here to the forks of Thompson's River is fine and nothing to hinder Canoes from going up – La Patchun Came with 10 Beaver newly killed, for which he traded 2 Blankets of 2 ½ pts.[8] He went off Immediately having meet [met] his friends on his way up. Towards evening four Indians from above Called here on their way to Vancouver's Island. They had property to redeem. Some women and Childrun [children] who were taken in the last Battle above – They informed me that they killed 10 men on the Spot, took away 10 women & 10 Children along with them. {It may not however be unnecessary to observe that the most implicit Confidence is not to be put in these Stories for by a singular Coincidence we find them make use of the Number *Ten* – and this with many other Circumstances we are obliged to record here proceed from our imperfect Knowledge of the language.}

Sunday 23rd. The Indians {Penaults} that Came here last night returned back being afraid of the Yeukeltas, So that the poor women must Content themselves with Serving the Cowitchens a longer time than they expected.

Monday 24th. Showers of rain with intervals of Sunshine. All hands Clearing and preparing ground for potatoes etc.

Tuesday 25th. A Continued pour of rain all day. Nothing else going on.

Wednesday 26th. Showers of rain and Hail with blinks of Sunshine. Fagnaint planing boards, Boisvert sick. Baker ill of the venereale [venereal] – the Couteaumens that went down Friday Came back. They Sold a Yewkeltas Slave to Skaniwa for a Gun, a Blanket and 2 yards of Collar wire. La Pitchun Came up along with them. He left 4 Beaver Skins here until his return.

Thursday 27th. Showers of rain with intervals of Sunshine. The men begane [began] to burn & gather the rubbish about the garden ground. No Indians about.

Friday 28th. The man on the watch last night observed a Canoe full of men Coming Closs [close] to the wharf. Five of the number debarked at Skanwa's lodge ap[p]roached it very quietly but on finding the lodge empty, they embarked and went off – Skaniwa thinks they Intended to kill him had they found him there, but this fortnight back he takes the precaution to Sleep in the fort. Lapitchen passed down. He traded the Skins he left here on his way up. He being a good Indian I lent him a Trap, the first article lent Since our arrival here.

Saturday 29th. Clear Calm weather. The man on the Gallery called out that he heared [heard] the report of a Cannon. We are in hopes the *Cadboro* is at the entrance – The men are Still at the Same work, a Job that will employ them Sometime.

Sunday 30th. Cloudy with rain. A few of the Penaults passed down on their way to Vancouver's Island to the Cowitchen Camp to redeem the women and Children taken on their last war excursion. Two Kutches brought 10 Beaver Skins which they traded for Blankets of 2 ½ pts.

Monday 31st. Frost and a Clear day – All hands at their usual work.

Tuesday 1st April. Clear weather with a Strong gale from the NE, which blew down a great number of trees. Thirty were thrown down in the Sight of the fort. No Indians about.

Wednesday 2nd. The weather Clear and warm. Skaniwa who went up the river to hunt Beaver Came back. The Slave he bought a few days ago deserted from him and Stole his gun and Some other articles. The Slave is Yeukeltas who was taken when young – Some rascally Quaitland Stole his traps, nor Could he get them back but by giving a Small Copper kettle for them. He had 4 Traps which he only Set one night and Caught 4 Beaver. He Could not remain to hunt as the Indians began to Steal his property.

Thursday 3rd. The weather as yesterday, work etc. the Same.

Friday 4th. A fine day. The Indians {Penault ambassadors} that went to the Cowitchen Camp Came back. They Succeeded in getting back 3 of the women by a large price for them – A Quaitland was rather insolent on the wharf, for which he got a few Sound Kicks from Mr. Annance. Mr. Skaniwa Seemed to take this in a very high Dudge[o]n and Spoke a good deal before the Indians, till I was under the necessity to give him two or three knock down blows which Soon brought the great man to his Senses.[9] {He will undoubtedly be the better of it, for he has been taking great footing on the protection he has in the Fort – not however as he ought, by Showing gratitude to the whites.}

Saturday 5th. The weather Clear and mild. The men going on with their usual work – Towards Evening, Indians were heard Speaking in the woods below – Mr. Annance embarked in a Small Canoe and paddled towards the quarter from whence the noise was heard, and in turning the point he heard them very distinctly, but being alone he did not think it advisable to go too near – We Cannot Imagine who they are unless Some more war parties from Vancouver's Island going up the river.

Sunday 6th. Weather the Same – Mr. Annance with some men went down to see who those Skulkers were. He went as far as the Nanaiman Village – Saw plenty of fresh marks in the woods, and tracks along the beech [beach]. I suppose being perceived, they thought proper to turn back – Or at least [they have] gone down the river for a few days. Some Indians from the little river Came to tell us that the Yeukeltas had been attacking the Musquum village, that two of the latter tribe had run away and told them of the affair. The Indians about here are So much ad[d]icted to telling fals[e]hoods that out of ten words you Can't believe two.

Monday 7th. Weather the Same as yesterday – Shienten Came to the fort. He has a few Skins and [a] Canoe load of Shell fish – He gave us no news except the wonderful Story of the Yeukeltas Coming to burn our fort. He Camped in the woods. He pretends [to be] or is really afraid.

Tuesday 8th. Fine Clear weather. The men busy at their usual work. A Cowitchen from Van. Island Called here on his way to the Quaitland village, nothing Strange from that quarter – Skaniwa went up the river to gather Some debts owing to him in that quarter as he intends to be off very soon to the Cowlitz. I begin to despair of the people who went to Vancouver.

Wednesday 9th. No Change in the weather. Some Penaults Came down with a few Salmon. They Speak a different Language from the Quaitlands – They Say all the Indians are rising Camp upwards, afraid of the Indians from the Gulf.

Thursday 10th. Cloudy with Showers of rain. Lapitchin Came with 2 Beaver. Skaniwa Came back from the Quaitland Camp, brought a few Skins.

Friday 11th. Incessand [Incessant] rain all the forenoon. The latter part of the day Clear and agreeable. Got a line arrenged [arranged] and Set for Sturgeon.

Saturday 12th. Weather the Same – No Stir about the fort.

Sunday 13th. Rain – Indians about fishing but don't like to part with it. The men kept Clearing ground.

Monday 14th. Rain with a Strong breeze. Caught a Sturgeon of 100 lbs. this morning and another Small one of 20 lbs. in Course of the day. A large one got off by breaking the Hook. We now entertain hopes of Catching a few with our hooks, a very desirable thing, as the Indians of this river put a great value on every thing in the Shape of provisions.

Tuesday 15th. Heavy rain all day. About 3 P.M. we were happy at seeing Mr. Manson arrive Safe from Vancouver. I must own that I was very anxious about him, knowing that the trip was a dangerous one, So Soon after the affair of Mr. McKenzie & party being cut off by the Clalams – which I am grieved to find from Mr. M is true[10] – He took his passage back in the *Cadboro* which he left a reach above the Cowitchen village waiting for a fair wind – Mr. Annance went back with [the] Boat.

Wednesday 16th. No Change in the weather. Captain Simpson and Mr. Annance Came up to the fort; left the Vessel above Pitt's River.

Thursday 17th. The Same weather as yesterday. The water rising fast. The vessel will make but Slow progress against the Strong Current.

Friday 18th. Heavy rain all day. At 7 A.M. the *Cadboro* anchored before the Fort and began to unload Such articles as the rain could not hurt.

Saturday 19th. No Change in the weather. The vessel finished unloading – and began Cutting firewood for her use back. Several Indians about fishing from whom we got a Sturgeon.

Sunday 20th. A Clear day. Five men Cutting and Carrying wood for the vessel, others putting the Potatoes {received from the vessel} in the Cellar and measuring them.

Monday 21st. The men employed about the Gardens and the wood for the *Cadboro* – In the evening having every thing ready She anchored out in the Channel {with 7 Bales Furs in addition to those of last Summer on account of outfit 1827 and about 130 Skins on the ensuing outfit,[11] besides a Bale of Slops and Camus, & some Iron we return to Ft. Vancouver being much required there itself}. Mr. Barnston went on board and takes his passage in her to Vancouver {being in a very poor state of health here for Some time back}.

Tuesday 22nd. Fine day. The *Cadboro* Started at day break. The men employed as follows: Bouchard, Plumondon, Fagnaint & Ettue preparing to begin the frame of a House, Pierre Charles arranging his Traps, Kennedy and Arquoitte burning Stumps, all the others preparing ground for Potatoes.

Wednesday 23rd. Cloudy with Showers of rain. The men began a House of 44 feet by 24. The others at work as yesterday. Five Canoes of the Whooms [Squamish] passed up the river with their families.

Thursday 24th. The weather as yesterday. The men at the Same work.

Friday 25th. Cloudy and Showers of rain. A great many Indians of different tribes about. The men employed as yesterday.

Saturday 26th. The weather Still Cloudy. A Canoe with five Cowitchins passed up. They report that the Cowitchins are preparing to go to War on the Clalams on account of the death of Joshia's father {father-in-law}, who they Suppose was killed by the Clalams, from the Effects of bad medicine. Every thing here goes on the same as usual.

Sunday 27th. Heavy rain all day. Four more Canoes of the Whooms tribe passed up. Quaitlands fishing about, from whom we got Some Sturgeon. The men at their usual work.

Monday 28th. Weather as yesterday – A Quaitland brought us 25 Beaver Skins which he traded for Blankets. The little fishes which the Chinooks Call Ullachun [eulachon] begin to make their appearance here, and are Joyffully [joyfully] hailed by the Indians of the river. Laputchine brought back the Slave that ran away from Skaniwa Sometime ago {but not the Gun}.

Tuesday 29th. Rainy day. The men began to hoe ground for the Potatoes. Ettue Cut his arm badly with his axe and is off duty – We made a trial to take Some of the little fish Chinook fashion {with the rake}, and proved very Successful as enough were taken to give a prog[12] to all hands.

Wednesday 30th. Cloudy with Showers of rain. The men at the Same work as yesterday. Indians in numbers fishing before our door. Our men take Enough to keep the kettle going.

Thursday 1st May. Heavy rain. Old Lecham a Quaitland Chief brought nine Beaver Skins for which he got Blankets – also Some Sturgeon. No Change in the work.

Friday 2nd. Fine weather. Many Indians fishing, and altho they kill plenty of Sturgeon, they will hardly part with any, So little are they in want of our goods, except Blankets. It is only when they have more than they want for their own use that we can get any at a reasonable rate. Our friend Skaniwa went off to the Cowlitz – he is a great rascal to say the least of him. Trade 25 Beaver & Otters.

Saturday 3rd. Cloudy day – Set the men to their work. Skaniwa Came back in Course of the night. He Says the Indians were near killing him. 50 Canoes of Musquiams Came to the wharf with their families. They went and Camped opposite in the little river. They say they have a few Beaver among them.

Sunday 4th. Clear day. A great many Indians going about. More Whooms going above with their families to the fisheries. Some are Camped opposite. Got Some Sturgeon. Two Nanomins Called here *En passant*. They Say their Chiefs have a few Skins among them, and will Come Soon – They Say the Yeukeltas and Quo-quals [Kwakiutl] are employed by Joshia to assist him against the Clalams – A Musquiam traded 7 Beaver for a Blanket & Beads.

Monday 5th. The morning very Threatening. Thunder & heavy rain in the afternoon. Traded a Sturgeon from a Quaitland for an axe. Six Penaults passed down to Whitlakenun's Camp. The men employed about the Gardens.

Tuesday 6th. The weather Still rough. The men at the same work. Indians Continually about the gates. Bought a Sturgeon from the Quatlands – We hear from the Indians that there is a Ship [the *Parthian*] at the Clalams trading Skins. I have no doubt the Yankees will pay that Quarter another visit which will injure our trade much, and will furnish these rascals with their wants, especially ammunition. In the afternoon a Canoe passed up (as he said) to advertise the Indians to keep their Skins and that the Ship was Coming to the entrance of the river.

Wednesday 7th. Fine day. The men at their usual work. Indians Continually about us. Traded Some Sturgeon. After dusk the Cry of Yeaukeltas was heard from all quarters. Immediately all the women and Children in the Camp embarked in their Canoes and went up the little river and hid themselves in the woods. The men made a Shew of remaining at the Camp or rather in [the] Skirts of the wood. Any one unacquainted with the Indian life would imagine all the furies of the infernal regions were let loose at once, however once the women Children & dogs were off things got quieter the rest of the night.

Thursday 8th. Fine day – men at work at the Gardens – The Indians Came across in great numbers – told the Yeukeltas had killed a Musquiam

Chief down at the Cowitchin Summer Village. They wanted that we Should give them Shelter in the fort. Great friends for Sometime, but unfortunately these Brutes know of no middle State. You must either allow them all the liberties they please, or keep them at great distance, for no Sooner you Seem kind towards them, than they begin to Steal and pilfer every thing they Can get hold of. And while the most decent among them were begging for Shelter from their Enemies, the rest were running about the men and picking every thing they Could – To be Short we were obliged to Send them off every one good, bad, and indifferent, and Stick to the good old Custom of keeping them to the bank of the river. Traded a few fresh Salmon that an Indian from above brought.

Friday 9th. The weather very warm. Several families of the Whooms who were encamped opposite, removed downwards – Musqueams about the Fort all day, Striving to keep up the price of their Sturgeon, which they Could easily do, but for the Supply we had from Vancouver not being out yet. The last affair with Yeukeltas keeps them in Continual alarm.

Saturday 10th. The weather the Same – Men employed at the Garden – Indians about us with no trade.

Sunday 11th. No Change in the weather. Indians about as usual. Traded 5 beaver for a Blanket and a Sturgeon for an axe. {These mercenary rascals are doing all they Can to keep up the price of the Sturgeon in which they would easily Succeed were we not So well provided with Corn, pease & Grease.} Our friend Skaniwa preparing to be off for the Cowlitz the Second time, and is only waiting the darkness of the night when the Indians give up fishing. I wrote Chief Factor McLoughlin by him.[13]

Monday 12th. Indians about fishing. They begin to Supply us well now and at a more reasonable rate. Trade 2 Beaver for beads – The men at the garden. The weather Cool and agreeable.

Tuesday 13th. Weather the Same as yesterday. Indians always about the Gates. The men Clearing and burning Stumps for the Potato ground. No trade.

Wednesday 14th. Fine day – Indians of all tribes (Say) Kawitchins, Whoomes, Musquiams, Keitches, and Quaitlands about us – Traded a few Beaver Skins for Beads – Sturgeon Scarce.

Thursday 15th. Fine weather. Some of the men Carrying in the frame of a House. The others at the Garden & Sawing boards – The Sills and Six posts of the big house were laid. Indians as usual about. A few Indians Called the Squaals [Douglas Lillooet] Came to the Fort. They inhabit the upper parts of Pitt's River or rather Some other Branches that fall into Fraser's River, from the northward as they seem to be perfectly acquainted with the men of Thompson's River. They named a number of them, Such as Jacques & Champegn[14] etc. They must have Seen them when trading Salmon on Fr's. River – We Could get but little Information from them as we Could not understand them. A Couple of Nanaimons passed up to the Quaitlands. They are from Vancouver Island.

Friday 16th. The weather the Same. Men employed as yesterday. Indians Continually about us. There is a report among the Indians that Skaniwa was killed by the Cowitchens about Point Roberts, and only his Yeaukeltas Slave escaped. He had a great deal of property which would tempt them – They got by this deed, 32 Blankets, a Gun, Kettles, Traps, Axes, Capots, Shirts etc. etc. However they want no booty to add to their Barbarous inclination. Blood and that alone Satisfies them when they Can get it without much risk to themselves. He had his wife and a Child & two Slaves with him. Trade to day two Sturgeon.

Saturday 17th. Cloudy with Showers of rain. Men at their usual work. Fewer Indians than Customary. Trade a Couple of Sturgeon.

Sunday 18th. Showers of rain all day. A great number of Quaitlines and Musqueams Straggling about the Fort. A dispute arose betwixt a Musquium womon [woman] and a Quaitland young girl about their virtue. The women Continued the dispute for Sometime, then the men took a Share in the Quarrel. Several Speeches were made upon the occasion by both parties – The Musqueams went off for their arms – The Quaitlands remained about the fort but Sent off a Canoe to their village for a reinforcement, they being only five of them. In a few minutes about 50 men of the Musquams Came across armed and began Harranging [haranguing]. Each orator Spoke in his turn, defying the other party by all the wild gestures and grimaces imaginable which was answered immediately by the five Quaitlands in the same way. After Continuing this for about a half an hour and now expecting that the reinforcement was at hand, the Musquams went back to their tents leaving the few Quaitlands again about the Post and in a few minutes 40 Quaitlands arrived but no enemy on the ground, So that this great Battle ended in words – We observed to them they had only knives. They said they would Close in with their Enemy, take hold of each other by the hair and then make use of their knives. I was sadly disappointed it ended So, as it would give us an opportunity of seeing their mode of fighting.

Monday 19th. Fine day. The men at work as usual. No trade.

Tuesday 20th. No Change in the weather – Got the roof on the Big House. Planted five kegs of Potatoes in the morning – The men began their usual work afterwards – Eight Beaver Skins were offered for trade {[by] an Indian from Pitt's River} but two being wanted of the number, he took them back. Bought 3 Sturgeon from the Quaitlands. Every thing we had was offered to him for his Beaver. Nothing would do but two Blankets. He said he would be back with two more soon.

Wednesday 21st. The weather very Gloomy & Close, with a lttle rain. Men at the gardens – No Trade.

Thursday 22nd. Thick fog in the morning but Cleared up at 8 A.M. Six fishing Canoes that were down the river gave the war Cry of Yeukeltas in Sight, and were paddling home as fast as they Could. There were about 60 Musquiams & Quaitlands about the Fort who ran to their Canoes and paddled to their villages – In a moment the women and Children were Sent to the woods, and the men under arms ready to follow –

This alarm like the rest turned out false – as they were a Couple of Large Canoes of Whooms {with about 15 men ea} who were going up after a Slave that deserted Sometime before and was now with her friends the Penaults – About 30 Musqueams in two Large Canoes Came and Sang and danced in their Canoes before the Fort for about two hours. {We presume this was in the way of devotion to the Fort, & assurance that they mean us no harm in passing in Such numbers – } No Trade of any kind. The men at the Gardens.

Friday 23rd. Fine weather. {Now that the Big House of 44 feet long & 24 wide is up} Bouchard, Ettue & Pierre Charles began to Square wood for another {building} of 30 feet by 20 at the Gate {for two ground compartments only} – Planted 5 kegs of Potatoes in the morning. The rest of the day their usual work of Clearing and rooting Stumps. No trade to day.

Saturday 24th. Cloudy with a Strong Gale from the N.W. Faignant & Plummonden planing boards for the flooring of the House. The others employed as yesterday – The Musquaims brought in two large Sturgeon. A Cowitchen brought news that Joshia was preparing a war party to kill the Quaitland. A Musqueam brought 4 Beaver.

Sunday 25th. Clear warm weather – A great many Indians about the fort – More war news – The Indians going off in all directions.

Monday 26th. Weather as yesterday – 7 kegs of Potatoes were planted before Breakfast. The men the rest of the day at their usual work – Traded 20 Beaver from the Quaitands for Blankets.

Tuesday 27th. The weather the Same as yesterday – The water keeps rising – The Sea Breeze is very regular, Sets in at 11 A.M. and continues till 4 P.M. – The Musquiams left the little river. They are going down to the Sea {to collect Shell fish}. Quaitlands about fishing – Pierre Charles is making a Spear handle of 72 feet long – to try and kill Sturgeon Cowitchen fashion. Therrien[15] & Perreault making a bag net Such as are used at *Lac La Pluie* for Sturgeon[16] – in order to try all ways possible to be independent of the rascally Indians of this place. The rest of the men employed at the Garden etc.

Wednesday 28th. Cloudy and threatening rain – The men at the Same work – Trade a Sturgeon.

Thursday 29th. The weather as yesterday – The men at their usual work. Laputchun and his friend Dolla paid us a visit. They brought 15 Beaver Skins for which they bought a Couple of traps etc. They are Just getting fond of Traps. Trial was made of the Seine this Evening. But from the men knowing nothing of the management of it, two Sturgeon that were taken in it escaped. I am in hopes that it will prove useful.

Friday 30th. No Change in the weather. The men at their usual work – Another trial was made with the net but no better siccess [success].

Saturday 31st. Weather much the Same – Work etc. as yesterday. No Indians to day, a Strange thing at this Season.

Sunday 1st June. Incessant rain all day – few or no Indians.

Monday 2nd. The Same weather as yesterday – Made another [trial] with the net – but Stuck fast at the bottom to a Stump and in attempting to get it Clear the two Maitres [main lines] broke and the net remains at the bottom. So much for Experiments. Trade a sturgeon – Indians about all day. Planted 6 kegs of Potatoes.

Tuesday 3rd. Cloudy with rain – Planted 4 kegs Potatoes. Two Indians from the Cowitchen's Camp told us that Skaniwa was killed by the relations of the Indian that was drowned here last Spring {whose widow it be recollected returned home to the Southward immediately, & very probably made Complaints there of Schannawa's Conduct to her husband during life, and to herself after his death, which I believe very far from being liberal on the part of the Scamp be his fate what it may} – Trade a Sturgeon. Work going as usual.

Wednesday 4th. Some rain – The men working at the Garden Sawing and Building the House.

Thursday 5th. Showers of rain. The work going on as yesterday. Lapatchin's Son Came with 5 Beaver to get a Blanket. Bought Some Ceder [cedar] bark from the Quaitlands.

Friday 6th. The weather Still Gloomy – Indians bringing bark. Traded a large Sturgeon. The men at their usual work.

Saturday 7th. Clear blowy Day – Traded 10 Skins from the Quaitlands for a Blanket, Beads, and Brass wire – Two Canoes of Whooms passed downwards. Traded two Skins for knives – Got Some Sturgeon & Bark – The men Still busy at the Gardens.

Sunday 8th. Clear warm day – A Skadget Indian passed downwards. He Confirms the report of Skaniwa's death.

Monday 9th. Weather the Same – Indians about with nothing to trade except a few pounds of Sturgeon and Bark – The men Clearing Ground for potatoes.

Tuesday 10th. Fine day – The men at work at the Potato ground. Trade 5 Skins – and Some pieces Bark.

Wednesday 11th. The weather very Sultry – The men at work Squaring, Sawing, and Clearing ground – The Yeukeltas have been paying another visit to the Musquiams a few days ago – Killed Six men and took away 30 women and Children – This is the first report; it may not turn out So bad – Trade a Sturgeon and bark.

Thursday 12th. Weather the Same. The heat would be very oppressive without the regular Sea Breeze – The Musquiams who were visited by the Yeukeltas are run[n]ing away up the river. They lost 3 men, 30 women & Children. One Yeukeltas was killed – The Country her[e]abouts is in [a] Continual State of fear by their powerful and Blood thirsty enemies from the Gulf of Georgia and Johnston's Straits.

Friday 13th. Fine day – Planted 12 kegs of Potatoes this morning. The men the rest of the day at their usual work – Bouchard and two men Covering the new House with Cedar bark. Indians about as usual. Trade 3 Small Otters and Bark.

Saturday 14th. The weather very Sultry – Planted 12 kegs Potatoes. The rest of the day the men employ'd as follows: 4 men Carrying home pieces for a House of 30 by 20. Bouchard etc. Covering the big House. Fagnaint and Plomendon planing boards – Ettuu, Perriault, and Arquoite making a Chimney. The rest Clearing grounds. Lapatchun Came here with 20 Beaver, traded a Kettle, a Beaver Trap – half axe and Beads. His friend Dolla had 2 Skins. They are on their way up to the forks, to make Salmon; I gave him a letter to forward to Thompson's River.[17] A few more Musquiams passed up. They look very Grim.

Sunday 15th. The weather Cloudy and blowing a Breeze from the South East. The men at work as yesterday. Indians about as usual. Trade a Sturgeon 12 feet long.

Monday 16th. Rain all day – The men doing little Jobs inside. No trade of any kind – {We have now 75 Kegs [potatoes] in the ground.}

Tuesday 17th. Showers of rain during the day. Planted Potatoes in the morning – Faynaint & Plummonden planing boards. Bouchard, Sauve, Pierre Charles & Ettuu working at the new House – The rest of the men Cutting down trees. No trade.

Wednesday 18th. Fine day. One of our Quatland friends Came down with 21 Beaver Skins – for which he traded Blankets and Beads – The men at work as yesterday. Trade a Sturgeon.

Thursday 19th. Cloudy with Showers of rain. The men at work as Yesterday. No Trade.

Friday 20th. Rain all day. Fagnant laying the flooring of the big house – The others at their usual work – No Trade – A party of Musquaims passed up to the fishing.

Saturday 21st. Cloudy and Showers of rain. All hands at their usual work – Indians about with nothing to trade.

Sunday 22nd. Dull Cloudy weather – Thunder in the afternoon. The Indians throng about, with nothing but Berries – {that is to say they Come with their wives & daughters.}

Monday 23rd. Weather the same as yesterday – The men busy Clearing ground. Indians about as usual.

Tuesday 24th. Still, Cloudy, and threatening rain: Bouchard and two men began a house of 20 feet Square. Fagnaint and Plummenden at work in the big house. The others Clearing ground and hoeing the first [potatoes] planted. 18 men of the Quaitlands passed down to See their Chief Whitlakenum who is very Sick {who is dieing [dying] in the lower Village}.

Wednesday 25th. No Change in the weather. The men at the Same work as yesterday – A Quaital Came with Six Beaver Skins and asked for Shells. {Monterry [*monterey* – abalone] Shells – a large Shell of about 8 In. in diameter that Shines inside something like mother of pearl and first brought from there by the *Cadboro*} – When that Could not be had he asked for a green Blanket, then an Embossed Blanket or fine Scarlet. When neither of these articles Could be given him he took off his Skins and Said he would keep them until Such articles Could be had.

Thursday 26th. Heavy rain all day – Ten Canoes of Whoomes passed up with their families. The Cowitchens and Nanaimans are begin[n]ing to make their appearances.

Friday 27th. Showers of rain – Bouchard finished the House. The rest of the men Clearing Ground & Hoeing Potatoes. Trade two Sturgeon for Brass wire.

Saturday 28th. Cloudy day. A Musquiam brought 7 Beaver and 3 Otter Skins, which he traded for a Blanket & Brass wire. Several Indians loitering about the Gates.

Sunday 29th. Fine Clear weather. Few Indians about.

Monday 30th. Warm weather. The men employed as follows: Fagnaint and Plummonden working inside the big house. Bouchard, Sauve, and Pierre Charles putting up a House of 30 ft. by 20 on the west side of the gate, Rabaska Ettue, and Perrault Squaring. Therrien, Dominique & Pepin Clearing ground. Jno. Kennedy, Peon Peon, and Ettue Sick. Traded 5 Beaver from a Musquiam.

Tuesday July 1st. Fine day. The men at work as yesterday – 7 Canoes of Whooms passed up – no Trade.

Wednesday 2nd. Showers of Hail during the day. One of the fair Laddies [ladies] of the Fort presented her Husband with a Son & heir, he being the first born in this quarter (I mean among the whites). He was named *Louis Langley* {with the Cheerful Consent of the parents}.[18]

Thursday 3rd. Fine Clear weather. Planted 16 kegs of potatoes. Men working at both houses – 8 Canoes of Whoomes passed up to the Fishing place. Traded 5 Beaver Skins from the Quaitlands.

Friday 4th. Fine weather in the forenoon, Showers of rain and distant Thunder in the Evening. Some Nanaimans Came to the Fort who told us the whole tribe were arrived at their old village, and that they had a few Skins. Quaitlands about as usual.

Saturday 5th. Rain all day. The men at different Jobs about the Fort – Some of our new neighbours {Nainaimous} Came to pay us a visit. They brought nothing to trade. They Say a few of the great men have Skins.

Sunday 6th. Fine day – Several Indians up and down the river. The Cowitchins killed 2 Quatlands a few miles down. They are Just arriving from Vancouver's Island to kill and Cure Salmon for about 2 months – Kutches trade 6 Skins. Report also Says the Cowitchins Killed 5 of the Kutchies, a weak tribe up Pitt's River. The poor tribes of this quarter Cannot attend to any thing like hunting while their Powerful Neighbours from Van. Island are allowed to Murder and Pillage them at pleasure.

Monday 7th. The weather as yesterday – A Nanimous woman brought 5 Skins for a Blanket. She says She has Some more. They began their old trade of thieving but as it did not pass without the punishment it deserved; I hope it will have a good effect.

Tuesday 8th. The weather thick and Showers of rain. A young man Stole a Smoking bag[19] belonging to one of the men, but on menacing to send them away, the bag was brought back. A wedding party passed up and down before the Fort Singing – Arquoitte and 3 men began to make Chimnies [chimneys] in the new House.

Wednesday 9th. Clear weather. The men employed as yesterday. Some Musquiams passed up to the fisheries – We were under the necessity of Sending all the Indians away on account of thieving – but matters was [were] Soon made up as the article was brought back.

Thursday 10th. Thick fog in the morning but Clear and warm afterwards – The Nanaimans paid us a visit headed by the two principal Chiefs, Pinnis and Squatches. The former began by offering two Land Otter tails and Said he wanted a knife each for them. After that he would bring his other Skins to trade – They then asked to be allowed to go all in the Fort to see how it was arranged. They were told that every one who had Beaver to trade should be allowed to go inside with his Skins, but them who brought nothing must remain on the bank. At this Monssr. [Monsieur] Savage got upon his high horse – Said he had plenty [of] Skins, but as we did not allow the Indians out and in as they pleased he would not allow his tribe to trade any – As this was a thing I would not agree to on any Condition, but especially as a threat followed – they were immediately told to be off the ground as fast as they Could and never to Shew their faces about the Fort. This prompt behaviour Soon took down Mr. Chief to his level – and [he] Said he would trade quietly the next time he Came. Nothing would now do with us but they must be off, So they went away very quietly – The men at their usual work.

Friday 11th. Fine day – Early this morning two Indians arrived with a note from Captain Simpson. He was then at the Sand Heads.[20] As the wind is favorable I expect him here in a few days – Sent back the Indians immediately with an answer to Captn. Simpson's note. Indians about us in Numbers. Hardly an hour of the day but they provoke us to harsh measures towards them in spite of all our endeavours to be on friendly terms with them.

Saturday 12th. The weather the same – The men busy at their usual work. Indians about with nothing.

Sunday 13th. Mr. Manson and 7 men [went] down to the vessel. He found her below the Island {Johnstones} beyond the Nanimous village. He was back in [the] afternoon with the letters.

Monday 14th. Incessant rain all day. No work out doors.

Tuesday 15th. No Change in the weather – I went down with Mr. Annance to the vessel. She is Still in the Same place.

Wednesday 16th. Still rainy. The *Cadboro* Came up about one mile. Traded 10 Skins with the Nanoimous.

Thursday 17th. Rain. Indians passing in great numbers up to the fisheries. Joshia passed the vessel. He says he has 50 Skins. The vessel got to the Fort.

Friday 18th. Fine weather – The vessel unloaded, and took in 5 Boat load[s] of wood the men of the Fort Cut and Carried to the water edge for them. Jashia traded 40 Skins for Blankets, a Quaital traded 5 Skins. Captain Simpson and Mr. Birnie[21] took leave of us as they are to be off early to morrow. Messrs. Manson & Annance went on Board with them {Spent a part of the evening with our friends}[22] – Indians passing up in great numbers.

Saturday 19th. Fine day – The *Cadboro* left this at 5 A.M. Gave the men their advances {which is far less than their order, but I believe this defficency [deficiency] is not Confined to them, as Goods there have been rather Scarce} – 250 Cowitchens passed up. A great many of them are Camped opposite. They are getting out of the way of the Yeukeltas & Quo-quals who are Coming to attack the Fort. Should such a thing take place, I trust they will meet a warm reception. Joshia brought 10 Skins and a few more was [were] got from the passants. The Cowitchins behaved well Considering their numbers.

Sunday 20th. Fine day – Indians passing up by Hundreds. An Indian brought 8 Skins to get 2 Blankets, and he being two Skins Short he was offered one Blanket with other things, but nothing would answer. He went off with his Skins. Great numbers about the fort all day.

Monday 21st. The weather fine – At noon a Strong breeze up the river as usual in dry weather. Fagnaint Cutting doors in the upper Stories of the Bastions in order to get into them from the Gallery – Indians about in great numbers – Some of them rather Saucy – Trade 5 Beaver & otter. Some other Skins were offered but not agreeing about the price they took them off.

Tuesday 22nd. Fine weather. The men at work as yesterday – Indians passing up by hundreds. No Trade.

Wednesday 23rd. Cloudy thick weather – Indians Still going up. They have an Od[d] Skin but unless he has the means of purchasing a Blanket nothing else will please. Trade 8 Beaver Skins – They now begin to menace us with the Clalams.

Thursday 24th. The weather the Same – A Nanaiman traded 8 Beaver and 2 Otters – he got 2 Blankets 2 ½ pts. in return – The men are kept busy Clearing Ground and finishing the Building for want of better work to employ them at, the nature of the Country not allowing us go much about.

Friday 25th. Fine day – Squatches brought 10 Beaver Skins for two Blankets. Indians throng about the Fort.

Saturday 26th. Fine day – The men Hoeing potatoes. Two of the Nanoimens brought 15 Skins. Indians about the Fort in numbers.

Sunday 27th. No Change in the weather – Indians passing up in great numbers – Trade 5 Skins – 13 more were brought but Could not agree about the price {a sure sign they have been trading with Coasters}. They try all they Can to reduce the prices, a thing easily done but will answer no good purpose as far as regards the Indians of this river, as they are out of the way of Strangers.

Monday 28th. The weather fine and Clear – Indians about us all day – Work going on as usual.

Tuesday 29th. Fine day till about noon when it Came on rain and very loud Claps of Thunder. Indians about all day – Several families of Whooms and Musquaims as well as Sanatch passed up. Our Friend Joshia and his little Camp was kept upon the alert last night, being afraid of a tribe Called Squaals who inhabit the upper Country about Pitt's River – Joshia's oldest wife who was at the Kutches arrived – She had 7 Beaver in her Canoe. It would seem Jo. keeps the old wives off for Beaver while He remains at home along with the young ones – Work goes on much the Same.

Wednesday 30th. The fore noon Fine and Clear. The afternoon the Same as yesterday. No Trade.

Thursday 31st. Cloudy with light Showers of rain. Indians of all tribes about the Gates. Some Skins were brought but not enough to get Blankets So they took them back – The men Hoeing potatoes and working inside of the fort.

Friday 1st August. Fine weather. The men employ'd as follows– Faignant and Plummenden Squaring wood, Bouchard, Pierre Charles arranging the inside of the last made House, Arquoitte and Perreault arranging Chimneys – Kennedy, Como, Ossin, Therrien, and Pepin taking in mud {clay}, the others Cleaning Ground. The two Nanoimon Chiefs paid us a visit. Complaints all over of the Scarcity of Salmon. Trade 5 Beaver and 3 deer Skins.

Saturday 2nd. Sultry and warm – Indians as Customary about us. No Trade Except 2 Deer Skins.

Sunday 3rd. The weather as yesterday. Our friend Joshia Came across with 20 Beaver Skins. He took a fancy to our poultry and nothing would do but he must get a Couple for which he offered 2 B. Skins – A few minutes after he got home the Dogs killed the Hen and the old fellow Sent his son to Change the dead one for another. I promised him one when he left the river for the winter which pleased him well.

Monday 4th. The weather the Same – The men employed burning and Clearing away the woods – Indians about always. Trade 5 Beaver Skins and 3 deer Skins.

Tuesday 5th. The weather Still warm and oppressive, Claps of distant Thunder in the morning – Some Cowitchins are returning downwards with their families, owing to the Scarcity of Salmon above.

Wednesday 6th. Fine Clear morning. Rain and Thunder in the Evening – Indians report the Coutinemuns are Coming down to war on the Cawitchins – The men Employed as yesterday.

Thursday 7th. The weather very warm – Indians about fishing, but get very few fish. Trade 3 B. Skins and two Otters – The men Clearing ground.

Friday 8th. Fine day. Nothing out of the usual way – No Trade.

Saturday 9th. Fine warm day. Sent off Pierre Charles with Four men to Hunt. The rest of the men at work as usual. Ettue one of the men that were [was] with Pierre Came back to let us know that they killed a Buck red Deer. Sent off 2 men in a Canoe up the little river for the meat. Indians Continually Going up past.

Sunday 10th. Fine day. The men Sent for the deer Came home. They brought home the meat of a very fat Buck – Jashia Came across with 40 very fine Beaver Skins which he traded for Blankets {of 2 ½ pts. indeed to do away with the possibility of any arguments as to the Size we show them no 3 pt. ones} – He also brought over a large piece of Sturgeon which he Said he intended as a present, however he was not above taking a knife and a little vermillion for it before he went off – He has now given us 110 Skins Since the 20th July – {true, they are Skins that the real owners would have traded were he not here at all} – I made him a present of a 2 ½ point Blanket – and told him I would give him one for every Hundred he brought – Betwixt that and a piece of the Deer meat he went back in very good humour with many fair promises – Sent back the men again.

Monday 11th. The weather Cloudy and threatening rain. Our men Came home with the flesh of another fat Buck deer. Several families of Musquiams passed up. Shientin their chief is Just arrived from the Yeukeltas where he went to try and recover his wife and Daughter, who were taken along with 30 more women & Children in the last attack. He did not get them as they were already Sold to Indians further to the northward – He tells us the Yeukeltas and Quo-quals are preparing to Come and make an attempt on our Fort. The Musquaims are always rather impudent when they come to the Fort – One of them asked for some of the deer to eat in a very rough way – No notice was taken of [him] for Some time, until he became troublesome. At last Mr. Annance asked him what he had to give for a piece. "Nothing," says he, "but I have a Cock," putting his hand on it. "Perhaps you want it." No Sooner Said than he got Such a kick on the very Spot, which Settled his talk – and [a] Couple more Sent him down the hill. They went all in a very short time – They are the very people who were so insolent to the Deceased Mr. McKenzie & party last winter – We Can't help having a bad feeling towards them – and little passed them with impunity. {We are determined to allow them but little indulgence, & certainly nothing with impunity.}

Tuesday 12th. The weather the same as yesterday – About 100 Canoes of different tribes went up with their families – They had a few badly Stretched Otters – which they offered for an axe each – and as they Could not get that they Carried away their Skins – The flesh of the 2 Buck deer weighed 1000 lbs. The men at their usual work.

Wednesday 13th. The weather very Sultry. Diable a Nanaiman traded 10 Skins for 2 Blankets – Huskennum {Awskinnum} the Sanatch Chief paid us a visit. He brought nothing – but says he gave his Skins to Joshia Some time ago. He says Salmon is plentiful about Point Roberts.

Thursday 14th. No Change in the weather. Trade 10 Skins from the Nanaimous – Pierre Charles Came home. He killed two more deer within two miles of the Fort on his way home. He says tracks are Scarce towards the Grand Prairie [Langley Prairie].

Friday 15th. Fine day. Sent 10 men off for the flesh of the two Bucks that were killed yesterday – They Came back at half past 7 A.M. The flesh of both animals weighed 1260 lbs. Salted Salmon, the first this Season.

Saturday 16th. Cloudy – The men hoeing the potatoes. Squaring and planing boards – Trade an Otter from Squatches and 10 Salmon.

Sunday 17th. Cloudy in the fore noon. Heavy rain the latter part of the day.
Indians fishing. {Their mode is the Scoop net.} Salmon about but offer
but few for Sale.

Monday 18th. Rain all day – Indians fishing before the door but Catch but
few – Le Diable brought 3 Skins to get a Small Blanket. As we had none
for him he took back his Skins till he get[s] 2 more. The men Cutting
down trees and Clearing ground.

Tuesday 19th. Incessant rain all day – very little work going on out doors.
Trade 14 Salmon.

Wednesday 20th. Cloudy day – The men at their ordinary work. The Indians throng about us with nothing. It's impossible to Spur these useless
rascals to exertion in the hunting way.

Thursday 21st. Clear weather – The men Cutting and Clearing ground. A
young Nanaimans brought 3 Beaver Skins and a few Salmon.

Friday 22nd. Fine day. Trade a few Salmon. The men employ'd Squaring
and Clearing ground.

Saturday 23rd. The weather fine. The [men] at the same work as yesterday.
Chilakeltel a Nanaimous Chief brought 5 Skins for a 2 ½ pt. Blanket.
Some Cowitchens offered dried Salmon to trade but we Could not get
any except at a very dear rate. Jashia is much alarmed at the Squaals
Coming to kill him. He Sends the Women & Children to Sleep in the
woods every night this three nights past. Report Says the Cowitchens
are gone on a war excursion to the Yeukeltas in a hundred Canoes. If
true they must be a Strong party.

Sunday 24th. Incessant rain all day – Trade a few dry Salmon.

Monday 25th. Showers of rain – Joshia brought a few Skins to trade for
ammunition but Carried them back as that article Could not be given
him. The men employed Clearing Ground & about the Buildings.

Tuesday 26th. Thick fog in the morning – Clear and warm the rest of the
day. Trade a Sturgeon and a few Salmon.

Wednesday 27th. Weather the Same as usual – Indians Continually about
us – Trade Salmon fresh & Dried.

Thursday 28th. Cloudy weather – Indians throng about us. Traded a few
fresh and dried Salmon – A Couple of our Cowitchen friends received
Some Salutary Chastisement not for their good behaviour. They begin
to understand us better now – than first we Came among them.

Friday 29th. The weather as yesterday – The men at work in the woods.
Some of the Nanaimans young men, who went to see them were rather
insolent and went So far as to make menaces of Shooting arrows at them
– From one thing to another a quarrel ensued. Two of the Indians got
good thumps in the ribs which made the whole [lot] Scamper into their
Canoes. I dare say they will be good fellows, the next visit we have of
them. {The men themselves however may have been to blame in Some
degree & they are forbid to encourage them their way in the least.}

Saturday 30th. Fine day – Indians up and down the river in great numbers – No Trade Except a few Salmon.

Sunday 31st. Weather as yesterday. Jashia brought 27 Beaver Skins {all for Blankets, and had a few loads ammunition to boot} and a Sanch Indian 5 Beaver Skins. Nothing else except the usual Stir of Indians about us.

Monday 1st September. Fine day. The men Cutting and Clearing wood Some Squaring – others Sawing etc.

Tuesday 2nd. Thick fog in the morning, mostly since 20th of August the fore part of the day is foggy – but after that Clears away, the weather is very agreeable. Le Diable a Nanaiman traded 5 Beaver. A number of Quaitlands Came down with Salmon.

Wednesday 3rd. Our neighbour Jashia got a fright last night. He thought his Camp attacked by the Squaals. The men made a great noise, fired a few randum [random] Shots into the woods, Sent their women and Children to take Shelter alongside of our Fort – They Said they Saw Some Indians lurking in the woods. They were Calling us to their assistance. No vestigages [vestiges] of any Indians Could be Seen next day So that they must have got a false alarm. Indians about us all day with nothing to trade.

Thursday 4th. Fine day – The men at their usual labour – Trade one Beaver Skin.

Friday 5th. Weather the Same – Men Squaring wood for the Cellar of the Big house. The rest at their usual work – Indians about all day.

Saturday 6th. Fine day. The men Carrying in wood for the Cellar – Others Squaring & Cutting down trees etc. Trade 5 Beaver Skins and Some Salmon. One [of] the Whooms tribe pointed his musket at one of the men perhaps with no bad intention – however to let the fellow know that such Jokes are not agreeable he met with the Chastisement he deserved. The others went off very quietly.

Sunday 7th. The weather rather Cloudy – Indians very numerous about us. News of Some Cowitchens being killed up at the fishery – Jashia who went a trip to Point Roberts Came back. He brought 5 Skins with him. All quiet in that quarter.

Monday 8th. Fine day – The accounts of yesterday regarding the people killed proves false – They say altho they fought all day none was killed. Trade 3 Beaver Skins from Jashia – and a few Salmon.

Tuesday 9th. Thick fog in the morning. Finished the Cellar and a Black Smith's Shop. Nothing in the way of trade.

Wednesday 10th. Showers of rain all day – An Indian told us that Waskaladget – a Sinihoom Chief, was at the Nanaiman village – and that he had a few Beaver.

Thursday 11th. The weather Overcast and Some drops of rain. The Sinihoom and 3 of his friends arrived early – and passed the day Smoking – He tells me that the Skadgets and Clalams are gone to war on the Yeukeltas in 37 large war Canoes – He also assures us that the deceased Mr. McKenzie nor any of his party gave the least offense to the Clalams –

that his guide Ai a waston was the Sole Cause of his being Cut off – Our friend the Francois had only thirty Beavers which he traded for Blankets – I paid more than Ordinary attention to him on account of his influence over the natives of the Sound. He promised to be back soon with more Beaver.

Friday 12th. The weather the Same as yesterday. The men differently employed. Our Sinihooms visitors Smoking and Chatting with the Cowitchins – 30 Canoes passed down bag and baggage from the Fisheries for their wintering grounds.

Saturday 13th. Fine weather – Our Sinihooms visitors went home Seemingly well pleased. We heard that the Scadgets and Clalams had quarrelled with the Nanaimons, and that the former turned back – 25 Canoes passed down from whom we got a few dry and fresh Salmon. The men are kept Constant at the Clearing of the woods in order to have a Crop next year to make people independent of the Indians.

Sunday 14th. Incessant rain – all day. Two Canoes of Cowitchins passed down. {Indians passing down in Brigades of 10 and 15 canoes.} Salmon is very Scarce with them. They will hardly part with any. What a difference from last year.

Monday 15th. Rain – The men at work as usual except Buchard and Plummenden who are getting timbers for the Boats. An Indian {of the Quatline tribe} from above Called the *Doctor*[23] Came down with 20 Beaver Skins, 10 of which he traded with us and the other 10 to Jashia for a young Slave Child. 35 Canoes of Cowitchins passed down – A young Nanoimous traded 3 Beaver Skins for Brass wire.

Tuesday 16th. Fine weather. The men at their usual work. 10 Canoes [of] Cowitchins went down. We got a few fresh & Dried Salmon from them – Traded 10 Beavers from a Nanaimans for [a] Blanket. The Doctor went back in perfect good humour with many fair promises of killing Beaver.

Wednesday 17th. Cloudy – 3 Canoes of Cowitchens passed downwards. Jashia Traded 21 Beaver Skins for Blankets – Bouchard finished raising the timbers of the Boats – and began Squaring wood for other purposes. The Others kept Clearing ground.

Thursday 18th. Heavy rain. The men at their usual work – No trade. Pierre Charles Came home with 2 Beaver to begin his fall hunt. 6 Cowitchin Canoes went down.

Friday 19th. The weather heavy & dull – The men employed as follows Fagnant & Ettew arranging the inside of the Small House, Bouchard & Plummondon putting a gallery round the big House, Arquoitte and Perreault arranging Chimneys, Baker & Peon Peon Sawing Boards for the Boats – Sauve, Rabaskie, Kennedy, and Ettienne Cutting wood for Coals, Ossen & Therrien Splitting wood – Bois Vert door keeper – Pierre Hunting – 47 Canoes passed down to day.

Saturday 20th. Very rainy day – 3 Cowitchen Canoes passed downwards. Traded 5 Beaver from the Nanoimous.

Sunday 21st. Showers of rain – The men at their usual work. Few or no Indians going about to day.

Monday 22nd. Thick fog in the morning, but Clear and warm the rest of the day – The men employed making Coals, Sawing, finishing the inside of the Houses – Burning and Clearing away wood Stumps etc. – 150 Cowitchen families Stop[p]ed at the wharf to trade. They have but few this year – There are now 345 Canoes of Cowitchens already passed from where [whom] we made a Shift to get about 3000 Salmon. From the Same number last year we might trade 20,000 with less trouble. They behave well Since they began to Come down.

Tuesday 23rd. The weather as yesterday. 160 Canoes of the Cowitchs traded a few dried and fresh Salmon. {Each [canoe] seldom contains more than one man with the family, and generally about half a dozen dogs more resembling Cheviot Lambs shorn of their wool.} The men mostly kept about the Fort while the Indians are so numerous about us.

Wednesday 24th. Fine day. 60 more Canoes of Cowitchins passed. We got a few more Salmon – Removed the goods out of the Store into the Garret of the big House – Intending to make a fish House of the Store.

Thursday 25th. Thick fog – 200 Canoes of Whooms Stopped along Side of the wharf – They are on their way to Burrard's Canal for the winter[24] – They are a very bold impertinent Set, and always disposed to give trouble – They never trade any thing – but Steal as much as they Can – We were Obliged to get very rough towards them – and Sent them off without much Ceremony – A few that were behind traded Salmon, and behaved very quietly. They had the Body of their Chief, who died 3 days ago, Carrying him to their lands up Burrard's Canal. He was an Excellent Indian and much attached to the Fort.

Friday 26th. The mornings are always foggy this Sometime past but the rest of the day fine and warm. The men put the Salmon in order, and [are] preparing wood for the Boats [and] Clearing and burning wood. Two families of Cowitchens gave us 74 fresh Salmon.

Saturday 27th. The Usual weather – No Indians about – The men at the Same work as yesterday – Our trade of Salmon from all those bands of Indians that passed amounts only to 5000 pieces of Dried Salmon {each the third of a Salmon} and 10 Barrels {Tierces} of Salmon we Salted – {Far from being enough but our Potatoes will be a famous Stand by.}

Sunday 28th. No Change in the weather. Pierre Charles and Ettienne who were out there 4 days back Came home. They killed 8 Beaver, brought home the meat of 3 of them – Bought a Sturgeon from the Cowitchens wt. 400 lbs. the Guts out.

Monday 29th. Weather the Same – Sent off Pierre Charles again with Ettienne – The men at their usual work. The last two Lodges of Cowitchens went down this day. Shienten a Musquiam Chief passed up on his way from the Shishals a tribe to the north of Burrard's Canal – He traded 6 Beaver Skins. He Says the Shishals intend Coming here Soon to trade the few Skins they have.

Tuesday 30th. Weather Cloudy, with Showers of rain – The men employ'd as follows, Some preparing Boat wood, others burning and Clearing ground, Peon Peon & Baker finished Sawing the Boat wood, Rabaskes,

Sauve, and Arquoitte Securing the fish Store, Jno. Kennedy & Bois Verd making Coals {burning a coal pit} – No Trade.

Wednesday 1st October. The weather Overcast – The men employ'd mostly as Yesterday. No Indians about – We had a trial of our potatoes – and are the finest I ever Saw in the Country.

Thursday 2nd. Fine day – The men at their usual work – A few Indians Came down from above. They Say some of our men were killed about the Coulomun Country.[25] They also say the upper Indians are Coming down to trade a few Skins they have.

Friday 3rd. The weather very fine – The men busy at work. No Indians, of Course no trade.

Saturday 4th. Fine day. The men at their usual work. No Indians about.

Sunday 5th. The weather fine – Every[thing] quiet. No Indians.

Monday 6th. The mornings always foggy, but the rest of the days fine and warm – Bouchard, and Fagnaint began putting the verringues [*varangues* – ribs] in the Boat – Plummonden & Ettue arranging the Cellar for the Potatoes, Sauve Stuffing the Chinks with moss, the rest of the men Clearing and Burning away the Stumps etc.

Wednesday 8th. Incessant rain. Since the 6th no Stir of any kind. The men doing little Jobs about the Fort.

[This is the last entry in James McMillan's handwriting, an indication that the post journal was not always written daily. After the arrival of the Simpson expedition on 10 October, Archibald McDonald began making the entries and continued until the book was filled on 30 July 1830.]

~

ARCHIBALD McDONALD

Archibald McDonald, a Highlander from Glencoe, came to North America in 1813 in charge of a group of Selkirk settlers emigrating to the Red River. In 1820, his thirtieth year, he entered the service of the Hudson's Bay Company, and the following year was sent to the Columbia District. There, while working as an accountant at Fort George, he married Chinook Chief Comcomly's daughter, who died soon after their son, Ranald, was born. In 1825 he married Jane Klyne, and together they raised Ranald, seven more sons, and a daughter. In 1828 McDonald was made a chief trader and attended the Northern Department Council meeting at York Factory, returning to the Pacific with the Simpson expedition. In 1833 he established Fort Nisqually before going on furlough, and from 1835 until his retirement in 1844 he was in charge of Fort Colvile, a large, successful operation that combined agriculture and trade. In 1842 he was made a chief factor.

Governor Simpson's *Character Book*, written when he was ill and despondent, has frequently been criticized for the mean-spirited tone of many of his remarks. It is interesting to compare his description of McDonald with the man who reveals himself through his journals and letters. He was, according to Simpson,

> A shrewd, clear headed Man, who Studies his own interests in all things, obsequious in courting favour, but would be overbearing if in power. Rather inactive and 'tis thought does not possess much nerve, but a generally useful Man who will not do any thing really bad or tell a direct falsehood: fond of conviviality, enjoys a Glass of Grog and I suspect would soon become addicted to Liquor if exposed to temptation and not under restraint. Expresses himself tolerably well on paper and is better informed, and would make a better figure on our Council board than many of his colleagues or even than the majority of those now Seated there. (Williams 1975:197)

Even McDonald's friends poked mild fun at "Archy who is always fond of talking of great men" (Tod 1842), and in his correspondence with the governor and council he appears anxious to impress and deferential to authority. The changes made when copying the journals indicate that he

Archibald McDonald. "A shrewd clear-headed Man."

Jane Klyne McDonald was the daughter of
Michael Klyne of Pennsylvania Dutch descent and
Suzanne La France, child of a Native mother and a
Canadien. Jane was a competent woman, at home in the
wilderness, among the white settlers at Fort Colvile or in
the "civilized society" of St. Andrews, Lower Canada.

was aware of his readers at headquarters. McMillan's entry for 11 August
1828, for instance, was reworded so that the Native's rough talk was reported as "indecorous expressions." The "debauch" of New Year 1830,
which became "the Spirit of the Day," is another example of the refining
process. He was undoubtedly pressed for time in preparing the 1828-9 journal and made the task possible by shortening the entries. Many of his omissions relate to women in the fort. None of these changes would classify
him as obsequious, but he seems less straightforward than either Barnston
or McMillan.

On the other hand, the journal provided useful information as he took
charge of the fort, and he probably saw the value of maintaining a fort
record that would be a reference for himself or helpful to his successor. He
began to add to the copies material that the council would appreciate, and

he appears, on occasion, to have used the journal to prepare the first draft for letters and reports.

Simpson's admiration for physical prowess could only be gained by someone as tough as McMillan, but McDonald's success could never have been achieved by an inactive man. There is a great deal of bravado in his accounts of confrontations with the Lekwiltok, but the isolation, the numerous rumours, the size of the Native population, the murder of Edward Driver, and the Clallam massacre certainly gave good reason for fear. McDonald made use of these facts to maintain two clerks at the fort, the importance of which had been seriously downgraded. There was a great deal of "nerve" in his decision to attack the Nanaimo village, but it was a faulty judgment probably made because of concern for his reputation. The handling of the Delannais case could be said to reflect an "overbearing" master, but venereal disease was eliminated at Fort Langley, and the firm control McDonald exercised was undoubtedly approved of by Simpson. There is considerable evidence that McDonald was talkative and convivial, but the fact that he used the "debauch" to renew the men's contracts is clear evidence that he was capable of restraint when it served the interests of the company.

In addition to possessing an elementary Scottish education, McDonald was provided with several months of training in accounting and medicine by Lord Selkirk, an opportunity he seized eagerly. William Tolmie, after meeting McDonald, remarked that he displayed "a very laudable desire for self-improvement, seldom met with in men his age" (Tolmie 1963:201).

His reports show his ability as an accountant, his attention to detail, his desire to provide information of use to those making company policy, and his competence in making intelligent suggestions. He was the type of man the company required after the amalgamation, a good manager who would implement policy to the best of his ability.

Excerpt from the post journal in Archibald McDonald's hand.

Like George Barnston, McDonald had been inspired by David Douglas to take an interest in natural history and to collect specimens. Both traders derived great pleasure and satisfaction from their large families, which were drawn closer when the Barnstons' eldest son married the McDonalds' only daughter. In 1861 Ranald McDonald and John Barnston worked on a road from the coast to the interior of British Columbia, and Ranald was with Alexander Barnston on the Vancouver Island exploring expedition led by Robert Brown.

McDonald was a prolific writer. Much of his correspondence has survived, and the journal he kept on the 1828 trip west has been published. His writing was cramped and often difficult to decipher. The fact that we have access to both the original journal and his copy is of limited help because of the numerous changes he made in the annual copy. The copy has been reproduced here. No attempt has been made to show every change, but significant information from the post journal that was omitted from the copy has been included in {braces}. Words consistently spelled incorrectly have been shown initially and subsequently corrected without comment. McDonald made considerable use of dashes, adhering to the breath pause system of punctuation by varying the length of each from a single dot to long wavy extravagances. These have been retained where possible but, when combined with other punctuation, the dash has been dropped, and each entry has been concluded with a period.

[October 1828]

Thursday 9th.
Friday 10th. The Carpenter's part of the Boat finished, and only requires gumming[26] that Mr. Manson & a party of 8 or 10 men may immediately proceed up the river for the purpose of examining the navigation.
Saturday 11th. About 8 O'Clock last night we had a sudden Call from the man on the watch of Canoes & singing down the river[27] and in a few moments had the agreeable Surprise of taking our Governor in Chief by the hand – he is accompanied from York Factory by Mr. Chief Trader Arch. McDonald and Dr. Hamlyn[28] and 20 men exclusive of Mr. James M. Yale[29] & 7 men from New Caledonia & Thompson's river – They left the mouth of that river in the morning of the 9th & to there from Kamloops House took them a day and a half. It would appear the river is worse than any idea we Could have formed of it and renders the practicability of opening a regular Communication this way with the Interior most doubtful.
[Sunday] 12th [Monday] 13th [Tuesday] 14th [Wednesday] 15th. Since the Governor's arrival here it has been Settled upon that Mr. McMillan be allowed to avail himself of his rotation of forlough [furlough] next Season and as a Change of this kind may be attended with danger and inconvenience in the Spring, he now accompanies the Gov. to

Vancouver, and Mr. McDonald assumes the Charge of this place keeping Mr. Yale in the room of Mr. Manson and the Complement of men reduced from 20 to 17[30] – Mr. Annance Continues Indian Trader – The furs now procured on account of Outfit /28 are 716 Beaver and 208 Land Otters including 96 Beaver & 39 otters Shipped in April – N.B. The Journal will now be kept by Mr. McDonald.

Thursday 16th. After a preparation of five days building another Boat – gumming and arranging the one built before our arrival & the one brought down from the interior {Thompson's River}, the Governor, accompanied by Mr. Chief Factor McMillan – Doctor Hamlyn & Mr. Manson with Thirty men left us this afternoon for the Columbia River by way of Puget Sound – The usual honours from the Garrison were of Course bestowed upon him.[31] To remove their Chagrin after parting with Some of their old Companions and Changing Bourgeois [North West Company term for an officer in charge of a district or fort] our men were ea. allowed a pint of Liquor this evening and Certainly had the effects of drowning all the cares of this world.[32]

Friday 17th. Nothing particular going on – {Our men indulging themselves after the debauch of last night & doing nothing} – towards evening made some effort to recover a fishing line that disappeared in the Stream two days ago, but to no purpose. {Took Inventory of all Goods – provisions & Stores at the place.}[33]

Saturday 18th. With the exception of the Carpenter – Cook – Gatekeeper and Fisherman who is directed to another attempt in that way – all hands have been in the Potato fields & housed 45 Barrels – Two Indians from up the river brought us 70 fresh Salmon, nothing to trade them with, but Scalpers, Buttons and very inferior Beads they Seem to put no value on.

Sunday 19th. {A good deal rain in the forenoon –} On visiting our Line this morning it was evident that the Sturgeon was at it: four or five of the Same lines had given way & the Hooks in various places Snapped in two – we have now doubled the Small lines, & got a few larger Hooks made by the Blacksmith. {No work to day of Course.}

Monday 20th. {Fine day –} Nothing from the fishery – Something is Still wrong – Housed 66 Barrels potatoes to day.

Tuesday 21st. A few Indians about – one of them from Point Roberts Called I believe in this Journal Anskinnum traded 20 Skins – he and his followers also brought about 100 Small fresh Salmon & 10 or 12 Larger ones Such as we See in the Columbia, but both far from being in their prime now – {They take them in great abundance in the little rivers.} The Sturgeon derange every thing Connected with our line – tis therefore withdrawn for the present.

Wednesday 22d. Much rain in the forenoon – Consequently Could do nothing at the potatoes – in the afternoon however we got in 30 Brs. – Three men were digging a Cellar in the fish House the whole day and the Carpenter {Faniant} Salting Salmon – The Point Robert's Chief {Chiche,nooks} and young men Supplied us with 200 more of this very essential article notwithstanding its quality, and every encouragement is given the old Gentlm. to further exertion.

Thursday 23d. {Dry pleasant weather – 39 Barrels of potatoes housed to day – which finished the whole of the ground on face of the hill, & in all yielded 240 Barrels = 720 Bushels} – Got another 100 Salmon today from new Commers [comers] – They take them now in the little Creeks without difficulty – They are by no means So much reduced as the fall Salmon in the Columbia or even in the interior of this river at present – Messrs. Yale & Annance made a Short round over the Swamp on other Side the river for wild fowl but met with little Success.

Friday 24th. {Weather Continues fine.} Traded 10 Beaver Skins from two different Indians of this neighbourhood; we have also had upwards of 300 Salmon at which the women and 4 men have been employed all day – {Rest of people of Course in the potatoes – Housed from lower field 58 Barrels, including Eight of the red, which is in the Cellar of Fish Store} – Being much in want of a Small Canoe or two, one was obtained to day.

Saturday 25th. {Traded another Canoe to day.} To day our friends brought us no less than 550 fish, which in all for the last four days is equal to 16 Tierces [measure equal to 42 wine gallons] and with our prospect of a Superabundance of potatoes the Establishment must be very independent indeed for the ensuing Season – {housed 38 Barrels potatoes} – we have now upwards of one thousand kegs in the Cellars.

Sunday 26th. Three or four of our men were allowed to go about a little with their Guns to day, but were not very Successful. Still the disappointment is not great as a little relief to themselves from the Fort was more the object than anything else – Enough Salmon came in to day to give all hands prog for two days.

Monday 27th. Early this morning it was discovered that a Slave Boy belonging to Mr. Annance's woman had decamped & with Annance's Riffle [rifle] too – Indians on the beach {among them Mr. Manson's brother-in -law} were immediately dispatched and Soon returned with the fugitive – The Rifle not appearing excited increased rage against the Scoundrel, and I was about demonstrating to him with a drawn Sword how I would cut off his head if it was not found – a little explanation and a few minutes delay led to the discovery that the Arm was only mislaid by Mr. Annance himself in another house – The Chap however had to run the gauntlet and among the other dreadful punishments he was to Suffer, a rope was put round his neck, and [he] was to have been hung to the Flagstaff for the henious [heinous] Crime of opening the Gate in the dead of night for the Indians to Come in to Cut our throats, if he did not find Security for his better Conduct !! A display of this kind was necessary, & with much appearance of Sincerity in the eyes of the women of the Fort – I think the little fellow will not risk his neck a second time. {This is not the only instance in which Slaves disappeared – women of that class in the Fort left their husbands before now[34]...Housed 61 Barrels potatoes.} Traded 22 Skins for Blankets in fact there is nothing else to Trade with – Rewarded the Indians with a Sm. axe for Securing the Boy – Fort Gate made fast with a Lock and Key.

Tuesday 28th. {A little light rain in the morning which did not permit our working out doors – Four men in the forenoon digging a Cellar out Side for the remainder of the red potatoes – housed to day 48 Barrels which in all make 155 Barrels of Red in Fish House to night.} Traded Six Beaver Skins and a few Cranberries – also Salmon enough {20} to give rations to all hands.

Wednesday 29th. With the assistance of the women we housed 220 kegs of potatoes to day {17 Red & 56 Barrels white all in the outer Hole...People have been served out with 15 days' rations in dried Salmon – that is with as much potatoes as they can eat.}

Thursday 30th. To prevent the dried Salmon moulding in the fish house we have removed a certain quantity of it to the people's own houses where it must all be forth-Coming – One of the Nannimous Traded 10 or 12 Small land Otters of no great value. {From the Specimen I see already of the hunts in this quarter the proportion of Otters is greater than I have Seen in any other part of the Country.} Notwithstanding the vast number of Indians that Seem to have passed down here on their way to Vancouver's Island before we arrived, I see a few Canoes Still drifting down from that quarter.

Friday 31st. {Commenced work as usual in the field this morning, but rain & bad weather Coming on we Soon desisted – people therefore variously employed about the Fort principally in making drains and digging places for a building of Convenience.} Got a few otters to day again – and so did in the fall Salmon – they Still eat well with Potatoes.

Saturday November 1st. *Tous Saints* – being a day on which the Engaged in general are exempted from work all over the Country – nothing was done to day; and to this indulgence was added a pint Rum per man on his individual account. {The day passed without a quarrel or any disagreeable noise among our people.}

Sunday 2d. A couple of young lads brought us 12 or 15 Salmon this morning – with the exception of Friday last, and two or three mornings we have had uncommon fine weather to work at our potatoes – three days more will finish them, in mean time we propose a trip up the river as those planted the beginning of July are not yet overripe.

Monday 3d. Mr. Annance with a party of Eight Choice men was dispatched up the river to day in a large Bark Canoe to examine the country and the mouth of the river between this and Simpson's Falls – they are allowed an absence of 10 or 12 days – Here we remain with the Same number of men – viz: The Carpenter – the Blksmith – two Sawyers – door-keeper – Cook and two men at outdoor work – The Carpenter and two of them Commenced places of Convenience in the Fort for both man and Master – improvement that is very desirable. {Four or five of the Indians of the neighbourhood Came in with a few Geese and ducks they now take by means of net.}

Tuesday 4th. {Raining the whole day.} The Blksmith has a man with him making nails, which I believe is the *ne plus ultra* [acme] of the Chap's pretentions [pretensions] to the Trade of which he will be a member. Sent more of the dried Salmon to the men's houses where it will be infinitely better preserved than in our outhouses.

Wednesday 5th. All of a sudden this afternoon 7 or 8 of the Indians of the Village below here (the Nanimons) arrived at the water Side with a warning to us that the Yewkultaus – to appearance the formidable & Common enemy of all the Indians within this river – were just at hand – Being a Stranger myself, and the Fort rather reduced in number, the manner in which this information was Conveyed and the apparent tenor of the news being heavy themselves I Should have felt rather alarmed too had I not perused this Journal and Seen how unfounded these alarms are – we keep a strict look out however, and our neighbours have Tellegraphed[35] this intelligence onwards.

Thursday 6th. The night passed quietly – nothing more Seen of the enemy and a few Indians that Came about from the Village begin to explain the Source of their alarm by telling the women of the fort that distant Shots were heard near the mouth of the River – but on our Suggesting to them that it might have been Trees falling they immediately admitted the probability! Late in the evening we were Surprized to see Mr. Annance & party back – They did not arrive at the mouth of the river that is the main object Harrison's river – [36] till yesterday morning – about a league further on they found 3 or 400 Indians making a fall fishery, taking a Couple with him as Guides, they Continued a Short distance thro' a lake, when the Indians at once directed them to a Small Creek of *black* water & the outlet of the Lake is *Clear green* & to the right hardly passable for a Small Canoe and [it is] Said this was the only Stream falling into the Lake – Somehow or other the party without proceeding to what appeared to be the *end* of the Lake, returned upon the Strength of this information – Slept last night a little beyond the Indian Camp, & on arrival there this morning found them all under arms in Consequence of the news of Wednesday evening having reached them during night – Mr. Annance did not remain with them long, and as he was given to understand on his way up that the river to the Southward [Chilliwack] was not navigable with a large Canoe any distance, he retraced his route to the Fort – he brought us the meat of a Couple of Beaver.

Friday 7th. Much rain for the last three days – very little doing about the Fort – {In the Afternoon the New Comers were Sent out to Cut Pickets except one of them finishing a WheelBarrow he began before he went off and another Squaring Wood for the Sawyers.} 9 P.M. The man in the Watch fired a shot and before we Could gain the Gallery fired a Second – Nothing human Could be seen, & however possitive [positive] Master Delenais as to the object of his firing, I am almost Sure he Saw nothing – neither was he heard Challenging any one – In Such Circumstances he is told how to act in future – he is a new hand in the Fort – No one ought to fire that early in the night on Indians at the wharf without Consulting the Gentlemen within first.

Saturday 8th. Still very disagreeable weather outdoors. {Six Men taking the pickets cut yesterday home halfway – Three Commenced building a Small House of Convenience for the men themselves and the rest variously employed Sawing – Squaring – Clearing away earth and Conveying it into hollows inside the Fort – A Small Canoe with two of the Indians of the Neighbourhood in it Came down the river in the afternoon and Say they passed up last night dreadfully alarmed at the Yucletaws, & were fired at.}

Sunday 9th. Nothing particular. {Weather wet and disagreeable.}

Monday 10th. Commenced Cutting and Sawing a parcel of pickets for enlarging the Fort: and the Owhyhees have accordingly moved down to the Pit on the Point.

Tuesday 11th. Dirty disagreeable weather. {The bad weather we presume detains the Indians expected from above with the Beaver – few or none of them are moving about at present.}

Wednesday 12th. We have now the materials on the Spot for extending the Fort by 33 feet, finding a space of 135 x 120 even with the present buildings too Confined – a neat little House here of two rooms 20 by 15 feet each is now finished, & the Blksmith bad as he is was for Some days making Hdles. – Hinges etc. etc. for the doors and Cupboards.

Thursday 13th. The Quaitline Chief Nicamuns and his brother Came in with 20 Skins Small & large – which they traded for Blankets – these, being the principal Indians of the neighbourhood & who at all exert themselves to Collect Beaver, we have thought it good Policy in Mr. Yale to form a Connection in that family – and accordingly he has now the Chief's daughter after making them all liberal presents – In addition to which with the view of increasing their Stock of goods to barter with the distant Tribes we have given them two Blankets & a Couple of Traps for a fine large Canoe of theirs we Stand in need of to enter little rivers with in preference to a Boat or a Bark Canoe – Before we begin the Fort 'tis necessary to Secure the remainder of our potatoes – got in 35 Barrels more to day. {Thick Cloudy weather.}

Friday 14th. The Quaitlines left us with flattering promises of Converting their Blankets to great advantage. {[They] are Soon to visit Some of their Customers to the Southward, Inland from here – 40 Barrels potatoes housed to day – Remainder of our dried Salmon turned into the Men's houses, where they will evidently be better preserved than in the Store.}

Saturday 15th. By 12 o'clock to day had our potatoes in – the whole crop yielding 670 Barrels = 2010 Bushels after 91 put in the ground and which at a moderate Calculation Seems amt. per amt. better than the Common run on the Columbia – all hands had a dram, and towards evening each was allowed a pint on his account and permission to struck [strike] up a dance to injoy [enjoy] themselves at for a few hours.

Sunday 16th. We finished our harvest in good time – the rain Since yesterday afternoon is a perfect torrent.

Monday 17th. {Still Soft disagreeable weather.} The Carpenter and Eight men Commenced {extending} the Fort – two squairing [squaring] wood for that part of the Gallery – Islanders regularly at the Saw and our wood Cutter Cook & Gate Keeper of Course at their respective avocations.

Tuesday 18th. The Quaitline Chief Came back already with 20 Skins but did not go So far for them as we Could wish.

Wednesday 19th. Still, a number of the Indians continue to descend the Stream with a vast deal of Stuff between Salmon – dogs and Children piled up on huge Rafts supported by a Couple of Small Canoes – they all give us a Call, and offer Scraps of dried Salmon at a rate not justified by the present State of our provision store.

Thursday 20th. The incessant rains we have had for the last five days rose [raised] the river to an unusual height at this Season of the year – it is within a foot of the Summer Fresh-shot [freshet] – By this flush the Indians are tempted to try the Sturgeon fishery – we have Come in for about 120 lbs. from no less than five of them as they have the very Selfish habit of trading their provisions by piece-meal.

Friday 21st. Messrs. Annance & Yale made a turn into one of the little Creeks and Shot a Couple Geese {& ½ doz. Ducks.}

Saturday 22d. In Spite of all we Could do this week from bad weather and Short days – only the Side Stockades are extended and the Bastion up in its new possition [position] – this much however is done without any imprudent breach in the Garrison. {One of the Quitlines gave us a call with 4 or 5 Skins, but declined trading them until he has a greater quantity and [he] proceeded to his Village up the river with them.}

Sunday 23d. A few of the Musquams traded 8 or 10 Skins on their way up, and had a Sharp Set down for being a few days ago Concerned in taking away a piece of Salted Salmon we had Soaking in the river – they like good lawyers, of Course denied all knowledge of the theft for want of the proof.

Monday 24th. Wet – dirty, Cold weather.

Tuesday 25th. The Fort is once more Closed in and the artillery mounted – An Indian that calls himself a Scadshot gave us a Call previous to his Setting out for that quarter and had a pressing Commission from us to send them here with the Beaver – he had a little Tobacco, but I doubt the Gentleman's Sincerity – {WhitlaKenum, the Quitland Chief, Came in to day but had nothing – He understands that in Consequence of a message we have Sent to the Scatshats they are Coming here with Beaver, and he now makes a merit of proposing to go there himself – This we forbid him because, if he goes at all – which I do not think he in reality has the least thought of – tis to prevent the Scatchats coming this way & claiming from himself heavy damages for giving away his daughter in marriage to Mr. Yale who was already the lawful wife (in their way) of a Scatchad.}

Wednesday 26th. {Previous to WhitlaKenum's departure to day, his Brother who was here with a few Beaver 4 days ago Came in with a grand total of ten and three or four Young Girls to dispose of them in marriage if he can – To mend the matter it turns out they are all married wives & of course all negotiation with the men broke off.} Although we apprehend no danger from them – yet the Indians of the vicinity have become very troublesome – ever Since the fields are Cleared of the potaotes [potatoes] – Swarms of women & Children are daily Sauntering about Collecting what they can and this unavoidably leads to a meeting with our men, who rather Seek than avoid it and I believe the fair ones themselves with the additional selfishness of the relatives are little inferior to the Chinooks – A positive instruction has only produced a formal application for wives, & of the two evils perhaps is the least & according[ly] two or three of them have obtained permission when Suitable Connections can be formed.

Thursday 27th. {People working at the Galleries – although the weather is excessively disagreeable – One of them came in to me this evening and made a most impudent application though we ourselves [are] partly to blame – He and a party of them proposed to go out and Stop for the night with Master Quaitland's Indian and his Seraglio – The proposition was answered with indignity of Course and a resolve made if not this very night early tomorrow morning to have the whole Gang banished from the plantation [area outside the fort where Indian visitors camped]. Nothing particular.

Friday 28th. One of the Iroquois – Etienne – Set a Beaver Trap last night in a Small Creek about 1500 yards from the Fort, and this morning had the good luck to bring home his prize. He and John Kennedy who knows where they are were Sent off to day for 10 or 12 Beaver Traps left in *Cache* by Pierre Charles but on account of the high water in the marshes Could not get in – Gallery and corner Platform finished and Swivels mounted thereon. {WhitlaKenum in his turn arrives with more women for the accommodation of the Fort and as this Commerce now with them Seems to Superceed [supersede] the Beaver Trade – the whole Concern was ordered off and I believe Mrs. Yale in the number.}

Saturday 29th. The two men by another direction gone for the Traps & Plemonden and little Louis {Satakarota} have been fitted out with Six from the Store to try their Chance up the river. {Rest of our men leveling the new ground inside the Fort – Scamps of Kitchies that were fishing Sturgeon in this vicinity touched at the wharf with two, but took good Care to put their new price upon So rare a Commodity – We took none.}

Sunday 30th. Etienne and Kennedy again returned unsuccessful. So are the other two – They saw visible appearance of Beaver last night, but when in the act of setting the Traps, they discovered themselves in the immediate vicinity of Indians and did not think it Safe to expose them[selves] & accordingly returned home until the party Can be made more formidable.

Monday December 1st. Four men Cutting & Carrying home Pickets to Shut up the Space between the Front Gate and the Houses – others Squaring and bringing home wood for Stairs to the Galleries, and a number of Logs for the Saw while all hands are about – Two have been Securing the Chimneys of the New House with Bark as our heavy rains here are destructive to every thing of the kind. Stone or Brick will be the only thing that will answer. {Boisvert Collecting our little Coals & putting it under Cover – } Three or four Quaitlines with their families encamped on the beach here but brought nothing.

Tuesday 2d. Dirty weather – a good deal of Snow fell last night – Before the winter fairly Sets in Mr. Annance with Six men is dispatched up the river – they have 12 Beaver Traps – provisions for 7 days and [are] otherwise well equipped – they cannot be expected to go far – Beaver hunt – Elk hunt or anything in the way of discovery will answer our purpose – The Blksmith and a man with him Contrived to make us 12 Small axes – The carpenter is indisposed in Consequence of a Strain in the Small of the back Carrying home firewood last night – The vagabond Indians we indulged with their own breadth of the beach last night decamped before day light with a Capot & pair [of] Trousers one of the men had the Sillyness [silliness] to leave out to dry in the Fort Pickets and which they could easily effect without the notice of the watch. {They were also at [a] small patch of potatoes belonging to one of the men.}

Wednesday 3d. Carpenter not better. Had been bled & Physic'd this morning – of the ten men now at the House, four are squaring wood for mechanics shop etc. etc. the Islanders of Course at the Saw – One Cutting firewood – the old man at the Gate and Annawaskum in the Kitchen.

Thursday 4th. Constant rain.

Friday 5th. {Weather rather better to day – Mrs. Yale Came home again.} Of a number of Indians that were about to day, three or four Seemed determined to Stop at the water Side, but the misbehaviour of the last party rendered this inadmissible – at length they pushed off, & just as they entered the little river opposite they let go two Shots. {We understand from Whitlakenum's family, that Some one of them has accompanied Mr. Annance & party.}

Saturday 6th. {Got a Small patch of potatoes belonging to Pierre Charles taken up, and Secured for him in our own Cellar.} Our four Squaring this week. Count 42 pieces – nothing extraordinary for *two* hands but as ours are mere beginners in this way we don't Complain and the weather Continues very unpleasant outdoors.

Sunday 7th. Nothing particular. Traded a Couple of Skins. {The Quitlines that came here two days ago went off, & a few Misquams that passed downwards traded an otter & a Small beaver Skin for one of our very inferior Sm. Axes made by Pepin.}

Monday 8th. A perfect torrent of rain all day.

Tuesday 9th. Faneant the Carpenter who did nothing for the last Eight days is again on duty, but not quite well.

Wednesday 10th. Mr. Annance and party returned – they have had excessive bad weather ever Since they went off – about 25 miles up they turned into a small creek to the right which in a few hours brought them to a lake[37] of 10 miles long and 6 wide at the extreme end of which there is a Considerable extent of low Clear Country – intersected with numerous ponds and little Channels well adapted for wild fowl – here they Spent the best part of two days and killed 4 Swans 3 Cranes 10 Geese & 40 ducks – after gaining the main river again they went up as far as the Chil whoo yook which was recommended to Mr. Annance on his last trip – but they could not mount the Current beyond the distance of 10 miles – near where they returned there was appearance of Beaver: being the Common thoroughfare however of all the Indians in that quarter every Lodge was distroyed [destroyed] – They Saw Canoes *en cache* but none of the natives – Two Beaver is all they brought – Saw no fresh track of Elk.

Thursday 11th. In course of the day Messrs. Yale & Annance with Six men, Crossed over and visited the Indians in the little river [Kanaka Creek] with the view of Calling them to account for their insolence in firing two Shots after leaving this the other day – They were also remonstrated with for the theft Committed ten days ago, which very unexpectedly produced a delivery of the Capot – It would appear it found its way there not many days ago, being ourselves Satisfied that the thieves Carried both articles up the River, but regretting their temerity and Sure of being detected Sent it back to the neighbourhood.

Friday 12th. Nicameus and family traded about 18 Skins, and with much difficulty got them all off, for while they do hang about here they will Stroll all over, and Set [an] example to others – these brutes Cannot appreciate kindness in its true light. Plemenden & John Kennedy with a few Traps, were allowed to make a trip up the river.

Saturday 13th. Our squaring produced about the Same number of Logs this week.

Sunday 14th. ½ our men allowed to go out with their Guns to day {by way of recreation}.

Monday 15th. In Case we have occasion for a Boat here towards the Spring the wood is Squared – three men rebuilding Chimneys. Rest Cutting firewood – {Carpenter has finished & fixed up against one of the Gallery Corners Stairs of 16 feet by 4 – Another of the Same Size is preparing for the opposite Angle.}

Tuesday 16th. {The two men yesterday Squaring Boat wood are now employed after Logs to fill up 5 of 12 large windows left in the New House and which Still can be fixed in without disfiguring the building – Carpenter and one man preparing the pickets that were Sawn Some days [ago] to Shut up the passage between the Houses and front Gate – Another alarm of the Yacaltas is driving up the Indians from below in Swarms – The wretches have nothing.} Another alarm of the Yewkultas.

Wednesday 17th. Plimenden and Kennedy have returned with 6 Large & 3 Small Beaver bodily – a good hunt Considering every thing – they were up a small river about 8 Miles from here {which Schamawah the late Chief, hunted last year, and Still left a few there – Traded 8 Skins to day.}

Thursday 18th. No less than four Inches Snow fell last night. Yet it Seems to disappear fast – The pair of Trousers lost with the Capot was taken back to day with many apologies from Some of the buttons being wanted.

Friday 19th. I hope we Shall now have Something like Winter – Mr. Annance and 6 men with our large wooden Canoe descended the main river and are to strick [strike] back to the Southward behind Point Roberts in Search of Elk – they leave their Craft at a place Called "HBC" tree Some distance below this – The Beaver hunters dressing & Stretching their Skins – The Sawyers at Boat wood and our other four or five men at firewood.

Saturday 20th. {I understand Mr. Yale has found means to get rid of his Lady that has Cost So much goods – } Plemenden and Kennedy accompanied by the lad in the Kitchen went out here to look for animals – Two Indians from the neighbourhood of Bellingham's Bay brought us 10 Large Beaver Skins and 7 or 8 Cawaitchin Canoes from the Island direct traded 18 Large & Small. It would Seem they are all gathering to a feast & dance given by the Quaitlines.

Sunday 21st. Our three men returned without Seeing any thing – more of the Cawaitchins passing up – their Canoes are loaded with Kamas [camas] which I believe is procured in abundance on the Island – with it and the Salmon they left *in Cache* last fall they propose living well for the Winter.

Monday 22d. Serene – dry frosty weather – {Most of the men at the house Chopping and Carrying home firewood. This is rather a laborious work to provide for 8 or 9 fires without a horse or dog to make use of however near the wood.} A few more of the Bellingham Bay furs Came in to day – Two Indians fishing in front of the Fort harpooned a very large Sturgeon which took them Several hours to exhaust & get ashore – no part of it as yet found its way here – Got our Corner Swivels[38] Covered with Cases.

Tuesday 23d. Hitherto in Serving out our Salted Salmon each man had a piece but this appearing not Sufficiently exact with all parties we got up a kind of Beam by which we now Contrive to serve each with 4 lbs. and as much potatoes as he can possibly make use of – Every Second day they have per man 3 pc. dried Salmon, which is exactly a whole fish.

Wednesday 24th. {Ten or 12 Canoes descended from Ni,cam.meus' Village where they had been assembled on a dancing party.}[39] In the evening Mr. Annance and party returned with the meat of two Elk and a small Chevx. – all they Saw – There being no Snow was much against them – they are Satisfied however that that quarter is not without animals. {The party did not go above three or four miles back from the main river 3 leagues below this.}

Thursday 25th. Our men have this a Holy-day and with a good proportion of the meat of yesterday and each a pint of Rum on his account they enjoy themselves to their heart's Content – Traded 5 Beaver Skins – every appearance of Winter.

Friday 26th. {Most disagreeable weather – People Cut a little Cord wood in the afternoon.} Lepitchin a very good little Indian and I believe the most industrious Beaver hunter in this quarter, came in with his fall hunt of 30 fine well Stretched Beaver which he traded for Blkts. in addition to which we gave him a few Skins on Credit as he proposes going on a trading excursion up the Country as far as Simpson's Falls – a distance of about 70 or 80 miles from here, & where Governor Simpson & party Slept their last night from Hudson's Bay.

Saturday 27th. Very little doing – {Got two or three pieces wood Squared and Carried to the pit.} Carpenter finished us a Couple of Tables and four Chairs.

Sunday 28th. Wet Weather again.

Monday 29th. Carpenter & three men filling up extra windows and blank space behind Chimneys of Big House – the whole length between the Posts – rest of our people variously employed.

Tuesday 30th. We had the big Quaitline doctor here to day for the first time Since my arrival and brought a few Skins – Soon after Joe, the Cawaitchin Chief made his appearance from Vancouver's Island & also has a small pacton [bundle] – he went up to the Quaitline Village and returns to-morrow to trade his Skins, and have a talk with us on the politics of the Country. {Plomondon & Etienne Oniaze indisposed.}

Wednesday 31st. People allowed this afternoon to Chop their own firewood. Joe returned – but did not Trade.

Thursday January 1st. At an early hour, received the usual Compliments of the day from our men, and in his turn each was Regaled[40] with a pint Rum, 3 lb. Flour – ½ lb. Grease and each House ½ Gall Pease – a quarter of Elk meat & a whole Beaver, with which to make merry rest of the day – Joe traded his furs – 37 Skins – all for Blkts. – he was to be indulged with a Gun in part payment if he had a mind, but declined it in Consequence of the difficulty in obtaining ammunition – {He tells us that the unfortunate affair of our people in the Sound is the cause of much trouble now among themselves.} He is to be back in a Couple of months, after visiting the Yewklatas and Tribes still further to the Northward along the main Shore. Went off well pleased of Course with fair promises of doing well – Our people, with the exception of one no wise irregular, were allowed lights[41] and the use of a House to enjoy themselves at a dance this evening – mean time the watch was mounted, who discovered early in the night that the drunken Sot Delannis had Contrived to haule [haul] one of the Quaitline damsels up by a port hole in one of the Bastions – At first we apprehended there were more than one in the Complo. But no. And even him, there being no irons at the place am at a loss what to do with him.

Friday 2d. Having obtained the necessary information beyond doubt as to Louis Delinnis' guilt in the affair of last night, he was Called in and in the presence of two of the most Credible men among themselves laid open before him the Criminality of his Conduct – He was told that had there been Irons he Should have felt the weight of them for Some time, but now that one half his year's wages – Eleven pounds – Should be the forfeiture of So unpardonable a Crime[42] and to take no liquor during the present year of our Lord – he did not Seem to think his Sentence hard – Said not a word in justification and with all appeared penitent – Situated as we are tis highly necessary to take this formal notice of these indiscretions – Plemmenden and Etienne are off on another attempt for Pierre Charles' Traps and will make a round in Search of Beaver.

Sunday 4th. {An unusual Squad of Men, women & children Strolled thro' the field to day in Search of potatoes & *also* we have no doubt with the view of accommodating our people – They were turned off more peremptory than usual.} Every thing quiet.

Monday 5th. Nicameus the Quaitlen Chief and friends brought us 30 Skins to-day. {He also brought back his Daughter in Consequence of her husband regretting having given her Conge [discharge] Some days ago.}

Tuesday 6th. {Weather appears to have taken a favorable turn.} Our men variously employed – two raising knee timbers[43] for Boat, two working at *dalles* [flagstones] for the Houses – rest Squaring, Chopping etc. etc.

Wednesday 7th. Took account of the dried Salmon in the Safe keeping of the men themselves and have no Cause to Complain of their management – {Say 1450 pieces which we find a few less than it ought to have been.} Carpenter fixing up a Small Stair to the Garret of the Big House.

Thursday 8th. Two or three of the Penaults Came down to day with a few Skins for the first time Since my arrival here, but I have no doubt many of the Furs traded by the Quatlains came from them, who make it a point to take all the Credit they can for bringing them to the House & discourage the actual hunters Coming near us at all. In the afternoon Mr. Annance and Six men moved off on another trip down the river, & as hunting is the main object Mr. Yale is allowed to breathe a mouth full of Sea air also. About an hour after *their* departure our other two hunters returned with good Success – To arrive at the *marais* [swamp] took them two whole days walking knee deep in water – their third night they Set 7 of the {9} Traps, which produced 4 Large Beaver – the next 3, and last night on their way home found an 8th in one of two Traps they left Set as they went along – besides this, they found a lodge perfectly entire not far off – So much for Beaver in the vicinity of Fort Langley.

Friday 9th. {Soon after the Gate was opened this morning, the Pellalts of yesterday were at the water Side in their Canoes & in a few minutes a little Slave Girl belonging to Mr. Annance's woman disappeared – They were suspected, pursued & brought back with the prize by five of our men – an old woman, who appeared to be the mother made a doleful appeal to our humanity for the offence – I signified to her [the] Girl was not mine, but that I should procure her freedom for 10 Beaver Skins & that until they Came back with the Beaver her daughter would be taken good care of – During this altercation, who arrives but the Scamp Ni,ca.mous – the Quaitline Chief; that traded the girl here without I believe Coming by her himself in the most lawful manner.} Plemenden & Etienne arranging their Beaver Skins.

Saturday 10th. The Beaver hunters {Plomondon and Etienne Oniaze} off again with an additional man by way of Security.

Sunday 11th. A regular fall of rain Since yesterday morning – Having now but Seven men in the Fort the look out is more Strict than usual.

Monday 12th. Carpenter, Blacksmith and Delinais making Some preparations inside the Fort to begin building a Boat – The Owhyhees at the Saw – Thirien Chopping, & Charpentier about the Kitchen – this will be our avocations till the rest of our people return.

Tuesday 13th. {A little before noon, a good deal of Shouting & noise was heard up the river, and soon after no less [than] 16 Canoes were Seen rounding the point – As they advanced the men were at arms in the Gallery – Self & one of the women went out to Speak to them - It was Mr. Yale's Father-in-law – the Quaitline Chief: who, with his tribe was bound for a dancing party among the Kitchies – None of them Stop[p]ed ashore but himself being forbid[d]en – He without much ceremony asked his daughter for [a] Blanket & she just as unceremoniously walked in – took it out, & with a pin buckled it on round his neck – I however with Still less Ceremony took the liberty of removing it & told Master Nicamous to be off with his own good new white Blanket & accordingly away they went to the Masquerade.} To-day 15 or 20 Canoes of the Quaitlines went down on a feasting visit to the Kitchis – Nicameus alone Came ashore – seeing so many was not agreeable to us.

Wednesday 14th. Every thing quiet.

Thursday 15th. Our neighbours returned from the *tout* {their party of pleasure} given by the Kitchies and say they understood our people were firing away about the mouth of the River.

Friday 16th. Traded a fine piece of Sturgeon today.

Saturday 17th. One of the Sandish [Saanich] Indians – Anskinnum {Chinuck} – Came in with 18 Skins and is accompanied by an Indian from the Southern part of Puget's Sound who has got about half a dozen – This is the first time the latter was at any of the Establishments & had much to Say on the politics of the Sound.

Sunday 18th. Our hunters are back, with the greater part of the meat of 5 Elk, which they with difficulty Contrived to Collect to the water Side, out of as much more they left behind – After leaving this, they discovered the band on Point Roberts, but immediately made to the Southward – next day they rounded the point and again Started them on the borders of the bay – and followed them across the neck of land to "H.B.C." Tree – The Gentlemen give a horrid account of the face of the Country they traversed in this Chase – Here & there, there are a few high ridges with Strong wood but in general extensive quagmires, interspersed with patches of overgrown Chalaal [salal] & deep water holes. Even this Country produces appearance of Beaver – They Set three Traps there one night and took 2 Beaver – in the third, they found the paw of a large one, who it would Seem had recourse to the expediency

of Cutting it off rather than Submit to an unpleasant Confinement –
This is an evil all our young hunters Complain of where there is but
little water – This afternoon also Came home the man Sent out with the
Beaver hunters on the 10th with five large Beaver and Says that from
the Same cause they lost four.

Monday 19th. John Kennedy and Ossin Sent out with Eight more Traps to
join Plemenden & Etienne in the *Grand Marais* and to follow the stream
Some distance down which is supposed to fall into Birch Bay.

Tuesday 20th. One of our men Pierre Therrein was allowed to take a wife
out of Aiskimnum's {Chinuck's} family – He gave a Gun & 4 Blkts.

Wednesday 21st. Lepitchin the Indian that had the Credit from us some
days ago, Came down to day {from his Village a little above here} with
a pressing invitation for us to go to a *Rout* {a kind of party} he is in his
turn giving to the Kitchis and Quaitlines – he had three or four of the
Indians of Simpson's Falls with him & of Course [they] were treated
kindly {with Something to eat.}

Thursday 22d. Messrs. Annance & Yale with Six Men were at the Indian
feast, and returned with 16 Beaver as their Share of the distributed property – I believe this is a Common practice with the principal Indians,
and the real motive not so much from a professed Spirit of liberality &
greatness as from avarice & gain, for tis well understood that every one
who receives, acknowledges a debt of at least 20 per Cent above the
actual value of what he got! Five or Six new & old of our Blkts. – about
as many of their own manufacture – 15 or 20 white Sheep Skins – 5 or 6
fathoms of the fine Beaver Bead – a number of Cassors or Kettles –
Leather Shirts – and the Beaver to our Gentlemen were the principal
presents – I understand there was but little to eat.[44]

Friday 23d. Our Boat is finished, & the Carpenter & two men have begun
extending a Gallery from beyond the log House to the main one. {4 of
our people now employed in the low point near the river Side to Clear
away wood & prepare Same for a Coal-pit – others Squaring.}

Saturday 24th. A party of our men are now employed Clearing the low
point of woods beyond the Creek.

Sunday 25th. Nothing new.

Monday 26th. One of the Sandish Indians Came in with 20 Skins he procured at the Scadschads, from whence he is but just returned and Says
there is Beaver in that quarter, but that they wish to keep them for larger
Blankets than ours which the Ships promise to bring them Soon.

Tuesday 27th. {A number of the Indians of the vicinity have Encamped not
far from us on account of the Cursed Yeaucaltas of whom they Seem in
eternal dread.} Everything quiet, & nothing worth mentioning.

Wednesday 28th. Cold frosty weather and a good deal of Snow.

Thursday 29th. No change in the weather.

Friday 30th. All hands clearing out the Snow – not an Indian to be Seen – In
the evening our Beaver hunters Came home all the little Creeks being
frozen over – The two that went out on 19th took eight – but Plemenden

& Etienne have Eighteen fine Large beaver which with the thirteen we had from them on two former occasions make a total of 31 Skins Since the 3d. of the month – It would appear that the nature of the Country requires great precaution in Setting the Traps to advantage – and to do it with a degree of Certainty – a man must wade thro' water to his middle for a Considerable distance before he Can find a patch of ground to lay his Trap on – This in my opinion accounts for the difference in the two hunts whatever is Said against the quality of the Traps.

Saturday 31st. There being a good deal Snow now on the ground 10 men are employed hauling home a parcel of Logs for the Sawpit – two after firewood, & the four hunters arranging their Beaver.

Sunday February 1st. A very Constant fall of Snow. All hands Clearing it out.

Monday 2d.
Tuesday 3d.
Wednesday 4th. } During these three days, a regular turn out at the Snow in the mornings, and the after part of the day hauling home the wood intended for building – River as yet not fairly taken, but Choked up with drift Ice & Snow – which Constantly keep moving to & fro at the influence of the Tide – Weather not very cold – indeed this afternoon it has broken up a regular thaw.

Thursday 5th. People variously employed about the Establishment.

Friday 6th. Three men off Collecting Gum and others making preparations about the Boat.

Saturday 7th. Until to day we were fully bent on Sending to the Scatshits for the Stock of beaver they must now have in that quarter, in Case our own Vessel does not Come round this Spring and the furs of Consequence going to Strangers – but be the Consequence what it will we Cannot Consistent with prudence Send – Admitting that I remain here with Six men, the two Gentlemen & the other 10 ever So well arranged would hardly be adequate to the troubles they might possibly met [meet] with & accordingly the idea is given up.

Sunday 8th. Mr. Annance & another party preparing for the Elk hunt – for we get not a mouthful from the Natives.

Monday 9th. Hunters made an early Start – Two of our men at the House are endeavouring to dress a Couple Elk Skins for we are Completely destitute in that way & I fear this attempt will not Succeed.

Tuesday 10th. Had our furs examined – they would have been the better of an airing, but the thing is impossible with the weather we have throughout – Got Six to day from the Indians of the falls.

Wednesday 11th. Nicameus here but brought nothing.

Thursday 12th. {In Course of day it was discerned that the little Slave girl in Mr. Annance's house was again gone – but too late to follow them.} Six of the Chilquiyooks Came down late this morning accompanied by as many of the Quaitlines and they seem to have a few Skins.

Friday 13th. Fine Sunshine day, the first we have had for a long time – Traded the few Beaver from our friends the Chilqueyooks for Beads & they Seemed agreeably disappointed at the quantity they got. {Three or four of the men with the Carpenter about the Galleries and three more of them Commenced Cutting into lengths & afterwards blowing up with Powder, any large Tree in the vicinity of the Fort.}

Saturday 14th. Fine day again, & had our furs well aired & dusted – four men have Commenced a part Gallery to the Big House, with the Carpenter – We were fully in expectation of seeing Mr. Annance and party back this evening whether or not they found the Elk.

Sunday 15th. About 4 P.M. we were Suddenly alarmed at the Sight of Annawaskum, one of Mr. Annance's party bounding out of the woods behind the establishment, in utter dismay himself – In a few words he told us the rest of the party were Cut off by the Natives; & upon further examination the facts elicited were these – Yesterday morning the two Owhyhees and Pepin being left in the Encampment – he, Delinais & Etienne accompanied Mr. Annance to the hunt, but dispersing in the woods in Course of the day, he was returning alone a little before Sunset, & as he advanced to the near vicinity of the encampment he all at once Saw a good many Indians – Say 7 or 8 – Some with white and Some with Blkt. or dark Capots running in all directions and two of them in particular with a menacing aspect making for him, where he Still Stood in the edge of the woods – Apprehending that the three men left in Camp in the morning were inevitably destroyed, he ventured no further & forwith put his trust in a speedy flight to the Fort – This is all he Can Say of the fate of any one – The party were in a Bay to the Southward of Point Roberts & saw no appearance of any kind of Indians before this event – However unfounded may be this melancholy tale it is Sufficiently alarming to render a Search necessary and accordingly Mr. Yale & Eight men with the Boat Started immediately for the point below this called "H.B.C." and to Cross by land to the Bay in question – I remain of Course with two men & the poor exhausted lad just arrived – however in any case I hope the lost party will not be absent above 36 hours.

Monday 16th. Every thing quiet – Gate locked from morning to night. {A few of the Quaitlines Came to the water Side, but Soon returned & Seemed much Concerned at what has happened.}

Tuesday 17th. All hands on guard last night – About 10 A.M. we were quite overjoyed at the echo of a distant Paddling Song up the river – & that all was well was Soon Confirmed by the arrival of both parties in their respective Canoes, which met with our hearty Congratulation by a discharge of two of our Wall pieces [small cannon]. It would appear that Indians *were* at the Encampment as Annawaskum reported, and in numbers Sufficient to excite Some alarm. As Mr. Annance himself, who it Seems arrived at the Encampment a short time *before* Annawaskum, was Struck with their appearance and actually thought like the other that they were wearing the Capots of our men, but in reality were our people mixed with the Indians – They proved to be from Birch Bay & Soon moved on. Etienne & Delenais arrived late – the latter having killed an Elk but of Course no Sign of Annanaskum that night – next day they got home the meat, Still Concerned at the fate of their absent man, which increased into a serious alarm that night and to the moment our people from the House fell upon them about 10 O'Clock yesterday morning – Words Can hardly express the mutual relief this meeting gave to the parties. After a sumptuous repast on the meat of the Biche, Mr. Yale and five of his party embarked with Mr. A. & arrived at "H.B.C." about 11 at night where they found the other three men that Came across by land the Same way they went in the morning – With so much uneasiness in the minds of us all, & detached as we were in three Separate parties yesterday morning tis most Satisfactory to find that here we are, all met again in perfect Safety – the thoughtless looking on the past as a mere laughable event. The alarm having this happily ended I believe it in like manner terminates the occurrences of a round year for, by reference to the beginning of these Sheets, it will be found that the many actions Connected with Outfit 1828 commenced on the 18th February and our arrangements to Close the accounts of that year are made accordingly.

Archibald McDonald Chief Trader

JOURNAL KEPT BY
ARCHIBALD McDONALD, 1829-30

Journal of Occurrences at Fort Langley
1829-30

[February 1829]

Wednesday 18th. It was on this day to the month that the Packet [mail boat] left this place for Fort Vancouver and commenced the Journal of occurrences connected with last Outfit, which is just Closed and ready for a start in like manner, had we only had the means of Carrying it – With this date on Shall also consider Outfit 1829/30 to begin. Our people are allowed this day to repose themselves after their overexertion on the late alarm, which happily turned out so well.

Thursday 19th. Sent out Plomondon & Kennedy for a few days to set Beaver Traps in a direction where they are not likely to be molested by the natives – The Carpenter with a man works inside – two men have Commenced a Coal pit – two are Squaring – two Sawing – four Clearing ground and two Cutting firewood, Carrying it home, & Cooking Salted Salmon and Potatoes for us twice a day.

Friday 20th. Had a visit from Lepitchin and Son-in-law today. He is the young man we always had in view for Sending up the river with the Packet & is not averse to the undertaking but has no inclination to go off immediately, & rather than force the Chap against his inclination, we Consent to his Spending a few days down here with his young wife {which will answer our purpose as we intend to await the Vessel till the 25th}.[1]

Saturday 21st. {Drawing out & explaining their accounts to the men.} The two men Sent out on Thursday Came back without doing any thing – They Say that there is too much ice and Snow yet in the Swamps where they proposed setting their Traps.

Sunday 22d. To appearance the rainy weather has recommenced – a canoe just arrived from the Coast inform[s] us that Joe the Cawaitchin Chief who winters regularly on the Island has been killed by one of his own followers – the result tis said of family acrimony.

Monday 23d. The Snow is going fast.

Tuesday 24th. Nothing particular.

Wednesday 25th. Plomondon and Kennedy again off to the Beaver hunt, as it is not desirable that the waters Should rise too much.

Thursday 26th. The Quaitlines here all moved off to Some distance above where it is Said they will more easily procure the means of Subsistance – When we Say the Quaitlines we very often mean any one of the distinct Tribes Called among themselves – Quaitlines, Musquams, Kitchis and at a distance even the whole collectivity are better known by the appellation of Cawaitchens as that Tribe is the leading nation in this quarter.

Friday 27th. Nothing particular.

Saturday 28th. {This week four men were Constantly Clearing ground on the Point – two Squaring – two at the Coal-pit – two Sawing – two at Carpenter's work & two Cutting & Carrying home firewood, & Cooking Salt Salmon & potatoes twice a day.} One of our Engages – Louis Ossin is allowed to take a woman from the Camp & each man had a half pint liquor on the occasion in the evening – We got three or four Skins to day to begin the new Score with.

Sunday March 1st. It is now ten days Since our letter man left us, & his not returning yet is no good Sign of his being a man to his word for Carrying despatches to the interior – however, if he does not come there is hardly any other alternative.

Monday 2d. Most of the Indians have again returned from above and the Quaitline Tribe fixed their Camp not many hundred yds. off – They are not what may be called bad Indians Still there is no good arising from their being too near – they will Saunter about the premises: & their inherent disposition to pilfer & to pick up every little trifle they can, must at times lead to unpleasant harshness – Our people resumed nearly the work of last week – Old Boisvert takes his Station at the Gate – the night watch is in like manner regulated with greater Strictness than it was in dead of winter.

Tuesday 3d. Another of our men – Louis Delenais – is permitted to take a wife. Heretofore it was thought desirable to have no connection of this kind with the Cawaitchens, and the few women that were admitted were from a distance – The plan however does not Seem to answer our purpose, for these Laddies [ladies] in themselves have nothing very worthy or Conciliating about them, when they come to have intercourse with the natives here: & like all Indians their attachment to their own lands and friends keeps them for ever on the wing to be back again, which Cannot fail leading to the Same disposition in the husband – Again those of the men that had not been lucky enough to Come in for a Chance of this kind have no inducement at all to remain at the place. We have therefore, thought that if Indian Connection is at all countenanced the one is as judicious as the other, & to reconcile the bucks to Fort Langley without Some indulgence of this nature is utterly out of the question – to leave them to prowl about in the Camp would be the worst policy of all – What remains for us then, is to make the best & wisest Selection we Can for every man of them, which I think will be tantamount to a few yearly Contract[s] & the evil be not quite So great as was first apprehended.

Wednesday 4th. Nothing new.

Thursday 5th. Fine warm weather.

Friday 6th. We have now given up all idea of Seeing not only the Vessel but also the young Indian that promised to be the bearer of a packet to the interior and have resolved on another expediency Should nothing Cast up before the 12th.

Saturday 7th. Como – an Owhyhee, & one of our best men here is married to the Sister of Nicameus – the Quaitline Chief – all hands had a half pint & a hop on the occasion. Our hunters returned in the evening with 11 large Beaver taken during Six days of the twelve they were absent which upon the whole is not So much amiss – They Say that about the place when they returned appearances were more favourable, but, in Consequence of their being required at the house by a Certain day, Could not continue out longer – The swamp where they have been is about 15 miles from here in a SW direction, & yielded to us upwards of 50 Beaver this winter, that the natives would never trouble themselves about, from the uncouth nature of the Country.

Sunday 8th. Every thing quiet.

Monday 9th. A Couple [of] Canoes arrived from Vancouver's Island, contradict the report of Joe's death Some days ago – Four men with our large Canoe made a trip 5 or 6 miles up the river for Stones to build Chimneys with, as the Clay will not answer[2] – & three are levelling part of the river bank for laying our Craft on {our Canoes and Boat}.

Tuesday 10th. Not the apppearance of a Beaver Skin from the wretched Indians of the place – Indeed if others don't bring them their way I see hunting them themselves is perfectly out of the question – their dread of the enemy is incredible. At the very risk of Starving they will not appear in the main river in any Shape when the Yewkaltas are reported to be near, & that is not Seldom.

Wednesday 11th. Messrs. Yale & Annance & ten of our best here viz. Faneant – Plomondon – Delenais – Charpentier – Pepin – Ossin – Terrien – Faron – Puopuoh & Como, are preparing for a Start tomorrow the length of the Cowlitz Portage – They are Served out with 10 days provisions in potatoes & Salted Salmon – The packet, exclusive of private letters is made up with the Journal up to 17th Feby. – District account Book of Course Comprehending Inventory & Returns – Men's winter advances – Men's orders for ensuing Season, and the Requisition for Current Outfit, beside Letter to Governor and Council, and two to John McLoughlin Esqr. Chief Factor.[3]

Thursday 12th. At a few minutes past midnight, a Girl[4] was born to Plemendon, and precisely at 2 a.m. our party was under weigh [way] – They have near upon 100 Skins in Trading Goods, in Case the Indians of the Sound may Come to them *Enpassant* with Beaver, that would be desirable to have out of their hands before the Coasters have time to Come along, as our own Vessel now is not likely to be here in a hurry – they will return from whatever part of the Portage they meet with a trusty Indian to Carry the Packet to Fort Vancouver – Until their return I shall be here with but Six men – namely the Cook – Gate-Keeper – one that will assist to Speak a little with Indians – the Chimney builder {Arquoitte}, who can always work inside – and the two Iroquois, one of them unwell – Our little Artillery was hardly examined & loaded anew, when the Yewkeltaws were announced – no less than 20 {no less than 30} Canoes, but Should it even be true I have no doubt the number is exaggerated by one half.

Friday 13th. Nothing alarming transpired during [the] night, but as Soon as our Indian neighbours {the Quaitlines} had time to assemble, the advance of the enemy was given out as admitting of no doubt; & that their Scouts of the night discerned the force to be 30 {up to 50} canoes at least – They made every thing Secure themselves, & only a few resolute fellows Kept peeping at a distance So as to have one glance at the enemy – before an actual retreat to the woods Should be Commenced: when, to their great ease of mind, four or five Small Canoes of the Whoomes Tribe hove in Sight round the first point below, which put an end to their Yewkelta terror for the present. It is impossible to describe their Continual alarm at the very name of this formidable foe: and can only proceed from the little mercy they have to expect from those atrocious villains when any of them unfortunately fall into their hands – Although those here abouts are themselves pretty numerous and ought to be able to make a good Stand before Strangers Coming upon them, yet on this occasion they Seem to put their greatest faith in the protection of the Six White men in the Fort – However in Case Something may be pending over us, we keep them all alike at a distance.

Saturday 14th. Every thing quiet – Nothing more heard of the enemy.

Sunday 15th. Fine, Clear mild weather.

Monday 16th. Got about 30 lb. fresh Sturgeon today, which gave us all a mouthful – Arquoitte & Kennedy at the chimney – the other two men with the Cook levelling the Fort & laying Gutters – Boisvert in the lookout, and the Gate key in my pocket – The women allowed out only morning and evening for water & firewood {and this to appearance is quite enough; for, even during those few minutes, they contrive to Create a little disturbance among the Indians about the beach with their batter of words this evening, but all women warfare & Consequently not very alarming}.

Tuesday 17th. We attend to very little work now on account of our night watch is doubled.

Wednesday 18th. One of our neighbouring Indians {Aquaitline, and the father of one of the women that made the noise last night} brought us 15 Skins today, that he traded for Blankets of Course.

Thursday 19th. Late last night the Young man with whom we Settled to be the bearer of our packet as far back as the 19th of last month, came in, accompanied by Laitzie one of Coutamine Chief[s], and another Indian – They have about 20 Skins mostly belonging to the Stranger – {The Stranger traded 10 of them for a Couple of Traps and a Small Kettle – 8 remain untraded.} Latzie made me a present of two, of Course from Selfish motives – He looks pitiful having lately lost his wife & child and being a good Indian to my own knowledge he has had a Blanket with which to Cover his nakedness – he is the Same Indian that Came down with Governor Simpson & myself last fall: but I find the Gentleman has not delivered notes that he was entrusted with going back, to our friends in the interior relative to the Gov's. final arrangement here for his journey to the Columbia, and were according to his account he & them were upset in the river.

Friday 20th. Last night as late as 10 O'clock our Eleven women in the Fort Created a most unconscionable row among themselves, & two Couples actually proceeded to blows – They are all Indians true, but they Seem of the very worst description – be it remarked however that all the heroines on this occasion are the enlightened ones from the Columbia[5] – {Tis impossible to learn the precise cause of their quarrels – Scandal no doubt has a great Share in them – } Arquoitte has finished a very neat Chimney in the big House – the other men Still running the Gutters – Wrote a few lines up to Thompson's river by Laitzie who is anxious to be off tho' Should wish him to remain until our party returns.

Saturday 21st. Fine, Clear, Calm, dry weather the whole of this week, which gave us Sanguine hopes of seeing our people back, this being their 10th day – & happily are not disappointed: for a little before Sun Set the Song was heard, and a few minutes brought the Boat with flag flying in Sight – Sure Signs at all times that everything is right, and is also the Case now, but the party's rencenter [*rencontre* – encounter] this morning with the Yewkeltas at the mouth of the river had nearly proved fatal to them all, & evidently were Saved by their own resolute & firm Conduct – As near as Can be Collected from the relation of the Gentlemen themselves the particulars were as follows – By way of elucidation it may not be amiss to observe, that the Southern branch of the two main ones into which the river divides itself a few miles from the Coast again forks off within half a league to the Sea, and Coming up the least of these Channels it was that our party discerned the enemy in a point to the right hand exactly at the forks – On perceiving our people they evidently wished to Conceal themselves behind the point with the exception of two Canoes Containing about 30 men each – these boldly Stood out into the Stream, with the manifest intention of amazing the Boat, but by this time every thing in a few minutes having been made Snug on board & a resolution taken to rush through with Flag up & a Cheerful Song, the Gentln. Stood up & fixed a watchful eye upon their motion – they failed in their design of decoying the Whites into a Snare as they hoped or of passing them down that Channel so as to get in their rear. They instantly Stemmed the Current and were the two nearest of a half moon formed out on the river with Seven other Canoes equally well manned, as the

Boat gained the point – No shot was fired until our people were fairly within the Small Bay above & right abreast of the Canoes that at that time might have been about 150 yds. off – As they Commenced firing they gradually approached – the Boat never getting out of slack water had to Contend with a Strong Current alongside a Steep bank, of which Situation the Savages took immediate advantage, and the very two Canoes that first recon[n]oitered, made for the Shore – A Battle now being unavoidable, the Boat also dropped on shore: but from Some neglect amongst themselves in the hurry, all was thrown into an alarming dilemma for a moment, by allowing the Boat to Shear out again when but Seven men had landed – these however being directed to fire, kept the Indians that landed below at Sufficient distance until the two Gentlemen with the other three men hook or by Crook got ashore with the ammunition and rendered the position taken So formidable to the blood thirsty villains that in about 15 minutes the whole rest of them – not an Indian under 240, was Completely repulsed & down the main branch into the open Gulf before our brave little party reembarked. Although their Guns (generally old American Muskets) Carried well with Seemingly no want of ammunition among them it is a most fortunate Circumstance that none of our people was hurt – neither is it likely with the exception of Mr. Annance and his Rifle, that our Small Trading Guns made any great execution among the Indians – Our Blunderbusses if they did not carry their length at least made noise – no Small Share of the Battle with these hunters of human beings – Whether they had a fixed design upon the Establishment – on the party, or merely Came to Catch at what they Could is very uncertain: however had they ever appeared before the Fort when I was here with but Six men I flatter myself they would require to fight more determined than they Seem to have done to gain much by it. The Indians here abouts have all come round to Congratulate us on the wonderful triumph over the invincible Yewklatus – that never yet from them met not only with their match, but even the Slightest resistance and all this from a handful of *white men* – Some of their own friends that were down that way Slily for Shellfish had but a narrow escape, & Confirm all that happened and a great deal more as regards the extent of the havock [havoc] made, which, it is not the best policy to Contradict – altogether no Set of Indians ever entertained a higher opinion of the prowess of a white man than the Quaitlines do of us this evening – Immediately on this intelligence two men were dispatched after Latzie who only left us about noon, as, by this means we may yet Contrive to push letters in to Fort Colvile before the middle of April – the time the Express is likely to leave that place.

Sunday 22d. An unusual concourse of Indians about us the whole day, and every fresh arrival gives additional account of the great destruction made in the battle; which is not Surprising for they all have a happy [k]nack of making a good Story out of nothing, and of course, a trifling event gives them licence to exaggerate to an extraordinary degree: how far then from the truth must be *their* account, of so memorable an affair!

Two Canoes were fairly annihilated – three with but four men in each, that could barely work home their Canoes – one Celebrated Chief had a Ball thro' the Eye, & their disasters of minor importance are innumerable! One thing Certain however that the blood thirsty hounds on their return at the mouth of the north branch got hold of two young men & a woman whom they instantly displayed – the poor old man who was also there, is now here in a doleful Condition. Our two men had the good luck to come with Laitzie before he left Camp this morning, & all are now here again – he will again start after a few hours rest and has a letter[6] for the Governor, Chief Factors, & Chief Traders on the affair of yesterday & its happy result – It unquestionably has produced three good effects viz. assures our people of the necessity of a vigilant lookout – of their own Strength even before numbers, when displayed with firmness & Courage, & undoubt[ed]ly proved to the enemy as well as those Indians nearer the door what we are Capable of doing if pushed to it.

Monday 23d. Laitzie and associates {two of his own friends} left us during the night, and however thoughtless and dilatory these Indians in general even when we evince great anxiety to have them to be punctual, I am in hopes from the great encouragement given this Indian, besides his own personal Knowledge of the Cause of the dispatch that he will reach Thompson's river in ten days but then again time will be lost if the forwarding of the Letter will entirely depend upon the natives. Eight men were up the river today for Stones, that we may have every thing of the kind at hand before the Indians begin to Collect.[7]

Tuesday 24th. Early this morning our large Canoe that was employed yesterday for Stones was missed – It was designedly left in the water So as to make another trip with today, tho' not I believe too well Secured – Whether it was taken away, or drifted with the tide we know not. The two Gentlemen with the Boat & ten men went down the river for four hours after it to no purpose – down that way they Saw the Indians taking up the Body of the poor wretches that were butchered the other day – Late in the evening, Waskalatchat, Commonly Called the Frenchman, a Sinnahome Chief, arrived – he is accompanied by another active Indian of that quarter, and has a Note from Governor Simpson dated 19th Feby.[8] which our people understood at the Portage had passed on to the Sound, but were not able to pick it up as they Came along – The information it Contains has no allusion to an apparently well founded report among the Indians that two Boston Vessels[9] have arrived in the Columbia river, tho it is perfectly possible that these Ships may have Come in Subsequent to the date of the Gov's. note and was [were] the Cause of their having dispatched 3 men from Fort Vancouver about the 10th of this month with a liberal supply of Trading Goods, that was afterwards Consigned to the Charge of an Indian (St. Vincent)[10] whom our people had seen on the portage and was also full of the news of the new Comers. St. Vincent was directed to proceed to the Sound with his Outfit, and then according to his own account, to deal it out sparingly for what ever he could get, {which appears highly probable even from the tenor of the Gov's. note to myself}.

Wednesday 25th. Got home our last haul of Stones, having now a Sufficiency for our Chimneys and an Oven – The Sinnahomes gave in about 40 Skins, for which we mean to pay them well before they leave us – Our people now are put upon regular work at the Sound of a Horn having no Bell – Fences & farming will be the avocation of at least one half of them, now that we understand by the Governor's Communication, though not an official one, that Cultivation and the rearing of Cattle will in Some degree be prosecuted here also – The face of the Country immediately round the Establishment will not admit of any *extensive* operations that way; but a few miles higher up on the river, there is a good deal of fine open plains that would answer the purpose to any extent were it [not] for the natives & [for being] so far from the House.[11] {Same real danger that was to be apprehended here at the Commencement of the Establishment is Still equally probable by a rush in from the more distant Indians.}

Thursday 26th. Nothing particular.

Friday 27th. Dirty wet weather – The Frenchman has no idea of leaving us with Such unpleasant weather, & he Seems perfectly reconciled to the disappointment – he & friend with their families lodge within & have the full freedom of the Fort with what other indulgence we Can Shew them – One has about him a very Strong, tho' Coarse, red ground Embossed Blanket that found its way from Chinook this Spring, & there as they Say fetched but Three Blankets – Such articles ought unquestionably to have been at our disposal here, although the Stout White Blanket will always be the grand demand.

Saturday 28th. Still raining – This week we Succeeded So well with our Cawaitchin women as to get them to turn over all our potatoes, and a very desirable job it was, for in this moist climate that is never very Cold, they Shoot most rapidly.

Sunday 29th. The Sinnahomes left us, well loaded with Potatoes and a Small Share of our little douceurs [trifling gifts] – In Blankets also their Stock is greater than I ever knew before going out of a Fort for the Same quantity of furs – For 35 Beaver and 10 Otters, they have Eleven Blkts., a pound of Beads & a pound of {Brass} Collar wire, besides a long String of the usual Small presents we have the Satisfaction however to Know that they went off uncommonly well pleased & of Course with faithful promises to return loaded with Beaver before the Season is over – their fulfilment notwithstanding, we know will very much depend upon the inducement they meet with at home from the Coast Traders – that they will meet with better is doubtful, and it is more than likely that these very Indians will not trade in the Sound even for the Same Tariff we now allow – a Blanket of 2 ½ pts. which is always the Standard, they have for Three Beaver Skins; but notwithstanding this uncommon advantage, I do not think it will be the means of urging them to increased exertion in their hunts – however, the end is answered, if it be the means

of bringing in Skins that would otherwise have gone to an opposition &
be entirely lost.

Monday 30th. Our people have resumed nearly the work of last week –
namely – Six of them at fence-wood – three at Carpenter work – Blksmith
& Stone Masson [mason] at their jobs – the Sawyers at theirs – One at
the Gate of Course and the other two employed between the Kitchen &
firewood – On a former date we had occasion to allude to a little Slave
Girl that one of the Chiefs traded with the women of the Fort Some time
ago, and afterwards, as we Suspected, winked at the owners carrying
her away – in Consequence of his not Coming too honestly by her himself – These distant Indians Conscious of having acted wrong though
not in reality their fault of Course Keep Shy with the Establishment &
listen to whatever tales Master Nicameus Cho[o]ses to tell them – In the
Same manner we Suspect his dealings with respect to the Canoe we lost
the other day (for it Came from him) and this morning thought it advisable to have him Called to account, and Satisfy him how Confident we
are of his knavery. In a few hours he brought Beaver to Compensate for
the Girl and has in Some degree undertaken to recover the Canoe.

Tuesday 31st. Every thing quiet.

Wednesday April 1st. All appearance of Spring – Vegitation [vegetation]
Coming on rapidly – a man's labour now is an object; we have therefore
got 10 or 12 of the natives to Carry home our fence-wood – a work they
Cheerfully undertook for a good mess of potatoes, but our generosity
extended to a little Vermilion and a few Beads.

Thursday 2d. No less than 20 of the Indians in our employ today for much
the Same reward as yesterday.

Friday 3d. Nothing new.

Saturday 4th. Very fine weather the whole of this week, with occasional
Showers, the two men at our fence for the last three days got over a
Space of about 600 yds. made with excellent Cedar wood Seven feet
high: and will prove of great Service against all encroachment from the
Indians – The Carpenter and a man principally working in the big House;
and Plomondon fixing a railing all round the Fort Gallery; Four men
Scrapping [scraping], Cleaning & Gumming our Boat as the Vessel will
now be expected every day – no Beaver, & Sturgeon equally Scarce.
{The Natives are actually starving.}

Sunday 5th. The Quaitlines gave Some tidings of our Canoe today, which
may be true, though it is only one of the hundred different accounts we
have had of it Since its disappearance.

Monday 6th. Four Indians {Quaitlines} volunteered their Services this
morning to recover our Canoe which they also effected – tho' not from
the very quarter they gave out on Starting, but this Change in their route
it is possible may have arisen from our not thoroughly understanding
each other – however it is Clear they went Some distance down the
river, as two Indians from below accompanied them to receive Some
reward for their good office being the first that Secured it. What great
mustery [mystery] Soever appears in the whole affair the Canoe is now

here and we shall endeavour to take better Care of it in future – no Suspicion now attaching to any particular individual, all Concerned in its recovery here have been less or more rewarded.

Tuesday 7th. Three or four of our friends the Chilquihooks dropped in upon us before the Sun rise today with about 25 Skins {Beaver}; and were Soon followed by a band of the Quaitlines {headed by Nicamous}, who did not blush in an earnest request that we Should sell our Blkts. dear to the Stranger – Their drift of course was too plain to blind any one – It is these upper Indians that kill the Beaver that the others generally bring to the Fort, and now Seeing the hunters themselves find their way to us & [are] encouraged, not only do the Quaitlines lose the Credit of trading at the house, but also the profit made in the original Barter – the Change is particularly mortifiying at the very time the trade Tariff is reduced. {Our interest of Course is to give every encouragement to the Beaver *Killer* and in fact every distant Indian.}

Wednesday 8th. The Chilquihooks left us remarkably well pleased, but would not promise to be back with any thing worth while of their own killing for two or three *moons* – we are taking Steps to form a family Connection in that quarter if possible – Coming down last fall, the mouth of the river they hunt in Called the Titun [Coquihalla][12] was on our left hand about 10 O'clock, and is likely to receive many of the little Streams adjoining the waters of Okanokun or rather of the Schimilicamich [Similkameen] River.

Thursday 9th. Eight men Commenced breaking new ground with the Hoe, and turning up roots – work that Can advance but slowly. We have also a Couple of men not far off, breaking up the Beaver dams that overflow a space that may yet become good pasturage – Several shoal ponds are in the neighbourhood and will easily admit of the same operation – To begin with we got a few Gallons potatoes put into the ground today.

Friday 10th. This afternoon again, had one of our Yewkatla alarms, that at length caused our neighbours to at least a Shew of making a Stand, & of rallying to one point: but, as I believe they surely expected – proved unfounded – The new Comers are two Indians with their families from the Sound, who, after landing here for a Short time Continued on to the Camp – One of them was here with the Frenchman about the middle of Sept. last, & [it] was rumoured that he was Concerned as well in the murder of our people, as being the very actor in the affair of Schannawah: which, however did not appear to Mr. McMillan of Sufficient weight to take further notice of.

Saturday 11th. The Strangers and their friends here were on the beach early, Smoking their pipes, and the Suspicion in the Sinnahomes or rather in the Skiwamus [Skykomish] a Small inland tribe to the Southward of them, increased considerably through the day; not only from further reports industriously Circulated to his prejudice but from the numerous articles about them apparently the property of our deceased friends – He Somehow or other Suspected our unfavorable opinion of him, & Contrary to his intention in the afternoon, thought it advisable to rise

Camp in the evening & again Sleep with the Quaitlines {Indians of the plain}.

Sunday 12th. A crowd of Indians on the beach and about the Fort today again with their curiosity much excited at what was in the wind – The Stranger drifted down in his Canoe to the wharf, & preferred remaining in it basking himself before the Sun to Coming on Shore – At length, the unusual indignation of our people against him, with all these Supposed trophies of his infamy, prompted us to order him ashore thro' his own Companion; which he immediately did without the least Sign of dismay – All the articles in question – namely – an old Blue Coat – a Blkt. – Guncover – a large Red Fire Bag, a powder Horn and a Cap, being Collected and placed before him in course of the enquiry, were at the Same time minutely examined by all our people present, that could have had any previous knowledge of them: But to the great good fortune of the Criminal not one item of them Could be identified as ever having been the effects of the deceased however Sanguine were the jury – neither Could much be made of the various rumours Since last year against his Character principally Coming thro' one of the women of the Fort & the daughter of the very Schannawah [Plamondon's wife] of whose death he was also accused – He behaved with great Coolness throughout, except the moment he was deprived of his Dag [knife] which threw him into great agony, but recovering himself, he did not Seem to think any unfairness in the proceedings, Conscious I believe of his own innocence – though Sure enough, it was perfectly possible for an innocent Indian to be possessed of Some of the articles Searched after – As the things were returned to them one by one (for the whole was not about his person) he was assured, that, joined with what was generally Said of him, had we been able to trace about him the property of our unfortunate friends, our determination was to hang him up immediately by the very Guncoat, rigged out with all the other rewards acquired by So black a Crime: & that Such Should be our Sentence on any Indian that ever fell into our hands under Cimilar [similar] Circumstances: but on the other hand equally assured him, that, so far are we from going to wanton extremity with any of them, now in the absence of Sufficient proof he Should be allowed to return to his friends unmolested. While this decision was given two of the Quaitline Chiefs were present, & Special Care was taken to impress upon them how applicable this resolution Should be to every mother's Son of them So Caught, to which the Savage part of the audience Seemed to acquies[c]e most Cheerfully – Without receding in the least from the force of this threat we afterwards Showed kindness to these Chaps and gave them ample proof of our disposition to show no unjust ill-will to any of them: and towards evening they left us Seemingly not disgusted with the Judicature of Fort Langley[13] – From all that has taken place, I think that neither they nor our neighbours here will in a hurry Strut about with any thing they don't honestly Come by – This Indian left us his Gun to be repaired and will Call for it in a few weeks when he shall have Beaver. Ai.a.waston, poor McKenzie's own Guide, appears, by the unanimous information of every one we have questioned in this unfortunate affair solely to have been at the bottom of it, and whose death by a bold Stroke would most unquestionably have produced a Salutary effect all over.

Monday 13th. Four men today Sent up the river to a Lake [Sumas] about 30 miles off where we understand there is this Season of the year a great quantity of wild fowl – They also have a few Traps, & are accompanied by Nicameus & brother – rest of our people employed in usual way.

Tuesday 14th. It would appear the Sturgeon Season has commenced as 8 or 10 were Caught last night – The Small fish in the Columbia called ulluchans [eulachon] is also within the river, but not yet this high – Blksmith making us a few Small axes – not an easy job from the materials we have.

Wednesday 15th. While 20 or 30 Canoes were industriously fishing a Short distance above, every thing was thrown into Confusion & grief at the sudden disappearance of one of them – the unfortunate fellow got his Scoop net entangled, with which they work for the Sturgeon in a great depth of water – made two or three fruitless attempts to disengage it, & at length went down to rise no more. {So there is an end to the fishing for the present.}

Thursday 16th. Blowing a perfect gale of wind last night and the greatest part of today – The d----d Yewkultas again beyond doubt within the river, for a Boy of about 14 as naked as the day he was born and dreadfully torn up in the woods, managed to get off from them yesterday evening: & is Certain that his Father (the big doctor) and rest of the family are destroyed – The Indians here will have it that they absolutely have a design upon the Fort – Mean time we Can only keep a Strict look out and ourselves in perfect readiness for action when necessary.

Friday 17th. This, according to our account being Easter day, our Canadians agreeable to their Montreal *contrime* {habit} will have it a fast day at least a day exempted from work – Two of our hunters Came home with about 60 Geese and half dozen fine fat Cranes – the other two forked off in the afternoon to Set Traps in one of the Small rivers – In the evening a melancholy Cry was heard from below which Soon brought a swarm of the Quaitlines to our Wharf, concluding from the account given by the boy yesterday that all was not right, & this Suspicion was immediately Confirmed by the arrival of the other brother with the headless body of the father – and a most moving Scene it was – The poor doctor was by far the most decent Indian we were acquainted with in this quarter – He went down towards the mouth of the river about Six weeks ago & rather imprudently threw himself in among numerous Small channels generally overflowing with the Tide and wholly Secretted with Reeds & high grass from the eye of any one passing by the river, where he was making a very Successful Beaver hunt – Collecting a Stock of Wabbitinns [wapatos] & living upon Shellfish when Suddenly discovered by the monsters – The head, arms, and legs were severed from the body and in this State was found by the terrified Son when he ventured back to the

Spot – All but himself Succeeded in making off with themselves – He & family were part of those that escaped the day our party was attacked: and the very young man that arrived this evening with the body that day Conversed with our people not 1000 yards. above the Scene of action just as he was peeping out of his place of Concealment – Latterly it would Seem that they felt Some Security in having a number of the Cawaitchins that Came across to fish Sturgeon in their vicinity: but they also on this occasion experienced the unmerciful hand of the Common enemy – There is not an Indian now between this and the Sea, Consequently the less Chance have we of hearing what progress they make from below – Tis to be hoped our people on board the Vessel are full on their guard.

Saturday 18th. Plomondon & Kennedy Came home, finding the passage of the Creek impracticable at present {from want of water}.

Sunday 19th. Four or five of the Titans [Taits] came in to-day with about a Couple Skins each. In the afternoon for [the] first time Since I Came here, I went out with a Canoe and Eight men accompanied by Mr. Annance to examine the nature of the Country in the neighbourhood, and the practicability of Cultivating a good Spot with but little labour – an object however I am Sorry to Say that is not easily attained within a reasonable distance to the Establishment – even the plain we had in view above this, is not only a distance of 3 miles off, over a very bad Country, but is I am certain too wet of itself and always Subject to the overflowing of the river in Summer to Calculate much upon a Successful farm there – further on & more in the back Country, there are other very extensive openings, & I believe good Soil that might give Satisfaction but then at that distance the farming and rearing of Cattle Could not be Carried on without a distinct Establishment, which perhaps would require a greater force than the intended Speculation would afford – Here itself, for the ordinary purposes of the Establishment, ground enough can be wrought under the very eye of the Fort Bastions; but nothing more, unless we look to the tedious result from the Clearing of Strong woods not in the best of Soil, and from the draining of fens & marshes that would be equally tedious & unsatisfactory. Of about 15 acres now open, 5 of them is low meadow – 5 fine mellow ground fit for the plough, & the rest full of Strong Stumps & roots fit only for the Hoe for many years to Come: and pasture for more than a few Beasts, is out of the question. The possibility of its being hereafter proposed to extend the fields of Fort Langley Suggest these observations now.

Monday 20th. Cold & boisterous weather – most of the people overhauling a quantity of potatoes in another of our Cellars that much required it, and is now Conveyed to an upper Garret – the rest of them with the women Cutting the Seed.

Tuesday 21st. Weather very little better than yesterday, & our people are employed much the Same – The natives begin to take the Sturgeon now, but are extremely Selfish with it; and we have reason to be thankful for our good Stock of potatoes & Salted Salmon.

Wednesday 22d. Ten men to day grubbing away with the Hoe among the Strong-wood Stumps, that we may get a Small patch Cleared & prepared for a Bushel or two of Seed that Came to the place last year.

Thursday 23d. Sowed a little wheat, {about a Bushel} and had it rather imperfectly covered with the Hoe only – A very Current report today Says that the Yewkultas were again on this Coast, and Committed a dreadful havoc on the Indians to the Southward {of Puget Sound and Cawaitchens on Vancouver's Island}.

Friday 24th. Last night Scheenuck the Sandish Chief, & this morning Joe the Cawaitchin Chief arrived both from Vancouver's Island with about 70 Skins between them large & Small, with the usual great proportion of land Otters, and give full and ample Confirmation to the rumour of yesterday – It is Certain that the enemy after the attack upon our people, made the best of their way home – i.e. the Country on both Sides the Channel not far beyond point Marsil [Marshall] where the *Cadboro* had the man killed in autumn 1827 – and returned as Soon as they Could with 18 Canoes exactly double their first Strength. On the 15th they butchered the poor Doctor and two Cawaitchins; then Continued their Course along the Coast to the Scadchds, & about the night of the 17th fell upon that Tribe with the Same brutality & Carried off a number of their women & Children {that offered all the information we have yet had on that part of this distressing side of extermination, as, in their Captivity, they were met in the Gulf by the Nanimoos, a Kind of neutral party}. On their return tis Said that they got hold of three more Cowaitchens – thus, making that Campaign the most extended & destructive the Yewkultas have been upon for Some time back, and as is very natural has Struck dreadful terror in the minds of those around us here – The Cowaitchens have determined on a vigorous resistance or even on an attack in their turn when able to Seize a fair Opportunity – for this purpose Joe now Came across with Furs to buy for himself a gun and 300 rounds of ammunition for distribution among his followers that are already armed – So much amm. to one man in this part of the world & in times like the present may Seem imprudent; and must Seem Still more So when I remark that heretofore the article was entirely withheld from them: but keeping our own immediate hunters and Traders in this defenceless State, will I presume appear equally impolitic – What is more the natives of Vancouver's Island and all along the Coast Can have no difficulty in obtaining elsewhere for their Skins ten times the quantity of amm. we give, if totally refused them here: & how varied Soever may be opinion on the impropriety of giving arms & amm. in Trade, I am myself Convinced that an Indian refused this reasonable demand according to his notion of things, is not likely to be the first to repeat the visit – Indeed from the general horror at present of the Yewkaltas by all the Indians we have to do with, I think the more we promote the ruin of that detestable tribe, the more effectually we secure the good faith of those nearer home, & convince them of the acquisition they have gained by the Establishment. In Short, tis my firm belief that even the *Complete annihilation* of this truly barbarous banditti would be no loss to the human race. Joe returned home in the evening apparently well pleased – It may not be improper to observe here that Joe himself is Strongly Suspected of having been engaged in the attack upon our people in March, & to Confirm this suspicion our Quaitline friends tell us that a brother of his has disappeared ever Since that time: for my own part I am not disposed to believe all that is Said to the prejudice of this Indian for family feuds are very prevailant [prevalent] among the Indian Chiefs of this part of the world.

Saturday 25th. During these three days we have Contrived to put a keg and an half of wheat, & rather more than as much Pease in the ground – Obtained enough fresh Sturgeon to give all hands what they have not had for Some time back – a day's rations {tho' the Natives continue to take a good many}.

Sunday 26th. Nothing particular.

Monday 27th. Very fortunately for the grain put in the ground, we have fine growing weather, but not quite So favorable to the work we had in hand to day burning Logs that were heaped up Since last year – Our house Galleries in front & rear, now finished & all pretty desently [decently] railed round.

Tuesday 28th. Carpenter dressing plank for Cases into which we mean to pack our Furs – Plemenden began resquaring the wood we have at home for Tradesmen's Shops etc. etc. Rest of our people hewing down large Trees in the way of our gardens and otherwise enlarging them – Traded 15 fine large Beaver again from one of the Cawaitchens for a Gun, and we have Collected Sturgeon enough by piece meal to Serve us all for two or three days – So far things go on well.

Wednesday 29th. Work Same as yesterday.

Thursday 30th. Nothing remarkable.

Friday May 1st. ⎫ Ten men for these three days Clearing & levelling
⎪ new ground intended for a Kitchen Garden. Fanient
Saturday 2d. ⎬ & Charpentier indisposed. Blksmith to day repairing
⎪ axes. Got a few Skins from the Chilquehooks who
Sunday 3d. ⎭ also brought us down 2 or 300 lbs. Sturgeon.

Monday 4th. Had about 15 of the young Indians employed to Carry home Logs and Fence-wood before the ground is Sown & enclosed; for which they were paid with large Kettles full of potatoes now that we find of this very essential article we have more than we Can make use {now it's becoming impossible to preserve them}.

Tuesday 5th. Eight men at fences that our little Crop may be Secure when once in the ground.

Wednesday 6th. To make the most of our ground we have broken up a few yards of the low meadow all round in addition to the field of last year, which however may Suffer by the Summer flood but the disappointment Cannot be great as the potato seed is all we Can loose [lose] by it.

Thursday 7th. Planted 18 Kegs potatoes & Traded 15 or 20 Skins – So far well.

Friday 8th. Put 12 Kegs in the ground.

Saturday 9th. [Put] 9 [Kegs in the ground.] A few of the Mace [Sumas] Indians Came down today with 10 or 12 Skins & brought us 4 fresh Salmon best tasted & richest I have ever Seen in this Country – They weigh about 6 lbs. I understand 'tis always the Case for a Short time at this early period; but are Seldom or ever taken before they reach the first rapids: and then not in great numbers.[14] We Continue digging away with the Hoe among the Stumps.

Sunday 10th. Nothing new – {Digging away among the stumps.}

Monday 11th. Faneant & Plemenden, with the little assistance they Can at times have from the Gate-Keeper & Cook, have Commenced laying the foundation of a new building 42 x 21 feet in a line with the men's house of 60 feet – leaving a Space of 12 between.

Tuesday 12th. We have near upon a Bush. Barley in the ground to day, upon however but a very indifferent Soil – Yesterday & to day 4 men at fence wood & making an enclosure of about 60 yds. Square in a Suitable place not far from the fort, for the live Stock expected by the Vessel – Got a 300 lb. Sturgeon this evening – the first in an *entire* State we have had this Spring.

Wednesday 13th. Fine Spring weather – {We have now all our Pease – 4 Kegs – in the ground, and 50 Kegs Potatoes.}

Thursday 14th. Sowed 2 Bushels more of Barley which is our whole Stock of Seed, and is to be regretted as we Could always make Shift to find room for a Couple Kegs yet with a Small quantity of Indian Corn had we only had the Seed.

Friday 15th. Got another half dozen fine Salmon from above and 10 Beaver Skins equally acceptable.

Saturday 16th. Twelve men regularly in the field – the other three and the Cook got the new building this week up to the Wallplate – Employed 15 or 20 of the natives again to Collect & Carry to the Spot our Coal wood etc. etc. and as usually for little jobs are paid in potatoes – Yellow folders [yellow-handled folding knives] com. Beads or a little Vermilion.

Sunday 17th. Weather very fine and warm last week & but little rain.

Monday 18th. Faneant and Plemendon Squaring Rafters – 12 men in the field – Boisvert & Annawaskum with ourselves taking Care of Fort.

Tuesday 19th. The Indians from above brought us upwards of 30 Skins to day, but were traded thro' the hands of Nacameus & brother – a Common Custom with the home-guard[15] – The water now is about the height it Came to last year middle of June, & threatens a more than ordinary high flood – Two pretty little Beaver we came by a few days ago, & that were thriving well in a Snug enclosure made for them inside the Fort, were both in an unlucky moment devoured by two useless Dogs we had about us – they Soon followed the fate of the two poor Beaver & we have another Couple yet to preserve.

Wednesday 20th. Three Indians from below this afternoon inform us that big Guns have been heard at Sea yesterday, & again at Sun rise this morning; & more that one of them actually Saw a Vessel off Point

{Roberts} – All this may be true, although tis but one of the many reports of the kind Carried to us during the Spring.

Thursday 21st. For Some days back it was rumoured amongst the natives here that a Vessel was in the Sound[16] trading with the Clalams & Scadchads, which we think probable enough however great the Correctness of it would be against ourselves & our interest, as we are in daily expectation of Seeing Some of the latter this way with their Skins; but a Canoe from the Island to-day Seems to Confirm the account beyond doubt – Nothing further is heard of the Am. Said to have been Seen near the mouth of the river two days ago, & we must still live in doubts & fears with respect to our own – Indeed, if all is well, under existing Circumstances her delay So long to have a peep in this way is unaccountable.

Friday 22d. Water, about the height of last year, & is quite enough for our low Spots of ground in Cultivation. {Got a few Beaver to day from the Musquams.}

Saturday 23d. In addition to those of last fall, two more of our men took wives from the Indian Camp – {So much for our alliance with the Cawaitchens.} Plemenden & another went out this morning with Traps to a Beaver lodge they knew of in the vicinity, but as they apprehended was already destroyed & the dam broken up by the natives. {Heavy rain all day.}

Sunday 24th. Nothing new.

Monday 25th. Owing to the high State of the water now, the natives take but few Sturgeon; and our daily bread at present is potatoes & the Salted Salmon.

Tuesday 26th. A Constant fall of rain for the last 24 hours.

Wednesday 27th. Every thing quiet.

Thursday 28th. Nothing worth noticing.

Friday 29th. Very little of interest going on with us here now – The Indians have a few Skins among them, but Somehow or another having got the notion into their head of Soon Seeing the Vessel here with a vast quantity of goods & of Course (Considering the great bargains got by every one now to the Southward) as Cheap as dirt, will not part with them while buoyed up with this impression – neither will they move about to procure more.

Saturday 30th. Ten or twelve men this week regularly Clearing & hoeing up new ground – The Carpenter & two others got up the frame of a Kitchen adjoining the big House, & to-day he and Plemendon are allowed to make a turn into the woods after deer {to go out with a few Beaver Traps}.

Sunday 31st. Nothing new.

Monday June 1st. Our two men returned, & have not been unsuccessful – {Came back without making any thing of the Beaver, having found as usual the Indians breaking up the dams.} Yesterday they killed an Elk and this morning a Small *Chevreuille* {its young}.[17]

Tuesday 2d. Now that we must give up all idea of Seeing the Schooner before She Comes for good and all with our Outfit after the arrival of the European Vessel in the Columbia we have Commenced planting more potatoes in a patch of fine ground reserved for a fair experiment with Indian Corn.

Wednesday 3d. A number of the Indians hereabouts that went up to the first rapids in quest of Salmon Came back without much Success – the flood having Carried away their Stages.

Thursday 4th. The weather for this Season of the year remarkably Cold – Snow falls daily in the mountains in our vicinity, & this day we have had no less than an inch of hail in the very Fort which however Soon disappeared.

Friday 5th. Had a few words altercation with our Carpenter to day, which led to an explanation of his Contract – Being Engaged as *bout de Canot* {builder} he thought he was not Strictly bound to work as Tradesman – of Course he found his mistake.

Saturday 6th. Four of our people went out this afternoon after wood animals – rest Continued at work till 4 and then ea. had a half a pint of rum on his acct. which in Some degree tends to remove *J. Baptiste' ennui* for the work at the head of the Hoe – a few Beaver Come in, but very Slowly.

Sunday 7th. Our hunters Came home early without killing anything but had a Shot at a Blk. Bear, and another at 3 or 4 Elk.

Monday 8th. {As the Season now is too far advanced to expect much from the Seed that may Come in the Vessel, we discontinue that work.} The Carpenter {Faniant} with 4 men now preparing wood for a good Bridge in a Small Creek that divides our little farm, and Cannot at times from the influx of the tide be Crossed without – two Cutting fencewood – three putting up a Chimney in Blksmith's New Shop – the Owhyhees again at the Saw – Plemenden – the Gate-Keeper – Charpentier & Annawaskum variously employed about the Fort.

Tuesday 9th. Arquitte & three men gone up the river a Short distance for more Stones.

Wednesday 10th. Much rain today and very little work going on outside – Gave another cleaning to our potatoes & think we Shall now make them and the Salted Salmon nearly See the fresh Stock of both 'tho the former are rather on the decline in quality. {The water is again rising, & the Sturgeon fishing entirely discontinued – A number of Indians encamped in the little river opposite, have moved off to Some distance below.}

Thursday 11th. Nothing new – torrents of rain Still falling.

Friday 12th. Lepitchine Traded 15 fine Skins of his own Killing – He is the only real Beaver hunter among them here – Another good hunter of the Sandish Tribe Came in with Eight, but as he Could not get a Gun for them – the value of those now traded by the Vessel in Puget Sound, he took them away until he Could procure a few more – unfortunately for the fellow however he did not go far until he lost them all – It appears the Nicameus family had a female Slave that disappeared a few days ago, & fixing their Suspicion upon him as accessory to her flight, took this Summary way of paying themselves – It has led to a quarrel among them in which however we don't interfere as the Suspicion Seems Strong.

Saturday 13th. { We got more potatoes planted yesterday.} Arquoitte & a man yesterday Commenced building kitchen Chimneys and an Oven adjoining – The assemblage of a number of idle Stragglers now in the Quaitline Village close to us becomes rather troublesome – When we Surrounded our little fields & made other enclosures about the Fort, we left an avenue for their accommodation, which we now find by one half too Convenient – Every man woman Child & Dog of them as regular as the Sun is up parade down & occupy the very Chinks of our Gate until with Some difficulty we get them off at 8 O'clock at night. Yesterday evening after the watch was Set two or three of these Stragglers Continued about: and one of them, on being preemptorily ordered off, when he found himself at Some distance did not Scruple to let us See that he Carried a knife – Kind & mild treatment is I believe the maxim prescribed for us to observe towards all Indians – but *here* from their numbers it will not do – they must So far be kept in awe of us that treating them with mere justice & fairness & Some especial notice of those that deserve it, must be owned Sufficient indulgence – The Quaitlines themselves are not wicked – at least they don't find it [in] their interest to be So with us – but are wo[e]fully indolent, and Selfish with what little they may have – rather than fish or move about in any way for the means of living, they hang about us to Catch at any trash they Can; & unluckily our Superabundance of potatoes this Spring affords them in Spite of all our precautions but too great an encouragement – The insolence of the Chaps last night has obliged us to Shut up the only pass to the Fort but by water, which we Conceive field quite enough for them, as on landing they will be allowed the Same privilege of Sauntering between the bank and Gate as heretofore: and we hope the Step will at least Compel them to Come more Seldom, if not induce them to employ themselves to better purpose – Of all the Stout Strapping Indians I am alluding to, perhaps Collectively they don't *kill* 10 Beaver in the year.

Sunday 14th. The Natives pay due regard to our new fence – {One of our men wounded another Blk. Bear to day, at no great distance off – This evening for the first time Since the Commencement of the Summer we have a pressing alarm of the Enemy, but [it] is I believe quite unfounded.}

Monday 15th. Having got most of our field work {planted the last two Kegs of our Potatoes} out of hand for the present, ten men in two equal parties Commenced Squaring & preparing wood for a new Store {of 53 feet, which will require at least 240 pieces – } in lieu of a temporary one already up.

Tuesday 16th. Etienne Oniazis[18] indisposed – were this man at Chinook from appearance about the groin I would have pronounced him on the *black list* but having left that place 14 months ago and no dangerous Subject in this quarter I feel easy on that head particularly as he himself assigned it to a fall he had over a Stump the other day.

Wednesday 17th. To day we prevailed upon the Nicameus family to trade 40 of their Beaver – they have Still more than as many to meet the fancy Goods they expect in the Vessel – With the proceeds of these furs we now get them off a Short distance to the Southward in hopes they will Succeed in draining from that quarter the Skins that will otherwise be possessed by the Scadschads & ultimately fall into the hands of the Coasters – On this principle it behoves us to give great encouragement to these petty traders, that they may afford to undersell the Strangers; but in gaining this point the Sacrifice in goods must be Considerable – Force of property alone will now Secure Skins in this quarter – An Indian from the Southward is here now & has about him a three pt. Blanket not inferior to ours that Cost him but 2 Beaver Skins.

Thursday 18th. Sent Lepitchine up to Simpson's falls to See what the Indians there are doing. {Our provisions will Soon fall off now and the Salmon from there must be our first relief.}

Friday 19th. To day was fortunate enough in getting Sturgeon for all hands – no appearance of the Salmon yet.

Saturday 20th. A Good Stock of potatoes being always a grand Stand-by, and having plenty Seed & unoccupied ground, one of our Squaring party was to day employed planting 8 Kegs in excellent Soil.

Sunday 21st. Nothing particular.

Monday 22d. Three or four of our Quaitline Traders Came in to day with about 50 Skins, and we have allowed them Guns & a reasonable proportion of amm. in payment; which in the routine of trade they make over to the Beaver hunters that are not by them permitted to visit the Establishment themselves – These Guns they have for 10 Skins, that they may not be losers in giving them for 11 or 12: but from their thoughtless way of Bartering among themselves the probability is that they give them for even less than 10 Skins – The little presents they get here & the Consequence they are anxious to acquire at the Fort is in fact their only gain.

Tuesday 23d. The Quaitlines despairing of Seeing our fine goods traded a few Blankets to day.

Wednesday 24th. Nothing new – Mrs. Annance brought another Boy into the world last night.[19]

Thursday 25th. Water Still rising, and is now Some inches higher than last year – part of our Barley is already affected by it {and several patches of potatoes}.

Friday 26th. By way of Consoling us in our incessant anxiety about our Vessel, that was to have been here very early in the Spring we are informed by the natives that She was wreck'd on the Coast to the Southward of Cape Flattery;[20] and that the vast number of *Blankets* picked up by the Indians has made them independent for ever: a remark that Seems to us to falsify the Correctness of the Story of the Ship, as we expected no Blkts. in our Vessel – The rumour is brought us by a young Indian of this neighbourhood that was taken prisoner by the Yewkaltus the very day our people were attacked & has effected his escape from them thro' the Cawaitchens towards the South end of the Island.

Saturday 27th. {This week we have had 5 men Hoeing & weeding our potatoes.} Our Store wood finished for the present – Faneant & a man putting up Shelves & a Counter in Indian Shop, & making a few necessary articles for the Bake House.

Sunday 28th. Our oven has afforded us all a few Loaves today.

Monday 29th. With the assistance of 25 Indians our people got all the heavy wood intended for the Store Carried to the head of a Small creek, from whence we easily rafted them home Stick by Stick across a perfect lake which now overflows Potatoes – Barley, Meadow & every thing else in the low neighbourhood.

Tuesday 30th. The last day of June, and not a word from Columbia.

Wednesday July 1st. Nothing particular.

Thursday 2d. A Young Whoomes whom we Supplied with a Trap 15 days ago Came back this evening with 5 Skins – the fruits of his first attempt as Beaver Hunter – He is the nephew of the Chief of that Tribe that died up this river during the Salmon Season of '28, {who is} Said to have been a very good Indian: and we hope the young man will prove deserving of the indulgence we mean to Show him as leading man.

Friday 3d. Seeing the river rise Considerably beyond its height of last year I was to day induced to make another visit to the low open Country above this and found the inundation was even worse than I apprehended in the Spring – nothing but a few narrow ridges remained above water. {By a portage of about 100 Yds. we Came out with one Canoe in the neck of land alluded to on 19th March that divides the upper end of that large opening from the main R. Our family Connections among the Indians here being a Subject on which much Stress is laid, it behoves us to watch its tendency with the Strictest attention & Keep these dames always within due bounds – To day the old *farrow* of one of them Came about, and easily obtained a good Share of her Society about the Fort Gate, without any regard to her husband – On being remonstrated with by him, She watched her time and walked off to the camp: After his work was over he followed her, & requested her return, which with the Concurrence of her relations and others around was positively refused under frivolous pretexts that She was not Kindly treated or entirely Secured as yet with the necessary property – As this way of going off is a trick of theirs they have already oftener than once practised under different pleas, by which if permitted to pass with impunity they Could easily Screen their clandestine Commerce when the husbands are bound down never to Correct them: & as the drift of the one in question was Clear – namely an opportunity of gratifying her paramour & when Convenient return to the Fort & to the arms of her outwitted husband I resolved to interfere, & finding neither of the Gentlemen with me disposed to anticipate my wish on this hand I called 5 men under arms immediately & with them proceeded to the Village when with very little gallantry in my address I ordered the lady to the Fort & acquainted the Natives that it would be best for them never to put us to Such trouble again, a Step which I hope will have a very good effect & When it becomes necessary to cut Short with any of them I am determined to have at least the Satisfaction of *turning them* off & never on any Consideration to re enter the Establishment.}

Saturday 4th. With the assistance of the Indians again our people today Carrying home all the wood Squared this week – {About 50 Logs.}

Sunday 5th. The young Doctor brought us a few Beaver Skins.

Monday 6th. That a great proportion of our potatoes is irretrievably gone now we Still threw a quantity of Seed in the ground – which may probably yet Come to maturity; & while Some of our hands are employed in this way and hoeing the rest – others are raising Cedar Bark of which we want a great quantity {but having nothing to encourage the Indians with, we Send 5 of our own men out for that purpose}.

Tuesday 7th. Rumours of a Vessel about the mouth of the river, is very prevalent to day; and in the evening Sent two of our Indians with a note to the Commander.

Wednesday 8th. Understanding from the natives that the 3 Gentlm. on board the Vessel are Strangers; which report, joined to their being so long outside, & to as yet having heard nothing direct from themselves, induced us to have a look that way without delay – accordingly about 11 a.m. I left this with a Boat & ten men well armed accompanied by Mr. Annance – by 4 we reached the mouth of the river, and in two hours more boarded the *Cadboro* in the Gulf with no new face on board[21] – Then, & only then, did we for the first time learn the melancholy fate of our people in the Columbia & the loss of the *Wm Ann*. Saw what might be Collected from the rumours brought us 12 days ago – Lieut. Simpson also brings us the first Confirmed account of the American Traders fixing themselves in the Columbia, & of the Blanket being actually down to One Beaver Skin – This is a sad blow to the Trade, & here I fear it will be particularly felt – according to the Tariff at the time, when we made out our requisition in the month of February, we had Blkts. enough for another year, & only Sent for a few other primary articles – these unfortunately are not Come, nor any additional Blkts.

Thursday 9th. A little before noon left the Schooner at anchor abreast of the Cawaitchin Village & got here in the evening.

Friday 10th. Sent Mr. Yale & 6 men down for Some of the goods – two men after Biche – Carpenter and another began one of our Packing Cases with 200 nails I borrowed from the Vessel yesterday, none being Sent ourselves.

Saturday 11th. Mr. Y & party returned early this morning with the men's Equipments & 2 Bdles. Rod Iron from its Smallness literally good for nothing – no Small disappointment as without nails we Cannot get Cases made for our furs – The Nicameus family Came in with about 20 Skins this afternoon to have a view of the new Goods – they traded them for a Green Blanket & Some Red Strouds – We at [the] Same time treated one of them (Sandish) with a Capot & Hat & well he deserved it altho the mere Carrier of the Skins he traded – I fear however we must begin this mark of generosity with others not quite So deserving – Cheenuck {Chihinuck} – one of our best Traders from the South end of the Island is in with only 5 Skins – a sure Sign he has been alongside the American {but he denies it}.

Sunday 12th. Nothing in the Shape of provisions Coming for us in the Vessel, and every thing now getting low here, Messrs. Yale – Annance & ten men were dispatched early for the Falls, where the Salmon in any quantity first make its appearance – They have the means of Salting 4 or 5 Casks besides what fresh & dried they Can bring – Their object also is to See the Indians in that quarter before we are reduced in number here – a measure I fear rather hurried at the Columbia – The *Cadboro* is within 3 miles of us – Our hunters returned without killing any thing.

Monday 13th. Received our Goods & pigs this morning by the Long Boat. {One of our men's wives decamped this morning.}

Tuesday 14th. We received the *Cadboro* alongside this afternoon with a Grand Salute from our little artillery.

Wednesday 15th. Our Indians came in with a few Skins, but are Sadly disappointed in our variety of Goods – It is ascerted [asserted] by the Indians, & I fear with Some truth, that the American Ship is not far from Point Roberts.

Thursday 16th. Traded a few more Beaver to day, & with the half dozen men now with me here Contrived to pack our Furs.

Friday 17th. Packed & Shipped three more Cases furs on account of Current Outfit – making a total of 9 Cases in: 200 Skins, & a Bale of 100.[22] The Schooner of course ready to Sail, having taken on board her firewood & a quantity of potatoes {required for their own Consumption & the seed demanded by Mr. McLoughlin}. In the evening agreeable to appointment our people returned from above having met with a hearty reception from the natives, but their Stock of Salmon as yet is but very Scanty – They got upward of 30 Beaver on the trip.

Saturday 18th. {An Indian Came in this morning with 2 Beaver and asked for a fathom [the length of two outstretched arms] Strouds [cheap woollen cloth] in exchange although Said he, 'The Ships give a Blanket for *one* –' However as yet we have insisted upon the three tho' bad policy; but our Stock of goods will not admit even of that reduction.} The expediency of withdrawing from this place a Gentleman & 5 men being in Some measure left by Mr. Chief Factor McLoughlin to my own discretion, I only dismiss 2 men[23] – Still keeping a Complement of 15 men & the two Gentln. – and will endeavour to make the Surplus number pay their own ways by hunting Beaver when we can Spare them Consistent with Safety from the Estabhs. and move about without any great danger – Captain Simpson got under weigh in the afternoon.

Sunday 19th. {Delivered to the men their Flour & Sugar.} Had the good luck to obtain a few fresh Salmon from below this morning – I believe they are now fairly within the river.

Monday 20th. Two men Commenced making a Seinie [seine] with Twine just received by the Vessel, that we may try the Salmon fishery by this mode – the rest of our people giving the Second Hoeing to our potatoes.

Tuesday 21st. Threw a quantity of a Garden Seed in the ground in addition to a few Sewn the other day, but I am not very Sanguine as to our Success – the Season is far too much advanced.

Wednesday 22d. Three or four men employed about nets – Three weather boarding the Kitchen – & four have Commenced a Coal pit. {Etienne unwell.}

Thursday 23d. Tried our Success in the river last night with a Scoop net between two Canoes, which yielded 15 Small Salmon; but the Scoop was found too unwieldy being made with Sturgeon Twine & have now begun another with Holland Twine – with these and about 30 from the Indians, we Can go without our Salt-Salmon for one day – indeed, that grand Stand-by itself is now Coming to the fag-end, for we have not above a Couple Tierces remaining – of the potatoes there is yet an abundance & will be eatable for a month to Come from the Care we take of them. {Got a few Beaver to day.}

Friday 24th. The Indians of the Gulf begin to appear. {Cawaitchins & Nanimous...encamp in the little river opposite to us.}

Saturday 25th. Made use of our light Scoop last night with tolerable Success {took but 7 – The natives even don't try yet.}

Sunday 26th. A number of the principal Cawaitchins have arrived in the river – among them, the Yankie and brothers – they have Encamped on the opposite bank of the main river, and Say that Joe their brother-in-law is Come across but has remained lower down very unwell. From all we Can pick up from them regarding this Indian, Combined with many other Circumstances related of him by Lieut. Simpson we doubt his Same dark and treacherous motives in his whole behaviour – It will be recollected that the last time he was here, he had an unusual quantity of ammunition under the plea of making war upon the Yewkaltus – now however it turns out that So far from this he went direct with that amm. to them[24] – To think of Strai[gh]tening either him or the Yewkaltus in that article now Conducted as the Coast trade is, would be absurd: but this does not justify the Clandestine Conduct of Master Joshua – These Indians that are about us now have few or no Skins – they say that the Strange Ship is back Some days since & was half way between McLoughlin's Island & Point Roberts. {Their success we can only infer from our own deficiency from that quarter.}

Monday 27th. Our people now keep more constant about the Fort – five of them were getting home Bark today. {One attending to the Coal-pit – Blksmith & Faniant at work inside.}

Tuesday 28th. Our people for more Bark.

Wednesday 29th. Our friend Joe has at length made his appearance, with about 30 Skins Lar. & Small, and fully aware of the Standard of trade {enormous prices} to the Southward – In addition to his Blkts. we have made him a present of a Capot, Shirt, & Hat – As for the proof of his collusion with the Yewkaltus it is not an easy matter to establish nor are we in a Condition to Come to any Serious altercation with them – to his face we Conceive it the best policy to Seem to harbour no Suspicion at all of him, at Same time of Course to watch his motions.

Thursday 30th. {Twelve of our men Carrying Bark from the woods behind all day.} The natives Seem aware of the arrival of the Salmon – they now advance up the river in large brigades – The Nanimoos as yet Shew themselves the most forward – They also are a numerous tribe and live mostly on the Island – during the Salmon Season they occupy a large Village they have about 3 miles below this on Same Side the river. {Ever since they arrived in the vicinity, they have been less or more picking at our Coal wood – To day though repeatedly Cautioned to keep off they persevered So much in Carrying it down to their Canoes in defiance of all we Could Say, that at length we were forced to fire two Shots over them before they desisted.}

Friday 31st. Joe at us with a few more Skins he Collected among the Nanimoos – the present Tariff is very tempting to those that dab in the trade amongst themselves, and, they are very adroit in Concealing the advantage they gain – Often Some of them have not the means of Squaring the acct. until the Beaver is traded – one of those {a Quaitline} Came to us yesterday evening accompanied by the owner, whom he took the precaution to leave at the water side – having traded a Couple of Blkts. & a fathom Baize [felt-like woollen fabric] – he very deliberately handed the latter article to one of the women of the Fort, and with the Blkts. Settled the acct. with his Customer – Joe behaved something in the Same way today – in fact they are all Consummate rogues when they can – when he was remonstrated with by the trader he very ingeniously answered that we Should be no losers by his making the inferior Indians pay a little more for their Goods for Said he, "If I have a profit in the Trade I shall naturally See that the Furs are not thrown into another Channel." {Got our new building Commenced Some time ago Covered to day.}

Saturday [August] 1st. The Quaitlines having no great love for the Cawaitchins, or a desire of being at all in their neighbourhood they moved off from here today higher up – We Continue to exercise with our Scoop net every night abreast of the Fort & get nearly enough. {To day for the first time Since I came here we are obliged to give Grain for the people's rations.}

Sunday 2d. Every thing quiet.

Monday 3d. Sent P. Charles & three men out after Elk, in Case we may Succeed in Collecting a little Grease none being Sent us from the Columbia.

Tuesday 4th. Our Elk party returned unsuccessful – they always avoid broad day light both in going out of the Fort and returning; & once in the thick wood we apprehend no great danger for the natives themselves never like to quit their Canoes for any time. {It would Seem the natives themselves are now occasionally out after them [elk] with their dogs in this vicinity.}

Wednesday 5th. Joe, who went down towards Point Roberts a few days ago to Collect Beaver returned today – and Says that the quantity of Salmon now Caught there is immense and that all the Indians on the Coast to the Southward have resorted to the Point R. village. {The natives are too numerous for us to Send there.} I am Sorry to Say his number of Beaver is not great.

Thursday 6th. A few of our men we Still venture to keep in the woods close by, raising & Carrying home Bark – rest in Sight of the Fort.

Friday 7th. Nothing remarkable.

Saturday 8th. Weather at present remarkably dry – we therefore avail ourselves of it to burn a quantity of rubbish & underwood in the vicinity to prevent its taking place by accident when not So well prepared & when the wind might be unfavorable – Casks of water were previously prepared, & fortunately all ended well.

Sunday 9th. Some of the Quaitlines Came down & brought us a few raw Salmon being almost the first we have had in this State: for, the natives here also like those in the Columbia & indeed all over think it Sacrilege to give them otherwise to the Whites at first.

Monday 10th. We are now rather quiet, for the bulk of the Indians are past & I Cannot Complain much of their behaviour; true on our own part we avoided every thing like harsh measures with them – As, of their own accord they Strictly respected our fences, it Saved us the necessity of violent remonstrances – nevertheless it was always necessary to Shew a warlike appearance.

Tuesday 11th. Having nothing in the Shape of a Barn erected, we have today Constructed a kind of Shed with a threshing floor for our little grain that will Soon be ripe – Blksmith making us a Couple Sickles. Traded about 50 Salmon from the Nanimoos.

Wednesday 12th. Four men out with the Scoop last night brought in 30 pieces & in the morning we traded near 150 – In Course of the day dispatched Mr. Yale & Eight men Some Short distance up the river with our Seine and here I am now with Mr. Annance and 7 men attending to nothing of Course but the Fort. {Weather fine and warm.}

Thursday 13th. Procured upwards of 600 Salmon today principally for Cartouche Knives [all-purpose knives] – Rings – Buttons & Vermilion – and our friend Joe brought us a few Skins.

Friday 14th. Mr. Yale & party returned with little more than 100 pieces – The Shore he Says as far as they went is very unfavourable for the Seine and the net itself far from being the thing – it is both Short & narrow – This arises from the want of Twine & the necessity of tacking pieces of old Indian nets received from the Columbia to what we make ourselves. {I am *unwilling still* to give an opinion of the Success a fishery of our own would have, but I think we may lay it down as a probable rule, that in years of Scarcity, which must at times be expected to intervene, the best regulated fishery will not Secure Salmon, and that in years of abundance the *Seine* would be quite unnecessary as at the rate we now trade, the expense of our Twine & Agris [*agrès* – equipment] would almost equal the Cost of the Goods we give in Barter as may be Seen by the Subjoining Scale, Commenced three days ago. To day traded a Beaver and two Otters for a Blanket.}

Saturday 15th. Four men pulling up our pease – & the rest entirely attending to the Salmon trade – Carrying it up – Cleaning & Salting.

Sunday 16th. No Holiday – all hands about the Salmon – {Traded and cured upwards of a thousand Salmon.} One of the wives of one of our Quaitline Chiefs hung herself last night after a quarrel with her husband – She was a young widow, the wife of the Whoomes Chief of whom mention is made in an other place – It may lead to quarrels.

Monday 17th. Salmon Trade remarkably brisk – before 8 A.M. had upwards of 1000, & were obliged to refuse all that came in afternoon for want of means to Cure them – We even now have more than enough for our Tierces, and our quantity of Salt very little more than will be required to Complete about 50; with the remainder however we have Commenced dipping a quantity of the Salmon for 48 hours in brine, and then hanging them up in Smoke – In Case the Salmon fishery at Fraser's river may hereafter become an object of attention I here give a view of this Season's Trade:

STATEMENT OF SALMON TRADE AT FORT LANGLEY FROM 10TH TO 20TH AUG. 1829.

[Date]		[No. of] Salmon	[Trade items]		[Value]		
August	10th	37	1 Com: Half axe		–	2	8
	11	52	81 " Sm: "	1/5	5	14	9
	12	145	2 Hand Dags	1/6	–	3	–
	13	654	4 1/2 doz Scalping Knives Gro	69/	1	5	10
			8 1/2 " Roach "	46/6	1	12	–
			1/2 " Folding "	12/	–	–	6
			5 1/2 Gro Brass Rings	6/3	1	14	6
			3 1/3 doz T.C. Looking Glasses	3/4	–	11	3
	14	677	1 1/12 Gro: M. C. Buttons	7/6	–	8	1
	15	1177	1 1/6 " M. Jacket	6/	–	7	–
	16	926	1/3 doz. 8 in flat files	8/	–	2	8
			1/2 " 7 in "	6/6	–	3	3
			125 Large Cod Hooks	8/11	–	11	1
			50 Sm: Kerbey "	7	–	–	5
			3 lbs Com: Canton Beads	1/	–	3	–
	17	1014	2 yrds Cop and brass W. Bands		–	2	–
	18	640	10 Sm: Chisels - T: L made	1/	–	10	–
	19	572	1 1/2 lb Vermillon	3/9	–	5	7
	20	1150	1/3 doz. Com: Horn Combs	2/8	–		11
			2 " Indian awls Gro	5/3	–	–	10
			1 lb Leaf Tobacco	3 1/2	–	–	–
			–Red Baize ⎫ in Great	–	–	–	–
	24		–Collar Wire ⎭ demand	–	–	–	–
[Total]		7544	Avge 6 lbs = 85 Tierces Cost	£	13	19	10

Tuesday 18th. This morning again made a push to trade all the Salmon brought us; but as yesterday, many were turned off with it in the afternoon – Joe with a few of his immediate followers is encamped right opposite – we get but few Salmon from their Village, & more we understand that the liberality of the Nanimoos, has even given offence – He was here himself a Short time in the forenoon, & Certainly if he is possessed of *a bad heart* he takes good Care to Shew nothing of it when with us – After his return however we all at once observed him bringing up to [a] very high pole 4 or 5 fathoms red Strouds – and not long after about 50 Nanimoos in 4 Canoes paddled up, and landed at his Village – Short harangues passed between them – then Master Joshua took down his Ensign – Cut it & a number of Blkts. into Small pieces, & gave ea. of his guests one – 'Tis Said that a few of the Blkts. he extorted as a kind of homage from our Quaitline neighbours – The Nainmous quietly returned home in the evening – What all this means we are unable to unfold – various reasons are assigned – Some Say the Chief gave a thrashing to his little Girl and that he makes this Sacrifice to prove his parental affection – others again Say and with more appearance of truth, that he adopted this Seemingly generous way of paying for Furs he gets from them from time to time – Of Course we watch them in all these manoeuvres.[25]

Wednesday 19th. Have as much as we Can do in the Salmon way.

Thursday 20th. Before 8 A.M. had upwards of 1100 Salmon traded, and were under the painful necessity of intimating to our friends the Nanimoos that we Could trade no more at which they Seemed much disappointed – notwithstanding the abundance of fish, & their readinesss to trade; we never by any Chance made them pay more than the first Tariff with which we Started, &, as may be Seen by the annexed Statement is in all Conscience as Cheap as provisions Could anywhere be had – Let me here remark that the axes which Came to nearly half the amount are overvalued, being shabby little things got made here by ourselves. {Exclusive of what Came in to day we have now 2000 pieces Smoked and 45 Tierces well Salted with our 60 Bushels Salt.}

Friday 21st. This morning turned off upwards of 40 Canoes with their fish.

Saturday 22d. Every thing going on in the usual quiet way, Saving lots of rumours of war – killing and destroying every thing about the Establishment, which is really not worth more [than a] minute's notice at present – Our little Crop has been Collected this week, & tho' the wheat is not thrashed it may be estimated thus – Wheat Bush: 25 Peas – 20 – Barley 10 –

Sunday 23d. Uncommon fine weather for the last Six weeks.

Monday 24th. {People variously employed about Hay – Coals – Salmon – and two are Cutting drains adjoining a Beaver dam Close by that is now dry.} Took in a few more Salmon to day to Complete our quantity of Salt, and the Stock may now be Considered as follows viz.

Salted in various Sized Casks, pipes etc. =

Salmon	50 Tierces	avg: 90	= 4500
partially salted & in Smoke	<u>35 Tierces</u>	" "	<u>3150</u>
	85		7650

Double necessity compelled us to this mode of preserving the last quantity – Casked of Course it has [been] Saved and did not take above ¼ the Salt required for curing them in Pickle – Altho this is but the first attempt they look remarkably well & I think in the event of Salmon becoming an object here a certain quantity in this State might meet with a ready market provided it was not kept too long in hand here.

Tuesday 25th. By an Indian just arrived from the mouth of the river we understand that the assemblage of natives in that quarter is very great – On Point Roberts alone he Says that no fewer than 200 Canoes landed the last week from the Southward.

Wednesday 26th. {Now that our Stock of fresh Salmon is procured, our little harvest over, and nothing particular to do about the Establishment except that tedious & upon the whole unprofitable one – beyond what is absolutely necessary for the maintenance of the place – of clearing & breaking up with hoes new ground. A party of 5 or 6 will for a few weeks be employed at making Shingles, 2 or 3 Squaring & Sawing – The latter with a Couple more hands are now erecting a new pit – one attending the Salmon in Smoke – Carpenter trying to Colect [collect] the means of heading the Casks – one at Gate of Course – This, with the Cook at his avocation, is the most judicious distribution we can make of what is Called the heavy Establishment of Ft. Langley.} Had a visit from two worthless fellows from the Southward today – One of them our prisoner of last April – not however agreeable to promise with a lot of Beaver. Their whole trade Consists of a Sm. Otter – a three quarter Beaver & 2 Climik or Elk Skins! Their main object is a friendly visit among the Indians here to whom they are Connected by marriage & I would as soon they had remained at home – Their Constant theme is boasting of Boston men's liberality.

Thursday 27th. Nothing new.

Friday 28th. Every thing quiet.

Saturday 29th. Very little doing this week out of Sight of the Fort – Got about 30 Skins from the Nanaimoos – the proceeds of a Short *Durwaine*[26] made by three or four of them to the northward this week. {We have now about 6,000 Shingles in the rough of Cedar of Superior quality.}

Sunday 30th. We once thought it a good opportunity to write to the Columbia by the two Strangers upon essential points relative to this place, but Such a Step in Consideration being thought imprudent So many goers & Comers now on the Coast, we merely Sent an insignificant note.

Monday 31st. {To day & yesterday we got the rest of the Nanimoo Skins – great part of them are very inferior Otters – Still we make our price inviting.} Sent Pierre Charles and three men upon another attempt after the Elk – & in mean time were provident enough to get a Sturgeon that measured no less than 12 feet long – Cost a fathom Red Baize.

Tuesday September 1st. Rain to appearance has Commenced – {and unfortunately our wheat still on the ground}. We have now Since middle of July 350 Skins.

Wednesday 2d. Most of our people removing the Smoked Salmon from the rain into a Secure place.

Thursday 3d. Nothing remarkable.

Friday 4th. A good deal of rain for the last three days.

Saturday 5th. {In the forenoon had our wheat untied & exposed to the Sun, and in the evening was Secured into a Small heap in a tolerable good Condition – Our hunters not returned agreeable to appointment – This week headed nearly a Sufficient quantity of dried Salmon for our Winter Consumption.} This week we ventured to Send 4 men out to work at Shingles not far from the Fort; being an article we understand much in demand at the Owhyee Islands – we have also employed a squarer and two Sawyers to prepare plank for the Same market and may pay, but not an object of great advantage while a mill is elsewhere employed for that purpose – this week they turned off about 500 feet.

Sunday 6th. Our Hunters have returned but with little or no Grease – they Shot two animals but of very infirm Constitution. {Saw some appearance of Beaver.}

Monday 7th. {Four men at the Shingles.} Two men thrashing our wheat today. {Blksmith at nails & Axes.}

Tuesday 8th. The Indians are now a good deal upon the move, that their Stock of Salmon is Secured – they occasionally drop us a Skin.

Wednesday 9th. Faneant having made a Shift for Some days back to head the most of our Salmon Casks tho' none of them what may be Called pickle tight, is now Sent out to dress the Shingles: but Sensing alarms about the Yewkultus being near in the afternoon induced us to recall all hands to the Fort – After passing up in the luggage Canoes all the women, Children etc. etc. about 30 Indians in a war Canoe went down to reconnoitre, but I doubt it will all end in Smock [smoke]. {I do not think the alarm is well founded.}

Thursday 10th. Notwithstanding a vigilant look out last night one of our Sm. Canoes disappeared from the beach; but between threats & bribes [we] got it back – they Say it was used in the panic of yesterday.

Friday 11th. We can hardly get fresh Salmon enough now for the daily prog; but another kind of fish exactly of the Same Size but of very inferior quality is most abundant – It has no Scales, and the male is encumbered with a remarkable high Shoulder forming at times nearly a half Circle and tends greatly to distort the head & the loss of its own equilibrium. {They are by no means good eating, & we seldom trade any – There were none last year, & are we presume followers of the Salmon.}[27]

Saturday 12th. {Our little Grain now is Secure in the Store – say about 50 Bushels in all – A good deal of ground burned & cleared away during the fine weather of this week.} Our Sawyers this week Counted 560 feet {of 2 in. Plank} – The wood is the bastard Fir.[28]

Sunday 13th. A good deal of rain in these days.

Monday 14th. It being very desirable to prepare a quantity of Staves here in Case we may undertake a more extensive fishery another year – 4 men were Sent back into the woods to examine the different qualities and returned with a fair Sample of the white pine – Commonly Called in this Country *le Pin Blanc* [*Pinus monticola* – western white pine] and not at all Common in this part of the world – In the absence of Oak however it may answer our purpose – Wrote a few paragraphs to day for Mr. Chief Factor McLoughlin upon the business of this place which we may have an opportunity of Sending by Indians round Thompson's river.[29]

Tuesday 15th. The natives begin to drift down towards this vicinity now.

Wednesday 16th. Our 4 men did not proceed to the woods {to the staves, but were employed nearer home at the Shingles} today.

Thursday 17th. From the number of Indians now Coming down, & apparently disposed to fix themselves in our neighbourhood for a few days, all our people are kept about without making it appear that we have any dread of an attack although in fact various idle rumours of the kind are afloat however they bring us the Beaver – had 20 from one of {the Quaitlines} today.

Friday 18th. Had our Bastions newly Covered & arranged, & Completed our night watch Shed over one of the Corner Galleries. {Raining most of the day – Another of our men took to himself a wife.}

Saturday 19th. Nothing new – Every thing notwithstanding rumours, keeps quiet.

Sunday 20th. The rain for Some time now is very frequent.

Monday 21st. That the natives may not Conceive our Suspicion a half dozen men to day are employed in Sight of the Fort erecting a Bridge we had prepared Some time ago, and others hewing down trees that obstruct the view on the river bank & that will otherwise be useful – all of Course with their arms by them.

Tuesday 22d. Very fine weather – The Indians as they Come down, all give us a Call and make a tender of their Surplus dried Salmon for Knives Axes etc. etc. but having already laid in our stock in that article – Say about 7000 pieces, we are obliged to decline it, and especially as our Small goods are now fairly aground – In Some respects it would be an act of Charity to accommodate them in this way being Indians that were entirely out of our reach while the regular trade was going on, and naturally [they] dipart [depart] disappointed, & without any good reason to acknowledge the advantages brought them by the Whites; Still, in Such a year as this it would be impossible to please them all, and by entering into no traffic with them we get rid of much trouble and annoyance.

Wednesday 23d. Nothing particular.

Thursday 24th. {As the Cawaitchins were about making a move this morning the Cry of "Yewkaltas" flew about in every direction – The report said that they had been about the mouth of the river doing great mischief there – Two Canoes one from the Nanimoo & the other from the Cawaitchen Camp with about 30 warriors each immediately got under weigh to reconnoitre but returned in the afternoon with rather a favorable account – The enemy was on the Coast, but not quite so near as was said – They seem Satisfied this is no imminent danger – accordingly they Shoved off in the evening & I cannot Complain of their having been too troublesome Since they Came in to the river – We used them kindly & made no display of whatever suspicion we had of them.} Our Bridge of 45 feet long & 12 wide is finished, and well railed in on Side next the main river, where two loopholes are Cut out and a berth for a swivel which peradventure may be made use of; but is more for Show in that respect & the name of the thing than any thing else.

Friday 25th. Ventured to have Sent 5 men out to work the Staves.

Saturday 26th. With four men & a Small Canoe I visited our people in the woods up the river – we have now about 1000 excellent Staves of the kind – The wood looks uncommonly fine & well adapted for all household furniture – 'tis a pity we are not in the way of Securing a quantity of it for exportation – The Country is too level for a Mill Seat & the nature of the bottom I believe not favorable for dams neither is the wood itself very Common.

Sunday 27th. The Nanimoo Tribe left us to day – we previously had a few of their principal men up, and acknowledged their good behaviour with a few Loaves of Bread and molasses for their families, besides a little Ammunition for themselves.

Monday 28th. The men at the house now, burning away & Clearing ground while the weather is fine – Pierre Charles went out 2 nights ago and Shot a good fat Blk. Bear – These animals now begin to infest the banks of the little Streams for dead fish.[30]

Tuesday 29th. Nothing remarkable.

Wednesday 30th. Joe our Cawaitchin friend was across today & traded a few Skins previous to his departure for winter quarters. At his own earnest request we made him a present of one of our little male Goats received this Summer from Columbia & a Cock – even Should he be treacherously disposed this mark of Confidence in him Can do no harm – upon the whole however the fellow is very Cautious in all his intercourse with us.

Thursday October 1st. The Quaitlines bring us a few Skins, but they plead hard for the price given the Gulf Indians.

Friday 2d. The Whoomes Tribe passed down today, but were unable to enter into any trade with them also Saving a few trifles given for Salmon Oil. {We could afford to buy nothing from them Saving a few Bladders of Oil.} Our newly Created Young Chief was not with them – at first they Seemed rather Shy, which we knew to proceed from Some dread they had of us; and that that dread originated in idle Stories Circulated by the grumbling to the prejudice of the Others – we of Course assured them that whatever might be the differences between them they had nothing to fear from us & with which they Seemed perfectly Satisfied – They Consist of about 40 Canoes & pass the winter in Burrard's Canal.[31] {P. Charles & Plomondon brought us home another large Bear with which and a pretty decent Sturgeon we have now in Store we Shall manage to live tolerably for a few days – Joe left us to day, & promised us a friendly visit Soon.}

Saturday 3d. To day {with Mr. Annance} I visited another Small Stream in this neighbourhood for the Site of a mill, but [it] is not the thing.

Sunday 4th. Every thing quiet.

Monday 5th. Very fine weather – Our Billy Goat, the father of the flock was Castrated to day for mischevious behaviour.

Tuesday 6th. Four men to day and yesterday Cut[t]ing Hoops – Blksmith & another dressing up our Hoes for the potatoes – others arranging Casks and three fixing up a Shed for our Pigs and Goats. Hunters off again.

Wednesday 7th. Commenced {housing} our potatoes, but [they] yield miserably – hardly 1/3 the proceeds of last year from the Same Space of ground – To day we have also to remark the arrival of what is Called the fall Salmon – They are at least a Couple of pounds heavier than the Summer fish & far from being bad eating[32] – Last fall they did not Come for 15 days latter [later]: yet we Salted of them from 15 to 20 Tierces that our people never Complained of. {This Season I think a great many of them Could have been procured before the end of the month. Hunters returned without doing much.} The Quaitlines brought us about 20 Beaver.

Thursday 8th. Heavy rain – {Blksmith only, at work.} Our Billy Goat did not get over the operation.

Friday 9th. Mr. Yale with four men gone up the river {to hunt wild fowl}.

Saturday 10th. Six men today employed Carrying Staves {and Hoops} to waterside.

Sunday 11th. Nothing new.

Monday 12th. Got home most of our Cask materials {& Faniant with another rising wood of the Same quality for a Desk.} One of our Sows pigged yesterday, but have the misfortune to lose them all – the brute is So fat that the little ones Could never get at the mitch [milk] – however I hope the other will Succeed better, although there is lots of grease there too.

Tuesday 13th. Pierre Charles found 2 Beaver in his Traps today. {We in like manner had one from Lepitchin's family.}

Wednesday 14th. Much rain and bad weather this week.

Thursday 15th. Mr. Yale and party returned – they Saw a few Indians with Beaver but will Soon be in with them themselves – Of wild fowl they brought us upwards of 100 Swans, Geese, & Cranes with a few Ducks – Four men today Cutting a road thro' the woods to get at our Shingles.

Friday 16th. The rain incessant.

Saturday 17th. Faneant has finished for our little Counting-Room a very neat Desk, made of the white fir. Got home 10,000 Shingles. {Of the 10,000 made we have now in the Fort 8,900 – the other 1100 were burned in the woods by accident.}

Sunday 18th. Our young Woomes Came in with a few Beaver and part of an Elk – Annawuskum McDonald our {Kitchen} Servant, having taken a woman last night, our people were treated with a decent Ball on the occasion, which, with other moments of relaxation they have, Seem to make them think that they Cannot be much happier in any other part of the Country.

Monday 19th. Re-commenced {housing} our potatoes, having done nothing at them last week. A Canoe from the mouth of the river passed up this afternoon and dropped us 4 Beaver, meat & all – a sure Sign the Beaver is not exhausted. {One of our men had the misfortune to lose his wife this morning by her running away: but as I was Strolling about one of our furthermost off Gardens there I discovered her and after giving her a sound drubbing Sent her home to the disconsolate husband!}

Tuesday 20th. {Made another attack upon the potatoes, but did not house above 70 Kegs owing to hail & bad weather.} Pierre Charles & Plomondon again visited their Traps – got nothing, but Shot another Bear.

Wednesday 21st. Weather very bad.

Thursday 22d. Change of weather – dry and frosty – all hands in the field – the patch we are now upon being new ground yields remarkably well.

Friday 23d. Again, agreeable weather – Our potatoes now being in, Saving a small field adjoining the Fort & every thing apparently quiet I have resolved on a visit to the Columbia, Conceiving it now improbable that we Shall See the *Cadboro* on her return from the northward as was hinted at in Some of my Communications with Mr. McLoughlin – we are now reduced to 150 Blankets the only trading article we have: and to add to our disappointment my letter of 14th Sepr. did not find its way to the Interior – The move has been a profound Secret to this moment when the party was advertised & even now the trip is given out merely to the Sound – As I start tomorrow with Mr. Annance and Eight men, Mr. Yale with Seven is entrusted with the Charge of the place and has my letter of instructions of this date.

Monday November 23d. Returned here late last night with my whole party all Safe and well, after a journey of 30 days to and from Fort Vancouver including a Stay of 12 days there – delay that was at least 8 days more than would have been the Case had the York Express only arrived any thing like the ordinary time: but the worst of it was the necessity of Coming away without Seeing it arrive at all, and Consequently Mr. McLoughlin's difficulties in Coming to any decisive Steps with respect to the various projects Contemplated for promoting the Company's interest in this part of the world. While there, I perused the Governor's letter of arrangements for the West Side the R. Mountains last Spring, and noticed his opinion on the expediency of reducing Fort Langley to a Clerk and 12 Men – On this head, as well as other matters Connected with the place I addressed a letter to Mr. Chief Factor McLoughlin acquiescing in the reduction; but Confining ourselves to the very duty and protection of the Fort only – See Letter 14th Novr[33] – Among other arrangements, the Superintending Factor proposes to attach the Schooner

Vancouver[34] to this Establishment for the protection of the Gulf and Sound Trade, that will otherwise fall into the hands of the Americans now fairly established in the Columbia to the unspeakable loss and inconvenience of our business – *There*, a very inferior Beaver Skin fetches a 2 ½ pt. Blkt. – In Puget Sound they are in equal estimation – On our return we could have procured a very few at the Scadchads at that rate, but by giving it there it would only be bringing our own Fort Tariff at once to the Same Standard: and this I am in hopes we Shall be able to avoid here for perhaps 4 months yet – more, the 2 ½ Skins at which we now make a Stand is no more than our little Stock of Goods will require – By means of the Fort Langley Vessel it is in like manner in Contemplation to form a Saw-mill Establishment on this end of Cowlitz portage to be Connected with this place – The Mill Seat Certainly appears to possess the requisite advantages – Doctor McLoughlin moreover, for the Sake of a Salmon fishery would like to keep the Strength of this place Still up to 15 men: but the unfortunate delay of the York Factory Express has left every thing in an unsettled State – We now Came to no understanding as to the manner of receiving or despatching the Packets – The Vessel's employment this winter will altogether depend upon the advice received from Head-quarters – Consequently we Shall turn our Shingles and Boards to the Compliton [completion] of our own Garrison & our Salted and Smoked Salmon we Shall use ourselves with the potatoes in preference to the dried as it will not keep for another Season. Here every thing went on Sufficiently well during our absence – The natives gave little or no trouble & Mr. Yale managed to Collect from them about 80 Skins – Upwards of 1000 lbs. Sturgeon & near 100 Geese and Ducks – The only uneasiness they had at the Fort arose from the various rumours Carried to them, by every fresh arrival, of our destruction in the Sound etc. etc.

Tuesday 24th. Nothing doing to day – Indeed, were we even disposed, the weather is much against out door work; & the little jobs within were entirely attended to during our absence for the Sake of Security.

Wednesday 25th. I am Sorry I have to remark that the lutter [litter] brought forth by our other Sow was no more fortunate than the first – Out of 11 young not one of them Survived 48 hours – altho my aid was given them to Suckle the mother – Our pigs are Certainly too fat for breeding and here tis not an easy matter to keep them lean – we have determined on Shutting this one up for the knife & will make Some amends for the disappointment in Grease.

Thursday 26th. Incessant rain ever Since our arrival, & now I understand very little less during our absence.

Friday 27th. Early this morning Joe & Cheenuck visited us from the Island with about 50 Skins – The former had about him the very great Coat of the deceased Mr. McKenzie which he had from the infamous A i o waston personally. {Nor did our Chief Seem very Squimish [squeamish] in Sporting it about while here. Let me not however be understood to mean that he made any boast of [it].}

Saturday 28th. The two Chiefs after visiting their friends the Quaitlines a few miles higher up, returned this morning with a woman {of that tribe} in bondage – To give Some idea of the Selfish & unfeeling disposition of these Indians I shall in a few words Say how this unfortunate woman became their prey – It has been Seen about the end of June that a young Quaitline taken by the Yewkaltus Some time before Succeeded in getting off from them, and on gaining the Cawaitchin Country – where it appears he was instantly recognised as a fair prize – was by Joe made over to Cheenuck, & he upon parole allowed the young man *En attendant* to proceed home and that he would Claim his Sister at a future period – hence the visit of yesterday – The old man who is himself by birth a Musquam married to a Quaitline, was very unwilling that his Son Should again be turned into Slavery and equally loath to part with a young Girl, proposed to accompany the Claimants to the Lodge of a married daughter of his, which they did & entered at dead of the night – the husband however Contrived to give a death Stab to his father in law before the lady was Carried off in triumph – She is now in tears at the waterside & far gone in a State of pregnancy {to her late husband. Joe and friend promise to visit us again Soon – We Still obtain their Beaver at the rate of 2 or 2 ½ pt. Blanket, but at this rate Cannot expect them to make an advantageous trade for themselves & us to the Southward where the price is more liberal.}

Sunday 29th. The Cawaitchins left us this morning – no Change in weather.

Monday 30th. A good deal of Snow fell this forenoon. {Pierre Charles & Plomonden went out with their Traps – two men about firewood – Six Set about preparing our New Store & the rest variously employed about the Establishment – Falling Snow most of forenoon.}

Tuesday December 1st. Removing Small bark bits inside the Fort to make room for the new Store.

Wednesday 2d. Took down the old Store and in the mean time had our Salmon Casks Secured under the Gallery.

Thursday 3d. A favorable Change in the weather.

Friday 4th. To day & yesterday had all hands employed in Carrying out the old building & reerecting it for the accommodation of our live Stock {expected from the Columbia} in a Small enclosure Close to the Fort but must remain uncovered for want of Bark – the old being required for the new building.

Saturday 5th. Laid the foundation of the Store.

Sunday 6th. Winter Set in. Still the Quaitlines brought us upwards of 20 Skins {which he [the Chief] traded for a Gun & a few woollens}.

Monday 7th. Turning out the Snow has occupied all hands today – {& making a temporary abode for our Hens – Goats & pigs inside.} Pierre Charles and Plemenden whom we Sent out a few days ago, returned with 4 Beaver and the best part of a Bear. {We also got a little Sturgeon to day bad as the weather is.}

Tuesday 8th. A Continual fall of Snow.

Wednesday 9th. To day and yesterday most of our people hauling home in trains the Log wood intended for our Store which had been Squared at a distance Some months ago.

Thursday 10th. The Snow Continues falling, and the weather is So Cold – 7° below freezing point – that the river must Soon take – Not an Indian on the move. {Our people are employed – Some hauling home firewood on hand Trains [probably hauled on sleds] – Some turning out Snow & others squaring & hewing wood.}

Friday 11th. Change of weather Thermo. up to 34° above Zero, and the river Seems more Clear than yesterday.

Saturday 12th. To day a perfect deluge & of Course very unpleasant about the plantation – The Indians don't Stir – In this vicinity they are at present Closely engaged in one of their winter medicine parties. Described at Some length in Journal of last year {Jan. 22, 1829}.

Sunday 13th. Sent Mr. Yale with the Hunter and 5 men down the river this morning for Something to relish with the Salted Salmon again[st] Christmas – Bad as the weather is we Continue to pick up a few Skins.

Monday 14th. Nothing new.

Tuesday 15th. {The Carpenter & four men at the Store.} The two Owyhees recommenced Sawing.

Wednesday 16th. Nothing worth remarking.

Thursday 17th.   do do

Friday 18th.   do do

Saturday 19th. For the last 5 days nothing could equal the torrents of rain we have had – The wind has been westerly & the Thermo. from 38° to 42° – Last night one of our young Goats of little more than 10 Months old brought forth 3 young Kits of which however but one Survives.

Sunday 20th. Fair – and the Glass down to 30° at noon.

Monday 21st. A fresh fall of Snow last night – & Sleet & rain all day.

Tuesday 22nd. Had 15 very fine Beaver from one of the Titens – In morning we killed our Hog, & is of a pretty decent Size. {One of the Sonese Indians Came in with about 10 Beaver.}

Wednesday 23d. {Nicameus Came in to day with a few Beaver he had from the Indian that traded with us yesterday.} Weather Still most disagreeable – & I fear our hunters will return unsuccessful.

Thursday 24th. Bad as the weather is three or four of the Harrison River Indians came in with from 35 to 40 very fine Beaver Skins – Our hunters also made their appearance rather late with their Canoe loaded – i.e. the meat of 4 Elk and three Beaver with their hides respectively – So much for the good things of Langley. {The men that Straggled about a little & had an opportunity of Seeing some of the Country, Speak with Confidence of the Success that Could be had there with Beaver Traps.}

Friday 25th. Christmas day – Our men have each had a pint and a regale of Vinison [venison]. {We also got a few Beaver Skins from the Chilquihooks.}

Saturday 26th. Nothing new.

Sunday 27th. {At the earnest Solicitation of Some of our people themselves I have Consented to Equip 5 of them with Traps.} Four of our men went off this morning with a few Traps to try their Chance at the Beaver near their hunting ground last week – in Such Severe weather there Can be no danger from the Enemy.

Monday 28th. Nothing new Stirring.

Tuesday 29th. Weather Cold but Scerene [serene] and agreeable.

Wednesday 30th. For the last three days, the Carpenter and four men have been employed about the Store – the wallplate is now on; but must I apprehend remain in this State until we can rise Bark next Summer for the Covering for without nails we Cannot Succeed with the Shingles – It is 55 feet long – 22 wide & 13 high and altogether So far pretty decently finished.

Thursday 31st. Weather Continues Cold with Some drift and Snow – The hunters returned in the evening with Eight Large Beaver notwithstanding the unfavorable Season. {Their Course was down the river & did not go beyond the distance of 10 or 12 miles.}

Friday January 1st. The new year was ushered in with the usual Compliments: after a Salute from all the Guns of the garrison the men and in Succession the women were received into the Hall & treated with just enough of the "Oh be joyful" – precaution however was taken that there Should be no excess of drinking to day, So that we could all again meet *in the evening with propriety*

NOTE OF REGALE ETC. ISSUED –

	Pts. Rum	Loaves	lbs. fresh Pork	no. Beaver –	lbs. fresh Elk	Gals: Pease	lbs. Salted Salmon	No. Smoked – 2 lbs. ea	No. dried "	Galls. Potatoes	pts. Molasses	
14 Men – Regale & Extra Rations	14*	14	35	4	112	14						*only ½ delivered now
14 Men – Ration for 4 days	–	–	–	–	112	–	56	21	56	56	–	
To their women for good behavior	–	–	–	–	–	–	–	–	–	–	–	
[Total]	14	14	35	4	224	14	56	21	56	56	12	for 4 days

{Fine hard frosty weather, Still the river has not taken but is Sufficiently obstructed with ice to prevent Crossing it in either way: however, one fine fellow of our Savage neighbours on hearing the report of our big Guns, Contrived to find his way to us thro' the woods with a handsome Beaver *tout rond* for Dinner.}

Saturday 2d. As was intended, our people with their fair ones met in the Hall yesterday evening: and the amusement went off very well without any indecent frolick: but to day the fellows are at it tooth & nail.

Sunday 3d. Still Some Glee going on among our Champions. {Very little relaxation in the drinking way.}

Monday 4th. {After a debauch of three days we tried the people's disposition to renew their Contracts...} Our people being Still disposed to keep up the Spirit of the day, we Seized the opportunity of Calling them to renew their Engagements; & having made a good beginning all has ended well – As many as we require are engaged for two, and Some for three years; and Several of them at reduced wages – to wit – The Blksmith and a Couple of *Bouts*[35] – All we now require is a Cooper in room of one of them.

Tuesday 5th. We have now what may fairly be Called a regular winter for this part of the world yet 'tis remarkably Changeable: one day Snow – another day rain and the next frost or hail – Now however the frost and Snow Seem to prevail Ther. this morning in Shade 5° below. That our Enemy the Yewkaltus are not likely to Cruise about with Such weather is pretty Certain – we therefore Send the Beaver hunters out again.

Wednesday 6th. Nothing new. {Of the nine men at home – two are at the Saw – two Constantly Chopping & Carrying home our firewood – the others variously employed.}

Thursday 7th. Two of our hunters returned home last night finding too much ice in the ponds – they attempted to trench, but unwilling to disturb the Beaver desisted.

Friday 8th. Every thing quiet – nothing new Stirring.

Saturday 9th. The rest of our hunters Came back owing to the Same Cause with the others; but in other respects had a flattering prospect before them, having Stumbled upon no less than 8 or 12 Lodges.

Sunday 10th. Another row amongst the Indians of our neighbourhood – this afternoon one of two Quaitlines that Came down upon a Special visit to the Musquam Village right opposite to us, was brought to our wharf lifeless with 7 or 8 arrows Still Stuck in his body & otherwise much mangled with the Knife – This butchering now is in revenge for the death of the old Musquum that was killed by his Son-in-law in the upper Village latter end of Novr. – nor is the difference likely to end here – One of our men with two of the women happened to be in that direction at the time making ashes: The poor wretch on being mortally wounded made an effort to throw himself into their Canoe, but his pursuers were too much bent upon their purpose to be defeated by this Screen. {One of our people was present during the affray.}

Monday 11th. A good deal of reconnoitering going on all night between the two Villages – In Course of the forenoon the Quaitlines amounting to about 60 men in 12 Canoes came down armed best they Could, and Seemed to muster from 10 to 12 Guns of one Sort or another – They made it a point to Call upon us first & tendered us a large Sturgeon for *ammunition*, which we refused them for a variety of reasons 1st they

Can afford to give Beaver – next they are not absolutely in want of that article and lastly had they got it they would always contrive to make that a price of their being Supported by the whites – They then wished one of the Gentlm. to accompany them to the Musquam Camp – this was also refused from the Same motive. After repeated Calls & visits Coming from both Sides the Quaitlines Crossed, and fixed their Camp on the opposite bank of the little river, where the negotiation Could be Carried on with greater Convenience – If we did interfere tis possible the parties for the present would acquiesce in our decision; but [it] would only be involving us in endless treaties among them without producing any permanent good – we therefore make it a point to keep Clear of all Indian broils: for, like the generality of their race, they have a happy knack of turning every thing Said or done to their own advantage in Cases of this kind.

Tuesday 12th. The trouble Continued on the other Side till late today – Ever since the Quaitlins Crossed they fired occasional volies [volleys], which, with other Signs of hostility did not indicate a peaceable disposition – they now tell us that two of the Musquams are Slain – which we doubt much, as with them I find a man is dead when he *acknowledges* his life in the hands of his enemy! When the Quaitlines Came down yesterday they told us they had already killed 2 Musquums above, which on further inquiry proved to be a death of this mild nature.

Wednesday 13th. It is ascertained that two Indians were actually killed & one of them very luckily the identical man that took the life of the other on Sunday – here ends the business for the present – Two of our men {Plomondon & Ossin} in another attempt after Beaver.

Thursday 14th. Two more of our people {Kennedy & Therien} gone out with their Traps – Our Blksmith, that he is now Engaged for two years, is allowed to take a woman.

Friday 15th. Nothing new – Very dirty wet weather.

Saturday 16th. Kennedy and associate that left us on Thursday again obliged to return: the Lake along which they have their Beaver lodges is Still Solid ice, and the little Creeks in an overflowed State – all very unfavorable for their purpose.

Sunday 17th. Every thing quiet.

Monday 18th. Francois Faneant who never made a Keg in his life I have prevailed upon to undertake Cask-making – I think he will Succeed, but his progress will be very Slow – with other disadvantages, all the tools we are able to muster for him are not the most perfect – Our other disposable hands in the wood.

Tuesday 19th. Plomondon and Ossin Came home in the evening with Eight very fine Beaver they took at not the distance 12 miles from here, notwithstanding the State of the weather – Where they worked was less exposed to the recent flush in the little rivers than where the other two were.

Wednesday 20th. Three or four of the Titens Came in this morning with Beaver. They were accompanied by the principal men of the Quaitlines who come this way now for the first time Since the late campaigne [campaign] – they seem on their guard for they are well armed.

Thursday 21st. An arrangement has been made with four of our best hands {P. Charles – Plomondon – Kennedy & Therien} to proceed Slily to the Lake discussed by Kennedy, and there in Common for their mutual defence hunt the Beaver – the direction they are in {below this} is not the most Secure, but later in the Spring it will be Still less so.

Friday 22nd. A few men at present Squaring wood for an Indian House, of which we Stand in need outside.

Saturday 23d. Weather very bad – Nothing new Stirring.

Sunday 24th. Every thing quiet.

Monday 25th. Our friend Josua Came across to day, but without a Single Skin; what is worse he's rigged out from head to foot with American Slops & Candidly owns they are from a Small Vessel for Some weeks back near the South end of Whidbey's Island.

Tuesday 26th. Master Joe has made the round of the Indians, but his Council is far from being agreeable to us – to blab about even the truth is what we don't want at the present moment; but he goes beyond it and exaggerates to the highest pitch the goodness of our rivals. {Kennedy & Therien Came back this evening with news from that party – They had 12 Beaver when he [they] came off.}

Wednesday 27th. Got in about 10 Beaver to day in Spite of Josua's logic and prevailed upon a few of the Musquams to make a trip to the Shee Chals in Case they may pick up Skins among their friends there.

Thursday 28th. Very dirty Cold wet weather.

Friday 29th. Weather rather better.

Saturday 30th. Ever Since Joe was here, we determined on Sending a Small party to the Southward to the interior of the Osaak [Nooksack] Country as he and the Indians of the Sound Seem determined to engross that trade for the benefit of the opposition; Mr. Annance and Six men accordingly Started this afternoon – for the best part of two days they go by water, and then tramp it – they have 4 Beaver Traps besides lots of dried Salmon for their maintenance {6 days rations} after they Come to leave the Canoe – I am now here with Mr. Yale & 5 men.

Sunday 31st. The Quaitlines have returned to their Encampment of last Spring in this vicinity – they Say that Sandish their Chief has accompanied Annance – and Confirm a rumour we have had Some days ago that three of the Osaaks were killed by the Scadchads and their auxiliaries that help to drag the Beaver to the Southward, for Sharing a disposition to give preference to this quarter.

Monday February 1st. Our doings here now are very limited – two men at Cooper work 2 Cutting & Carrying home firewood – Cook of Course at usual avocation.

Tuesday 2d. Very fine weather.

Wednesday 3d. Nothing new Stirring – Got a fine Sturgeon today.

Thursday 4th. Every thing quiet – hard frost.

Friday 5th. Much drift ice the whole day – Late in the evening Mr. Annance and party returned – they left their Canoe yesterday morning in a Small Creek beyond Goose [Sumas] Lake and after walking for a few hours to the bank of main river there took another Canoe to Come down with – Mr. A. with 4 men & the Indian got to the Osaak [Nooksack] or Whullumy [Lummi] river their first day from the Canoe, which proved to be fully as large as we expected, but Saw nothing of the natives, Seemingly having abandoned that part of the river after the Slaughter Committed amongst them by the Scadchads or rather their friends in Bellingham's Bay – The other two of the party remained behind with the Traps & with which they took 4 Beaver in a Couple of nights.

Saturday 6th. Our Musquam Traders have returned from the Sheechals, with however but very few Beaver. {This is the third week Faniant is at the Casks & he has Continued to turn off 15 of about 25 Galls. ea. assisted by a man to dress his hoops,[36] no great doing for 2 men.}

Sunday 7th. Nothing particular.

Monday 8th. In addition to the 4 men already out with Traps two more are Sent to day, and 4 to raise Staves.

Tuesday 9th. Pierre Charles – Plemendon – Kennedy & Therien came back this evening with 43 Beaver – {44 very fine Skins viz. 36 Large – 6 Small & 2 Otters} prime quality which is well worth looking after – all in the Course of 20 days of very unfavorable weather between ice & high waters – All these they took round a Small Lake not two miles in Circumference and not above 15 miles from the Fort – neither did it appear that the natives ever troubled themselves about going that way – being below this & to the N. W. of the river, it is rather dangerous.

Wednesday 10th. Incessant rain for the last 5 days. {Our wood men Came home with a few Staves & returned again.}

Thursday 11th. Got 12 or 15 of the Musquam Beaver & another Sturgeon.

Friday 12th. Our two men that went out on Monday Came back with 4 fine Beaver notwithstanding the unfavorable State of the weather – they found a few Lodges not far off.

Saturday 13th. Our Stave men {Ossin & Delinais} Came home with a Canoe load.

Sunday 14th. Got about a dozen Skins from above today.

Monday 15th. Four men Still after the Staves – and four more sent to Cut Hoops – this is an article of which we use an incredible quantity from want of the requisite means to go on with – An iron Hoop at each end of the Cask would greatly facilitate our Cooper work, but of every thing in this way we are perfectly destitute. Indeed the man now at that work is himself far from being an efficient hand – Since the 18th of last month assisted by another dressing his Hoops – they have only turned off 20 very indifferently made Casks – of 25 Galls. – A Cooper we must have, if it is at all intended to go on with the Salmon business.

Tuesday 16th. Took Inventory to day, being about the Close of the year: & I am anxious it Should be over in Case the Vessel be in upon us every moment – The proceeds is Close upon 1600 Skins, and notwithstanding the enormous Cost of Beaver in these days in this part of the world our principal goods expended upon them Consists of about 210 Blkts. 12 Guns 8 yds. Strouds & 30 yds. Duffles: and fortunately we have Still about that proportion to go on with for a Couple of months longer.

Arch McDonald – Chief Trader
Fort Langley
16th Feby 1830.

James Murray Yale.
In charge after McDonald left, Yale spent the next thirty years at Fort Langley.

Chief Trader Archibald McDonald descending the Fraser in 1828.
This is artist Adam Sheriff Scott's depiction of the event. It was used as a
calendar illustration for the Hudson's Bay Company in 1944.

Journal Kept by Archibald McDonald, February-July 1830

[February 1830]

Wednesday 17th. Our Sow that littered 11th of last October brought forth another family, but whose fate is no more Successful than that one – We have now about 30 Casks finished – a few men Still after Staves & Hoops – & in other respects things going on well.

Thursday 18th. Eight men in the lower point hewing down very large trees & P. Charles & Plomondon Commenced a packing press.

Friday 19th. Nothing particular.

Saturday 20th. Several inches of Snow fell today.

Sunday 21st. Cold frosty weather.

Monday 22nd. Our people employed much in the usual way.

Tuesday 23rd. Got a few Skins to-day – nothing new.

Wednesday 24th. 2 men packing our Furs.

Thursday 25th. Nothing new.

Friday 26th. This afternoon the French-man arrived here with a Budget [pouch] of private Letters for me from the other Side the mountains & a Couple from Mr. McLoughlin:[1] it left Vancouver 16th Decr. – & gives no proof of the Safety with which we Can trust to Indians to Carry our returned packet to the Columbia by the 16th of March.

Saturday 27th. People most of this week employed on the low point – Cooper has now 32 Casks finished & Annanaskum Commences with him.

Sunday 28th. Preparing a Small packet for Le Francois – viz. – a few duplicates of papers going by the upper route & of my letter to Gov. & Council – Our old goat brought an addition to our live Stock today no less than 4 kids.

Monday March 1st. The Sinnohomes have returned, with our packet – Had 8 Beaver Skins – viz. 2 Lar. & 6 Sm. – had 2 Blkts. for the former & brought away the latter as they Could not get one for Ea. also.

Tuesday 2nd. Four men again Sent for to raise Staves – Traded Eight Skins from a Nanaaimo Still at rate of 2 per Blkt.

Wednesday 3rd. Four men Sent for Hoops.

Thursday 4th. The parties for the Staves and Hoops are home – we have now materials to Complete about 150 Barrels.

Friday 5th. Nothing particular – men at various jobs laying up the wood.

Saturday 6th. Got a quantity of Logs Collected and Carried home before we Come to Set fire to the woods and otherwise Clear away the ground.

Sunday 7th. The Natives take a great quantity of Sturgeon now.

Monday 8th. Having Sent by the Sound Indians but a few papers on business and they not likely to reach Vancouver in a hurry – Mr. Yale and Eight men were Sent off today with our regular packet by the upper route: but having prevailed upon Lepitchin – one of our Indians here, to go on with it to Kamloops, the party will not accompany him beyond Harrison's river – Contents of packet – Report & General Letter for Governor & Council:[2] for Columbia Accomptant – merely – a List of the Furs – Inventory – and abstract of advances to people here during the winter – Columbia Superintendent a Short letter on business – duplicate of papers Sent for *him* by the Indians on 1st Inst. Such as Requisition – men's orders etc. etc. and a reasonable proportion of letters for private Correspondents – Parting with Lepitchin at the mouth of Harrison's river Mr. Yale & party will ascend it as far as they Can – They have 20 Traps with them & are allowed a month to make their observations in that Country.

Tuesday 9th. About 7 o'clock last night we had one of the most pressing alarms of the enemy being near I have witnessed Since I came here – At that time three men & two women arrived here out of breath – left their Canoe a little below this on seeing the formidable foe – namely a Canoe with 8 or 10 people in it – The Quaitlines in an instant were under arms – drew themselves up in Battle array – near our Bastion & Continued So for a Couple of hours when to their great happiness it was found out that Josua the Cawaitchin [Cowichan] Chief was the Source of all their terror – He with 7 or 8 of his followers is now here with about ½ dozen Skins & no more.

Wednesday 10th. Joe traded his Skins at the usual Tariff.

Thursday 11th. Nothing worth remarking.

Friday 12th. Joe left us with his usual fair promises.

Saturday 13th. Weather for the last 5 days, very unpleasant – much Sleet & rain – Faniant with 2 assistants regularly at Cooperage – he this week finished 9 Barrels of 36 Galls. ea. The others one dressing Hoops & the other Staves – Of the other 4 men now at the Fort one is in the Kitchen one Cutting & Carrying home firewood & the two Iroquois at various jobs about the Fort.

Sunday 14th. Nothing new.

Monday 15th. Nicamous Traded 2 Beaver today, and with much reluctance he gave more than *one* for his 2 ½ pt. Blanket: he has a few more, but like many others, Says that he is in want of nothing until the Ship Comes with the fine things.

Tuesday 16th. Our two Iroquois today & yesterday fencing in a fine piece of Ground for kitchen garden.

Wednesday 17th. From Lepitchin's Son just arrived from the Falls, we understand that his Father passed on Some days Since with our packet & that Mr. Yale & party were up Harrison's River – Sorry to say he has no flattering account of Beaver from that quarter.

Thursday 18th. Plomondon and little Joseph Klyne[3] went out this forenoon to visit 3 Traps that Simon had Set on Monday last, and in 4 hours returned with 2 Beaver.

Friday 19th. Weather most unpleasant.

Saturday 20th. Our Cooper turned off ten Barrels this week.

Sunday 21st. Nothing new – Mrs. Yale a young daughter.[4]

[Monday] 22, [Tuesday] 23, [Wednesday] 24, [Thursday] 25, [Friday] 26, [Saturday] 27 } Very little worth mentioning this week – The Cooper turned off 11 Casks –Plomondon and the Boy Klyne killed 2 more Beaver during a Couple nights they were out & the two Iroquois have been mostly about our new Garden – Clearing away & rooting up Stumps & Conveying to it the little manure we Collected from our Hogs & Hens that is now laid down for a hot bed – not a Skin Came in.

Sunday 28. Dirty weather – Sleet and Snow the whole day.

Monday 29th. No Change in the Season.

Tuesday 30th. To day and yesterday the two Iroquois Squaring.

Wednesday 31st. This evening I was glad to see Mr. Yale and party Safely back, after an absence of 23 days. Including 3 or 4 day's delay about Harrison's Lake, they reached Ermatinger's portage, from the Pishalcoe Lakes,[5] their 12th day – that distance Comprehends the aforesaid Lake of 12 leagues – a river not very bad of 20 leagues, and another Lake[6] of about 7 – at the upper end of which there is the portage, and beyond it the party Continued up the main Stream[7] for about 20 miles further, when the navigation became impossible – For particulars See Mr. Yale's report – The party killed 12 Beaver and Traded about 25 – with a few good Martens & Cats.

Thursday April 1st. Nothing particular going on.

Friday 2nd. Lepitchin the Bearer of our Packet to Kamloops returned to day – He has no letter, & accounts for it by telling us that Lolow[8] was the only one he Saw there – This is possible enough, but I suspect the fellow did not himself go quite the length of the Establishment – Still, I feel easy as to the packet getting there in good time – The Cooper & another man went out this afternoon with Traps for a few nights.

Saturday 3rd. Got from 12 to 15 Beaver to day from Several Indians – they now Come to present a Beaver at a time and make a bold push to pass it for a Blkt., but hitherto we have insisted upon the Two.

Sunday 4th. Weather Continues very raw and backward.

Monday 5th. Sent 6 men off to the pines, about 3 miles up the river, where the one half will employ themselves rising Staves & the other half Squaring a few fine logs which all we Shall easily get home when the water is high in the Summer.

Tuesday 6th. The two men that went out on Friday Came back with but 2 Beaver and an otter.

Wednesday 7th. Nothing new.

Thursday 8th. About 50 of the Fall Indians [Taits] in Eight Canoes arrived in the Musquam Camp this evening by Special invitation to eat Shell fish etc. etc.

Friday 9th. The Banquet has Commenced on the other Side, & the Quaitlines are invited to join – I believe there is very little variety in the way of eating; nor are the presents usually made on Such occasions likely to be very Splendit [splendid] or valuable – What is worse than all there Seems but little Sign of Beaver among So many Indians gathered together.

Saturday 10th. In Consequence of the very bad weather we have had throughout the whole of this week & of Course the little work done out doors: Our wood party is directed to remain above another week – Had a parcel of Indians employed to day carrying home about 200 planks we had Sawed in the woods in Case fire Should get to them in Course of the Spring.

Sunday 11th. A Canoe Came across from the Island belonging to Joe's Tribe, & informs us that Several people were lost by the upsetting of a Canoe from that place *going* to the Clalams a few days ago – The *Gros Nez* (Chechenuck) one of our best Traders from the Island, was of the party & escaped Safe with his Beaver for the Southern market.

Monday 12th. This morning one of the Cawaitchins that arrived from the Island yesterday Came in with 4 Skins he had from a Quaitline in the vicinity for a Slave Girl of 4 or 5 year[s] old; & for them boldly demanded a Blkt. the price he was Sure to get from his Clalam friends for them – the impudence with which the demand was made led to an alterkation [altercation]. He was ordered out of the trading Shop without the Beaver, and the Indian who gave them him was Sent for, and to receive the ordinary price of this Fort for them, which he did & Settled with his Customer afterwards – The Tetins gave us a Call before their return home – they are about 50 in number & had a regular Smoking match outside the Gate – They had few or no Beaver.

Tuesday 13th. We got 8 or 10 of the Osaak [Nooksack] Beaver today in spite of all the temptation offered them from the Southward.

Wednesday 14th. Having mustered Glass enough to Complete three frames, the Hot bed made last month is Covered with them, and the Seed put in today; namely – a little of the various kinds of Melons, Cucumbers, & even pumpkins & Gourds – besides a great variety of Cabbages – The incessant Cold rainy weather that prevails prevents our laying any thing in the main garden.

Thursday 15th. No change in the weather – John Kennedy, who Caught a Severe cold as far back as the beginning of February while Trapping Beaver is ever Since getting worse – His neck & throat this evening are

So much affected that 'tis with great difficulty he can breath[e] – I fear his case is dangerous.

Friday 16th. Last night and this forenoon had a regular fall of Snow, with very Cold weather – In the afternoon I visited our men in the woods – They have now upwards of 3500 Staves with a proportional Stock of Heads – & the Squaring 50 Logs of very Superior wood: but I apprehend without draught animals we Shall have difficulty in getting all to the main river – Two nights ago one of the party took a beaver, at a Small lodge and dam within 100 yds. of where they worked: the poor thing was quite alone – the male they killed in the winter and this Solitary inhabitant of the Stock appeared to have been very industrious making accommodation for the reception of 3 young She was about bringing forth – Its Case would incite the Sympathy of *the man of feeling* but what Can we do – a doctrine of this nature would ill accord with Short returns.[9]

Saturday 17th. About 3 oclock this afternoon poor Kennedy departed this world, and Certainly Sooner than his Strength & illness indicated – the day being fine he walked the Gallery for the benefit of purer air and then descended to the Kitchen, where he Conversed in the usual way with me previous to my going out to the Garden when I had Some work in hand, but was not many minutes there when the Cook ran to me to Say that he was choacking [choking] – the only expression he was able to utter after I entered was "Am done" and was perfectly lifeless in another minute.[10]

Sunday 18th. Very fine day – Had the poor deceased decently burried [buried] in the afternoon – Afterwards took Inventory of his little effects which were not great, and disposed of them for the benefit of his woman in conformance with his own desire.

Monday 19th. Commenced our little work in the fields again with the Hoe – Pierre Charles & Annanaskum went out to look for animal tracks.

Tuesday 20th. Yesterday & today put 6 Bushels wheat in the ground.

Wednesday 21st. Our hunters returned without seeing anything – Got about a dozen of the Indian women to overhaul our potatoes.

Thursday 22nd. The Indians of the vicinity often present themselves now with two Skins; namely one large & another rather larger than an ordinary Small one, to See if they Can Succeed in reducing the Blkt. to this rate.

Friday 23rd. For the last three days we were employed putting all the pease we Could in the ground – the quantity is about 8 Bush. of white & of Gray – Ground however very bad.

Saturday 24th. The Cooper and assistants turned off 10 Barrels – Had a few more Garden Seed put in the ground Such as Turnips – Carrots – Radishes – Red & white Currants – Weather Continues very wet – We had a few Beaver this week.

Sunday 25th. Pierre Charles visited two Traps he left out 5 days ago & got a Beaver. He also killed a Chevreuille.

Monday 26. Sent Plomondon & Annanaskum with two Boys up to Goose Lake to hunt wild fowl – To day & Saturday Sowed 5 more Bush. Pease – & Put more Seed into our Hot Bed as pr. Garden Bk.

Tuesday 27th. The weather Seems to have taken a favorable Change.

Wednesday 28th. Four men Sent up the River to Cut Fence wood – Three Clearing away in the field – One working in the Garden – Faniant at *his* work & the other three namely Pierre Charles Etienne & Domque unwell.

Thursday 29th. To day we were Surprised to See the Whoomus Tribe to the number of 60 Canoes up the river and encamped on the bank right opposite to us – They remain with us the whole Season – Our Goose hunters are home, but killed nothing – they arrived at the Lake too late.[11]

Friday 30th. Did not Send our Fence-wood men up the river today – and all hands are preparing more ground for wheat – a Grand Ceremony passed this afternoon between the Quaitlines & Whoomis on the occasion of the former receiving a woman from the latter – Had more Small Seed thrown into the ground, & Transplanted 3 sets Melons & Cucumbers.

Saturday May 1st. After 5 days' fine dry weather, a torrent of rain unexpectedly fell last night & most of this forenoon – rather too much for our Small Seed & even exposed on the Surface much of our field peas that was not too well covered for want of Harrowing – the whole process is with the Hoe. The Beaver trade we have of late entirely given up – our few white Blkts. they won't look at, unless for a Beaver ea. & any thing else is out of the question – indeed they are determined to see what the Ship brings – we Still go on with our casks.

Sunday 2nd. Still raining.

Monday 3rd. Five more Bushels wheat put in the ground, on dry ridge near the Fort – making a total of about 24 Bush. wheat & peas.

Tuesday 4th. Preparing ground for Indian Corn – Plomondon indisposed – The Small fish Called *Ulachans* [eulachons] are arrived.

Wednesday 5th. Early this morning One of Josua's wives arrived from the Island, with the very unwelcom'd information of their having an opposition Vessel[12] anchored there – of Course loaded with every thing – She did not remain long after She Secured half a dozen Beaver her husband had in Bond in the Musquam Camp – Annance & myself went over to warn the Indians not to part with their Skins before our vessel arrived. One of them traded 5 beaver in the morning for the usual Tariff – Late in the evening Three Ossaaks arrived in the Quaitline Camp with about 30 Skins – they paid us a visit, but their furs they gave up to the Quaitlines.

Thursday 6th. During [the] night two Cawaitchin Canoes proceeded up the river in Search of Beaver, & another today has Come among the Quaitlines to See what they Can gather there – Appearances all together are much against us – True the Indians of this quarter had no intention of disposing of their Skins elsewhere, but the difference in the two terms is too great an inducement to resist: even in launching out a 2 ½ pt. Blanket for a Beaver, it will not answer the purpose.

Friday 7th. Had 2 Galls. Indian Corn put in the ground today, bad as the weather is – yesterday our Blksmith from eating to excess of the Small Ullachans [eulachons], in Such abundance now among them, did not feel disposed to work, & today my Gentleman presented himself before me for Something *better than ordinary* to feast on while he Should keep the house – His tone & insolence, not at all uncommon with him, at length provoked me to lay the Ruler across his Skull, & I dare Say he will continue Some days Still off duty.

Saturday 8th. Weather Seems to have taken a turn – Planted 7 kegs potatoes & Traded a few Beaver notwithstanding our disadvantages.

Sunday 9th. Nothing new – Various rumours about Vessels.

Monday 10th.   ⎤ Fine weather – water rising fast – The Whoolmes
Tuesday 11th.   ⎬ take an immense quantity of the Small fish – & the
Wednesday 12th.   ⎦ Quaitlines are equally Successful with the Sturgeon.

Thursday 13th. Blksmith at work again – all hands about the potatoes except 4.

Friday 14th. The weather warm and the river rising fast.

Saturday 15th. Two or three of our men indisposed today – one in particular Delinais, who was Suddenly taken ill in the field yesterday evening – a Nanimoo in Spite of all temptation from the Coaster Came to us with 8 or 10 Skins that he traded for Blkts. though a Couple of Guns was the demand at first.

Sunday 16th. Three Indians from the Ossaaks Came down to day with about 30 Skins that went to the Quaitlines. A few of them Came to the Fort thro' their hands for Green Blkts.

Monday 17th. The water rising most rapidly; 'tis now the height of the Summer freshet in 1828 – and above what it Came to 19th May – last Season when the first flush began to Subside – We understand that two war Canoes from the Whoomus Camp went off up the river before day light, and Causes Some uneasiness among the natives here.

Tuesday 18th. In Course of today the warriors returned without having done much execution – Two Canoes of the Quaitlines gave them a hostile meeting as they arrived but as nothing of moment occurred above a few Shots by way of bravado from each was all that resulted from this re-encontre – The Smaize [Sumas] tis Said Stood Feight [tight], & the assailants did not cho[o]se to advance.

Wednesday 19th. The water Coming to an alarming height – almost every thing in the low ground is overflown.

Thursday 20th. Sent Pierre Charles & a man to examine the Situation of our wood up the river, & to See how Convenient it may now be to have it floated down to the main river – He Saw three Elk, but Could not get a shot at them.

Friday 21st. Traded 12 Beaver to day for our price Still of 2 p[er] Blanket – a man & 4 Indians brought us home a Boat load of Staves. Our own hands unfortunately again obliged to turn all their effort to the clearing of Ground: every thing hitherto Sown is lost, and potatoes we must have.

Saturday 22nd. One of our Quaitline Chiefs – Sandich – with 3 or 4 Whoomes went off to the Southward – his object is to reach the Scadchads – & there he will learn the true State of the System of Trade with the Coasters.

Sunday 23rd. Nothing new – Every thing quiet – water rising.

Monday 24th. To day we were obliged to Send a part of our Goats away from the place, and dropped them on an Island a little above this.

Tuesday 25th. The incessant rise of the water has Compelled us to abandon our Garden, and Commence making a new one in the woods behind.

Wednesday 26th. The women are again in the potato Cellar.

Thursday 27th. Shortly after we dismissed the women from the potato Cellar to day, we discovered they had made free with Some of our powder in the other end which happened not to be too well Secured.

Friday 28th. Small parcels of the powder was [were] brought home today, with an assurance it was all they had; be this as it may tis all we can make of it – We are to blame ourselves fully as much as the wretches that took it: & the loss altogether is not very great.

Saturday 29th. Sandich – The Quaitline that left us for the Scadchads last Saturday is back with lots of News – It would appear that on reaching there, he was accompanied by Neetlum & Whaskienum to Point Partridge where Thompson laid with his Vessel; & then he Saw his Companions hand over 10 Beaver for 20 Red Cloth Blkts. & what was Still more gratifying to him, himself presented with two – He further relates that he Saw Ouvrir[13] there with a Canoe & 10 men from the Cowlitze portage, and that he Concluded a peace with the Clalams & Sealed it with 20 Blkts. – he Saw the Boston man Set Sail for DeFucca's Straits, & according to Sandiche's account will again be back in two months – he Saw or heard nothing of our Ship – all hopeless enough.

Sunday 30th. Light rain today – a thing much required for our dry Gravelly Soil on the high ground.

Monday 31st. As every thing in the way of Gardening now is become hopeless Six men are Sent up the river to dress the Staves and to rise Bark during this week – of the rest, 3 Still Continue working outdoors – 3 at the Cooper work & dressing Shingles – Delinais has fallen into a relapse – and Domque as usual in the kitchen.

Tuesday June 1st. The water Continues rising – Had Indian Corn planted behind today – Cabbages transplanted & our Cucumbers, Melons etc. etc. with Glasses transported thither.

Wednesday 2nd. Mr. Yale and Pierre Charles visited our people up the river and on their way home, with the assistance of 2 Indians, found the Goats all well on the Island though we failed in two former attempts.

Thursday 3rd. Nothing worth mentioning.

Friday 4th. A good deal of rain for the last two days and the effect is evident in the rise of the water – Since the 21st of last month traded one

Beaver today for 4 feet Blue Strouds from the Same Indian that traded that day – this is the last of our Strouds.

Saturday 5th. Our 4 men Came home after rising 800 pieces of Bark – & the other 2 after dressing with the Axe & reducing to proper length 1800 Staves – In the evening all hands a half pint.

Sunday 6th. The water last night if any thing lowered – One of our Indians today Came with an otter & 2 Sm. Beaver, when he knew he could never have passed for 2 Skins heretofore – however he had his Blkt. for them & So gained his point.

Monday 7th. Another Indian of the gang of yesterday (Sandich) Came with 3 Large Beaver & obtained his 2 Blkts. & then declared he would trade all his Beaver at the Same rate.

Tuesday 8th. A third Indian Came in this morning with Six *very large* Beaver, & Showing the porportional value between a gun & the Blkt. tendered them for one of the former & succeeded in lowering them from 10 Skins: but notwithstanding this abominable reduction it will be no difficult matter to foresee that they will not for many days rest Satisfied with this Standard & even as it Stands now our means will not enable us to trade above 50 or 60 Skins.

Wednesday 9th. The 4 Bark Cutters were this week Carrying it to the waterside and took home Close upon 200 pieces – Pierre Charles & Annanaskum Came home with Some Hoops that we find not yet too much in Sap & induces us to Cut more.

Thursday 10th. Nothing in the way of Trade.

Friday 11th. A very pleasing Shower today for the Grain & Gardens.

Saturday 12th. During these three days most of our people planting potatoes in a patch of New Ground on the point, which the water did not reach & which we defer[r]ed, thinking it imprudent to make use of until we Saw the river fall, which is now the Case – Pierre Charles killed a Small Biche [doe] while for the Hoops – besides a Beaver and an otter.

Sunday 13th. The Indians offer us Beaver but as was expected at a Still lower rate – we have disposed of a few Blkts. at the Skin & a half.

Monday 14th. ⎰ These two days all our people with the Boat & two
Tuesday 15th. ⎱ Canoes getting home our Bark – Staves – Hoops etc. etc.
– Water falling much yet we have rain daily.

Wednesday 16th. Had our Store Completely & well Covered today – Pierre Charles & Annanaskum gone out after animals.

Thursday 17th. This afternoon the two Scadchats Chiefs – Neetlum & Wheskienum accompanied by a half dozen of others & Sinaughten the Sinnahomes Came here – They have about 20 Skins Lar. & Small – All we learn from them yet is that Thompson was in their quarter not long ago & that he is very *Pichack*,[14] because he gave them no presents after he gave them Guns for 2 Skins & Blankets at a proportional rate!

Friday 18th. The Stranger visited the Quaitlines in the morning & before they returned from them gave their 4 Guns for 12 Beaver. In Course of the day they Commenced trade with us & made a firm Stand at 4 Lar. Skins for a new Gun, however to no purpose – Had 2 kegs Barley Sown today in a narrow belt already left dry by the falling of the water, but two to one the 2nd flood will yet drown it.

Saturday 19th. The Scadchads gave us up their Skins large & Small about thirty, for 2 Guns at the rate of 6 each and the rest in Blkts. at 1 ½ and left us in the evening.

Sunday 20th. Water again rising – This evening in consequence of the nonarrival of the Vessel have resolved on Sending Mr. Yale and Six men to the Columbia – Wrote a few lines for Factor McLoughlin.[15]

Monday 21st. About 4 A.M. Mr. Yale & party left us, & will Continue his rout[e] to Columbia if he sees nothing of the Vessel as he goes along – He was accompanied by 3 men to the other end of the portage close by So as to avoid the mouth of this river.

Tuesday 22nd. Incessant rain today & yesterday which with the 2nd overflowing of the river has again drowned every thing lately put into the ground.

Wednesday 23rd. Sent 3 men up the river for our fencewood Cut Some weeks ago: but unfortunately the current is So Strong that they Could not gain Shore with it on arrival; & is now a mile or two below this – Our young Goat killed last night: 2 meals.

Thursday 24th. Had 15 fine Salmon from the Chilkuhook river where the natives now take them in abundance.

Friday 25th. Last night our Sow that was so very unsuccessful with her young of Oct. & Feby. has now brought forth a family of 4 that promise to thrive – Seeing the fate of the others we had her shut up & sparingly fed for the last three months.

Saturday 26th. No trade of any description – & the doing at the Establishment is very little – Faniant & his man Continue at the Casks – the two Iroquois [and] Therien hoeing the potatoes – Delinais always at Gate & on Gallery – Domque Cooks & P.C. indisposed.

Sunday 27th. Water rising – & Musquittoes [mosquitoes] increasing.

Monday 28th. P. Charles & Louis gone down the river after Biche – Sandich with them.

Tuesday 29th. We understand the Nanimoos & Cawaitchins are arrived in the mouth of the river.

Wednesday 30th. Sandich returned & says our hunters will be here this evening but as yet there is no Sign of them – He traded a Skin & a half for a Blkt.

Thursday 1st July. Nothing new.

Friday 2nd. No word of our hunters.

Saturday 3rd. P. Charles & man at length arrived with the greatest part of a half dried Elk – which he Shot three days ago Some distance from the river out of a Band of Six – This week our two disposable hands about the potatoes & Indian Corn; but the water has again done us great damage. It is now fully as high as it was beginning of June – another annoyance we have now although in the opinion of many would Seem a very trifling one, is the mosquitoes – they are beyond anything ever Seen in the Indian country. Our people now are literally unable to work – no relief from them day or night – The natives have mostly abandoned the vicinity either for the Falls or Sea Shore.

Sunday 4th. We understand the Yewkaltas have been making havoc among them at mouth of river.

Monday 5th. Report of yesterday Confirmed.

Tuesday 6th. 〕 Nothing particular excepting the distressing rise of the
Wednesday 7th. 〕 water. Another foot will overflow every thing we have
Thursday 8th. 〕 in the low ground.
Friday 9th. 〕

Saturday 10th. Early this morning Josua & Chechinuck the two great men on the Island Came to us for the first time Since beginning of March and between them had perhaps from 12 to 15 Skins for which they demanded 2 Guns & 10 Blkts.! They took them away of Course for we have hardly So much property in the Fort.

Sunday 11th. The water Seems at a Stand.

[Monday] 12, [Tuesday] 13, 〕 This week our principal work out
[Wednesday] 14, [Thursday] 15, 〕 doors is the potatoes but I am Sorry
[Friday] 16, [Saturday] 17 〕 to Say that what the flood left us is
on the eve of being devoured by the Caterpillars – the whole of the field planted 10th 11 & 12th June is reduced bare with the ground, which was our main dependence – Those vermin also got into our vegetable Garden & are in a fair way of destroying every thing – No appearance of Salmon yet. Still the natives begin to arrive – The Nanimoos got to their old place yesterday – & the Cawaitchins are about the mouth of the River – Faniant goes on with his Casks – We got about 10 Skins this week – Our goods now reduced to 12 Blkts. – no appearance of our people or the Vessel.

Sunday 18th. One of the Nanimoos here to day with one Beaver, & took it back because he could not obtain a Blanket for it.

Monday 19th. 〕 Since Monday the natives are ascending the river –
Tuesday 20th. 〕 they all encamp in our vicinity – To day one of them
Wednesday 21st. 〕 – a Cawaitchin put ashore here in a miserable State
with 5 grains of Buck Shot thro' his right arm which he received in a Scuffle with the Yewkaltas three weeks ago down at Point Roberts while to no purpose endeavouring to protect his family from them – On that occasion we are now Satisfied that besides a few wounded 4 Cawaitchins & one Nanimoo were killed – which disposed all the Tribes in this quarter to a furious war upon the Common enemy, but Soon ended like all their former determinations of the kind – Not a word of our friends or the Ship.

[Thursday] 22, [Friday] 23, [Saturday] 24. Now that the bulk of the Indians are up here they are on the move towards their fishing place higher up – They passed on very quietly – I regret to Say *all* our potatoes is now attacked by the Grubs & very little appearance of their desisting until it is Completely ruined.

Sunday 25th. Josua is arrived – has nothing – & what is worse tells us that another Ship is wrecked in the Columbia – possible enough.[16]

[Monday] 26, [Tuesday] 27, [Wednesday] 28. Our 3 disposable hands out doors, about the potatoes, knocking down & destroying as many of the Caterpillars as they Can – P. Charles & a man finished arranging our Barn as our little Pease will soon be ripe – Faniant & his assistant have completed the number of 200 Barrels & today Commenced a few Small Axes from a Bar of Iron taken out of a Chimney – for fresh Salmon we must have – the Potatoes is now at an end & *Salted* fish cannot be used without – I am most anxious now about the Vessel & something more than ordinary must cause this Suspension of all intercourse with the Columbia Since Decr. last – Late this evening we have an account of the Vessel being Seen off Point Roberts.

Memo:	*Lar. Beaver*	*Sm. Beaver*	*Otters*
P. Charles	11	4	1 ½
Plemenden	22	5	1 ½
Kennedy	15	2 ½	
Ossin	7	3 ½	
Therien	8	1	1
Delinais	1	3	
Louis			1 (Sm.)
Total hunt 29/30	64	19	4

Thursday 29th. The news of last night Confirmed by most of the Indians coming up the river & add that there is no less than three vessels – about 10 at night Mr. Yale & the party with which he left this on 21st June arrived – having left the Brig *Eagle*[17] & Schooner *Vancouver* near mouth of river and Lieut. Simpson with the *Cadboro* not far off.

Friday 30th. Mr. McDonald with Eight men went down to See the Squadron – And here we Shall Conclude our Short notes on the occurrences of the day; and by reference to the 30th of July 1827 it will be found to be the very day on which the Establishment was Commenced – hence this volume gives the history of Fort Langley for three round years.

Archd. McDonald

Letter Book and Other Notes Kept by Archibald McDonald, 1830-1

Extract from Journal referred to, in the case of the Owhyhee[1]

[August 1830]

Friday 27th. While at dinner to day a few Indians of the Nanimo Tribe about the Gate contrived to Steal the Key of our Indian Shop – One of them has had a Sound drubbing from Mr. Yale for it.

Saturday 28th. For the last three or four days a Couple of men thrashing the pease – The wet weather will not admit of our Cutting the wheat – mean time a few hands are employed in digging a larger ditch in the meadow we partly dried last Summer – four men putting up a stable – rest about the Salmon except Gate-Keeper and Cook.

Sunday 29th. Dirty wet weather.

Monday 30th. The Salmon fishery again thriving, though it Commenced 10 days ago it has been very Slack at intervals – to day we got Close upon 500 & among those that Contributed I am glad to find was the young Chap that was Chastised on Friday.

Tuesday 31st. Since about 7 o'clock last night we have a very unpleasant Sensation about one of our new Owhyhees – After work hour he in the usual way went out for a little firewood – then went out as is also Customary with all our people to wash after working in the Salmon all day – did not return immediately nor has he appeared Since – No one Saw him near the river or anywhere else Since the moment he Signified to his companions that he was going to wash himself – Search was made for him all round, & the edge of the river examined with a long pole to no purpose – With the break of day the Search was renewed in the woods as we had & Still have faint hopes that he betook himself there in a fit of mental derangement, for the other Islanders Say that he was Subject to fits in his own Country and often wandered about for days – Como further Says that in the passage from the Islands to Columbia he understood he threatened to throw himself overboard & Puopuoh adds that he was very melancholy of late – ate little or nothing & that yesterday afternoon in particular he Complained of being fatigued – we never had occasion to use a harsh word with him.

Wednesday September 1st. Had Some Indians most of the forenoon with their long fishing poles Searching for the poor man and our own people the rest of the day with the Boat without either of them discovering any thing – We are now utterly at a loss what to think of him. Some will have it that he deserted to the American Vessel [Owhyhee] in the mouth of the river. Wrote a note by the natives to Captain Ryan[2] requesting him up without making any delay at the entrance as we are getting more Salmon than we anticipated when he Sailed.

Thursday 2nd. Very fine day and between housing pease – Cutting wheat & attending to Salmon we have just quite enough to do. The Key that was lost or rather Stolen a few days ago is brought back with various Stories about it, but no word of our unfortunate Owhyhee – much thunder & lightning this evening.

Friday 3rd. Traded no less than 1350 Salmon to day, but Some of them now of very inferior quality – Wrote another note to Ryan requesting him up with the Vessel. Should gain the mouth of the river any time before the 10th – The rainy weather to appearance Coming on, I fear our wheat is in a bad State.

Saturday 4th. Thompson whom we understood had left our vicinity is again back to the mouth of the river after looking into the Bays to the northward – Had a note from Mr. Annance of the 27th – They were then off the Clalam Village, quite Close with Captain Dominus.

Sunday 5th. All hands at the salmon.

Monday 6th. Contrived to get in about half of our wheat & Traded 1000 Salmon with a dozen of Beaver Skins.

Tuesday 7th. In the evening Mr. Annance arrived accompanied by Needlum the Scadchd Chief – They left the Vessel near McLoughlin's Island yesterday – Came across the portage & fell upon the river below the Nanimoo village – Their Sudden & unexpected appearance by that route gave evident alarm to the inhabitants, and according to Mr. Annance's opinion almost betrayed Conscious guilt in the affair of the poor Owhyhee – Mr. A. Says that Capt. Ryan got my note of 1st & would accordingly endeavour to Come up without delay – They left Dominus in Port Protection trading what Skins he Could and procuring Spars – Thompson they met with two days ago beyond McLoughlin's Island returning from this quarter. With Such zeal on all hands to Collect Beaver it Cannot be doubted that they are obtained with great difficulty & unheard of price. Our Vessel Seems to have good [got] about 120 Skins Lar. & Small for about 85 Blkts. White – Green & in Duffles besides a very long String of heavy presents – They found Dominus in the midst of the Clalams of Course making his own use of the rupture between them & us – When they left me I was decidedly for their Seeing that Tribe & opening trade with them without Coming to any explanation touching old differences – The *Vancouver* visited the Sinnahomes Bay also.

Wednesday 8th. Traded upwards of 1600 Salmon. In Course of the day many rumours afloat about the fate of our man – Needlum who paid a visit on the other Side the river to Joe the Cawaitchen chief, learned there that the man's clothing is in possession of the Nanaimoos. That he had been destroyed by the natives is pretty Clear, but whether by the Nanimoos or Cawaitchins themselves is doubtful, for the latter are also Strongly Suspected & some other Indians go so far as to tell us in Secret that it was the Cawaitchains that waylaid our man at the water-side – Killed him immediately & to throw all the Suspicion off themselves sold the Clothing to the Nanimoos: but for my own part the most probable thing I think in this distressing affair is, that if he was murdered it must have been done by the Nanimoos, instigated to it by the drubbing given the fellow a few days before our man disappeared, tho' he got it deservedly.

Thursday 9th. Salmon Trade not so brisk – few or no Indians Came from below to day in Consequence of an alarm they have had that we are going to kill them; & it is but fair to remark that till now itself they betrayed not the Smallest uneasinesss. Man, woman & Child Came & hung about the beach perfectly unconcerned & apparently in the fullest Confidence of Security & safety for their movements & behaviour under such painful Circumstances we of Course particularly watched – The Schooner has entered the river & I have written a note to Ryan[3] so he will be on his guard. In the evening two very large & three Small Canoes full of Scadchads made their appearance at our wharf – Their Chief (Needlum) was already in the Fort – he immediately embarked with them & pushed over to Joe's Camp – All the great men of the river are now assembled there – Our night watch is doubled & every thing in readiness in Case of the worst.

Friday 10th. A great Ceremony – going on the other Side solemnising a marriage that took place last Spring between a Boy of Needlum's and a little Girl of Joe's – Canoes – Guns – Blankets – Slaves etc. etc. are exchanged on the occasion.

Saturday 11th. The Scadchads all Came across to see us in the afternoon. Their whole Trade Consists of 2 Beaver Skins & a quantity of dressed leather for which they would have nothing but Blkts. They had the deceased Mr. McKenzie's dble. Barrel Gun[4] with them in a ruined Condition offering it for Sale: however they took good Care to put their own price upon it & went off much dissatisfied because they did not get 40 Blankets for it, or what was the Same thing 40 Beaver the price given for it themselves to the Clalams – They returned to the Cawaitchin Camp in the evening & Spoiled Children they are.

Sunday 12th. Wrote to Captain Ryan – The Scadchads finally left us in the afternoon, & immediately on their departure Joe Came across on a visit & of his own accord related the following account of our lost man viz. that he ran away from here to get on board the American Vessel – that Some days after he appeared on the bank of the main river where two young men & a woman Came to him, & prevailed on him to embark

with them after trading his Clothes for fish – that when the Canoe upset, and the Indians were afraid of him & struck him in the head with a
paddle; but that Still he got on Shore and ran away to the woods – altogether a most improbable Story!

Monday 13th. One of the Quaitlines brought us about 25 Beaver that he
procured in the river Ousaak – In the forenoon Sent two Indians down
to the Vessel with a pressing message to Ryan to be up as Speedily as
possible as we had resolved on punishing the Indians before they left
the river – See letter Book of this date,[5] & another letter on the Same
Subject addressed to the two Gentlemen with myself – In the afternoon
an Indian of the Quaitline Tribe Came to us with a most Serious Countenance Saying that he was just arrived from below – that he went down
with the Scadcheds yesterday & that on their way they found our dead
man on the beach below the Nanimoo Village, all naked his head Split
in two [and] Several arrow wounds in his body – and his right Side
rupt'd open with the Knife "vertically" not Said he as we generally do
in Such Cases "horizontally" Shewing in his own body the difference –
This Indian further adds that the Scadchads for their respect to the whites
wrapped the body up in a new white Blanket and Carried it down to
the Vessel. Accounts altogether so Circumstantial as these, of the actual
fate of the poor man now left no doubt in our minds, & of Course whet-
ted our rage against Indians that we before but suspected. What, however must have been our joy mingled with awe & amazement when we
Saw this Same Said dead man walk in to the Fort in the dusk of the
evening in his Shirt a perfect Skeleton!!! Mr. Annance & myself were
walking round the Gallery suggesting the plans of attack upon the village when my woman who was at the time leaning over the front pickets Stopped us, & observed that there was Some person behind the fence
or in a bush whistling to some one at the Fort: we immediately flew for
our arms and in going out met the man in the Fort Gate already in conversation with Mr. Yale – He was taken in and a slight refreshment given
him for he is dreadfully emaciated – He then gave his own Story nearly
as follows – On leaving the Fort the evening of the 30th as already noticed, he *did* go to the river & wash himself, & immediately became as it
were blind and insensible & Strod off to the woods – was in that State
according to his own ideas now for perhaps 3 or 4 days – Then fell on a
Small river near the Village, where he Saw 2 Canoes one with a man a
woman & a Child, & the other with only an Indian: To the former he
tendered his Clasp Knife for Salmon but had none to give – the other
then approached – threw out one fish & took the Knife – The Chap then
Signified a wish to have the Salmon Cooked on the Spot – they made
Signs to him to cross with them to the other Side, to which he reluc-
tantly Consented. Both the Indians then got into one Canoe & one of
them took up a Stick with which the Owhyhee thought he was going to
make fire on the other Side to Cook the fish – when half way across the
Canoe upset & the natives immediately made for the Shore when the
woman Still remained with the 2d Canoe – in it embarked & pushed out

again & fell upon him with the Stick & paddle – he resolutely defended himself, Sometime above & as often under water, but Caught two blows in the head, and one Severe one in the wrist while endeavouring to upset them all by Seizing on their Canoe – The woman & Child now roared out So hideously that they desisted, & he in [the] mean time [dis]engaged himself of his pea doublet & Trowsers [trousers] & flew to the woods. From that moment the poor Creature wandered about he . does not know where, or how he Survived. There were Berries but for fear of poisoning himself would not venture to eat them, being Stranger to their quality. Two days ago he was fairly exhausted & gave up life, Still by little & little & seemingly keeping in the right direction he was gaining the vicinity of the Establishment, and this afternoon he fortunately heard our Bugle Horn which encouraged him to fresh exertion & in the dusk of the evening gained the Fort as is just noticed.

Thursday 14th. We have again resumed our outdoor work, for nothing of the kind was attended to of late – In the afternoon the Indians Sent down to the Schooner yesterday morning returned with a note from Capt. Ryan acknowledging rect. of mine per the Scadchads & giving a discouraging account of his own progress Since Mr. Annance left him – he also answered my note of yesterday: & all ready, Cheerfully has Come into the proposal for the attack – The winds unfortunately are bad, & he advances but Slowly – however, with respect to the attack, the expediency of having him here Soon is not so pressing, but it is nevertheless high time that he was now arrived on account of his Columbia voyage – The Salmon fishery is now about at an end – indeed for Some days we had no great inclination to take in more, from the difficulty we have in arranging them properly before they are to be Shipped; besides they are falling off much in point of quality.

Wednesday 15th. At 5 o'clock this morning received another note from Captain Ryan intimating that he is but 4 miles below the Nanimoo Village & impatient to know if he is to Commence the attack before our people get on board, which in the arrangements made was not intended as the two Gentlemen with one half our Complement of men were first slily to board him. But thank God one happy event has put an end to all warfare for the present & immediately wrote Ryan accordingly – The Safe return of our man Seems to Create a Stir among the natives – The principal men of the Quaitlins here most of the day – One of them went below and Soon after he & the two leading men of the Nanaimoos Came up with the Owhyhee's Clothing perfectly entire & in the State in which he threw it off – A long harangue was made to them all in the Hall – vengeance Sworn against any Indian in the river had the man not Come back & fifty other terrible things, which however was at last smoothed over with milder expression & Sweetened with Bread & molasses – Nothing of Course was given them for restoring the Cloth[e]s, for in doing So we told them, & they believed it, that they did more Service to themselves than to any other by Saving their Village and the lives of their women and Children. Instantly the two Gentlemen & Eight men in the Boat well armed Started for the vessel as much for a display before them all as any thing else: but told the Chiefs of Course that it was Solely for the purpose of Countermanding the orders given the Captain to attack the Village on his way up.

Thursday 16th. Our people returned from below about 2 this morning. And now every thing Seems quiet & settled, and having Closed the Subject of the poor man's wonderful adventure, which perhaps in the opinion of the reader I have followed with greater prolixity than the Case deserved, I shall assure that the whole is but a perfect Sketch of the daily occurrence, yet far from representing the full force of the painful anxiety which we endured during that alarming Crisis. The thing is now over, very happily, but it is Seen how much it was on the brink of being otherwise – Much Could be Said on the whole affair, & especially as to the extent of punishment we had in Contemplation, and the Consequences that might follow that punishment – Certainly Should we experience no trouble from them after Suffering under Such Circumstances a Severe Chastisement at our hands there Can be little hesitation in doing it when perfectly apropos: but on the present occasion there is great reason to be thankful that the man by a most extraordinary miracle returned just in time to put a Stop to a Scene that Could not (in resorting to arms) by any possibility have terminated more fortunate for our interest & peaceable repose than it is. To Conclude – knowing that in the event of things having gone to an extremity, at a distance it would be natural to attach blame Somewhere I should myself always have the Consolation to Say both for myself & all those with me that nothing was done rashly or without mature deliberation, & that at no Stage of it had we reason to reproach ourselves with negligence or inattention.

A. McDonald[6]

Friday 17th. Not a breath of wind.

Saturday 18th. Heavy rain the whole day – Still with perseverance and the use of the warp rope the Vessel gained port about 2 p.m.

Sunday 19th. The launch was extended between the Vessel & the Shore & this was all done today.

Monday 20th. The Cargo Shipped on the 18th of last month relanded, & So is also a good deal of the Ballast in order to Ship the whole of the Salmon now if possible – Great preparations for war now going on among the different tribes in the river to retaliate upon the Yewkultas the excursion they made to Point Roberts last July & to revenge the butchery Committed on So many of the Cawaitchins & Nanimoos.

Tuesday 21st. The Schooner full tonight, & the papers delivered: there is however 25 Barrels of the Salmon that She Could not Stow of the 210 intended for her. Very early today the war party was on the move – no less than 28 Canoes passed this place beside 10 that will join of Nanimoos 2 of Whoomes & 4 of Chishalls – making in all upward of 500 men, & hideous looking rascals they are.

Wednesday 22d. Schooner under weigh [way] by 5 A.M. Passengers Mr. Annance, Faneant & Plomondon with their families – Charpentier ahead. The next account in hand of this armament was the return of Same on 2d of next month (October) after a precipitate retreat from before the Yewkultas – day after day the Canoes Continued to arrive up to the 10th when it was found that no less than Eight with near 100 men stuck behind – It would appear that on the first onsett [onset] they were very Successful against a small detached village which they ransacked & destroyed without mercy – Satisfied with this plunder and returning in triumph, the main body pursued & surprised them – 4/5th of them took to flight without firing a shot, and the remaining 8 Canoes being better provided with arms & ammunition made a stand, but only to become Subject to the disaster that followed – The Yewkoltas drove them ashore on a large Island – forced them to abandon their Canoes – in this desperate plight kept those that Survived for about 20 days – Three of our principal Chiefs (One Cawaitchin – not Joe – one Nanimoo & the third a Muskuam) & 45 men were either killed or Starved to death, & the remainder of these wretches at length found means to cross to the mainland by Swimming or on frail rafts: & in a distressing Condition Contrived to gain this neighbourhood in Straggled parties the first week of Novr. So thoroughly Convinced now of the unfeigned & inveterate enmity Subsisting between these two very formidable bodies, & of the good policy it would be in us to keep it up by affording those among whom we are pleased, Some kind of Countenance; we thought no opportunity more favorable Could possibly present itself for laying Claims to their gratitude & friendship than assisting them to relieve those on the Island & with this view allowed a Second party that undertook to view the ground at least 100 rounds of ammunition & the loan of a half dozen Guns: but after 2 days absence, doubting their own Strength, the whole party returned & faithfully gave up every thing with which they were accommodated with apparent marks of Satisfaction: & more actually offered a Slave in the Strength of this league to resist the Common Enemy. If I am over & above particular in these Notes, it is from pure motives – When things go on peaceably and well, few inquiries are made, when otherwise there will naturally be animadversions, & I but too well know how easily and Suddenly a reverse may Come about.

Archd. McDonald C.T.
Fort Langley 10th July 1831.

The Perth Museum and Art Gallery in Scotland has a number of items donated in 1833 by Colin Robertson, who worked for both the North West and the Hudson's Bay Companies. These were collected for him by James Murray Yale in his early years at Fort Langley.

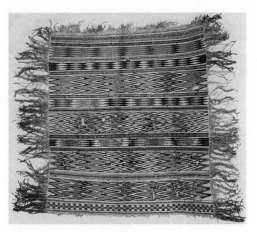

Classic Salish blanket.

Mountain-goat horn bracelets.

Model canoe. A Salish-style canoe nearly vertical cutwater.

Interior of a Lodge with Family Group.
Watercolour by Paul Kane, at or near Fort Victoria in April or May 1847,
showing a family section of the interior of a Clallam or Songhees plank house.
The dogs were probably the source of dog's hair used in weaving.

Flathead Woman Spinning Yarn.
Watercolour by Paul Kane, painted at
or near Fort Victoria in April or May
1847, showing a Songhees woman
spinning with the distinctive Coast
Salish spindle.

Fraser River Indian.
Watercolour and pencil by Paul Kane.

THE ETHNOGRAPHIC SIGNIFICANCE OF THE FORT LANGLEY JOURNALS

WAYNE SUTTLES

INTRODUCTION

Fort Langley was established in 1827 on the Fraser, the great river that flows into the inland sea that includes the Strait of Georgia, Juan de Fuca Strait, and Puget Sound. This sea and the lands around it, including the Fraser Valley, were the home of a large number of tribes now identified as Coast Salish. In his ethnography of a group of these tribes whom he called the "Upper Stalo," Wilson Duff (1952:25-6) used the Fort Langley Journals for its vivid picture of the annual flow of Native people across the Strait of Georgia and up the Fraser River, their activities on the Fraser, and their wide range of contacts within the region and beyond. In this essay I shall follow Duff's lead in exploring the value of the journals to ethnography, and I shall also try to show how ethnography can contribute to our understanding of the journals.[1]

The Journals

Fort Langley was established more than three decades after the first recorded meeting between the Coast Salish and Europeans. That occurred in the 1790s, with the Spanish and British exploration inside Juan de Fuca Strait (see the introduction to this volume). Then, apart from Simon Fraser's brief visit in 1808, there is no further record of contact until the Hudson's Bay Company expeditions of the 1820s. All of these earlier contacts were brief. The observations recorded are uniquely valuable, but they were necessarily limited to what could be seen in a few hours or a few days. With the Fort Langley Journals, however, we have a record of daily observations year-round over three full years. It reveals seasonal changes and patterns of activities that could only be guessed at and practices that could not have been surmised at all from the earlier records, and thus it adds immeasurably to them.

Like other early records, the Fort Langley Journals is limited by its purpose, the interests and preconceptions of the writers, and communication with the Natives. The purpose of a post journal was to record the weather, the trade, and visitors (see the introduction to this volume). We are fortunate that those who kept this journal did not confine themselves to these bare facts. As their entries show, their first concerns were for their own safety and profit for the company, but they evidently saw that those concerns were served by understanding the Natives. And as intelligent men they must also have been curious and eager to learn what they could of the Natives. But they also must have come with expectations based on their European origins and experience with the Natives of other parts of North America.

Communication with the Natives must have been limited. The Native languages are all very difficult for Europeans to learn, and it is unlikely that in the early years, if ever, any of the company people became fluent in anything but a simplified version of them.[2] They must have communicated with the Natives mainly if not wholly in Chinook Jargon, the simple "trade language" that had developed on the lower Columbia. The journal does not mention the jargon and only once records a jargon word (17 June 1830), but the jargon was no doubt known to most or all of the party that arrived to establish Fort Langley in 1827. The party included several Native women from the Columbia District, who must have communicated with their husbands and others in Chinook Jargon, and two Native traders who had visited Fort George, where they must have used it. It was probably not known on the Fraser at the time but would have soon spread among the Natives who regularly visited the fort. There is no evidence that any jargon based on a local language developed at Fort Langley, as it surely would have without Chinook Jargon.

With this limitation in communication and the cultural differences between the journalists and the Natives, it is not surprising that the journals tell us little about the mental life of the Natives, their attitudes and beliefs about themselves, their world, and the newcomers to it. Nevertheless, it tells us much about observable aspects of Native culture and much from which we may draw inferences about other aspects.

Ethnography

Ethnography is the attempt to describe the culture of a group of people, usually a group other than that of the ethnographer. The tradition of ethnographic writing (though not so called) goes back to classic times, and good examples are seen in some of the reports of the eighteenth-century explorers. By the mid-nineteenth century, ethnography had become a part of the emerging field of ethnology, first cultivated by people trained in other fields. Charles Wilson, an engineer with the Boundary Commission in 1858-62, and Robert Brown, a botanist who explored the interior of Vancouver Island (accompanied by the sons of George Barnston and Archibald McDonald) in 1864, both wrote on the Coast Salish of British Columbia.

A more professional style of work began with the arrival of Franz Boas in 1886. Boas had a research program, he was developing a method for recording and analyzing the Native languages, and he became the leading figure in North America in the science of anthropology, of which ethnology became a branch. He produced only a few short articles on the Coast Salish, based on brief visits during the 1880s and 1890s, but he worked extensively with people farther north, and his influence was profound. Early in the twentieth century Charles Hill-Tout's work with the Coast Salish was modelled after Boas's but was not much fuller. Nor was that of the photographer Edward S. Curtis. More detailed studies were not done until the 1920s on through the 1950s, mainly by Boas's students and their students (Suttles 1990:475). Duff's work with the "Upper Stalo" and much of my own work is in this Boasian tradition.

Boasian ethnography attempts to "reconstruct" Native culture as it was before it was greatly changed by the presence of Europeans. It is based on the observation of ongoing Native practices when possible but mainly on interviews with older people who have told what they experienced in their own lives and learned from those who had gone before them. Insofar as ethnographers have followed Boas's methods, we have also recorded terms and texts in the Native languages and explored the conceptual systems of the Native people.

Reconstructing a truly aboriginal culture would be very difficult. Even the earliest records do not reveal the pre-contact situation. There may have been earlier, unrecorded encounters, and there were certainly earlier influences. The explorers of the 1790s saw Natives with scars from smallpox, showing that they had already experienced an epidemic, probably in the late 1770s and no doubt from European sources. A second epidemic may have passed through the region around 1801-2 (Boyd 1990:137-8; Boyd 1994; but cf. Harris 1994). The first epidemic must have taken at least a third of the population, possibly much more. The second would have been equally devastating among those not exposed to the first. High mortality could have resulted in serious culture loss and even changes in social organization.

The earliest explorers also saw trade goods among the Natives, and in 1791 the people at Point Roberts seemed to indicate to Francisco Eliza that they had already traded with ships. In 1808 Fraser too saw trade goods, and at what is now Yale the people seemed to be telling him that white men came that far up the river from the sea. There is no evidence for this, but Native trade routes could easily have brought European goods from the outer coast. Indirect contact through Native trade routes must have also occurred as soon as the fur companies established posts – Astoria at the mouth of the Columbia River in 1811 and Forts Okanagan and Kamloops in 1811 and 1812. Fort George (as Astoria became in 1813) became a source of goods for some of the Coast Salish who later traded at Fort Langley. By the late 1820s, American ships were also entering Juan de Fuca Strait to trade with the Native people, as the Fort Langley Journals complain.

Thus by the time the Hudson's Bay Company established Fort Langley, the Natives of this region had been receiving European goods in trade for over four decades, they had probably suffered severe population loss from

Old World diseases, and some must have had direct contact with Europeans and non-Europeans who came with them – Iroquois and Abenaki from northeastern North America, Hawaiians and perhaps other Polynesians, and possibly Asians and Africans.[3] We have yet to assess what effect this influx of goods, population loss, and contact may have had on Native society and culture. Moreover, even a "truly aboriginal culture" was never stable; even in earlier times the Coast Salish must have always been experiencing some degree of social and cultural change.

When Boas came in the late 1880s, it had been nearly a century since the first recorded contact. When his student Erna Gunther published her *Klallam Ethnography* in 1927, a full century had passed since the founding of Fort Langley. By the late 1940s, when Duff and I were interviewing older Coast Salish, nearly a century and a quarter had passed. By this time the Coast Salish had experienced at least a century and three quarters of exposure to European diseases and goods, around a century of colonial or federal government, missions, residential schools, the rise of new Native religious movements, and, as Knight (1996) has shown, major involvement in commercial fishing, logging, and other industries. Discovering what life may have been like before these experiences would seem a formidable task.

However, there has also been continuity. The oldest people we talked with in the 1940s and 1950s were born in the 1860s and 1870s. They spoke one or more Salishan languages in preference to English. They had participated in traditional subsistence activities, as well as commercial fishing, and in traditional ceremonial activities, modified as they may have been by culture change. Most had been cared for and taught by grandparents, who would have been active in the middle of the nineteenth century. They could give genealogies and family histories going back several generations – well before European settlement and in some cases back into the eighteenth century. Their knowledge seemed to reflect a well-integrated Native culture that flourished in the nineteenth century, some of which survives vigorously today. I believe we can reasonably attempt to describe that culture.

Complementarity

Clearly interpretations of Native culture based largely on what our sources remembered and how they interpreted what they remembered must be checked not only with one another but especially with whatever earlier observations were recorded. The Fort Langley Journals provide the richest such resource for this region. The men who recorded them saw aspects of Native life that later ethnographers could not have seen. As a check on the ethnography of this region, they are unparalleled.

On the other hand, our understanding of the journals can be enhanced by ethnography. Ethnographers have asked questions that the early observers did not ask, in fact could not have asked, because they are based on an accumulation of knowledge about this region and about human beings in general. Ethnographers have constructed a picture of the Native social system and belief system of which the early observers could only have had glimpses. In the following pages I present a sketch of the Native culture of this region as seen in the Fort Langley Journals, supplemented by the observations of Simon Fraser and the expeditions of 1824 and 1825 and interpreted through ethnography. The Fort Langley Journals give us information that sheds light on Native society and culture in this region in the first years of continuous contact with outsiders. We can follow the seasonal movements of various tribes, see the network of intergroup relations, and trace intertribal conflicts. The people of the region often quarrelled, and members of one tribe sometimes pillaged, enslaved, and killed members of another. But paradoxically there was a regional culture and social system that allowed for ransom negotiations, intermarriage, and trade. The journals give us a view of this paradox. They give us our earliest look at Coast Salish potlatching and uses of wealth. And they give us glimpses of the careers of individual Native leaders who were profiting from and trying to cope with the presence of the fort. They also give us a clearer view of the relations between the Coast Salish and their neighbours to the north. They confirm much of what ethnographers have supposed, raise questions about other suppositions, and offer new data to interpret.

THE NATIVE PEOPLES

Names of many Native tribes[4] appear in the journals, some frequently, others rarely. (Table 1 in Appendix E identifies tribal names that appear in the journals with the Native forms and with modern spellings.) These include tribes who lived year-round on or near the Fraser River, those who habitually came to the Fraser in summer for fishing and other seasonal activities, those who had begun to come mainly to trade at the fort, and those who were known mainly as real or potential enemies. They came from an area that extended from the northern end of the Strait of Georgia southward nearly to the Columbia River and into the interior as far as the conflux of the Fraser and Thompson rivers. The population of this region, when the fort was founded, was denser than it seems to have been in much of Northern and Eastern North America, but we really do not know its size. It may have been between ten and fifteen thousand.[5]

Linguistic research (Thompson and Kinkade 1990) shows that these tribes spoke at least twelve different languages – eleven Salishan and one Wakashan. (Table 2 in Appendix E gives the linguistic classification of the tribes mentioned in the journals. Map 4 shows their home territories.) Ethnographic work, largely confirmed by the journals, indicates they formed a social network, within which language differences were relatively unimportant. As a consequence of intermarriage, many people spoke two or more languages, that of the group they grew up with and that of a parent or grandparent from another group. Language, it seems, was neither a basis for an alliance nor a barrier to forming one.

Fort Langley was built near the centre of the area in which the language we now call Halkomelem is spoken. This area extends from the eastern shores of Vancouver Island across the Strait of Georgia and up the Fraser River to the lower end of the canyon. The language includes three main groups of dialects: Island, Downriver, and Upriver. Island dialects are spoken by the Cowichan and Nanaimo, Downriver by the Musqueam, Katzie, and Kwantlen, and Upriver by the Sumas, Chilliwack, Pilalt, and Tait, to name only those tribes mentioned in the journals. The three groups of dialects are mutually intelligible, but to a non-speaker Upriver sounds remarkably different from the other two, and it is not surprising that McMillan wrote that the Pelalt language was different from that of the Kwantlen (9 April 1828).

The men of the fort seem also to have recognized the kinship of the Downriver tribes and the relationship among all tribes of the region. McDonald wrote: "When we Say the Quaitlines [Kwantlens] we very

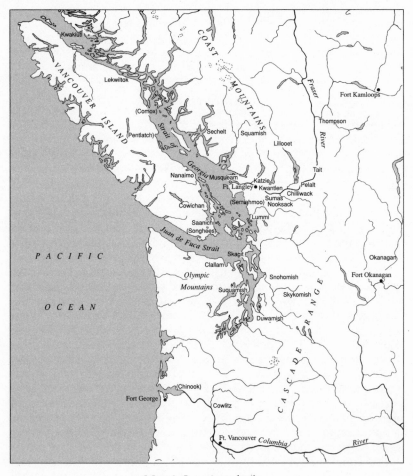

Map 4. Location of tribes

often mean any one of the distinct Tribes Called among themselves – Quaitlines, Musquams [Musqueams], Kitchis [Katzies] and at a distance even the whole collectivity are better known by the appellation of Cawaitchens [Cowichans] as that Tribe is the leading nation in this quarter" (26 February 1829). The phrase "the whole collectivity" probably refers to all of the Coast Salish of the region.[6]

The tribes mentioned most often are, of course, those who were seen or heard of most often, and they include the largest tribes of the region. But as we know from later ethnographic work, there were smaller tribes in the region who are not mentioned in the journals; perhaps they were known but thought to be a part of some larger tribe, or perhaps they were not yet known because another tribe was acting as intermediaries for them.

Each of these tribes had a home territory in which its winter villages were situated. Many also had camp sites and seasonal fishing and other rights within the home territories of other tribes, often distant from their own home territories. For several of the tribes mentioned, their most important seasonal sites were in the home territory of the Tait tribe in the Upper Fraser Valley and Fraser Canyon. Ethnographic work suggests that an extraterritorial seasonal right was originally granted, through intervillage

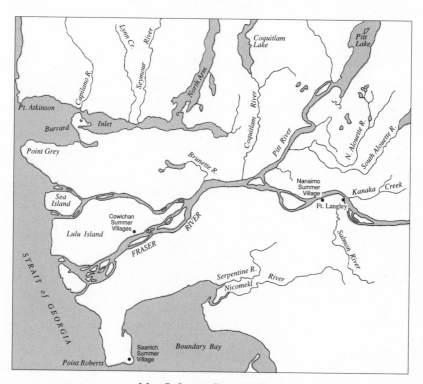

Map 5. Lower Fraser Valley

marriage, by a family in one village to relatives in another village, and that it was maintained through the continued acknowledgment or renewal of kinship ties. However, on the Fraser, it appears that fishing rights were not simply rights of families dependent on continued kinship but were rights assumed in perpetuity by whole tribes. Whether they had earlier depended on family ties is unclear. At any rate, the size and abundance of the Fraser fish runs probably would have made any attempt to control access to them difficult and perhaps pointless. Moreover, whatever the earlier situation had been, it was probably complicated by the virtual disappearance of some tribes in the earlier epidemics, opening access to their sites to others.

Year-Round Residents

Among the year-round residents of the Fraser Valley, the Kwantlen (written "Quoitlen," etc.) were the fort's nearest neighbours. This tribe evidently had a village below the fort on the Pitt River, called the "Quoitle" (Kwantlen) River in early entries, and another somewhere above the fort. References in the journals to Kwantlen chiefs indicate that Whittlekainum was the leading chief in the lower village, and that Nicameus was a leader in the upper village. In the spring of 1829 and again in 1830, there were Kwantlens camped "a few hundred yards" from the fort. One entry (28 November 1829) mentions Kwantlens being "a few miles higher up," a distance that seems too great to refer to what was usually called "the village above." They may have been at Hatzic Slough, where the McMillan expedition met Kwantlen in 1824. The Kwantlen became especially important to the traders as suppliers of fish, cedar bark (for roofing material), labour, and wives. They also played a major role as intermediaries; furs brought downriver often passed through Kwantlen hands before reaching the fort. In time they came to be known as the "Langley people."

According to Native tradition (Hill-Tout in Maud 1978, 3:68; Duff 1952:23), the Kwantlen had originally lived on the Fraser River at what became New Westminster, but after the fort was built they moved upriver to be near it, in part for the protection it gave from raiders. It may be true that at an earlier time the main Kwantlen village was downriver, but the move must have come earlier than the tradition has it. In the winter of 1824 the McMillan expedition encountered Kwantlen people (spelled "Cahoutetts," "Cahantilt," etc. by John Work) on the Salmon River, at a village farther up the Fraser at Hatzic Slough, and again farther downriver from a village either on the Pitt or the Brunette River.[7] One of the Kwantlen they met was Whittlekainum (so identified by Alexander McKenzie, who met him again in 1825). Thus two years before the fort was built, the Kwantlen were already wintering in their later territory.

A spread upriver may have become possible because the area had become vacant. The site where the fort was built in 1827, which later came to be called Derby, had earlier been the village of a tribe whose territory on the Fraser included Kanaka Creek and the Salmon River and extended southward to include the Serpentine and Nicomekl rivers and the eastern shore of Boundary Bay.[8] The Derby people, like those of several other villages in the region, had been largely wiped out by smallpox some time earlier (probably during the epidemic of the 1770s), leaving their territory to be taken over by tribes with ties of kinship to them. It would have been less exposed to raids from the Lekwiltok and from the encroachment of the Cowichans.

The two other Downriver Halkomelem tribes were based below the fort. The territory of the Katzie ("Kiji," etc.) included Pitt Lake, the Alouette River, and the lowlands south to the Fraser. The journals indicate that they had a winter village downstream, but it is unclear whether it was on the Fraser (where the Katzie later got reserves) or on the Pitt River. The wapato ponds to which people from all around came in the fall (see 5 October 1827) were in Katzie territory. Ethnographic work (Jenness 1955; Suttles 1955) indicates that the Katzie moved seasonally back and forth between the Fraser and Pitt Lake and its many sloughs.

Farther downstream, where the North Arm empties into the gulf, was the village Simon Fraser visited in 1808, identifying the people as "Misquiame" (Musqueam), making them the only tribe in the region identified by name before the 1820s. The journals do not mention this village, but it remains there today and was probably there when the fort was built. According to their own traditions, the Musqueam once had several other winter villages on Burrard Inlet and the North Arm, and during the summer they went up the Fraser as far as the Hope area for salmon fishing. This summer activity is attested in the entries for late August 1827, when Musqueams and Squamish came down from the fisheries with fish and went back upstream. On 1 October they came back down and camped at Pitt River, where they stayed through December (and menaced Alexander McKenzie). From the summer of 1828 on, the journals mentions a Musqueam camp or village on the little river (presumably Kanaka Creek) opposite the fort. This village was occupied in January 1830. The only Musqueam mentioned by name is "Shientan a Musqueam chief," who brought shellfish upriver for feasts and who acted as an intermediary in trade with the Sechelts. Known from later times but not mentioned in the journals are three other tribes who were adjacent to the Musqueam, the Tsawwassen, Coquitlam, and Burrard.[9]

Above the Kwantlen were a group of tribes who spoke Upriver Halkomelem. Those mentioned in the journals are the Sumas, on the Sumas River, which flowed out of the now-drained Sumas Lake; the Chilliwack, probably at that time up the Chilliwack River above Sweltzer Creek; the Pelalt, probably at that time near what is now Agassiz; and the Tait, on the Fraser from Popkum, just above the present Rosedale, to Sawmill Creek, above the present Yale.[10] The journals also mention "the Harrison River Indians" (24 December 1829). These may have been the Scowlitz, whose village was on the Harrison just above where it flows into the Fraser, or the Chehalis, from farther up the Harrison, or both. Not mentioned at all are the Matsqui, whose territory lay between the Kwantlen and the Sumas, and the Nicomen, who adjoined the Sumas.

These upriver tribes were the year-round residents of the area into which several thousand people came each year for the summer fishing season, their goal primarily being the rapids at the lower end of the Fraser Canyon, in Tait territory. During 1827 and 1828, the journals mention raiding parties composed of members of tribes who used the upriver fisheries (Cowichan, Nanaimo, and Kwantlen) attacking the Sumas, Chilliwack, and Pelalt, though not the Tait. Later, parties of upriver people begin bringing in skins, but they are accompanied by the Kwantlen, who have been acting as intermediaries and are not too pleased with this development.

Seasonal Visitors

The Nanaimo, Cowichan, Squamish, and Saanich came from outside the Fraser Valley. They came primarily for salmon, sturgeon, and wapato (see "Subsistence," below), but they also immediately began trading with the company people.

The Nanaimo and Cowichan were speakers of Island Halkomelem dialects whose home territories were across the Strait of Georgia, but they had large summer villages of permanent structures on the mainland, where they stayed during the summer and into early autumn and from which they made excursions upriver. The Nanaimo winter villages were around what is now the city named for them. Their summer village, estimated to hold four hundred people, was on the south bank of the Fraser just three miles downstream from the fort (see Aemelius Simpson's map, pp. 8-9), and thus for a part of the year the Nanaimo were among its close neighbours. The Cowichan winter villages were on the lower course of the Cowichan River and on Stuart Channel and the Gulf Islands to the north.[11] The Cowichans had a row of summer villages on the main channel shore of Lulu Island. After passing these villages on the *Cadboro*, George Barnston identified them with names we can identify as Somenos, Penelakuts, and Quamichan, three of the largest Cowichan villages. The first and third are on the Cowichan River; the second is on Kuper Island in the Gulf Islands. Presumably Cowichans from other villages either stayed in the houses of these three or had houses of their own. Barnston made a "rough guess" that the population was nearly 1,500 souls. In December 1824 Francis Annance had seen this "deserted village nearly a mile long," and estimated that it "must contain not less than a thousand men." Although their permanent summer villages were not near the fort, some Cowichans seem to have camped nearby fairly often. Most often mentioned among these was Shashia, later called "Joshua" and then "Joe" (see "Chiefs," below). Cowichans also crossed over from Vancouver Island to fish for sturgeon in April 1829, possibly not following a regular practice but to supplement their stores after a poor salmon run during the summer of 1828.

The presence of this large and formidable "nation" on the Fraser must have been the reason for an early disagreement about the name of the river. Reporting on the expedition of December 1824, both James McMillan and John Work indicate that the Natives identifed the Fraser as the Cowichan

River. But in August 1825 Alexander McKenzie was told, evidently by the Snohomish trader Waskelatchee, that the 1824 expedition had not been at the "Cowitchen" River but at another farther south called the "Quotlin" River.[12] On reaching what clearly was the Fraser, he recorded that its Indian name was "Quotlin."

The seasonal presence of the Cowichans of the Fraser was evidently not wholly approved by its permanent residents. On 25 August 1825 the Kwantlen chief Whotleakenum (Whittlekainum) indicated to McKenzie that he wanted to be considered "entirely distinct from the Cowitchens," who had "no business with the *Quotlin* [the Fraser] River."

The Squamish ("Chomes," etc.), who spoke a language not shared by any other tribe, came to the Fraser from the mainland to the north of the Musqueam. Like the Musqueam, the Squamish came earlier in the year than the Cowichan and Nanaimo, and they sometimes camped with or near the Musqueam on Kanaka Creek. McMillan's entry for 25 September 1828 says the Squamish were "on their way to Burrard's Canal for the winter" and also refers to "their lands up Burrard's Canal." According to the traditions of the Squamish and their neighbours, at one time the Squamish had all their winter villages on Howe Sound and in the Squamish Valley, and later they established winter villages on Burrard Inlet. Musqueam tradition has it that this move occurred after the first mills were built in mid-century, but the Squamish believe the move came earlier. If the journals are taken literally, it would mean that the Squamish were on Burrard Inlet by the late 1820s. However, the absence of any mention of Howe Sound and statements that the Sechelt were "beyond Burrard's Canal" (25 February 1828) and "north of Burrard's Canal" (29 September 1828) leaves open the possibility that "Burrard's Canal" was used to include Howe Sound and that the Squamish winter homes were still in their earlier homes.

The Saanich spoke a dialect of Northern Straits; other dialects of this language were spoken by the Lummi and by several other tribes not mentioned in the journals – the Semiahmoo, Samish, Songhees, and Sooke. The home territory of the Saanich was on Vancouver Island and in the Gulf Islands south of Cowichan territory. The journals put them at Point Roberts in early summer, locating a Saanich village there. Later in the summer the Saanich came into the river. The journals report (25 August 1827) a number of families from Point Roberts passed on their way up to the fishery. They were returning downriver in early October. During the fall a group of Saanich camped up the Salmon River, just above the fort, where they built weirs. The chief of this group was "Chaheinook" (one of several spellings of this name), also known as "Anniskinnum" and "the Gros Nez," who became an important trader. By the summer of 1830, he and Shashia are identified as "the two great men on the Island."

Ethnographic work (Suttles 1951) indicates that at Point Roberts in the late nineteenth century, Saanich fishermen took sockeye salmon in reef nets, as did fishermen from two other Northern Straits speaking tribes, the Semiahmoo and the Lummi. In good years, as 1829 must have been, they were joined by people from other tribes to the south as well as

Cowichans from Vancouver Island. But there is no ethnographic report of the presence of the Saanich on the Salmon River, in what would appear to be Kwantlen territory. Their presence there at the time of the journals may be explained by a Semiahmoo tradition. The Semiahmoo were a small tribe whose villages were on Semiahmoo and Birch bays. According to their tradition, they had marriage ties with the "Snókomish," (the Derby people), and when that tribe had largely perished from smallpox, they inherited the Nicomekl River. Some of the Saanich had close ties with the Semiahmoo, and they may have shared this inheritance and claimed the Salmon River.[13]

Traders

Small groups and even individuals from a number of other tribes visited Fort Langley primarily to trade. Clallam came from the southern shore of Juan de Fuca Strait, Lummi (or their neighbours) from Bellingham Bay,[14] Nooksack from south of the Chilliwack, Lushootseed-speaking tribes – Skagit, Snohomish, Suquamish, and others – from Puget Sound, a Cowlitz from farther south on a tributary of the Columbia, a Sechelt from the coast to the north, and Thompson (Ntlaka'pamux), Lillooet (Stl'atl'imx), and Okanagan from the Interior. During the three-year period, contact with several of these tribes seems to have been limited to one or two visits from each, while others had frequent or extended contact. Some had previously traded with the company elsewhere. The Cowlitz trader Scanewah and the Snohomish trader Waskelatchee ("the Frenchman") had traded at Fort George. The Thompson trader Lapitchine had probably traded at Kamloops.

Contact among these tribes was already broad. Several marriages between members of distant tribes seem to have existed before the fort was built – that of the Cowlitz trader Scanewah to a Clallam woman, that of the Kwantlen called "the Doctor" to a Lekwiltok woman, and that of an Okanagan man to a Duwamish woman. But trade with the fort probably broadened contact among the tribes who came there. It seems unlikely that, earlier, a Thompson (from somewhere around the present Lytton) could have sold a Lekwiltok slave (from north of the Strait of Georgia) to Scanewah (from near the Columbia), as he did at the fort on 26 March 1828.

Raiders

One tribe mentioned often, but never as coming to trade, are the Lekwiltok ("Yucletaw," etc.). These are the southernmost division of the Kwakwala-speaking people of the region around Queen Charlotte Strait. In the late eighteenth century this group lived on Johnstone Strait beyond the Comox, a Coast Salish people whose territory extended northwest as far as Kelsey Bay. By the beginning of the nineteenth century, if not earlier, the Lekwiltok had begun to assimilate some Comox villages and to raid others. By 1827 they were raiding as far south as Puget Sound. By the 1840s they had expanded their territory to include Cape Mudge and Campbell River, replacing the remaining Comox, who had moved south into Pentlatch territory.[15] The Kwakiutl proper of the eastern end of Queen Charlotte Strait are mentioned in relation to the Lekwiltok, but there is no mention of any tribes farther north. There is no evidence that the Haida, Tsimshian, or Tlingit came as far south as the Strait of Georgia this early.

An Unmentioned Presence

Not mentioned in the journals by name but represented at the fort were the Chinook and their neighbours on the lower Columbia River.[16] Several of the women who came with their husbands to the fort must have been from these tribes. There is some indication of difficulty between these women and the wives later taken from the Kwantlen and other local tribes, but "the enlightened ones from the Columbia" (20 March 1829) must have influenced the locals' perception of the newcomers and how to deal with them.

DOMESTIC LIFE

The Fort Langley Journals contain the kind of information about the movements of the Native people, their social relations, and the careers of individuals that could come only from long, continuous observation. But it says very little about the appearance of the Native people, what they wore, what they ate, and the houses they lived in. For this we can look at the reports of earlier visitors: Simon Fraser in 1808 (Lamb 1960); James McMillan (Merk 1968:248-50), Elliott (1912); and Francis Annance (1824-5) in the winter of 1824-5; and Alexander McKenzie (1825) and John Scouler (1905) in the summer of 1825. These men were seeing the people of this region for the first time and, in Simon Fraser's case, relying on them for food, shelter, and transport. As a result,they commented on things that to the writers of the journals were already familiar and probably needed no comment.

Appearance and Dress

From Work and Annance we learn that the Kwantlen they met on the Fraser in 1824 were generally short, though one man presumed to be a chief was about six feet tall; their heads were flattened, but less so than among the Chinooks; and older men generally had beards. A man's ordinary clothing consisted of nothing more than a blanket made of dog hair and bird down. To keep off the rain, he wore over his blanket a short cedar-bark cloak, with a hole in the middle for the head and open at the sides for the arms to be free, and on his head a conical hat. Annance (1824-5:18 December 1824) describes the tall chief as "finely dressed in his way with a clean European blanket and a large Chinook hat ornamented with white Shells, quite in the style of a Grandee."

Work and Annance do not mention paint, but in 1808 Fraser saw people near the present Hope having skin and hair "of a reddish cast," which he supposed came from "the ingredients with which they besmear their bodies" (Lamb 1960:101). Farther downstream he saw people who looked fair because of white paint. At Point Roberts in 1825, Scouler (1905:201) wrote that the Natives of this region painted lines on their faces with red ochre, charcoal, and powdered mica and applied a "prodigious" quantity of grease to their hair. The Fort Langley Journals do not mention face paint except in describing a war party, but the vermilion often mentioned as an article of trade may have been used for that purpose.

Fraser saw ornaments at the present Yale that were like those of the Thompson nation – "shells of different kinds, shell beads, brass made into pipes hanging from the neck or across the shoulders, bracelets made of large brass wire, and some bracelets of horn." Hats were of roots and conical in form, but some used head-bands of cedar bark "painted in various colours" (Lamb 1960:100).

Most visitors commented on the Native blankets. When Fraser reached the first Coast Salish village, he reported that the people had "rugs" made of mountain-goat wool and dog hair and that the dogs were "lately shorn." Later he wrote that the rugs "have stripes of different colours crossing at right angles resembling at a distance a Highland plaid" and that the dog hair was "spun with a distaff and spindle." Work describes the blankets of the Kwantlen as "some white and some grey or of black with varigated bands of different colors mostly red and white" (Lamb 1960:101). Annance (1824-5:18 December 1824) visited a lodge in which "we saw a sort of loom, with which they manufacture blankets with the hair of dogs and the down of ducks and geese."

The Fort Langley Journals indicate how numerous the dogs were. One entry mentions 160 canoes passing, each containing one family "and generally about a half a dozen dogs more resembling Cheviot Lambs shorn of their wool" (23 September 1828). The journal does not mention mountain-goat hair, but at an event that Annance and Yale attended in January 1829, both Native and Hudson's Bay Company blankets as well as "white sheep skins" were gifts. Conceivably these were skins of mountain sheep, which were native to the eastern slopes of the Cascades, though not "white," but it is more likely that they were mountain-goat skins. Ethnography indicates that Coast Salish hunters commonly hunted mountain goats in nearby mountains and traded their hides, which were valued because the white hair could be removed and used in blankets.

At Yale, Fraser had noted the scarcity of leather, from which he inferred that large animals were scarce, not yet appreciating that the dampness of the climate made other materials preferable. He later mentions hostile Natives wearing "coats of mail" and friendly Natives giving him several from which he might make shoes. These were probably shirts made of several thicknesses of elk hide, worn as armour for battle but not for daily use. The hostile Natives carried bows and arrows, spears, and war clubs of "horn" (antler or perhaps whalebone) (Lamb 1960:99, 103, 105). Scouler

(1905:201-2) mentions bows "frequently ornamented with the skins of serpents" and arrows "very short and armed with barbed pieces of bone, about six inches long."

Meals

Fraser and his party were served food at several places. He mentions mats spread out for them, salmon served in wooden dishes, salmon "cooked by means of hot stones in wooden vessels," sturgeon, oil, berries, roots, and "dried oysters" (probably clams) served in large troughs (Lamb 1960:98, 101, 102).

Houses and Other Structures

Fraser's journal shows that the Natives of the Fraser Valley built large shed-roof plank houses. This type of house had a frame of posts and beams supporting a single-pitched roof. Its roof and walls were of heavy planks, the wall planks running horizontally with a slight overlap and held between pairs of poles lashed to the eaves. A house seen at the present Yale was 46 by 23 feet; its walls 11 feet high (Lamb 1960:99). Farther downstream, probably somewhere below the present Mission, he saw a much larger structure – 640 feet long and 60 feet wide, with a front wall 18 feet high, actually a row of houses or "apartments" under one roof. These were 60-foot squares, except for that of the chief, which was 90 feet long. The entrance to the chief's dwelling was an oval opening in a post, above which was a carved human figure and "figures in imitation of beasts and birds." The floor was bare earth. There was a fire in the centre of each "apartment" and a hole above it to let out the smoke. Fraser (Lamb 1960:103-4) wrote that the "apartments" were divided into portions, possibly referring to the waist-high partitions seen in Paul Kane's illustrations of a house near Victoria.[17] He did not mention bed-platforms running along the walls, but they were probably there. He described the Musqueam village as a "fort" 1500 feet long and 90 feet wide, composed of both rows of houses and detached houses (Lamb 1960:106).[18]

This type of house was usual in winter villages and also at some seasonal camps. The Cowichan and Nanaimo summer villages on the Fraser must have been plank houses or at least the frames of plank houses to which the occupants brought planks during fishing season. At other sites occupied only seasonally, people probably more often set up makeshift frames for planks or mats made of cat-tails or tules. The "tents" of the Musqueams camped at Kanaka Creek (18 May 1828 journal entry) were probably mat houses.

Fraser also saw "tombs," that is, burial houses, at Spuzzum, the boundary between the Thompson and the Halkomelem, "of the form of a chest of drawers," about 15 feet long, with boards and posts carved with figures of birds and beasts. He commented that these structures must have cost much time and labour in the absence of "proper tools," suggesting that he saw few or no steel tools at this place, but farther downriver the Natives had "a large English hatchet." At the site of Yale he saw another tomb, with the posts "covered all over with bright shells, which shine like mercury" – possibly abalone (Lamb 1960:97-8, 100).

Canoes

The earlier observers say little about canoes, other than in relation to Fraser's problems in hiring them. In contrast, the Fort Langley Journals give some specific information that agrees with later accounts. It appears that the Native peoples had two main types of canoe – a common type, not described, and a large "war canoe." The ordinary canoes evidently ranged in size from those holding three or four persons to those holding up to eight or more. These were no doubt Coast Salish style canoes, with low, projecting bow and stern, probably measuring 12 to 30 feet in length (Holm 1991; Lincoln 1993). One variety is seen in the model in the collection at Perth. The smaller of these canoes were used for fishing or hunting, the larger for transport.

The "war canoes" are described in some detail by George Barnston (25 August 1827). They were obtained from people to the north and were used "as Luggage Boats" capable of holding "a great Bulk of Furniture & Baggage." Some were 50 feet long with a 6- to 7-foot beam. The bow was high, "at least 7 feet from the water." The stern was flat on top and bore a carved human face. The sides of both bow and stern were "very fancifully ornamented with circles and other regular figures which [were] laid on with various coloured Paints or Clay." Several journal entries mention war canoes with thirty men in each (21 March, 9 and 24 September 1829). These canoes were no doubt of the type sometimes identified as the "munka" (from the Kwakiutl name). They were probably obtained from the Lekwiltok or possibly from the Sechelt or Sliammon (Barnett 1955:114).

The "large Bark Canoe" used by company men (3 November 1828) must have been brought from the East by the company. The only bark vessels used by the Native people of this region were small makeshift craft made of cedar bark by hunters on inland lakes.

SUBSISTENCE

Reporting to London a few months after the fort was built, McMillan expressed some doubt about whether the company would be able to induce "our lazy naked Indians" to hunt beaver because the bountiful environment in which they lived made life too easy for them: "The Rivers in Summer are Swarming with Salmon and Sturgeon and when they retire to the Gulph and Islands: they are equally plentifully supplied during the Winter: Their wants in other respects are so trifling that but little exertion is required of them" (McMillan 1828a; see also Appendix B).

This view of nature's bounty and the ease of Native life persisted in anthropology until the mid-twentieth century as an explanation for the development of the complex social relations, arts, and ceremonies of the Northwest Coast; these were the product of leisure made possible by unfailing abundance. But it cannot have been that simple. As the journals show, while the rivers did swarm with salmon and there were other great abundances, these were limited in time and space and varied from year to year. There were good times but also hungry times. They show too that the winter was not simply a ceremonial season during which people lived on accumulated stores. There are many times during the winter when the Natives were seen out on the river to catch sturgeon.

The tribes' seasonal movements and their timing cannot be understood without reference to spatial and temporal limitations in the availability of resources and their qualities.[19] The great attraction of the Fraser River lay in the fact that within the region sockeye salmon ran almost exclusively in the Fraser, sturgeon were present in much greater numbers in the Fraser and around its mouth, and wapato grew most profusely in ponds and sloughs in the Fraser Valley. Of the tribes that visited the Fraser seasonally, the Squamish, Nanaimo, and Cowichan had smaller rivers in their home territories with runs of other species of salmon that could be taken in spring or fall, before and after the sockeye run in the Fraser. The Saanich had only one smaller stream in their home territory, which may have been why one group of them used the Salmon River above the fort. Having access to different species of salmon was important because of their different qualities and requirements for preservation. Sockeyes run in mid-summer and could be preserved outside, but they are fat and do not keep as long. Chums run in the fall and had to be preserved in a plank house over a smoky fire, but they are lean and when smoked well keep for a long time. Different species and even different races of the same species were valued differently for other reasons, including flavour.

Salmon Fishing

Salmon were of first importance in the Native economy (see Kew 1996 for an overview), and they were also sought after by the traders; thus the journals have a great many references to the taking and preserving of fish, giving a fairly clear view of the extent of the Native salmon fishery on the Fraser over a period of three years.

All five species of Pacific salmon run in the Fraser. According to information on the Fraser River runs gathered in the 1890s by fisheries experts (Rathbun 1900), there were two runs of chinook (or "spring") salmon, one beginning early and becoming heaviest in June and another from late September into October. The spring run spawned farther up the Fraser; the fall run spawned in its larger lower tributaries, such as the Pitt River.[20] Sockeye were first seen in late June or early July, but the main run came, some years in huge numbers, from late July through the middle of August or even early September. The bulk of the run went up the Fraser and through the canyon in order to reach spawning grounds in the Interior. Coho began to appear before the end of the sockeye season and became abundant in mid-September; the run in the Fraser lasted to the middle or end of October, but they spawned in smaller streams until November or later. Pink (or "humpback") salmon spawned in smaller streams from the latter part of September to the middle of October. Unlike other species they run only every other year, in odd-numbered years. Chum (or "dog") salmon could appear in September, but the run went on through October and November and even into December. In addition there was a salmon-sized anadromous trout, the steelhead, which ran in the winter.

The Fort Langley Journals use no names for the several species of salmon, but occasionally show that the company people were aware of the differences. The 21 October 1828 entry mentions "100 small fresh salmon & 10 or 12 large ones such as we see in the Columbia," probably referring to cohoes and chinooks. The 11 September 1829 entry describes what must be pink salmon. One the following month (7 October 1829) refers to "fall Salmon," probably cohoes, as opposed to "summer fish," no doubt sockeyes. A distinction is also apparent from the entry of 24 June 1830, which says the traders got "15 fine Salmon," probably spring chinooks, from the Chilliwacks, and one nearly two months later (12-17 July 1830), which says "no appearance of salmon yet," again no doubt referring to the summer run of sockeye. The traders came with some knowledge of the salmon in the Columbia River, but they were not yet familiar enough with the different species or the Fraser River races of the different species to have names for them. In fact, the English names now in general use for two salmon species were probably introduced on the Fraser, "sockeye" from Halkomelem sθə́qəy "sockeye" (or possibly Northern Straits sə́qəy̓, and "coho" from Mainland Halkomelem k̓ʷə́x̌ʷəθ "coho."

The different species have different habits and were caught by different means. Chinooks and cohoes were caught in the sea from winter through spring by trolling. In streams that were shallow enough, chinooks and other species were taken in traps set in weirs. The Cowichan caught spring-run chinooks in such traps before crossing to the Fraser for the sockeye run. On the Fraser, spring-run chinooks were taken in trawl nets and dip nets.

The trawl net is a bag-like net held down between two moving canoes, operated by four persons. Fraser saw it used near Yale in the evening of 7 July 1808, writing, "Their nets, that resembled purses, were fixed to the ends of long poles and dragged between two canoes" (Lamb 1960:114). It was used in streams deep enough, free of snags, and not too swift, as in the lower course of the Fraser and in its larger tributaries such as the Pitt. The journal mentions the Native use of "the scoop" net (17 August 1828). The term could mean either the trawl net or the dip net or both, but in a later entry (23 July 1829) the journals mention the traders' futile attempt to use "a Scoop net between two canoes" – clearly a trawl net.

The dip net is a net fastened to a hoop at the end of a shaft. It is generally used in eddies where the water is otherwise swift, operated by a single person standing on a rock or on a scaffold built out over the water (Duff 1952:62-3). Dip netting was the method used especially in the Fraser Canyon, the "fisheries" or "the rapids" mentioned often in the journals. The journals do not describe the method, but it is implied by the statement that Natives who had gone up to "the first rapids" for salmon came back "without much Success – the flood having Carried away their Stages"(3 June 1829).

Sockeye were taken in the sea in the reef net, a net suspended between a pair of anchored canoes. The most productive place for reef nets was at Point Roberts, where Saanich, Semiahmoo, and Lummi fished in the late nineteenth century. It was no doubt important earlier; the Spanish explorers saw "an incredible quantity of rich salmon and numerous Indians" there in 1791 (Wagner 1933:186–7). On 5 August 1829 the Cowichan chief Shashia reported "that the quantity of Salmon now Caught there is immense and that all the Indians on the Coast to the Southward have resorted to the Point R. village," and later another Native reported that "the assemblage of natives" at the mouth of the river was very great and that at Point Roberts "no fewer than 200 Canoes landed the last week from the Southward" (25 August 1829). It was very likely the success of the reef netters that brought them there.

It was the summer run of sockeye in the Fraser that brought large numbers of people past the fort on their way upriver. In the river, sockeye were taken in trawl nets and dip nets. During the summer the fish could be preserved by drying them outside. Especially in the canyon, a warm wind provided ideal conditions for preserving fish without the expenditure of fuel needed for smoking them (Duff 1952:18). Sockeye were also a source of oil. The journals mention (2 October 1829) the purchase of several bladders of salmon oil from the Squamish.[21]

The period covered by the journals begins early in the run of 1827 and ends as the Native people were preparing for the run of 1830, and the letter book contains some references to the catch of 1830. They show a fluctuation in the abundance of the fish over three years. In 1827 the fish arrived in early August, were abundant through late August and early September, and became scarce by late September. In 1828 the run was poor. The fish were still scarce in early August and remained less plentiful than in the previous year. On 14 September the journals reported that salmon were so scarce that the Natives would "hardly part with any," adding "What a difference from last year." On 22 September it reported that from the 345 canoes of Cowichans who had by then come down from the fisheries the fort had managed, by changing its price, to get about 3,000 salmon, while the year before from the same number of canoes they might have obtained 20,000 "with less trouble." But in 1829 the fish arrived in early August and were so plentiful by mid-August that the fort was turning them away. On 22 September the journals mention Natives trying to trade "their Surplus dried Salmon." In 1830 fishing began on 20 August, and after slack period was said to be "again thriving" on 30 August. The fort traded for fish in early September, and on 14 September the fishery was said to be "about at an end" with the quality of the fish declining.

The fall runs of cohoes, pinks, and chums were taken in smaller streams in traps set in weirs or perhaps with dip nets, harpoons, or gaff-hooks.

There are several references in the journals to Saanich people who spent the summer at Point Roberts, probably taking sockeyes in reef nets, and coming in the autumn to the Salmon River near the fort to build weirs for the fall runs. After the poor sockeye run of 1828, the fall runs provided some relief. The Saanich took them "in great abundance in the little rivers" (21 October 1828) and "in the little Creeks without difficulty" (23 October 1828). These fish were welcome at the fort.

Sturgeon Fishing

Sturgeon may have rivalled salmon in importance. These fish are much larger, and they can be taken through a greater part of the year. Biologists identify two species in this region: the white sturgeon, which can be up to twenty feet long and weigh perhaps as much as 1,800 pounds, and the smaller green sturgeon, which can be up to seven feet long and weigh up to three hundred pounds. Both species live in both fresh and salt water, but the white sturgeon is more common in the Fraser and its larger tributaries. It comes into the river in the spring to spawn and to feed on eulachon (Carl, Clemens, and Lindsey 1959; Hart 1973). The journals give no indication that the traders recognized two species; probably most of those seen were white sturgeon. The journals twice record trading for a sturgeon twelve feet long and once for one weighing four hundred pounds cleaned; its length was not given. The journals show that sturgeon became abundant in early May 1828, mid-April 1829, and early March 1830. They arrived just before the eulachon run in 1829, but nearly two months before it in 1830. However, some sturgeon must have been in the river at any time; there is at least one entry mentioning the Natives taking sturgeon in every month of one year or another of the three covered by the journals. Sturgeon fishing was evidently limited by the height of the river. In the fall of 1828 the journals report that heavy rain had raised it, tempting the Natives to try fishing for sturgeon, but for a time in the spring of 1829 the river was too high and the fishing was stopped.

The Natives took sturgeon with harpoons and with trawl nets. The sturgeon harpoon is described in the journals (31 July 1827), and its use has been described by later observers and ethnographers. It consisted of a long shaft ending in a pair of foreshafts, each bearing a head composed of two antler barbs and a blade of slate, shell, or iron. The shaft consisted of segments that fitted together so that it was variable in length; estimates are as high as seventy-two feet. Short lines attached to the heads joined a line that had to be much longer than the shaft. The sturgeon harpoon was used from a canoe in deep, slow-moving water. The harpooner held it vertically, and as the canoe was allowed to drift slowly downstream, he raised and lowered the harpoon, feeling for a fish lying near the bottom. Once he felt the plates on the back of a sturgeon, he thrust the harpoon into the fish. If a head penetrated, the line attached at its middle made it turn and catch in the wound; the shaft was then set free, the harpooner held onto the line, and the struggle began. The entry for 22 December 1828 reports, "Two

Indians fishing in front of the Fort harpooned a very large Sturgeon which took them Several hours to exhaust & get ashore."

The journal also mentions a "Scoop net" (trawl net) being used for sturgeon "in a great depth of water"(15 April 1829). On this occasion twenty or thirty canoes were out when one man got his net snagged, tried to get it loose, and was drowned.

The men at the fort appreciated sturgeon and were eager to get it, trading for it from the Natives when they could and trying various means of catching the fish themselves. It seems the Natives readily supplied them with sturgeon during the summer months but were reluctant to do so at other times, perhaps especially in the spring, when stores of salmon were probably running low. In early April 1829 sturgeon were scarce, and McDonald wrote: "The Natives are actually starving" (4 April 1829). This was the spring following the poor summer salmon run of 1828. McDonald complains that the Natives asked too high a price for sturgeon in the fall and that they rarely sold a whole fish. Selling by the piece, however, may have been less the result of sharp business practice than simply the Native custom of dividing a sturgeon among those who helped catch it or bring it in.

Eulachons

The eulachon, a member of the smelt family, ascends larger rivers in great numbers in the spring to spawn. The journals report their arrival in late April or early May (28 April 1828, 14 April 1829, and 4 May 1830), and that it was "Joyffully hailed" by the Natives. Biologists report that on the Fraser the "major spawning grounds appear to be along the stretch of river between Mission and Chilliwack" (Carl, Clemens, and Lindsey 1959:35). But they were abundant in the river before the fort, where Natives from different tribes took them. In May 1830 the Squamish were taking "an immense quantity of the Small fish." The traders tried taking eulachons "Chinook fashion with the rake." The Natives were probably using dip nets. On the northern coast, eulachon were a major source of oil, but on the Fraser, as on the Columbia, they were eaten fresh or smoked whole. A difference in oil content may have been the basis of this difference in use.

Hunting

The journals give little information about other Native subsistence activities. In 1808 Simon Fraser had observed a net that was used in deer drives. The Fort Langley Journals do not mention this or any other method of hunting deer and only once refer to the Natives' "occasionally" going after elk with dogs (4 August 1829). There is a reference to the Natives bringing in two deer skins (2 August 1828) but no mention of trade in deer or elk meat, which was supplied by company hunters. On one occasion (10 August 1828) the company people gave Shashia a piece of venison. There is a reference (3 November 1828) to the Natives' catching geese and ducks with nets, probably nets on pole frames used on dark nights in canoes with flares.

Gathering

Shellfish are mentioned in connection with the Musqueam. Their chief Shientin came upriver on 11 March and again on 7 April 1828, each time with a canoe-load of shellfish, the first time coming from Vancouver Island. Again on 8 and 9 April 1830 there is a report of the Musqueams giving a "Banquet" of shellfish. Berries are mentioned a few times. Women traded berries in August (5 August 1827), when they may have been black-berries, and on 22 June 1828, either salmonberries or a euphemism. On 28 October 1828, the fort traded for "a few cranberries," but no other berries are mentioned by name. The journals mention camas, rare in the Fraser Valley, being brought over from Vancouver Island (21 December 1828); these bulbs would have been dug the previous spring and preserved by steaming and drying. They also mention "a mass of Indians" gathering on the lower Pitt River to get wapato from ponds there (5 October 1827). But again nothing is said about any other of the bulbs and roots the Native people harvested. These omissions may not indicate that the traders were not aware of this variety of vegetable foods or were not consuming some in addition to their usual diet of fish or meat and potatoes. Perhaps the women of the fort were gathering them or getting them from relatives in small amounts, and the journalists did not consider this the business of the fort.

SOCIETY

Social Groups

In Native society there were groups sharing residence or territory at five levels: families, households, local groups, winter villages, and tribes. None of these groups was a wholly stable unit; people could move from one such group to another as kin ties permitted. Nor were the levels always distinct; a small local group could consist of a single household or a small tribe of a single village. There were also non-localized kin groups, each composed of persons descended from some illustrious ancestor or ancestral couple. In these, membership was permanent but not exclusive; because descent was reckoned equally through males and females, a person could claim descent from several illustrious ancestors in different places. The writers of the journals were aware of families, villages, and tribes.

The family consisted of the persons who occupied one section of one of the great plank houses in a winter village as their home base. It was generally composed of a man and his wife or wives, their minor children, perhaps dependent older relatives, and slaves. Each family had its own hearth in the house and its own equipment, dogs, stores of food, and one or more canoes, and it often owned the planks covering the frame of its section of the house.

When people made their seasonal moves, they often laid house planks across two or three canoes held eight to ten feet apart to make "rafts" ("catamarans" may be a better word), upon which were piled goods, provisions, children, and dogs (25 August 1827, 19 November 1828). These rafts and the occasional war canoe must have been occupied each by two or more families. They also travelled one family per canoe; an entry (23 September 1828) mentions 160 Cowichan canoes returning from upriver, each usually holding one man and his family and half a dozen dogs. In major seasonal moves, as those to and from the fisheries, large numbers of familes travelled together. There are also instances when single families made shorter trips alone, but this could be dangerous, as when the Kwantlen doctor lost his life and when the Musqueam chief lost his daughter. At a seasonal site, a family camped in a mat house, or if they took their planks, they used them to cover a frame. At some seasonally used sites there were permanent frames.

The plank house in the winter village was occupied by families who formed a household. They were related, usually but not necessarily, through males, and they co-operated in economic, social, and ceremonial activities. The frame of the house, the permanent structure, was identified as the property of those who built it, either several men co-operating or a wealthy man who could organize the labour force required. In either case the house had a head, whose influence over his house mates depended on his character and wealth rather than any formal authority.

The local group probably most often consisted of a wealthy household, which formed its elite, and other more or less dependent houses. The local group, or its leading house, was identified, through a tradition recounting its origin, with resource sites. The head of this house and those of his kin group who lived in the village were the managers of these resources. The local group was also identified with a winter village or with a section of a winter village shared with other local groups. A winter village might thus be identical with a local group, or it might be composed of several local groups. In the late nineteenth century, the Katzie tribe had a single winter village occupied by several groups who maintained control of separate resource areas that were said to be their original homes.

The largest social groups in Native society were the tribes. In the late nineteenth century there were tribes, like the Katzie, that wintered in a single village, but traditions suggest that earlier, before population decline, most tribes consisted of several winter villages. A tribe usually united to defend itself against a common enemy; however, traditions suggest that in conflicts arising out of disputes between individuals in different tribes, the local groups or houses might act independently.

Chiefs

"Chiefs" are mentioned often in the journals, but the term "chief" is never defined. References to more than one chief of a tribe (three men are identifed as Kwantlen chiefs) indicate that the term does not refer to the occupant of an office with authority over a whole tribe. This is consistent with the image we get from other sources, historic and ethnographic, that among the Coast Salish of this region a "chief" was an important, influential man, but at most the head of one of the local groups that formed a tribe. It was not the tribe but these groups or their heads that owned houses and rights to fishing sites and other localized resources. Within some tribes at some times the head of one such local group might be generally acknowledged as the most important man in the tribe, but there was no position of tribal chief that, like a European title or office, had to be filled at all times (Collins 1950:333-4; Barnett 1955:245).[22]

It is clear that even the wily Shashia, who was in later years reputed to be the "head chief" of the Cowichan (McKelvie 1945:244), was only one among several Cowichan chiefs at the time of the journal. He was not the leader in every Cowichan enterprise; although he led one war party against people upriver, Lammus led another. While a large war party was reportedly on its way to attack the Lekwiltok, Shashia was at the fort worrying that the Lillooet were coming after him. He may have achieved more influence later, but that did not make him into any kind of tribal chief.[23]

The journals suggest that chiefs were impressive orators and spoke on matters of war and peace, containing or provoking conflict. While the *Cadboro* was on her way to the site of the fort, a large number of Nanaimos tried to board her, "urged forward by an elderly man [later identified as a chief named Punnis] who gave out his orders with a loud Voice, and in a very determined tone" (25 July 1827) At the site of the new fort, people gathered from both upriver and downriver, and "many long and pithy orations were given by the leading men, who seemed to vie with each other in talking with vociferation, and noise" (11 August 1827). When a party of Cowichans and Nanaimos let it be known that they planned to attack the Chilliwacks, the Cowichan chief Shashia and the Clallam chief Stackeinum and others "harangued" them, after which they quietly went back to their camps (24 September 1827).

Some of the chiefs co-operated with the fort in recovering or trying to recover stolen property. That they did not always immediately succeed is consistent with leadership based on influence and personal character rather than on coercive power beyond the local or kin group.

Several of the chiefs were important to the fort as middlemen in the trade, bringing in skins from their own and other tribes. The chiefs mentioned most often were engaged in this business. Some, like the Cowlitz Scanewah, may have owed their prominence mainly to the property they had acquired through this trade.

The journals give one instance of the company's role in raising a younger man to prominence. In September 1828 the Squamish chief Whapplakainum, who had been useful to the fort and was "an Excellent Indian and much attached to the Fort," died at the fisheries upriver, and his body was taken back to his home (25 September 1828). The following summer the company supplied a nephew with traps, which enabled him to bring in skins, and on 2 October 1829, he is identified as "Our newly Created Young Chief."

Kinship and Marriage

The Coast Salish reckoned kinship, as Europeans do, through both the father and the mother, and they regarded marriage between relatives as distant as fourth or fifth cousins as improper. The ideal marriage was arranged between families of similar status in different villages. Usually the family of the young man made the first move, sending him and an older male relative to keep a vigil outside the house of the intended bride. If her family believed an alliance with his family was in their interest, they invited him in and began negotiating. The procedure involved the payment of a bride-price by the groom's family and a dowry by the bride's, the latter including hereditary names and perhaps other privileges for the children to come from the union.

In the letter book we learn of a marriage between a son of the Skagit chief Neetlum and a daughter of the Cowichan chief Shashia. Neetlum accompanied Annance to the fort on 7 September 1830 and visited Shashia, who was camped across the river. Two days later "two very large" and three small canoes of Skagits arrived, and Neetlum took them to Shashia's camp, where "All the great men of the river" were assembled. The following day there was a "great Ceremony...solemnising a marriage that took place last Spring betweeen a Boy of Needlum's and a little Girl of Joe's – Canoes – Guns – Blankets – Slaves etc. etc. are exchanged on the occasion" (10 September 1830). Probably the "marriage" of the previous spring had been simply the acceptance of the suit and conclusion of negotations, and this was the actual exchange.

Occasionally a girl or young woman was married not through negotiations begun by the groom's family, but simply by being given by her family to a powerful warrior to obtain his protection or to a powerful shaman as payment for his services. The offers that some of the earliest European visitors had may be seen in this light.

Most couples resided in the groom's village and household, but some resided in the bride's. The journals mention a Musqueam man who lived in his Kwantlen wife's village. It was expected that after a marriage there would be periodic exchanges of food and wealth over the duration of the alliance. If the alliance was valued by both sides and one of the couple died, the family of the deceased might provide a sibling or other close relative as a substitute so that the alliance might endure. In April 1830, eight months after the Squamish wife of a Kwantlen had hanged herself, the Squamish arrived with another bride for the Kwantlen; if she was not a replacement for the suicide herself, she was at least a means of continuing the alliance between the two tribes.

An alliance between important families in different villages was valued because it gave economic and political advantages to each village.

The exchange of food and wealth may have been especially important to villages with different local resources. The children of intervillage alliances provided kin links between the two villages, and because they inherited potential membership in either parent's kin group, they eventually gave one kin group access to some of the resources of the other. It also allowed for shifts in residence; if members of a family were not getting along well with others in a house, they might move in with kin elsewhere, even taking their house planks with them.

Because of economic advantages and shared kinsmen, villages linked by marriage had reasons to maintain peaceful relations and help each other against common enemies. To increase these advantages, a powerful man might take wives from several other tribes. The journals give examples of marriages linking distant tribes. The Cowlitz trader Scanewah's marriage to a woman from the Clallam tribe, at least 120 miles (193 km) from Cowlitz country, must have been motivated by economic and political advantage. So must have been the Skagit-Cowichan marriage, mentioned above, which may have been the first between these tribes. At least some of the alliances formed between the Kwantlen and the company were no doubt motivated by the same interests.

Women

Ethnographic work has suggested what the journals show: that in Native society women were used by their families to further economic and political ends; they were married off and perhaps remarried as suited their families' purposes. Young women seemed to have little choice in the matter. Perhaps a young man did not either. But for a young woman removed to her husband's village, there might be no escape from an unhappy marriage but suicide.

Men and women played different roles in conflict. Women might start a quarrel, but it became threatening after men got involved. When an enemy attack was expected, the men got their arms, while the women and children were sent into the woods.

Women were evidently seen as valuable property. If raiders were successful, they generally killed the men and captured the women and children. A powerful warrior might seize a young woman from a neutral party, as Lammas seized Shientin's daughter. A creditor might abduct a woman in payment for a debt, as Chehainook did in the Kwantlen village. A man who paid ransom for a sister-in-law might compensate himself by taking her as an additional wife, as Scanewah did.

On the other hand, women were evidently free to dispose of the products of their own labour and could be competitive in commerce. Before the fort was built women in canoes came alongside the *Cadboro* to trade berries for rings, buttons, and such, and the company traders found it "amusing to observe the spirit of Rivalry & opposition that in this species of trade pervades the bosom of our fair visitors" (5 August 1827). And at least some women, perhaps mainly older women married to prominent men, could play important roles. The Cowichan chief Shashia had four wives (5 October 1827). On one occasion (16-17 November 1827), he camped near the fort and sent one of them up to the Kwantlen village to trade for dried salmon, and she returned the next day with a canoe-load. On 29 July 1828, the journals noted that his oldest wife had been at the Katzie camp trading for beaver skins, adding, "It would seem Jo. [Shashia] keeps the old wives off for Beaver while He remains at home with the young ones." On a third occasion, one of Shashia's wives came over from Vancouver Island to collect beaver skins that "her husband had in Bond in the Musquam camp" in order to take them back to trade with a ship anchored off the island (5 May 1830). Other examples of women in responsible positions are a Nanaimo woman who traded skins at the fort (7 July 1828), and the Kwantlen doctor's Lekwiltok wife, who negotiated the ransoming of captives. We know from ethnography that women also had important roles in ceremonies, but the journalists were probably unaware of this.

Marriages with Company Men

The relationship between Native women and the men of the fort is sometimes unclear and ambiguous, perhaps deliberately made so by the journalists, but what is recorded reveals something of the cultural differences between the Natives and the company.

Some of the men had brought wives with them from the south, but these women are not specifically identified. One, we know, was the daughter of Scanewah and therefore a woman of high status who provided a valuable tie between company and Native traders. During the three years recorded in the journal, ten company men married local women. The first was James Yale, who married a daughter of one of the Kwantlen chiefs. Later the Hawaiian Como married her sister, and there were other marriages with Kwantlen women. Pierre Therrien took a wife from the family of the Saanich chief Chaheinook. Mention is made (8 April 1829) of a plan to establish such a tie with the Chilliwack, but nothing may have come of it.

Regarding Yale's marriage, McDonald wrote on 13 November 1828 that the company officers thought it good policy, and the chief's family was evidently pleased with the "liberal presents" they all received and with the connection. Evidently they saw it as a better connection than one with a distant tribe. It was learned a few days later (25 November 1828) that a Skagit already had a claim on the young woman and was threatening to collect "heavy damages" from her family. At this time the chief's brother brought a number of young girls to offer as wives, but it turned out they were all already "married wives," probably meaning that they had been betrothed through bride-price payments. When permission to marry was given to the next men, McDonald wrote (26 November 1828) that letting them marry was preferable to tolerating contacts outside the fort. The entries immediately following suggest that the Kwantlen chief had quickly moved from offering young women as wives to offering them for sexual services. Other entries suggest that some of the women were enterprising in seeking lovers among the company men. Elsewhere on the coast, female slaves were prostituted by their masters, and it is likely that some of the women offered here were slaves. The entry of 27 November 1828 suggests that this had been happening during McMillan's time. But in McMillan's entries, there is only one possible hint (22 June 1828) of relations between the company men and the local women.

Letting men marry created some new problems. McDonald wrote about his concern for keeping the men's Native wives "within due bounds" (3 July 1829). On that day the mother of one of them came to the gate and talked with her daughter, and after the husband complained, the wife slipped away. The husband went after her and asked her to return, but with the support of her family and others she refused, "under the frivolous pretexts that She was not Kindly treated or entirely Secured as yet with the necessary property." This was a trick played before, McDonald wrote, and merely a way for a woman to spend time with a lover and return to her too tolerant husband when it suited her. So McDonald and five armed men went to the village and took her back to the fort. On another occasion McDonald found a missing wife, beat her, and sent her home (19 October 1829).

In the first instance, it may be that the woman really had a lover. Having been married off to a complete stranger, probably without having much say in the matter, she may have been inclined to seek one. On the other hand, the "frivolous pretexts" offered for her absence from her husband may have had a real basis. By Native standards, she may not have been kindly treated, and her husband may not have lived up to the terms of a marriage, which require continued exchanges of food and wealth. By McDonald's standards, his behaviour suggests, a marriage conveyed a woman to her husband and that was that.

Another event suggests that the company traders, or McDonald at any rate, did not appreciate what the affinal ties required. In January 1829 a fleet of Kwantlen canoes passed on their way to what was probably a winter dance at the Katzie village. The Kwantlen chief Nicameus, whose daughter was married to James Yale, landed and "without much ceremony" asked his daughter for a blanket. She "just as unceremoniously walked in – took it out, & with a pin buckled it on round his neck." At this McDonald removed the blanket "with Still less Ceremony" and sent him off (13 January 1829). Probably what happened was this: Nicameus was going with his people to the intervillage ceremony and was in his own eyes making a proper request of his daughter for a public recognition of his affinal relationship with Yale and the company; his daughter was in no position to deny the request and so took a company blanket; but McDonald saw this as letting Nicameus get something for nothing and so took the blanket away from him, no doubt humiliating him in the eyes of any Kwantlen watching.

CEREMONIES AND FESTIVALS

Ethnographic work identifies several kinds of ceremonies and festivals. The only ceremonies performed for the benefit of a whole village or perhaps the whole of humanity were those honouring foods. The best known of these was the first-salmon ceremony, which was performed for the first catch of the species of salmon honoured. The species and details of the ceremony differed from tribe to tribe, but the ceremony generally had its basis in a myth telling of a contract between people and salmon, binding people to treat salmon in the proper ritual fashion and salmon to return another year. On the Fraser the species was the sockeye. At the beginning of the 1827 season Barnston wrote, "The arrival of this fish is hailed by the natives with joy & festivity" (2 August 1827), but he did not elaborate on the festivity. The only other suggestion of a ceremony is McDonald's statement that some Kwantlens "brought us a few raw Salmon being almost the first we have had in this State: for, the natives here also like those in the Columbia & indeed all over think it Sacrilege to give them otherwise to the Whites at first" (9 August 1829). These must have been simply the first raw salmon McDonald had seen, since Barnston had reported getting raw salmon two years earlier. Probably the sacrilege was allowing anyone to cut the salmon improperly, especially before the rituals honouring the fish had been performed. Such an act, in the Native view, might offend the salmon and keep them from coming again.

Other ceremonies known from ethnographic work were performed for the benefit of individuals or families. These include shamanistic curing sessions, the winter dance, and celebrations of changes in status. The journal does not mention anything that suggests the activities of a shaman – beyond the identification of a Kwantlen man as "the Doctor." But it does describe events that must have involved the winter dance and changes in status.

The winter dance (or "spirit dance") was a gathering at which women and men each in turn sang and danced possessed by the "songs" that they had acquired, earlier in life, from the vision powers ("guardian spirits") they had encountered on their vision quests. Changes in status given ceremonial attention included taking or bestowing a name, announcing a girl's puberty, marrying, wiping out a stain on family honour, and honouring the dead. The ceremony might include the display of an hereditary privilege (including masked dancers, rattles, animated stuffed animals, and so on) and required the distribution of property to the guests in payment for their witnessing the event. These ceremonies could take place at any appropriate time; a wedding ceremony took place when the bride was delivered to the groom. But often they were incorporated into larger ceremonial gatherings.

The Native languages of the region distinguish two kinds of ceremonial gatherings, identifiable in English as "feasts" and "potlatches." In the late nineteenth century, a feast was a gathering of guests from within a village

or from nearby villages invited to share an abundance of food or to partici-
pate in a winter dance and perhaps, but not necessarily, to witness a change
in status. A potlatch was a gathering of guests from other tribes invited for
the specific purpose of witnessing changes in status, celebrated with grand
displays of inherited privileges and lavish distributions of property. The
changes in status might include the bestowal of inherited names, marking
of a girl's puberty, honouring of the dead, and wiping away the stain of
some disgrace. The winter dance was necessarily held in the season when
dancers' "songs" return to them. The potlatch was more often held in
better weather, when guests could come from greater distances. In recent
times the winter dance has been an occasion when guests related to the
hosts, especially affines, could bring them food to be served or property
to be given away then and there, with the understanding that it would be
paid back with interest later. This was one way of accumulating the means
to give a potlatch. Late-nineteenth- and early-twentieth-century Coast
Salish potlatches were huge affairs, lasting a week or two, at which most
or all of the families of a village, one by one, displayed their privileges
and celebrated their changes in status. Whether these large potlatches were
a recent development or an old practice is not known. References to ceremonial gatherings in the Fort Langley Journals are important in what
they suggest.

The journals mention three of these that took place in the winter of
1828-9. The "feast & dance" given by the Kwantlens on 20 December 1828
may have been simply a winter dance, but it was attended by people from
some distance – two people from around Bellingham Bay, presumably
Lummi, and a number of Cowichans. Both of these parties sold skins at
the fort; this could have been their primary reason for coming this distance in winter, but it is also possible that the sale was to give them blankets to use at the affair. The Cowichans were said (in the following day's
entry) to have had their canoes loaded with camas, which, together with
cached salmon, would supply them well for the winter. But it as likely
they were bringing them to the "dancing party," which appears to have
lasted until 24 December.

On 13 January 1829 a number of canoes of Kwantlens passed the fort on
their way to the Katzie village for an affair that the post version calls a
"dancing party" and a "Masquerade," the occasion on which McDonald
removed the blanket from Nicameus. (The annual version says they were
going "on a feasting visit.") On 15 January the journals report that "our
neighbours," that is, the Kwantlens, had returned from the "*tout*" given by
the Katzies. The journal's use of the term "masquerade," if taken literally,
implies that this gathering included a celebration of a change in status
featuring masked dancers. Dancers in the winter dance did not use masks.

On 21 January 1829 McDonald wrote that the Thompson trapper and
trader Lepitchin, who was camped above the fort, came to the fort "with a
pressing invitation for us to go to a *Rout* he is in his turn giving to the
Kitchis [Katzies] and Quaitlines [Kwantlens]." He was accompanied by
three or four Taits. The following day McDonald reported:

Messrs. Annance & Yale with Six Men were at the Indian feast, and returned with 16 Beaver as their share of the distributed property – I believe this is a Common practice with the principal Indians, and the real motive not so much from a professed Spirit of liberality & greatness as from avarice & gain, for tis well understood that every one who receives, acknowledges a debt of at least 20 per Cent above the actual value of what he got! Five or Six new & old of our Blkts. – about as many of their own manufacture – 15 or 20 white Sheep Skins – 5 or 6 fathoms of the fine Beaver Bead – a number of Cassors or Kettles – Leather Shirts – and the Beaver to our Gentlemen were the principal presents – I understand there was but little to eat.

McDonald's brief account makes it very clear that this affair was either a potlatch or an event held to prepare for one. If early nineteenth-century potlatches were held in summer, as later ones were, then this event would have to be preparatory to a potlatch. The reference to repayment also suggests this. The "white Sheep Skins" were probably mountain-goat skins, valued for the hair's use in blankets.

This account contains what may be the earliest statement from anywhere on the Northwest Coast that property was given with the expectation that it would be returned with interest. The question of whether this was expected of guests at a potlatch has been debated in the anthropological literature. Franz Boas asserted that guests who received property at a potlatch were expected to return double the value at their own potlatches. However, several other ethnographers reported that return with interest was expected only of property given to relatives or affines by someone preparing for a potlatch. This was a means of accumulating property for it; at the potlatch itself the host gave to a much wider group and with no expectation of increased return. His reward was the reputation for wealth and liberality that he gained. But in the long run this in turn could mean continued control over his family property, good relations with his neighbours, and good marriages for his children.[24]

There is one other account of what must have been a potlatch. On 18 August 1829, Shashia was camped across the river from the fort, reportedly annoyed with the Nanaimo for their having been more liberal in selling salmon to the fort. McDonald reports that he was seen raising four of five fathoms of red stroud on a pole. Soon after a party of Nanaimos arrived, there were short speeches on both sides, and then Shashia took down the cloth, cut it and a number of blankets into small pieces, and gave one to each of his guests, who then went home. The company traders did not know what this meant, reporting that some said "the Chief gave a thrashing to his litle Girl and that he makes this Sacrifice to prove his parental affection," while others said he was paying the Nanaimos for the furs he got from them. McDonald thought the latter more likely. But it may have been both. If Shashia had publicly struck his daughter, a small potlatch would have "wiped away" the shame. And by inviting the Nanaimos as witnesses, he would have been putting them under some obligation to acknowledge his status as a "chief," that is, a wealthy and liberal person.

"THESE MERCENARY RASCALS": WEALTH AND COMMERCE

Ethnographers have stressed the importance of wealth in Native society. "Chiefs" were rich men. People without wealth were socially worthless. Wealth consisted of goods, such as canoes, containers, weapons, blankets, and hide shirts, and slaves. Blankets, which were made of dog wool, mountain goat wool, and bird down, were especially important as a measure of value. They could be taken apart, the wool used in strips and later rewoven. (Dentalia, the shells used on the Columbia and elsewhere as a kind of currency, were evidently less important in this region; they are not mentioned in the journals.)

The journals suggest that wealth was as important in the early nineteenth century as it was later. The number of shorn dogs seen shows that Native blankets must have been made in quantities, and the demand for Hudson's Bay Company blankets seems to have been great. Given a choice of trade goods in exchange for their furs, the Natives often insisted on blankets. They revealed their identification of blankets as wealth and power when they reported that a company ship was wrecked south of Cape Flattery and that "the vast number of *Blankets* picked up by the Indians has made them independent for ever"(26 June 1829).

The Native traders seem also to have been as deeply concerned with profit as the company. They haggled over what they should receive for their furs, especially when there was the prospect of trading with American ships. On one occasion (6 May 1828), a canoe came upriver advising people to keep their furs for an American ship that was coming. They tried to get the most for their salmon and sturgeon and often succeeded in keeping the price up, prompting the journal, with what seems pot-and-kettle irony, to call them "mercenary rascals" (11 May 1828).

Moreover, they seem generally to have been no less mercenary in dealing with other Natives. The more important Native traders were the "chiefs," who acted as intermediaries, bringing the furs of other tribes to the fort and using stratagem or force to control the trade of other tribes. When the Chilliwack came to the fort to trade (7 April 1829), the Kwantlen chief Nicameus asked the fort to sell its blankets at a higher price, evidently to discourage the Chilliwacks from dealing directly and causing him to lose the profit he had made as an intermediary. Native traders tried to conceal their profits from their Native clients. The entry for 31 July 1829 reports that a Kwantlen came with his client, left the man outside the fort while selling his furs, and entrusted a woman inside with the difference between what he got and what he came out with for the client so that the man would not know that he had profited by the sale. The next day the Cowichan Shashia acted similarly, and the journals add that when they could be, they were all "Consummate rogues." When the company trader remonstrated with Shashia, he pointed out that the company was no loser, because as long as he got his profit he would "See that the Furs are not thrown into another Channel." More serious measures may have

exclusive. The question of how important trade was to the summer gathering at "the fisheries" will have to be answered by other sources.

CONFLICT

The Fort Langley Journals contain several accounts of conflict, and these are especially valuable. Traditions of quarrels, fights, and battles recorded by ethnographers long after the events occurred are especially hard to evaluate. Filtered through family pride and changing values for several generations, they are not likely to be true and unbiased accounts. The journal accounts too are no doubt biased; the fur traders had their preconceptions about the Natives, and their ability to communicate was limited. But they were there and able to observe some of the events and to check what they were told against other reports and observations. Their accounts confirm what ethnography indicates, that disputes might be settled by speeches, a show of solidarity by kin or tribesmen, and the payment of wealth, but were not always settled. The fear of conflict was pervasive and well justified. A quarrel between individuals easily led to a quarrel between groups, and any loss of life was likely to be followed by retaliation, which could soon take the form of a large war party bent on ravaging whole villages. Moreover, a war party could easily be deflected from its original objective to any handy target. Smaller, weaker groups of people had good reason to fear attacks by larger, stronger ones.

Control of Conflict

Not every dispute led to physical violence; it would have been in the interests of most people to contain any potential fight. One instance of a quarrel that did not escalate began at the fort when a Musqueam girl and a Kwantlen woman got into a quarrel "about their virtue" (18 May 1828). The quarrel spread to the other women and then the men, Musqueams versus Kwantlens. After both sides made speeches, the Musqueams went to their camp for their knives. The five Kwantlen men who were there stood fast but sent for reinforcements. Soon they were facing about fifty armed Musqueams, who took turns haranguing them with "all the wild gestures and grimaces imaginable," to which they answered in kind. After a half hour of this, with the Kwantlen reinforcements due to arrive, the Musqueams withdrew, leaving the field to the Kwantlen. They later told McMillan that if they had fought, they would have seized their enemies by the hair and used their knives on them. But since they did not go for their bows and arrows and guns, it seems likely that they had not intended to go beyond a show of defiance. The close relationship between the Musqueam and Kwantlen, near neighbours and very similar in speech, may have made them reluctant to fight over what they may have seen as a trivial issue. Confrontations with "wild grimaces and gestures" have not been reported ethnographically for this region, but they are well known from South America, Oceania, and elsewhere.

Murder and Vengeance

Closeness, however, did not prevent lethal conflict. In another case (see 28 November 1829) involving the Musqueam and the Kwantlen, one killing led to another, with the conflict ending when it evened out. In June 1829 a young Kwantlen who had been captured by the Lekwiltok during a raid in March managed to escape and reach Cowichan country. There the Cowichan chief Shashia saw him "as a fair prize" and turned him over to the Saanich chief Chaheinook, who allowed the boy to return home, saying that he would later claim the boy's sister in his place. In November, Shashia and Chaheinook had arrived at the upper Kwantlen village to claim the girl from her father. The father, who was a Musqueam married to a Kwantlen, did not want his son to return to slavery nor did he want to give up his young daughter, and so he offered them an older, married daughter and took them to her place in the middle of the night. However, the older daughter's husband managed to stab the father to death before he was himself killed and his pregnant wife "carried off in triumph."

As expected, the trouble did not end there. In January 1830, two Kwantlens came down to the Musqueam camp opposite the fort, and one was killed, with arrows and knives, in revenge for the killing of the Musqueam by his son-in-law in the Kwantlen village. The next day about sixty Kwantlens in twelve canoes with ten or twelve guns came to the fort asking for ammunition and for one of the officers to go with them to the Musqueam village. These requests were denied. The Kwantlens crossed and made a camp across Kanaka Creek from the Musqueams, where they could negotiate with them. The stand-off continued another day with occasional shots fired, and the Kwantlens reported that they had killed two Musqueams. It turned out that two "were actually killed & one of them very luckily the identical man that took the life of the other on Sunday – here ends the business for the present" (13 January 1830).

It appears that peace prevailed. On an evening in April eight canoes with about fifty "Fall Indians" (presumably Tait from around Yale) arrived at the Musqueam camp "by Special invitation to eat Shell fish etc. etc." The next day (9 April 1830) it was reported that the "Banquet" had commenced and the Kwantlens were invited to join it.

Liability and Vengeance

Outright murder was not the only cause for vengeance. In the Native view, a person in some way liable for the loss of a relative was a proper target. The murder of the Lekwiltok wife of a Kwantlen known as "the doctor" seems to have been an instance of this. The motive was said to have been revenge for her not having rescued a relative from slavery. Another instance of blame being laid where there was no physical violence is implied by a report (26 April 1828) that the Cowichans were preparing to attack the Clallams because they believed that Shashia's father-in-law was killed by the Clallams "from the Effects of bad medicine." The term "medicine" is probably used in the sense of shamanistic or magical power; in a later entry a winter dance is identified as a "winter medicine party."

In some cases, the desire for vengeance could have been accompanied by other motives. The murder of Scanewah was one in which the victim may have been blamed for an accidental death, may have behaved badly, and must certainly have tempted his killer or killers with his wealth. The whole story illustrates the region-wide network of interrelations. Scanewah, the Cowlitz trader, was staying near the fort. In February 1828 an Okanagan man who had been staying with him went to buy a slave from the Katzie, fell through the ice on the river, and drowned. The Kwantlen chief Whitlekenum came down and gave two beaver skins to the widow, a Duwamish woman, who left for her home by an inland route through Nooksack, Skagit, and Snohomish country. Whitlekenum's gift to her may have been compensation for any liability the Kwantlen may have been thought to have had in her husband's drowning. But Scanewah was evidently not as generous as he should have been. He soon suffered harassment and decided to return to Cowlitz country. In preparation he bought a Lekwiltok slave from Thompson Natives who were staying with the Katzie; the slave ran away with his gun, but he was returned by Lapitchin, the Thompson trapper and trader, without the gun. Fearing for his life, Scanewah left the night of 11 May.

On 16 May it was rumoured that Scanewah, his wife and child, and a slave had been killed by Cowichans at Point Roberts, only the Lekwiltok slave escaping. McMillan noted that Scanewah had "a great deal of property" that would have been tempting – "32 Blankets, a Gun, Kettles, Traps, Axes, Capots, Shirts etc. etc." but added that the thirst for blood alone would have been enough. Later, however, Cowichans reported that Scanewah had been killed by relatives of the drowned man, whose widow had returned home and, McMillan suspected, had complained about Scanewah's treatment of her husband and herself, "which I believe very far from being liberal." Scanewah's murder was later confirmed by a Skagit. The following spring a Skykomish who came to the fort was rumoured to be the killer, but there was no proof, and he was allowed to go his way. The Skykomish are an inland tribe who may have had contacts across the Cascades with the Okanagan, and so the suspicion may have had some foundation.

"War"

The existence of a Native term for "make war" (x̌íləx̌), as distinct from "fight" (k̓ʷíntəl, perhaps literally "grapple with one another"), indicates that war was seen as a distinct state. A Native term for "warrior" (stámə̌š) designates a distinct status. The warrior was a man who had acquired a vision power of a special class that made him dangerous, even to his own people. His vision power might command him to test his strength by leading a raid on some village for which any pretext for attack might be found. He was believed to be inspired by his vision power to acts of berserker-rage, killing at random, cutting off his victims' heads, and drinking their blood (Barnett 1955:268). The writers of the journals recorded a number of instances of "war" (as defined by the Natives). But they seem to have been unaware of the special status of the warrior. The Cowichan Shashia led one expedition, but he does not seem to have had the character of the "warrior." Staying near the fort in fear of the Lillooet, as he did in the summer of 1828, was not in that character. On the other hand, the war leader Lammus in the one incident reported (see below) seems to fit the image.

Incidents in the journals indicate that bows and arrows were still used in fighting, but muskets were also commonly used and evidently valued. The journals do not mention the "coats of mail" seen by Fraser in 1808. This hide armour must have been capable of stopping an arrow, but by 1827 muskets may have already made it obsolete (cf. Gunther 1972:14 for the outer coast).

Both the journals and the ethnographic record indicate that a common justification for organizing a raid was revenge for a real or supposed injury. Another motive reported ethnographically was grief over the natural death of a relative and the wish that someone else should suffer (Barnett 1955:268). The journal gives no indication of this motive, but it may have been present in some of the members of the "war parties" mentioned, and this motive, together with the frenzy of the warrior, may account for the apparent redirection of aggression seen in the account that follows. Still other motives must have been material gain in the form of captives (who could be ransomed or sold as slaves) and plunder (goods and food) and more lasting political gain through the intimidation of possible rivals. But whatever the initial excuse for conflict, once it was under way it could be opportunistically redirected. Aggression seems to have been pursued when victory was assured but easily abandoned when it was not.

A series of events reported between August 1827 and April 1828 shows aggression initially directed toward the Chilliwacks redirected toward other upriver tribes. On 22 August 1827 Barnston wrote that eight Musqueams had been "cut off" by the Chilliwacks. He did not say what the Musqueams were doing up in Chilliwack country; they may have been simply passing by on their way up to the fisheries. On 24 September a party of Cowichans and Nanaimos passed, saying that they were on their way upriver to attack the Chilliwacks to avenge "the murders" of the Musqueams. The Cowichan chief Shashia, the Clallam chief Stackeinum, and others harangued the party (with what advice is not clear), and it disbanded. But on 11 October a party of eighty-six Cowichans and Musqueams passed on their way up to "make war" on the Chilliwacks, Barnston adding "tho' certainly their marauding excursions scarcely deserve to be so entitled." Two days later the party returned "without having performed any feat worthy of notice." However, one man had been wounded by an arrow. On 18 October another party of about seventy Cowichans and Musqueams went upriver to attack the Chilliwack. This time they were led by Shashia. The next day the Cowichans came back down. (Their Musqueam allies are not mentioned.) They had killed one man and one woman and captured several women and children to be made slaves. The head of one of their victims hung from the bow of their largest canoe, and most of the canoes were loaded with loot – "dried and fresh provisions, Baskets, Mats, and other Furniture, the Spoils of the Camp of the unhappy creatures that they surprized." These unfortunate people were not the Chilliwack but the Sumas, described as "a small and weak tribe ... not far distant." On 20 October a Sumas man came downriver intending to ransom one of the women taken by the Cowichans. Two days later he returned with his wife "and other females" (including children?), having paid everything he had taken with him.

There is no indication that the conflict was pursued during the winter. In early March 1828 there was a report that the Kwantlen had gone to attack the Chilliwack, but it was not confirmed. Then on 13 March a Cowichan war party passed on its way to "kill" the Chilliwacks. It was headed by Lammus (not mentioned elsewhere) and consisted of about 150 men in ten canoes and "painted to their very ears." The party soon met the Musqueam chief Shientin travelling with his wife and two good-looking daughters. Lammus took the elder daughter, threatening that if Shientin objected he would kill him and make slaves of his family. (It seems that the earlier role of the Musqueams as reason for vengeance and as allies was irrelevant; Lammus was simply using his superior force to seize a woman.) Again it was not the Chilliwacks who suffered. On 19 March some Katzies reported that the Cowichan war party had returned downriver after having killed ten Pilalts and taken a number of women and children as slaves. McMillan commented on how fear of the Vancouver Island tribes kept the local people in "Such Continual alarm" that they could barely look after their families.

On 22 March four Pilalt men came by on their way to Vancouver Island with property to pay as ransom for the women and children the Cowichans had taken, but the next day they came back fearing that the Lekwiltok might be about. McMillan added that the poor women would have to serve the Cowichans "a longer time than they expected," which suggests that paying ransom was the usual practice. A second Pilalt expedition passed on 30 March and the "Penault ambassadors" returned on 4 April 1828, having ransomed three of the women at a high price.

In 6 July McMillan wrote that the Cowichans had just come over from Vancouver Island for the summer fishing and had reportedly killed two Kwantlens and five Katzies, adding, "The poor tribes of this quarter Cannot attend to any thing like hunting while their Powerful Neighbours from Van. Island are allowed to Murder and Pillage them at pleasure."

It appears that if the aggressor was strong enough, the victims might not openly retaliate (as in the case of Lammus's seizing Shientin's daughter). However, they may have had another defence in the spreading of rumours. On 6 August 1828 McMillan wrote that "the Indians" (presumably the Kwantlens) were saying that the Thompson were coming down to make war on the Cowichans. There is no indication that this ever happened, but the threat may have kept the Cowichans in check. Later in July and in early August the Cowichan "chief" Shashia, who was camped near the fort, became so worried that the Lillooet were coming to kill him that at night he sent his women and children to sleep in the woods or beside the fort. Again there is no indication that the Lillooet ever came after him.

The attacks by the Cowichans on mainland people, while sometimes giving them slaves and loot, may have also been intended to intimidate the tribes into whose territory they were coming to fish. To some extent it seems to have worked. On 1 August 1829, after a group of Cowichans came to camp near the fort, the journals reported that the Kwantlens, "having no great love for the Cawaitchins, or a desire of being at all in their neighbourhood," moved on upstream.

A show of force could be enough to make a threatening war party back off. Before dawn on 17 May 1830 two Squamish war canoes went upriver, making the people near the fort uneasy, but the next day the war canoes returned without having done any harm. It was reported that they had been confronted by two Kwantlen canoes, each side fired a few shots "by way of bravado," and that was all. Farther upriver the Sumas had stood their ground, and the Squamish retreated.

Conflict with the Lekwiltok

Conflict with the Lekwiltok may seem to be a special case. Some of the literature on this region gives the impression that the Lekwiltok (or all tribes to the north) and the Coast Salish had a kind of predator–prey relationship, the Northerners always seeing the Salish as no more than potential slaves, and the Salish always fleeing in abject terror. During the early nineteenth century there was indeed a good deal of slave-raiding on the part of the Lekwiltok and a good deal of hasty flight on the part of the Salish, and there were a good many Salish who ended their days in slavery on the northern coast. In several entries the journals seem to support the image of the Salish as helpless victims, as when McDonald wrote (10 March 1829) that the dread of the Lekwiltok felt by the local people was "incredible" and that "At the very risk of Starving they will not appear in the main river in any Shape when the Yewkaltas are reported to be near, & that is not Seldom."

However, the Fort Langley Journals also show that the image of eternal enmity between predator and prey is false. The relationship between the Lekwiltok and the Salish may have differed from the relationship between any two Salish tribes in degree, but it did not differ in kind. It involved peaceful as well as hostile encounters, at least one marriage, negotiations for ransom, trade, and possibly alliances.

Lekwiltok raiders had been making forays into the southern end of the Strait of Georgia, Juan de Fuca Strait, and Puget Sound when the

Hudson's Bay Company arrived. They may have been coming for some time, but there is nothing to indicate when this began. The marriage of the Lekwiltok woman and the Kwantlen doctor must have been arranged some time before the company arrived, and this alliance implies a period of peace between their two tribes. The use of northern canoes by the Coast Salish implies trade. But in the summer of 1827 Lekwiltok raiders had evidently captured some women from the Skagit, Clallam, Kwantlen, and perhaps other tribes. While the fort was still under construction, a party of Skagit let it be known that they intended to ransom the women they had lost. On 7 September Barnston reported that the Lekwiltok wife of the doctor had arranged the ransom of Clallam and Skagit women, including the Clallam sister-in-law of the Cowlitz trader Skanawa. The following day Barnston learned that this woman had been killed by a Kwantlen, "because the poor creature had not been equally successful in recovering some women of his own tribe, which arose probably from the ransom offered not being sufficiently valuable." In October "two Indians from below" came to tell the Kwantlen that the Lekwiltok intended to punish them for the murder of the Lekwiltok woman. During early 1828 there were rumours that the Lekwiltok were on their way to attack the fort, but they did not appear.

There was another instance of a ransoming expedition in the summer of 1828. In June, Lekwiltok raiders attacked the Musqueams, capturing some women and children, and in August it was learned that the Musqueam chief Shientin had returned from Lekwiltok country, where he had gone to try to recover his wife and daughter, who had been among the women and children taken. He found that they had already been sold to tribes farther north.

There may have been an alliance between the Cowichan chief Shashia and these supposed enemies. On 26 April 1828 it was reported that the Cowichans were preparing to go to war with the Clallams because of the death of Shashia's father-in-law. Then, on 4 May, two Nanaimos passed and said that Shashia had enlisted the Lekwiltok and Kwakiutl to help him fight the Clallam. There is nothing later to indicate that this happened, but there are later reports of Shashia's dealings with the Lekwiltok.

There were reports of Salish retaliation. On 23 August 1828 it was said that Cowichans in a hundred canoes were going north to attack the Lekwiltok. If true, Shashia was not among them; at this time he was camped near the fort, worried about the Lillooet coming after him. On 11 September the Snohomish chief Waskelatchee reported that Skagits and Clallams in thirty-seven large war canoes had gone to make war on the Lekwiltok. But the journals make no further reference to these expeditions.

From the autumn of 1828 into the spring of 1829 there were a number of false alarms among the Native people who had camped near the fort for fear of the Lekwiltok. McDonald wrote (13 March 1829), "It is impossible to describe their Continual alarm at the very name of this formidable foe." But three months earlier Shashia had announced (1 January 1829) that he was leaving to go visit the Lekwiltok "and Tribes still further to the Northward along the main shore," presumably the Kwakiutl proper on Queen Charlotte Strait.

On 21 March 1829 there was the famous encounter at the mouth of the Fraser, when a dozen company men drove off a force of Lekwiltok estimated at 240. But Lekwiltok raiders returned in greater numbers in mid-April. They caught the Kwantlen doctor at the mouth of the Fraser and killed him, whether in revenge for his wife's death or simply as a random act is not known. They also killed two Cowichans and then went south and attacked the Skagits, capturing a number of women and children. This was learned by a party of Nanaimos, identified as "a Kind of neutral party," who met the Lekwiltok in the Strait of Georgia and talked with the Skagit women. After this encounter the Lekwiltok again passed the mouth of the Fraser and killed more Cowichans. It was also on this raid that they captured the Kwantlen youth who escaped only to be seized by Shashia.

Reportedly the Cowichans were now determined to resist or retaliate, and Shashia came to the fort seeking to buy a gun for himself and three hundred rounds of ammunition for his followers. McDonald weighed the question of supplying ammunition to the Natives and decided to let Shashia have what he wanted, even though he was suspected of having participated in the attack on the company party. This suspicion was evidently cultivated by the Kwantlen, and McDonald dismissed it as motivated by a family feud. However, McDonald later wrote (26 July 1829) that it had turned out that, instead of attacking the Lekwiltok, Shashia had taken the ammunition to them.

If Shashia had intended to placate the Lekwiltok, it did not work. They were back again in March 1830. But the success of the company men in the encounter at the mouth of the river may have encouraged the local people to stand fast. There was a report, which proved false, of a Lekwiltok war party coming, and the Kwantlens "in an instant were under arms – drew themselves up in Battle array – near our Bastion" (9 March 1830). Then, in early July, a Lekwiltok party made an attack at Point Roberts, killing four Cowichans and one Nanaimo. This event, McDonald noted, "disposed all the Tribes in this quarter to a furious war upon the Common enemy, but Soon ended like all their former determinations of the kind" (19-21 July 1830), suggesting that he did not believe the earlier reports of Salish expeditions to the north. However, the letter book reports that on 21 September 1830 a large joint expedition of "upward of 500 men" did go north to attack the Lekwiltok. In October, they straggled back, reporting that nearly a hundred men had been stuck on an island. A few of these later made it home, but many were killed or starved to death. McDonald sought to ingratiate the company with the Coast Salish by giving ammunition and lending guns for another attack, but those who took them lacked the confidence to use them and returned them.

Coast Salish warriors of different tribes did finally cooperate in at least one famous victory over the Lekwiltok, the "Battle of Maple Bay," but probably only much later. Meanwhile, a few years after the Fort Langley Journals were written, there was another attempt at alliance. In 1838 James

Douglas reported that the "'Coquilts' of Queen Charlottes sound," that is, the Kwakiutl proper, had been cutting in on Fort Langley's trade, diverting furs to Fort Simpson, which paid twice as much. To this end the Kwakiutl had "succeeded in opening a friendly intercourse with the 'Musquiams' inhabiting the country at the mouth of Frasers river" (Rich 1941:281). This relationship probably did not last long; no Musqueam tradition of it has been recorded.

SLAVERY AND RANSOM

Captives taken in raids, if not soon ransomed by relatives, became slaves. Once enslaved, they might be quickly sold to distant tribes from which getting home free was probably very difficult, especially for the young. The Lekwiltok sold by the Thompson to Scanewah was evidently a grown man, said to have been "taken when young" and so presumably raised in slavery. He left Scanewah once, but seems to have gone back to the Thompson (who returned him to Scanewah) rather than heading north for Lekwiltok country. Escaping one's captors did not ensure freedom. An escaped slave might be seen by people other than his own as property to be had for the taking, as was the Kwantlen boy whom Shashia and Chaheinook traded for his sister.

Interpretations of Northwest Coast slavery offered by anthropologists have varied, especially with regard to the economic value of slaves. One view, once popular, was that slaves cost more to keep than their labour was worth and were kept simply for the prestige that came from owning them. Another view is that they had great value in a Native economy that rewarded those who could control a large labour force, especially during the great runs of salmon. Still another suggests that their principal importance was as a commodity (Donald 1984; Mitchell 1984; Mitchell and Donald 1985).

The Fort Langley Journals give very little information on the daily lives of slaves that would relate directly to the question of the value of their labour. Scanewah took slaves along on his trips, and their labour may have been important, but he may have had no alternative than to keep them with him. There are instances of the purchase of small children, whose value as workers would not have been realized for some years. However, the journals do give examples of negotiations relating to captives and slaves that indicate their commercial value. Scanewah reportedly paid a ransom of "seven or eight Blankets, and some trifling articles of trade" for his Clallam sister-in-law, and he paid a gun, a blanket, and two yards of collar wire for the Lekwiltok slave. The Kwantlen doctor bought a young child slave from Shashia for ten beaver skins (15 September 1828). McDonald considered ten beaver skins a proper price for a little girl slave who escaped with a party of Pilalts. A Cowichan sold a four- or five-year-old girl to a Kwantlen for four skins (12 April 1830). The family of the Kwantlen chief Nicameus bought a female slave from a Saanich; when she disappeared, they blamed the seller, and when he left the fort, they seized the eight beaver skins he had as compensation (12 June 1829). Slaves were also used as wealth; they are mentioned as among the items given at the marriage of Neetlum's son and Shashia's daughter (10 September 1830).

There were evidently principles involved in the acquisition of slaves. In January 1829 a little girl slave belonging to Annance's wife escaped with some visiting Pilalts. A party of company men immediately went after them and brought them back. An old woman who seemed to be her mother pleaded for the girl. McDonald told her that the girl was not his, but he would buy her freedom for ten beaver skins and meanwhile see that she was well cared for. The child had been sold by the Kwantlen chief Nicameus "without," McDonald believed, "Coming by her himself in the most lawful manner"(9 January 1829). The next day the girl disappeared again, and this time she was not recaptured. Later McDonald suspected that Nicameus had "winked at the owners carrying her away – in Consequence of his not Coming too honestly by her himself" (30 March 1829). After being confronted on the matter, Nicameus brought in beaver skins to compensate for the loss of the girl.

Rules are also implied by the practice of ransoming captives, which was a possibility not confined to Coast Salish tribes, as we have two instances involving the Lekwiltok – the successful trip by the Lekwiltok wife of the Kwantlen doctor and the unsuccessful trip by the Musqueam chief Shientin. When the Sumas man went over to Cowichan country with a canoe-load of property to ransom Sumas women just captured in a bloody attack, why did the Cowichans not simply kill him and appropriate his property? Or when the Musqueam chief Shientin went all the way to Lekwiltok country to ransom his wife and daughter, how could he have assumed he could deal with them, and why did they allow him to return? There must have been rules, acknowledged by both the Coast Salish and the Lekwiltok. Perhaps one could *legitimately* capture or plunder only to compensate for a loss, as would have supposedly been the case with a raiding party out to revenge some real or fancied wrong. Perhaps then if the bearers of ransom appeared openly, in broad daylight, public opinion in the village of the captors ensured their safety.

While wealth implied power, safety did not lie in simply travelling with wealth; that did not help Scanewah. And safety did not come from being in the aggressor's home territory; that did not help in the case of the Saanich man who had sold the slave to the Kwantlen family. But in both the killing of Skanawa and the seizure of the Saanich man's skins, the perpetrators may have sought compensation. Perhaps you were safe only if you did not owe anyone anything.

COMPANY INFLUENCE ON THE NATIVES

Fort Langley influenced the Native people in some ways that are pretty clear and no doubt in many others that we can only speculate about. Little that the company brought was entirely new. The changes were largely quantitative and significant mainly in what they foreshadowed of qualitative changes that lay ahead.

Trade itself was not new. Archeological evidence (Carlson 1994) indicates it had been going on for millennia. There is also some linguistic evidence for its antiquity.[26] But did the hard bargaining seen in the journals date back to pre-contact times, or was it acquired through contact with pre-company traders or knowledge of what had been going on for several decades on the outer coast? The pursuit of wealth is reported ethnographically for the Native peoples from southeastern Alaska to northwestern California, and it is almost certainly old in this region. The speed with which the Natives showed themselves to be "mercenary rascals" suggests an old tradition of bargaining. But in earlier times, hard bargaining may have been the practice in dealing with strangers. The company traders were strangers from outside Native society, and even after they established marital ties with Native women, they continued to conduct their business in a businesslike way, preparing the Natives for the impersonal market economy to come.

European goods were not new but were now available in much greater quantities and varieties than had been known before. In earlier entries in the journals the Natives were accepting beads, rings, and "trifling articles of trade." But soon they were getting axes, knives, kettles, brass wire, and blankets, and later on guns and ammunition, steel traps, cloth, and more and more blankets, at prices increasingly in their favour. Trade blankets were being used by Native traders to exchange for skins from other tribes (14 November 1828) and probably beginning to replace Native blankets as a measure of value and medium of exchange.[27] The use of company blankets in Native transactions was in the interest of the company, and the company no doubt promoted this; it was reported that a representative of the company had "Concluded a peace with the Clalams & Sealed it with 20 Blkts" (29 May 1830).

The influx of European goods must have influenced the production of Native goods. Metal tools must have quickly replaced stone tools except for the hand-held stone maul used by woodworkers. Stoneworking became obsolete (and soon forgotten), while woodworking may have flourished with the new tools. Iron kettles supplemented but did not wholly replace watertight boxes and baskets, nor did trade blankets wholly replace the Native blankets. But, in time, production of these things declined.

In return for their goods, the company's highest priority was to receive furs. This demand was probably new here on the inner coast, and it may have diverted the efforts of some of the Natives from other activities to trapping (Collins 1950:335) and to expanding trade with other tribes. Still, the journals complain that the Natives did not exert themselves enough in killing beaver. On the other hand, they do not complain when the Natives were working hard catching fish, which the company also needed.

As the activities of the fort expanded, the company needed labour – men and women to work for wages. Working for some reward was not new in the Native economy. Persons recruited for co-operative fishing, hunting, and perhaps other activities received shares for their efforts. A person wanting to build a new house paid those who worked on it. A shaman was paid for his services. But the employer and the employees were also participants in a social network. The only other relationship in which one worked for another was that of master and slave. At Fort Langley the relationship was new in that the men and women who worked for the company were neither slaves nor, initially, participants in the same social network.

The Natives were paid with some of the usual trade goods and also with potatoes. These soon became an important addition to the Native diet, which was rich in protein and fat but may have been poor in carbohydrates. The company's practice of paying in potatoes and allowing people to collect any left in the fields after the harvest no doubt promoted an appetite for them, and hiring Native women to help raise them ensured that they knew how to do so. When the Snohomish chief Waskelatchee and his party left "well loaded with Potatoes" (29 March 1829), they were probably only one of many. But here again cultivating potatoes was an easy step from traditional practices relating to camas and other native food plants, and in a short time the practice spread throughout the region (Suttles 1987:137-51).

With the new source of wealth and changing emphasis in economic relations, changes must have occurred in Native society. Some Native leaders were better suited or better placed to take advantage of the new trade than were others. The company itself, in its effort to encourage trapping and trading, must have raised the position of some of the Native leaders by giving them favours, such as letting them camp at the fort, giving them traps, extending credit, and marrying their sisters and daughters. Company officers may also have lowered the position of some, including some of the same persons, by treating them badly in public. But it is unlikely that pre-contact society was rigid, and these shifts in status may not have been radically different from rises and falls in fortunes that would have occurred in earlier times as the result of natural disasters and wars.[28]

There may have been some increase in conflict as a result of the presence of the fort. Attacks on upriver tribes may have been motivated by a desire to monopolize trade, as the reported attack on the Nooksack was said to have been. But the new trade probably also promoted wider peaceful relations. We do not know whether the Lekwiltok were increasing their raiding at this time, but if so, it was more likely because of an increased need for a commodity – slaves – to trade with peoples to the north than because of Fort Langley.

The new trade may have had some effect on the status of women. Earlier, women skilled at weaving may have produced the bulk of the wealth used in ceremonial exchanges. The influx of trade blankets may have devalued women as producers of wealth. On the other hand, those few women who found employment at the fort or who entered into relationships with the company men may have risen in importance in Native society.

The journals tell us little about the health of the Native peoples, beyond mentioning hunger. There are no references to diseases. While some men came with a venereal disease, an entry (16 June 1829) suggests it had not yet spread. Alcohol was not yet a problem. Rum may have been brought by some of the trading ships, as told in a Lummi tradition (Suttles 1954:45), but Fort Langley was not a source. Tobacco was evidently not used when the company arrived. Native traditions indicate this, and in Annance's account of the expedition of 1824-5 he reports: "We presented a pipe to them to smoke; but they did not know how to make use of it." References to smoking in the journals refer to visitors from the south or upriver.

The company people did not attempt to change Native behaviour or values except as these directly affected business. They wished the Natives would spend less time fighting and kill more beaver, but they could only remain neutral in Native disputes and reward those who brought in skins. They did not tolerate theft or any threat or show of disrespect to themselves, and only in such cases took direct action.

They did not oppose slavery. The company evidently did not ordinarily engage in the slave trade, as some American traders certainly did, and its officers and men did not themselves ordinarily hold slaves, but it is clear from the journals that its officers tolerated and even supported slaveholding by the men's wives, some of whom may have originally been slaves themselves and seem to have been regarded as the property of their husbands. They were not about to preach abolitionism.

Nor did they practise or teach conservation. This seems clear from McDonald's comment on a female beaver his men had taken. Her mate had been taken earlier and she was evidently the last of her colony, but she had been industriously building a nest for the young she was about to bear. "Its Case would incite the Sympathy of *the man of feeling*," he wrote, "but what Can we do – a doctrine of this nature would ill accord with Short returns"(16 April 1830). Company policy was evidently one of take all while you can, while Native trappers, more recently and probably earlier, understood the long-range value of leaving a part of a colony to reproduce.[29]

Like Native society, the Hudson's Bay Company was hierarchical. But the company officers' methods of maintaining status in relation to both their own men and the Natives may have come as a surprise to the Natives – immediate and direct use of physical force, punching with fists and kicking with booted feet. When Scanewah objected to this abuse of a Kwantlen, McMillan "was under the necessity to give him two or three knock down blows which Soon brought the great man to his Senses" (4 April 1828). In this behaviour, as in its famous defeat of the Lekwiltok, the company demonstrated its superiority, again foreshadowing the domination that was to come.

The question, first raised by Joyce Wike (1958) and later taken up by Wilson Duff (1964) and Robin Fisher (1977), of whether the Natives were the victims of exploitation by the fur traders, as some historians have supposed, or controlled the trade and enjoyed a cultural enrichment, as some anthropologists have asserted, probably cannot be given a simple answer by the Fort Langley Journals or any other single document. But the journals do suggest that, during these first three years of permanent European presence, while some of the Natives were for a time in control of the trade and making a profit from it, some, like Scanewah, must surely have been learning that dealing with the Europeans meant risking one's dignity and autonomy.

OMISSIONS IN THE JOURNAL

There are a few surprising omissions in the Fort Langley Journals. There is no mention of gambling, yet we know from ethnographic work (Maranda 1984) that this has been important since the mid-nineteenth century as a means of publicly demonstrating vision power, acquiring wealth, and providing entertainment. The games played were changing during the late nineteenth century, but it seems unlikely that in some form they were not played earlier. Were they never played by the crowds hanging around the fort? There is also no mention of the ball game that we know of from Native traditions, but the game required a playing field, and there may have been none near the fort. We may also wonder about the absence of any reference to some of the tribes that we might expect the fort to know or know of. Were the people at the fort not aware of the Chehalis, who lived up the Harrison River, the Semiahmoo, Samish, and Songhees, who were kinsmen of the Saanich and Lummi, or the Comox, who were being driven south by the Lekwiltok?

Such omissions only raise questions. There may be others with implications I have not perceived. They certainly do not detract from the value of the journals. The data on "chiefs" and their activities support the interpretation based on ethnography. The careers of Shashia, Scanewah, and others invite further research and biographical treatment. The brief accounts of potlatch-like events and the importance of blankets extend ethnographic interpretation back in time. The accounts of conflict, even allowing for bias, challenge any tendency to idealize the old life as serene, while those of ransom negotiations challenge any tendency to view it as chaotic. The data on salmon, sturgeon, and trade invite quantitative analysis. The Fort Langley Journals should provide material for much more interpretation and for comparison with what occurred at other early posts.

APPENDICES

Appendix A:
The Clallam Massacres

When rumours of the murder of Alexander McKenzie and his four men and the capture of a Chinook woman by the Clallam in January 1828 were finally confirmed more than two months after the event, the dread some of the men had of Fort Langley seemed fully justified. The cause of this tragedy has never been satisfactorily explained. Native accounts preserved through oral tradition have been published, claiming the Clallam were seeking revenge for wrongs suffered at the hands of the traders.[1] Any unprovoked insult or abuse of the Natives would have been a serious breach of Hudson's Bay Company policy, and it seems unlikely that McKenzie would have deliberately offended them. Grievance there may have been, nevertheless. While aboard the *William and Ann*, McKenzie promised every group from Puget Sound to the mouth of the Fraser that he would return. He paid little attention to the urgent demands of the Clallam that he should not visit the Cowichan. Eventually the fort was built on the lower Fraser, contributing to the political and economic power of the Fraser River Natives and preventing the Clallam from achieving a role as intermediaries. It is possible that the Clallam considered this treachery and a betrayal of friendship.

It is also possible that the Chinook woman, held captive by the Clallam, may have played a role in the tragedy. She was the Princess of Wales, a daughter of the Chinook chief Comcomly and wife of Alexander McKenzie (Lambert 1972:19; Merk 1968:87, 104). A woman of wealth, she possessed many slaves, some of whom may have been Clallam. We can only speculate about the cause of the massacre, but we know that the consequences were serious.

McLoughlin reported to Simpson the news that Donald Manson brought when he arrived with the express from Fort Langley (McLoughlin 1829). The Clallam had murdered the men as they lay sleeping, after having left the Clallam village on their way back to Fort Vancouver. The chief (probably Auciatin), who had accompanied the party to Fort Langley, acquiesced to a plot by others after failing to dissuade them. He reassured McKenzie so that the men slept without keeping their arms about them, and he may even have been McKenzie's murderer.

McLoughlin noted that Manson had travelled safely through Puget Sound, whereas McKenzie had chosen to go by Hood's Canal because he considered his personal acquaintance with the Clallam a safeguard. McLoughlin assumed the men had been murdered for "the sake of their clothes and arms" and declared a determination to punish the perpetrators, but he was forced to wait till the brigade came down.

As the punitive expedition set off on 16 June 1828, McLoughlin reported his plans to the governor and committee of the Hudson's Bay Company (Rich 1941:57-8). Chief Trader Alexander Roderick McLeod, accompanied by three clerks – Francis Ermatinger, Thomas Dears, and James Yale – led fifty-nine men from Fort Vancouver via the Cowlitz to Puget Sound. Francis Ermatinger kept a journal of the expedition, which was copied several times and created a great deal of controversy.[2] His account reflected a savage desire to kill Natives and an enormous resentment of McLeod for his reluctance to take action, his failure to consult the clerks, and his dependence on Michel Laframboise and some of the free traders.

The party obtained canoes when it reached Puget Sound and set out to meet the *Cadboro*,[3] which had been dispatched to Admiralty Inlet. Shortly before the McLeod party met the schooner, a group of the men, passing two Clallam lodges, fired at the Native families sleeping inside and killed a number of them. Captain Aemilius Simpson, using Waskaladget [Waskelatchee] as a negotiator, had tried without success to obtain the release of the Chinook woman. The two parties converged off Cape Townsend, where the Natives, aware of these activities, had gathered in force. The Clallam moved to a village at New Dungeness and prepared for battle, and the punitive party followed. McLeod continued to negotiate, and an attempt to take hostages led to the death of a chief named "Tokin" and the capture of a wounded Clallam. Under cover of fire from the *Cadboro*, the brigade landed, burned the village, and destroyed or seized all the property as the inhabitants fled. The next morning only two children were to be found in the ruins. They were sent ashore with Waskaladget, and the woman was finally released in return for the wounded prisoner.

Satisfied with the success of the venture, McLoughlin reported to the governor and committee (Rich 1941:63-5), unaware of the gossip generated by the Ermatinger journal. Both the governor and the committee demanded further explanation and requested a copy of the written instructions McLoughlin had given McLeod. He was unable to oblige because his directions had been oral, and he was in the embarrassing position of having to defend the Clallam venture even though he had not seen Ermatinger's journal (Barker 1948:81-5). His support for McLeod was qualified, because he had been unhappy with McLeod's conduct of the Umpqua expedition. From Francis Ermatinger, McLoughlin demanded copies of the journal in order to send one to Governor Simpson and one to McLeod.[4] He forwarded the report written by Aemilius Simpson[5] and answers to questions put to Michel Laframboise (HBCA D.4/123:89-93), which contradicted Ermatinger's account. It is difficult to quarrel with McLoughlin's verdict that Ermatinger's journal did the clerks no credit, but the incident was devastating for McLeod and reflected poorly on McLoughlin.

No matter how much the committee deplored the killing of Natives, the policy in the country remained firm. The death of company people had to be avenged, and punitive action would be considered successful if no whites were killed. But it would appear that McLoughlin began to be cautious about advocating wholesale destruction. In the spring of 1832, two men were murdered by the Tillamook Natives. McLoughlin instructed Michel Laframboise to lead a trapping party of free traders from the Willamette to revenge the deaths "with the least effusion of blood." Six Natives were killed, and many captured women and children were released (Barker 1948:268-72). No gentlemen participated; the expedition was considered a success, and little more was heard about it.

Appendix B:
McMillan's Report to Governor and Council,
15 February 1828

Fort Langley 15th Feb. 1828

Gentlemen

I have the satisfaction to inform you that in pursuance of instructions given me, I have established this Post about 20 miles up from the entrance of Fraser's River, for the accomplishment of which I trust my proceedings will meet with your approbation.

My endeavors to encourage a Trade with the Natives has not been so successful as perhaps you expected or I myself would wish, but taking all circumstances into consideration, little more could be expected in so short a period our first year: the difficulties I have to struggle against requires patience and forbearance to bear up against them, and so far as regards the Country are not easily removed by any means over which I can have influence or Control. The Visit of the American to this Coast has been rather hurtful to the Trade, by giving the Indians such prices for their Furs, that I found it difficult to come to any terms with them except at the same rate those people carried on Their Trade. I at last got them to part with their Furs on the same terms as the Columbia Indians which price I intend to keep up unless we are again visited.

Our returns since last August amount to 938 Beaver and 268 Otters which valued according to the last price list sent us from the Columbia will I hope nearly clear the expenses of the year, which I am sorry to observe are very considerable, but from an examination of the accounts, the present Outfit bears a load from which succeeding years will in a great measure be free, to meet the charges of a year's wages of the people and a complete year's expenditures of provisions, of which I have omitted on the Inventory enough to answer the consumption of the coming Spring, we have only what can be reckoned a half year's trade of Furs, and the reduction of 20 pc on Inventory appears against this years Outfit – all these unfavorable circumstances will in a great measure disappear in the accounts of 28/29, and the only extra expenses will be the Men's wages who will be sent to releave [relieve] those whose Contracts expire and wish to leave the place; this is a disadvantage and will be felt while the Post exists for Servants hired at York in Summer do not arrive here before December and in February again those whose places they fill go off: we are thus called to pay a year's full wages of a number of Men additional to our complement of whose Services we have the benefit for only 2 Months of the year. Our Winter has been uncommonly severe, and the Weather is still far from being open, since early in December the River has been passable on the Ice, and is impossible for us to say how long it may last so: We have been made to expect the *Cadboro* here this month, if she arrives in the Gulph [Gulf] soon, she will in all probability have to wait some time before attempting coming to the Post. It is impossible for me at present to give any thing like a correct Idea of what may be the resources of the Post, and which in a great measure depends on how we can keep our numerous Indians in order, that there are Beaver is a thing that can hardly be doubted, but when our lazy naked Indians will be brought to hunt them time can only determine: The Rivers in Summer are swarming with Salmon and Sturgeon and when they retire to the Gulf and Islands: they are equally plentifully supplied during the Winter: their wants in other respects are so trifling that but little exertion is required of them still I would fain entertain hopes of this Post making good returns.

I intend sending of[f] the Express to the Columbia in course of a few days to be there on the 10th of March about the time it leaves Vancouver to the east side: By next opportunity I trust I shall be better able to give you a correct Idea of this quarter, meanwhile beg leave to conclude with assuring you that I am with good regard

Gentn,
Your very obedt. humb Servt.
signed *James McMillan*

Appendix C:
McDonald's Report to the Governor and Council,
25 February 1830

Feb. 25 1830.

The Langley district being perhaps less perfectly known to you than any other Section of the department, without going into an elaborate detail I hope I do not unnecessarily occupy your attention for a few moments in giving you the best Idea, in the Shape of a Report of its situation and other circumstances as I am able to put together.

Boundary – The district on its being first chalked out was to embrace that considerable tract of Country along the Coast from the South end of Puget Sound to the Northern extremity of the Gulf of Georgia including the Clalam Country and Vancouver's Island. Inland, from the first mentioned point it was to divide the trade with the Columbia by a line due East to the head of the Piscahoes river; and another supposed line from the coast to the Chilcoton Country might be said to terminate its limits in that quarter. In this case the back and Eastern boundary would be circumscribed by the lower part of New Caledonia and the Country from which Thompson's river and Okanakan derive their returns. A superficial glance over this immense space and conceiving its undisturbed possession naturally led to very high expectations in the way of returns; but the present state of the Coast Trade and the extraordinary inducement held out elsewhere to draw the Beaver out of the district, without alluding to the unproductive nature of much of the Country itself, will I presume in some degree account for the disappointment.

Navigable Rivers. – Over the space of the Country thus described it is but fair to suppose that a number of Streams exist, none of them however, with the exception of one deserves particular notice as Navigable Rivers: as far up as tide water mark, and while the Country is flat many of them do indicate tolerable size, but soon contract and are lost in the Mountains that are in no instance many leagues from the Sea Shore. This is also the case with the two streams falling into the main river that have already, I believe, gained some distinction: the rivers of Pitt and Harrison, both in the N.W. bank. The mouth of the former is about six Miles below this, the first reach in it presenting more the Character of a narrow Lake than a running Stream led no doubt to the mistaken idea of its magnitude. The other to my own certain knowledge comes from a greater distance, and is the same we visited from Thompson's river in Autumn '27 by the name of Lilliwhit. In its whole course however it is so bound up in perpetual Mountains as to afford but few advantages; we have been as far as the upper end of Harrison's Lake where the obstructed navigation begins, its junction with this river is about 40 miles up and near the same distance below Simpson's Falls.

Of Fraser's River itself I shall say nothing, that once interesting subject being now completely set at rest by the Governor's own observations. However from the part I have had myself on a former occasion to ascertain the practicability of its being navigated, to shew no inconsistency in my information then I hope I may be allowed to refer to the 2nd & 4th Paragraphs of my Report of Sept. 1826 which I presume is exactly in accordance with what Governor Simpson and myself have since experienced; but that I was egregiously misinformed by the Natives as to the real state of the River below the Falls whence I returned is very certain, although it was always my own conviction that the lowest possible state of the water was requisite to make any head way in those rivers.

Population. The Indian population in this part of the World is very great, and were it not for the continual variance among themselves, especially the Warlike Tribes, would have been extremely dangerous to a handful of whites. Beginning on the South side of De Fuca's Straits – rounding the Sound and following the East Shore to the mouth of this river; then ascending it to the point where my return made on this head from Thompson's river in 1826/27 in that direction discontinued: from Simpson's Falls keeping the N.W. Bank again to the Sea – Coasting it to about Lat. 50 and then crossing over to the Island and following that shore until we again come to the Sts. the following general Abstract is the attempt we have made to arrive at something near the number of men inhabiting that space. vizt.

Tribes		*No. Men*	*Names of Chiefs*
TLALAMS & W. OF SOUND			
1ST DIVISION			
Tlalams	[Clallams]	200	Stukeenum
Toannois	[Twana]	50	Soukeenum
Sqams	[Suquamish]	60	Awonastun
		310	
E. SHORE SOUTH OF FRASER'S RIVER			
2ND DIVISION			
Nisquallies	[Nisquallies]	40	
Pyallups	[Puyallup]	40	
Sinawamus	[Duwamish]	50	
Sinnahooms	[Snohomish]	100	Waskalatchat
Skewhams	[Skykomish]	50	are inland
Scatchads	[Skagits]	90	Neetlum

▶

Tribes		No. Men	Names of Chiefs
Soquimmy	[Snoqualmie]	50	inland
Smallons	[Smaliwhu]	40	inland
Sinnamy	[Swinomish]		
Whullummy	[Lummi]	50	
Ossaaks	[Nooksack]	40	Interior
Noheums		30	
Nahews		20	
Summcamus	[Semiahmoo]	40	
		640	

S.E. BANK OF RIVER TO FALLS & FROM THENCE BOTH SIDES TO FORKS OF THOM. R.

3RD DIVISION

Quaitlines	[Kwantlens]	60	Nicameus
Smaise	[Sumas]	40	
Tchulwhyooks	[Chilliwacks]	60	Koomilus
Pellaults	[Pilalts]	50	Tchoops
Skam & Swatch		100	Tamulston
Honellaque		90	
Kakumlutch		80	
Whuaquum		70	Kemwoon
Hutlehunssens		150	
Teitton	[Taits from Hope to Yale]	200	Sopitchin
Nakhustons		160	
Kullulluctons		170	
Asnons		130	
Harvanos		70	
Specums	[Spuzzum]	110	
Yalluachs		70	
Icquillus	[Lower Thompson]	200	
Skochuk		130	
Whee y kum		240	
		2180	

N.W. BANK FROM FALLS TO COAST

4TH DIVISION

Teets	[Taits]	40	
Tchunns	[Chehalis]	50	within
Squaltes	[Lillooet]	100	Harrison's R.
Musquams	[Musqueams]	50	Sianton
Kitchies	[Katzie]	20	
		260	

E. SHORE N. OF FRASER'S R.

5TH DIVISION

Hoomus	[Squamish]	90	
Shee-Challs	[Sechelts]	50	
Squaltes (interior)	[Lillooet]	60	mix with the above
Tloohooses	[Klahoose]	40	
Nonowuss		30	
		270	

▶

Tribes		No. Men	Names of Chiefs
VANCOUVER'S ISLAND			
6TH DIVISION			
Tchalhulls	[Comox]	50	
Nanimoos	[Nanaimos]	100	Squagis & Pinnus
Cawaitchins	[Cowichans]	200	Josua
Sanutch	[Saanich]	60	Tcheenuk
Tchanmus	[Songhees]	40	
Soaks	[Sookes]	50	
		500	

[*Note:* Modern terms for tribal names have been supplied by Wayne Suttles.]

4160 Indians tho' a great number would not be considered incredible were the number but better proportioned and it did occur to myself as rather curious that the 50 or 60 miles between the Falls and Forks of Thompson's River should accommodate nearly 1/3 of the whole: it is however the fact proved by the repeated examination of the Indians themselves and in particular the last mentioned chief on the 3rd division, who is mostly a resident here, & whose acct. of the lower Indians we *knew* to be correct. When Gov. Simpson & myself came down 2 years ago & when our speed gave them but little time to shew themselves, the number appeared uncommon: & the nature of the river & manner of living account for it. There is a perceptible difference between them and those of the Coast, & altho' they are perhaps fully as fond of property & of pilfering they have not I believe the same savage thirst for taking a man's life – The Summcamus are the only Indians that came near us from the 2nd division; but the Skins of the four last Tribes came thro' the medium of Traders. Of those of the 5th the first Tribe only, and that in the Salmon Season but are no hunters – Beyond the Nonowuss on one side the Channel & the Tchulhutts on the other are the formidable Yewkaltas that may be about 300 men, but armed and equipped in a superior style. All but the first and two last Tribes on the Island came this way in the Summer Season. The Tlalums we never see.

Establishment. List of Gentlemen and Men Attached to Fraser's River, with the Capacity and Family of each as follows, vizt.

Name	Capacity	Family		Remarks
		Wife B	G	
Arch. McDonald	Chief Trader	1	3	In charge
F.N. Annance	Clerk	1	3	attends to the Trade & Indians
James M. Yale	Clerk	1		attends to the People & Stores
1. Pierre Charles	Beaver hunter	1		re-engaged
2. Cha. Charpentier	Mid. man	1		Cook
3. Como	Mid. man & sawyer	1		re-engaged 2 yrs.

▶

Name	Capacity	Family			Remarks
		Wife	B	G	
4. Louis Delonais	Steersman	1			re-engaged reduced to £17 when present contract expires
5. Dominique Farron	mid. man	1			re-engaged 2 yrs.
6. John Kennedy	mid. man	1			re-engaged may in time assist as interpreter
7. Annawiskum McDonald	Foreman	1			re-engaged & reduced from £22 to £20 when he acts as cooper
8. Louis Ossin	mid. man	1			has a year to serve, recalled his notification
9. Etienne Oniaze	mid. man	1			re-engaged 2 yrs.
10. Peepeeoh	mid. man & sawyer	1			re-engaged 2 yrs.
11. F. Faniant dit Peitte	mechanic	1		1	unsettled with
12. Simon Plemondon	Foreman	1		1	re-engaged, is a good hand in woods & after Beaver
13. Louis Satakarata	mid. man	1	2	1	re-engaged 2 yrs.
14. Etienne Pepin	Blksmith	1			re-engaged 2 yrs. reduced from £25 to £22
15. Pierre Therrin	mid. man	1			re-engaged 2 yrs.

By this List we shew that all our Men have taken Women in this quarter – a measure once thought very impolitic nor do I affirm that in this condition they are preferable or perhaps equal to single men: yet I am happy to say that a year's experience does not forebode any frightful evil; besides, as may also be seen above, it has had the effect of reconciling them to the place and of removing the inconvenience and indeed the great uncertainty of being able to get them year after year replaced from the Columbia. Provisions for them they have none, save what they derive from the regular and ample allowance to themselves.

EXPENDITURE OF PROVISIONS

Imported	lbs. flour	lbs. rice	gal. molasses	gal. rum	bush. salt
Mess – Three gentlemen including Mr. McDonald's family	915	8	6	4	
Families of Two Clerks	60		3		72
14 Men exclusive of 1 in kitchen	155		1¾	11	
Indians (Flour damaged)	275		20	2	
	1405	8	30¾	17	72

▶

	Value		
Mess – 3 Gentlemen including McD's Family	17	16	2
Families of 2 Clerks	2	15	9
14 Men exclusive of 1 in Kitchen	18	17	10
Indians	6	11	
	£ 46		9

The Article Flour is the only item under the head of European Provisions that may seem extravagant: nor indeed would we at all have had recourse to anything like the quantity had it not been on hand since the formation of the Establishment and become perfectly unfit for future use. In time to come even with a hand mill, we shall be able to make Flour enough for ourselves: Indeed the 25 Bushels wheat raised last Season with the hoe would go a great way towards it now. As for the Country Produce, the real support of the place, I maintain, procured as it is at the very door without incurring any extra expense, that nothing can surpass it in cheapness as will be seen hereafter.

Including the salt, one year's expenditure under this head amount to	£20	17	6
European Provisions, exclusive of the ordinary mess allowance	25	3	3
	£46		9

The greater part of the Meat, Beaver and Wild Fowl we killed ourselves. Of the salt & salmon valued in this account more than ¾ of the whole is now on hand; but the place itself still requires a considerable quantity before the fresh supply arrives. When this business is regularly entered upon, of course the one Outfit must give credit to the other for such Stock, altho' the Plan no doubt will be to realize all the surplus before the close of the year.

State of Trade. The Beaver Trade at Fraser's River being of course the object to which we all look, I have the satisfaction to inform you that it continues on the increase, altho' in all probability still far short of expectations. As is elsewhere remarked the returns of Fort Langley must now be considered as the proceeds of a very small portion of the extensive District originally projected. To the Northward of Burrard's Canal the face of the Country is still more Mountainous than hereabouts and of consequence yields but few returns; the Southern Wing of the district tis true was always acknowledged rich in Beaver, but here the fatal effect of the existing opposition is particularly felt. Of the numerous and large tribes represented in another page and upon whose hunts special reliance was placed in the contemplated trade of Fraser's River, not the face of an Indian have we seen from the Southward of the Ossaak for the last 12 months, nor indeed can it be expected that we will while such liberal terms are held out to them at home. The American was in the Sound in April and on his 2nd visit in the month of July came within a very short distance of Point Roberts, there however, from the shortness of his stay and from the few furs being previously got in, I am satisfied he did not collect many Skins. This however will not always be the case; for, altho' our Indians are sufficiently fond of our Establishment and of our own indulgent treatment towards them (when they merit no worse) others with a Vessel for any time in or near the Mouth of the river, will always get Beaver from them. From our old Tariff of 4 or 4 ½ we came down to 2, 2 ½ & 3 Skins according to circumstance, but as the Trade elsewhere is carried on, to continue at even the lowest of these Prices will be impossible, to have given way to a greater stretch of liberality last year however was by no means sanctioned by our Outfit. When we made out our requisition our total ignorance of the Opposition already set up in the Country did not enable us to make that ample allowance to meet it which the nature of the Trade subsequently required, and the deficiency did not happen to be made up at the Depot hence the necessity there was of keeping up the Tariff at the Fort, and our total inability to annoy our rivals in the Sound. As it is including 50 had from the *Cadboro*, and with the help of the few Woollens I was able to take across the Cowlitz Portage from the Columbia in the fall, we have now little more than 100 Blankets to go upon, until the arrival of the Summer Outfit from England. Under all these circumstances, I trust that the result of the year's trade just closed will not appear unsatisfactory, and that with suitable means we shall be able to repeat it. Here we exhibit a comparative view of the returns of the three years, vizt.

	Beaver	Otter
Outfit 1827-28	940	250
'29	1135	300
'30	1205	378

£174. 11.7

Prime Cost is the charge thereof including all gratuities.

Improvements suggested. Fort Langley, [I] am aware, has the name of being extravagantly kept up, and perhaps a Clerk and 12 men the number lately proposed is as great a Complement as is generally allowed for the same returns; but if we satisfactorily shew that the surplus three men in addition to the greater security to the Establishment can more than pay their own Wages occasionally, hunting Beaver or at other merchantable employment at the Fort, I flatter myself that the propriety of keeping 15 men will appear sufficiently desirable, and especially when it can be done without calling upon Columbia for them. Hitherto the little Beaver hunt we made here was by mere starts and jumps in dead of winter, when we thought ourselves and the hunters in security; but now that we have acquired a little better knowledge of the Country and some confidence in ourselves among the Natives that we are accustomed to see, I think a small Trapping Party regularly employed in this way would pay well: and to effect this purpose with the greatest safety in our power to both parties, would be, towards the middle of October, when the Indians are out of the

River, to equip 8 good hands that would coast it to the Southward until they came to the Whullummy or Ossaak River – perhaps 80 miles from here – which as far as we can judge admits of Canoe going for some distance up, and near its source to hunt the Beaver: to return at the end of three months; and afterwards to be employed nearer home as they are at present, until the Natives again begin to assemble. If the Establishment is not curtailed a Gentleman could be sent with this Party on their first setting out. So confident are we of something worth while being in that quarter, that last month I sent a Gentleman and six men across Land to see the River and converse with the Natives, whom we know to be industrious, and whose Beaver find their way to the Fort thro' the medium of the Quaitlins. They are but few in number and wholly at the mercy of the Scatchads on one hand, and of our Indians here on the other. Of the two I believe ours pay them the best and generally get the Skins: the others however are not to be outdone in times like the present and what they fall short of in property they make up in terror and exemplary punishment and I am sorry to say that they have had recourse to this most oppressive measure in a marked degree not long ago. When I sent Mr. Annance I thought it possible to be able to ascend the River with a Craft, and to fix a small trading house in the back Country ensuing season that might be the means of keeping the bulk of the Skins found among the Scadchats and others from reaching the Coast at all, and this to be done under the protection of the proposed Trapping Party, but our people unable to ascend the river, and the Ossaaks entirely disappearing in consequence of the late trouble from those of the Coast returned rather suddenly; and any thing we now do in this way will altogether depend upon circumstances, and the manner in which the opposition is directed to be carried on in the Sound itself. The returns of this year includes 85 Skins killed by our own people, and placed to their respective credits at the rate of 5/ per skin; and as such they are estimated on the other side with the General Returns.

Among other returns that could be made from this place, last fall we had 3000 feet of Plank, and 10 m. Cedar Shingles ready for Shipment: the latter I should suppose would answer well, but the Boards with mere manual force can hardly be made worth the trouble when Machinery is in competition, should the demand for Timber continue we thought a Saw Mill here also an object of attention, but without exposing ourselves at too great a distance, the improbability of finding a good Seat where wood is in abundance is a great objection. There is however one strong inducement in this vicinity to make an effort: the occasional Bluffs of American White Pine (Pin Blanc) that is to be met with, & which I believe is no wise common on the W. side of the Rocky Mountains.

With respect to Salmon, in case our Journal cannot conveniently be consulted with this, the best idea of what is, and might be done in that way, must be derived from the following Statement.

Statement of Salmon Trade. Fort Langley from 10th to 20 Aug. 1829
[For this part of the report, see the journal entry for 17 August 1829.]

In addition to this Statement I have to observe that instead of awaiting the appearance here of the Salmon till the 10th or 15th of August, a good Stock might be procured near the Falls at least fifteen days earlier; as could well be inferred from what our own people saw when on a short trip up that way last July while at the Fort with six men I had the protection of the *Cadboro*. It may not be amiss also to remark that I think a detached Salting Camp within a very few miles of the Establishment during the last 20 days of August would succeed well, without being exposed to imminent danger so that by those means we could secure a period of 55 or 60 days instead of 20 – Ample time judging from last year's experience to procure 500 Barrels of Salmon. To conclude with this subject I must inform that we made several attempts ourselves last Summer with the Seine & hand Scoop net but our success by no means proved that we could do without Indian trade, nor does ever this appear to me a source of great disappointment as in years of Scarcity the best regulated fishery of our own would miscarry while in years of plenty such as last the expense in trade would hardly exceed the very cost of Lines and Twine.

STATE OF ESTABLISHMENT

For the nature of all the Business that is likely to be carried on here the Fort is now sufficiently well arranged. To finish the Buildings inside, a good spacious store of 55 feet long and a large Cooper's Shop are erected, both indispensable should anything extensive be undertaken in the way of fish curing. The man who acted as Carpenter and the only man Unengaged, we have kept at Cooper Work for the last Six weeks, assisted by another; but has not produced in that time above 30 of 25 Galls. not too well finished – they are made of the Pin Blanc having no oak or any other hard wood at hand – were two of our men good Coopers so much the better.

As to the farm little can be said of it. All our operations that way being confined to the Hoe the elevated ground near the Fort being already exhausted did not yield us above 25 Bushels Wheat, 20 of Peas & 10 of Barley. The little rich alluvial soil there is would have done better, but here again the Summer flush did considerable damage and it was only with the help of seed put in the ground first week in July that we were able to secure about 1200 Kegs Potatoes. For the seed of this Spring we have taken other precautions – of Kitchen Garden I can say nothing the seed of last year not coming to hand before middle of July.

Should the Trapping party be disapproved of tis my intention to dispense with one of the Gentlemen; yet, the two would greatly add to our Security during the Salmon operations & if it so happens that the contemplated Establishment on north end of Cowlitz Portage is carried on not only could the extra Clerk but a few hands also have been sent thither anytime after the middle of October & answer all purposes to be here again by the beginning of July.

I have the honor to be with great respect
Gentlemen –
Your very obed. Servant
Arch. McDonald
Chief Trader

APPENDIX D:
BIOGRAPHIES OF SHASHIA AND SIMON PLAMONDON

SHASHIA

The name of the Cowichan chief called "Chaseaw" by Alexander McKenzie has been recorded in the Fort Langley Journals in many ways, from Shashia and Josia to Old Joe, and as Saw-se-a, Tsawsiai, Soseiah, and Tsosieten elsewhere, the latter probably the best attempt to capture the Cowichan sound. He came from Taatka, one of the smallest of the Cowichan villages, but because of his abilities as a trader, Europeans considered him to be an important Cowichan chief.

Undoubtedly his ability to obtain arms and ammunition from Fort Langley made it possible for various Salish groups, united under his leadership, to deliver a decisive victory against the Lekwiltok at Maple Bay in the 1840s. (Humphreys, n.d., estimated the date to be 1840.) According to the account given to Edward Curtis (1913:33-5), Salish from Puget Sound, the lower Fraser, and the Cowichan area united to launch a retaliatory attack against the northern foe, whose aggressive acts were frequently noted in the Fort Langley Journals. They were joined by the Nanaimo, whose village had been burned recently (see Cryer, n.d., vol. 2). After this victory, peace treaties were made and there was intermarriage between the Cowichan and northern people, an extension of the network of alliances being formed at Fort Langley through potlatching and intermarriage. McDonald credits the chief with four wives, but Annance, testifying in Montreal in 1867, reported that he had ten (*Connolly* v. *Woolrich* 1867:228).

One of the chief traders at Fort Langley, the Cowichan chief also appeared at Fort Victoria, founded in 1843 in anticipation of the border settlement, and at Fort Nanaimo, established in 1849 to take advantage of the discovery of coal. James Douglas sent Joseph McKay and Thomas Cluamatany on an exploratory trip up the Cowichan River in May of 1851 under the protection of "Hosua" (Bowsfield 1979:180). The following September, the Cowichan chief shot a Nanaimo Native collier, to the dismay of Joseph McKay, in charge of Fort Nanaimo (McKay 1852a). "So-cee-ah," according to Douglas, committed the murder, "in consequence of your refusal to pay him for his services, in a former voyage to Nanaimo" (Douglas

The Cowichan chief Shashia is called Saw-se-a by
Paul Kane who highly romanticized him in this oil painting.
Alexander McKenzie said of Shashia: "This Indian had
Certainly the appearance of a Chief and his manly
Countenance Would Command respect anywhere."

1852). McKay denied any injustice (McKay 1852b), but soon complained of the lack of venison since the *fracas* with the Cowichan (McKay 1852c).

On 5 November 1852 a Cowichan and a Nanaimo murdered a Scottish shepherd named Peter Brown. Prominent among the Cowichan chiefs summoned to meet the large punitive expedition led by James Douglas was Sosieah (Moresby 1909:127-36: Gough 1984:52).

In the spring of 1853, two young Nanaimos fired at a Cowichan in retaliation for the death of the Nanaimo collier (Douglas 1853), but by October 1855 the rifts were healed when Old Joe invited the Sechelt and the majority of the Nanaimo to a grand feast (McKay 1855-7).

According to Agnes Thorne and her son, Abner, direct descendants of the Cowichan chief's uncle, Shashia had two sons, both of whom predeceased him. The eldest, who received his name, died after a boil was lanced. James Douglas makes reference to young Sacee ah, who received a blue cap in May of 1853 (Douglas 1853). The second son, Cul-chil-lum, was killed during a fight over a gambling game while visiting the Snohomish in order to arrange a marriage (see also Elmendorf 1993:132-3). Paul Kane, who painted portraits of both Cul-chil-lum and his father in 1847, declared the chief to be "a great warrior in his younger days" (Kane 1968:152).

According to Robert Brown (1870:346), Tsosieten traded as far north as Sitka, where he obtained guns from the Imperial Fur Company (the Russian American Company). These he mounted on the bastions of a fort he built on an island (probably Valdes), where he died in 1870, blind and childless.

Apart from the information supplied by Agnes and Abner Thorne, the details in this biography have come from records left by white people. We can only guess at the extent to which their misconceptions about the structure of Coast Salish society affected their perceptions of the role of the Cowichan chief. For more information, see Suttles, "The Ethnographic Significance of the Fort Langley Journals," in this volume. Suttles finds it difficult to believe that Shashia could have traded as far north as Sitka. He may, however, have obtained the guns through a trading network.

Cul-chil-lum, son of Shashia,
in an oil painting by Paul Kane.

SIMON PLAMONDON

Simon Plamondon was among the first Hudson's Bay Company employees to farm on Cowlitz Prairie, where he settled in 1837 with Emilie Bercier,
a widow who became his wife after the death of Scanewah's daughter. He
acted as a guide to Charles Wilkes, who declared, "a more useful man I
have seldom met with, or one that could be so well depended on" (Wilkes
1845 [4]:317).

His marriage, after Emilie's death, to Harriet Pelletier, niece of F.N.
Blanchet, one of the Roman Catholic priests who established a mission in
the area, and his appointment as Indian agent in 1855 is further evidence
of the respect he enjoyed.

However, with more settlement, things changed. Harriet lived with
her sisters in Vancouver and Oregon City, leaving Simon on his farm with
his large Native family. He began to have financial difficulties, probably
because of his illiteracy, and he was Indian agent for little more than a
year because he was judged to be too friendly with the Natives on the

Simon Plamondon:
voyageur, labourer, carpenter, farmer.

aggressive settlement frontier. His land was sold to pay debts, and he spent his old age (he lived to be one hundred years old) with various friends and relatives.

George Plamondon, one of Simon's white grandsons, wrote about the Plamondon family. Though not all his stories correspond with known facts, it is probably true that Simon was the youngest son of Catherine Gill, daughter of Louis Gill and Suzanne Gamelin, his French wife (Plamondon 1961:6). Louis Gill's parents, Samuel and Rosalie James, were New Englanders captured by the Abenaki as children, who married and raised their white family among the Natives. Francis Annance was also descended from the Gill family. If Catherine was Simon's mother, Annance and Plamondon were second cousins.

Simon Plamondon's life spanned a period of enormous change. This illiterate Canadien voyageur was one of many who spanned the continent and made possible the profitable fur trade. He served as a labourer and carpenter at various forts. When the early settlers arrived, his experience was highly valued until the cities began to grow and his skills were no longer admired or needed. The story of his life reveals much about the clash between the fur and settlement frontiers.

For a more detailed biography of Plamondon, see Wallin 1987; for information about Annance, see note 10 in the introduction to this volume.

APPENDIX E:
NAMES IN THE FORT LANGLEY JOURNAL

Wayne Suttles

The Fort Langley Journal mentions by name twenty-six or twenty-seven tribes. Many of the names are spelled in more than one way, and most spellings differ from modern English spellings, some so much as to be unrecognizable. The reasons for this diversity lie in the number of Native languages and in their phonological complexity.

The journalists must have heard most tribal names as pronounced by the Kwantlen in their Downriver dialect of the Halkomelem language. However, the fort was visited by speakers of Island dialects (the Nanaimo and Cowichan) and Upriver dialects (Chilliwack and others) of Halkomelem, by speakers of other languages – Northern Straits (Saanich), Squamish, Clallam, and Lushootseed (Skagit, Snohomish, and others) – and the journalists must have heard tribal names as given by these people as well.

The Native languages must have presented difficulties to all outsiders (see note 2, Suttles, "The Fort Langley Journals and Ethnography," this volume). All the languages of the region have systems of sounds (represented here with the phonetic symbols in general use among linguists working in the region) that make distinctions quite foreign to any of the languages of the employees of the company – English, French, Gaelic, Iroquois, Abenaki, and Hawaiian. While there are minor differences among the Native languages, in all there are glottalized (or ejective) stops and affricates such as $\dot{p}$, $\dot{t}$, $\dot{c}$, $\dot{č}$, and $\dot{k}$ contrasting with their plain counterparts p, t, c, č, k and so on; there are uvular stops and a fricative q, $\dot{q}$, and $\check{x}$ contrasting with velars k, $\dot{k}$, and x; there are rounded (or labialized) velars and uvulars k^w, $\dot{k}^w$, x^w, q^w, $\dot{q}^w$, and $\check{x}^w$ contrasting with their unrounded counterparts k, $\dot{k}$, x, q, $\dot{q}$, and $\check{x}$; there is a voiceless lateral spirant and glottalized affricate ł and $\dot{\check{\lambda}}$ contrasting with plain l; and in Halkomelem, the language spoken by the largest number of Natives who came to the fort, there is a glottalized interdental affricate $\dot{t}^\theta$ contrasting with an interdental spirant θ. Over half of the consonants of the Native languages of this region are lacking in the languages of the Europeans, Eastern North American Natives, and Polynesians who came into the region.

Ordinarily, when we hear an unfamiliar language we are simply not aware of the distinctions it makes that our own does not. In time we may begin to hear them, but without linguistic training we will not know what to do with them. Not surprisingly, then, Native names appear in the journals in a variety of spellings, none of them capturing essential features of the Native word. Table 1 lists the tribes by their modern spellings, the spellings appearing in the Fort Langley Journal, and the Native names as recorded in recent times in the phonetic symbols used by linguists working in this region.

The writers of the journals, speakers of English probably with some familiarity with Gaelic and French, generally did not indicate the distinctions mentioned, writing k, q, and q̓ as "c" or "k," distinguishing the rounded k̓ʷ, q̓ʷ, and so on from the unrounded initially but not finally, writing ł as "l" and ƛ̓ as "tl". But there is no consistency. An initial rounded velar xʷappears as "Ho-" or "Whu-" in "Holumma" and "Whullumy" for xʷlə́mi (Lummi), as "O-" in "Osaak" for xʷsə́ʔeq (Nooksack), or as zero, as in all spellings of xʷmə́θkʷəy̓əm (Musqueam). A final xʷ appears as "ch" in Barnston's "Nanimooch" for snənéyməxʷ(Nanaimo), but it is usually ignored.

A few journal spellings may differ from recent transcriptions of the Native names because of language change. The journalists write "s" for the Halkomelem θ, as in the various spellings of xʷmə́θkʷəy̓əm (Musqueam) and in Barnston's "Maes" for səmə́θ (Sumas), and they write "ch" for the Halkomelem c and c̓, as in the various spellings of qə́wəcən or qəwícən (Cowichan) and sc̓əlxʷíʔqʷ (Chilliwack). In twentieth-century Halkomelem, the θ sounds like English "th" in "thin," and the c like the "ts" in "gets," and the journalists' spellings may reflect a slight shift in the articulation of these consonants. (But surprisingly the Native š also commonly appears as "s" when final, as in "Chomes" for Squamish and "Soquams" for Suquamish.) In the names of Puget Sound tribes, Duwamish, Skykomish, Snohomish, and Suquamish, we find "m" and "n" in both the journal and the modern spellings corresponding to "b" and "d" in the names as recorded in the Lushootseed (Puget Sound) language in recent times. (The modern name "Duwamish" is a partial exception.) This may reflect Halkomelem pronunciation, which would have "m" and "n," or it may reflect an earlier Lushootseed pronunciation.

One kind of variation is due to the journalists' use of plural forms and their reinterpretation of a native final -s. The journalists generally use plurals with the English suffix -s or -es when writing of persons and use singular forms when using the name as a modifier, as in McDonald's "our friends the Chilquihooks [Chilliwacks]" (7 April 1829) and "the Chilkuhook river" (24 June 1830). But occasionally a final -s appears in a modifier, as in McMillan's "A Nanimous woman" (7 July 1828). Conversely, the final -s that corresponds to -š in the names of Puget Sound tribes is often interpreted as a plural, as in Barnston's "The Soquams traded" (9 October 1827) and his "The old Soquam chief" (6 July 1827).

Differences among the dialects and languages in the forms of Native names and the journalists' spellings allow some inferences about the journalists' sources and perhaps shifts in their contacts or interests. The Upriver and Downriver dialects of Halkomelem differ in many ways but perhaps most noticeably in the correspondence of "l" in Upriver to "n" in Downriver. From this difference we can infer from McMillan's "Penault" that he had learned the name of this upriver tribe from the local downriver people – the Kwantlen, and we may suppose from McDonald's "Pellalt" that he had been talking with the Pilalt themselves. The spellings "Titun" and "Titens" for the Tait also indicates a Downriver source, which was not changed to the Upriver forms. (I have not recorded the Downriver form listed, but such a form would correspond to the Upriver form "tittəl" given by Wilson Duff.)

Because of the difference in Island and Downriver Halkomelem pronunciation of the name now spelled "Cowichan," we can see that Barnston and McMillan were representing the pronunciation of the Cowichan themselves, while McDonald favoured the Kwantlen pronunciation. From the vowel in "Chomes," "Whoomes," etc., we can infer that the journalists got the name from the Squamish themselves, while the modern spelling implies a Halkomelem source. But from the middle "l" in "Tlallam," etc., we can infer that the journalists did not get the name from the Clallam, who pronounce their name with a "y." The spellings "Yucletaw" and so on for the Lekwiltok and "Quo-quals" for the Kwakiutl proper clearly indicate a Salish source. The several Salishan languages of the region all knew the Lekwiltok as the yə́qʷəłteʔx̌ or something very similar. This name probably came originally through Comox, which, like Clallam, substitutes "y" for "l."

The journal also mentions a number of Native men by name, a few again and again. Most are names of men who were important traders. No women are identified by name. As with tribal names appearing in the journal, most personal names are spelled in a variety of ways, none representing very well the Native original. Some of these names can be identified with persons appearing in genealogies recorded in the mid-twentieth century, and some are borne by living persons today. In these cases we can give the original Native form. The Kwantlen chief called "Whittlekainum," "Whittlekenum," "Whotleakenum" (in McKenzie 1825) was x̌ʷəλ̓iqínəm; the Squamish chief called Whapplekeinum" was x̌ʷəpəlqínəm (Randy Bouchard, personal communication); the Cowichan chief called "Shoshia," "Joshua," and "Joe" was ƛ̓ásietən or ƛ̓ásie for short; the Saanich chief called "Chaheinook," Chechinuck," the *Gros Nez*, and so on was čəx̌ínəqʷ; and the Skagit chief called "Neetlum" or "Needlum" was sníλ̓əm. It is likely that further research would identify most of the other personal names that appear in the journal.

TABLE 1. TRIBAL NAMES

Modern Spelling	Spelling in Fort Langley Journal	Native Source
Chilliwack	Chilcocooks, Chilcoyooks (B), Chiliquiyouks (McM), Chilquiyooks, Chilquihooks, Chilquehooks, Chilkuhook (McD)	sčəlxʷíʔqʷ(DH), sčəlxʷíqʷ(UH)
Clallam	Tlalam (B), Tlalam, Clalams (McM), Clalams (McD)	šxʷƛ̓éləm (H, NS, cf. Cl nəxʷsƛ̓áy̓əm)
Cowichan	Cowitchen (B), Cawitchens , Kawitchins, Cowitchens (McM) Cawaitcin (McD)	qʷə́w̓əcən (IH) qʷə́w̓ícən (DH)
Cowlitz	Cowlitz (B)	káwlicsk (Cz)
Duwamish	Sinuwames (McM)	dxʷdəwʔábš (Lsh)
Katzie	Kijis (B), Kutche, Keitches (McM), Kitchies, Kitchis (McD)	q̓íči̓ʔ (H)
Kwakiutl	Quo-quals (McM)	kʷákʷəł (H)
Kwantlen	Quoitle, Quoitlan (B), Quaitland, Quaitline, Quatlan (McM), Quaitline, Quaitlen, Quaitlin (McD) Quaital (McM)	q̓ʷá·ṅƛ̓əṅ (DH) q̓ʷá·lƛ̓əl (UH)
Lekwiltok	Yucletaw (B), Yewkeltas (McM), Yewkultaus, Yucletaws, Yacaltas, Yeaucaltas, Yewkeltaws, Yewkultas (McD)	yə́qʷəłteʔx̌ (H)
Lillooet (Douglas)	Squaals (McM)	sθqʷáł (DH)
Lummi	Holumma (B), Whullumy (McD)	x̌ʷlə́mi (H, NS)
Musqueam	Misquiams, Misqueams (B), Masquiam, Musqueam (McM), Musquam (McD)	x̌ʷmə́θkʷəy̓əm (H)
Nanaimo	Nanimooch (B) Nanaiman, Nanomin, Nanaimous, Nanoimon (McM), Nannimous, Nanaimoos (McD)	snənéyməxʷ (IH, DH)
Nooksack	Osaak, Ossaaks (McD)	x̌ʷséʔeq, nəxʷséʔeq (DH)

▶

Modern Spelling	Spelling in Fort Langley Journal	Native Source
Okanagan	Okinagan (B), Okinukun (McM)	(Interior Salish)
Pilalt	Penault (McM) Pellalt (McD)	pənáltxʷ (DH) pəláltxʷ (UH)
Saanich	Sanch, Sauch (B), Sanatch (McM), Sonese (?), Sandish (McD)	xʷsé·nəč (NS), xʷsé·nəc (H)
Sechel	Shissal, Shisals, Shee Chals, Sheechals (McD)	sxíxaɬ (DH), šíša ɬ (IH)
Skagit	Scadgat (B), Skadget (McM), Scadshot, Scadschads, Scadchds, Scadchads, Scadchats, Scatshat, Scatschat, Scatchad (McD)	sqájət (Lsh)
Skykomish	Skiwamus (McD)	sq̇íxʷəbš (Lsh)
Snohomish	Sinahomes (B), Sinahome, Sinahoom, Sinahooms (McM), Sinnahomes, Sinohomes (McD)	sduhúbš (Lsh)
Squamish	Chomes, Homes (B), Whooms (McM), Whoolmes, Whoomes, Whoomus (McD)	sqx̌ʷúʔmiš (Sq, cf. DH sqx̌ʷám̓əx)
Sumas	Maes (B), Mace, Smaize (McD)	səméθ (DH)
Suquamish	Soquam, Soquams (B), Sockwans (McM)	suq̇ʷábš (Lsh)
Tait	Titun, Titens (McD)...	[títtən (DH? cf. UH "títtəl")]
Thompson	Coutoomuns, Coutinemuns (McM), Coulomun, Coutamine (McD)	(Fr. Couteaux 'Knives')

Abbreviations:

B	Barnston	Lsh	Lushootsed
Cl	Clallam	McD	McDonald
Cz	Cowlitz	McM	McMillan
DH	Downriver Halkomelem	NS	Northern Straits
Fr	French	Sa	Salish [any of several languages]
H	Halkomelem	Sq	Squamish
IH	Island Halkomelem	UH	Upriver Halkomelem
Kw	Kwakwala		

TABLE 2. LINGUISTIC CLASSIFICATION OF TRIBES MENTIONED

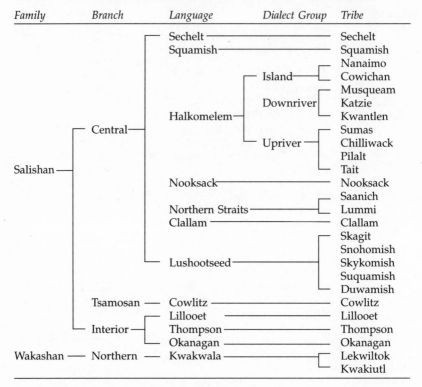

Family	Branch	Language	Dialect Group	Tribe
		Sechelt		Sechelt
		Squamish		Squamish
			Island	Nanaimo / Cowichan
		Halkomelem	Downriver	Musqueam / Katzie / Kwantlen
	Central		Upriver	Sumas / Chilliwack / Pilalt / Tait
Salishan		Nooksack		Nooksack
		Northern Straits		Saanich / Lummi
		Clallam		Clallam
		Lushootseed		Skagit / Snohomish / Skykomish / Suquamish / Duwamish
	Tsamosan	Cowlitz		Cowlitz
	Interior	Lillooet		Lillooet
		Thompson		Thompson
		Okanagan		Okanagan
Wakashan	Northern	Kwakwala		Lekwiltok / Kwakiutl

Note: "Coast Salish" and "Interior Salish" are terms used by anthropologists to designate cultural groupings. "Central," "Tsamosan," and "Interior" are terms used by linguists to designate coordinate branches of the Salishan family. The "Central" branch includes the languages of the Coast Salish of the Strait of Georgia-Puget Sound Basin. This term should not be confused with "Central Coast Salish," a term used by anthropologists for a cultural group of Coast Salish tribes consisting of the tribes who speak Squamish, Halkomelem, Nooksack, Northern Straits, and Clallam.

NOTES

ABBREVIATIONS

BCA   British Columbia Archives
HBCA   Hudson's Bay Company Archives
NAC   National Archives of Canada

INTRODUCTION

1 For the effects of early Native–European contact, see Suttles, "The Ethnographic Significance of the Fort Langley Journals," pp. 163-4, this volume.
2 Five years later, George Simpson became the governor of all Hudson's Bay Company territories in British North America. He was a hard-working and very capable administrator. For biographies, see Galbraith 1976; 1985:812-8; and Rich 1938:466-7.
3 Dr. John McLoughlin, a partner in the North West Company, played a key role in the negotiations that led to the union of the two fur trading companies. After amalgamation he was put in charge of New Caledonia and the Columbia District, which were merged. For biographies, see Barker 1959; Williams 1975:176; and Lamb 1985:575-80.
4 The *Tonquin* sailed north from Astoria on a trading expedition in June 1811. The crew was attacked and killed by Natives in Clayoquot Sound. See Lamb 1969:124-7.
5 For information about the introduction of Iroquois into the fur trade in western Canada, see Nicks 1980:85-101. The North West Company brought Iroquois to the Columbia District, where they were employed as a band under a leader who received their pay and under whose name their debts were listed. After amalgamation it was discovered that these debts were very heavy, and in order to collect them more easily the band members were listed individually (HBCA B.76/d:1-12). A large number were dismissed and encouraged to return east, but many settled in the country; some became free traders and were used on the Snake River expeditions, and those considered most useful were retained on contract.
6 For biographies of James McMillan, see Fleming 1940:450-1; Williams 1975:183-4; Thomas 1985:583-4; Devine 1994; and the introduction to the 1828-9 journal in this volume.

7 Michel Laframboise, born in Quebec, arrived on the *Tonquin* in 1811 as one of Astor's men. He subsequently worked for both the North West and the Hudson's Bay companies. He settled in the Willamette Valley in the early 1840s. For a biography, see Nielson 1933:284-6; Fleming 1940:444; West 1942:204-5; Davies 1961:142; Nunis 1968:145-70; and Munnick and Warner 1979:A-54.

8 With his father, Alexander McKay, Thomas reached the Columbia River on the *Tonquin* in 1811. McKay senior was killed when the *Tonquin* was attacked and destroyed. Tom's mother, Marguerite Wadin, became the wife of John McLoughlin. For a biography, see Nielson 1933:290-2; Rich 1941:347-9; and Lavender 1968:259-77.

9 For biographies of John Work, see Dee 1943:229-270; Rich 1941:356-8; Sampson 1976:850-4; and Williams 1975:199.

10 Francis Noel Annance's great grandparents were New Englanders who were captured by the Abenaki as children and grew up among them, marrying as young adults. His father, Francis Joseph Annance, was one of a group of four boys who, as a result of Protestant missionary activity, were sent to school in New Hampshire. Francis Noel attended Moor's Indian Charity School as a young adult. He was in the Columbia District in 1820 as an employee of the North West Company and was retained by the Hudson's Bay Company. He returned to the Abenaki village of St. Francis in 1845. For biographies, see Fleming 1940:426; Williams 1975:200; and Maclachlan 1993:35-9.

11 The term *Kanaka*, meaning "man," was frequently used to describe these workers. It did not come into common use until later in the 1830s and eventually came to have an unpleasant connotation (see Naughton 1983:3-5). In these journals the men are referred to as Islanders, Sandwich Islanders, Owhyhees, or Owyhees. For more information about the Hawaiians, see Duncan 1972; Barman 1995; and Koppel 1995.

12 The boats used were probably similar in construction to those described by Alexander Kennedy as the means of transport from Fort George to the posts in the interior:

> Of a peculiar construction, they are made in imitation of bark canoes, & have been much improved upon since the first invention by Mr. David Thompson. The boats now carry from 40 to 50 pieces, and are navigated by 8 men each. They are wrought by paddles instead of oars, and are carried over the portages on men's shoulders, but it requires the crews of two boats to carry one. The reason assigned for using paddles instead of oars is that the current is very strong in some parts of the River when these craft by the means of paddles are enabled to keep close in shore where the current is less felt than they could do if oars were used. (Kennedy 1824-5)

Simpson commented on the boats as being "more properly speaking Batteaux & wrought by Paddles instead of oars," probably drawing on Kennedy's report as well as personal observation (Merk 1968:38).

13 Pierre Charles was described by William Fraser Tolmie as "a middle sized broadchested Indian, a Banakir [Abenaki] from near Montreal, aged 40 & the best deer hunter of the Rocky Mountains" (Tolmie 1963:203). He probably came to the Pacific with a group of Abenaki who appear to have been recruited from St. Francis by the North West Company after the union. It is not surprising that Francis Annance was sent to look for him. Charles was on the

Snake River expeditions of 1825-6 and 1826-7, but became an employee of the Hudson's Bay Company and joined the party that founded Fort Langley. He was sent to Fort Nisqually from there and finally settled in the Cowlitz Valley. The *Catholic Church Records* show his name as Pierre Charles dit Langlois.

14 McKay's journal has not survived, but Work's is in BCA A/B40 W89.21 and was published (Elliott 1912). Annance's is in HBCA B.76/a and also has been published (Thompson 1991:5-29). None of the maps has survived, but apparently the Clallam expedition used Work's.

15 Alexander McKenzie was a Scot who joined the North West Company in 1812 or 1813. He spent the summer of 1815 at Spokane and was stationed at Fort George (at the mouth of the Columbia River) in 1820. His untimely end was a matter of great concern for the people at Fort Langley. For a biography, see Fleming 1940.

16 The *William and Ann* was a cedar brig built in Bermuda in 1818 and purchased by the Hudson's Bay Company for use on the Pacific coast. It reached the Columbia on 11 April 1825, but repairs were required, which delayed the voyage north until late in May.

17 The details that follow are from McKenzie 1825. The names of Indian tribes have been modernized, but McKenzie's spelling has been retained for names of individual Natives.

18 Auicactin was believed by the people at Fort Langley to be the Clallam responsible for the death of Alexander McKenzie and his travelling companions in January 1828.

19 The traders usually referred to the Cowlitz chief as Scanawa or Skaniwa. According to Delbert McBride, a direct descendant, the name is spelled Scanewah and pronounced Scán-e-wah.

20 In his lifetime, the Snohomish chief established many contacts over a large area. He was frequently called "le Francois" or the Frenchman "because of his whiskers," according to Roman Catholic missionaries. He listened to their teachings and they have left us a description of the tall chief as he arrived at one of their meetings. "Witskalachee, arrayed in French style with trousers, shirt, jacket, *sous-veste*, topcoat ornamented with a star fashioned from porcupine quills, hat, cravat, everything complete, appeared at the head of his people accompanied by several underchiefs" (Landerholm 1956:61, 66). He was used as an emissary by the leaders of the punitive expedition to punish the Clallam and became one of the principal traders at Fort Nisqually after it was established in 1833. Chief Trader Heron elicited confessions from several chiefs about murders and thefts; only Waskelatchee had none to admit (Tolmie 1963:223). This may explain, in part, the strength of his network or merely the extent of his discretion.

21 In neither the Work journal nor the Annance journal is any mention made of an encounter with Saanich Natives. Only one presentation of clothing was recorded. According to Work, a chief's clothing was presented to the principal chief of the Cahoutilt (Kwantlen) and a common coat to a younger Kwantlen chief. According to Annance, the party clothed the chief and his son.

22 Various trade and ship journals contain many references to these dogs, long extinct, and to the blankets made from their hair. For a survey of references in the literature see Howay 1918:83–92, and for more information see Suttles, "The Ethnographic Significance of the Fort Langley Journals," p. 176. See also Paul Kane's sketch, *Interior of a Lodge with Family Group*, p. 162, this volume.

23 Chaseaw became a familiar figure at Fort Langley, where he was variously
    called Shashia, Josia, Joshua, Josua, and Joe. For a biography, see Appendix D
    in this volume.
24 Evidently Whotleakenum, the Kwantlen chief, had given the clothing to the
    Saanich chief.
25 The winter homes of most of the Cowichans were in the Cowichan River Val-
    ley, but thousands of them travelled up the Fraser to their summer villages to
    fish. See Suttles, "The Ethnographic Significance of the Fort Langley Journals,"
    p. 172-4.
26 Aemilius Simpson, 1792-1831, a relative of Governor George Simpson, was
    appointed hydrographer and clerk in the Columbia District when he arrived
    overland from York Factory. He was given command of the *Cadboro*, which
    arrived at Fort Vancouver on 8 June 1827. He was one of the few captains on
    whom McLoughlin could rely, but apparently he was not an accomplished
    hydrographer, so George Barnston did much of the necessary work (Brown
    and Van Kirk 1982:52-3). Aemilius Simpson was "efficient but somewhat ec-
    centric," donning kid gloves before issuing an order. "Form was nine tenths
    of the law with him, and the other tenth was conformity," was a judgment
    made by A.C. Anderson (Bancroft 1884:477). Commenting on his death,
    Archibald McDonald said, "I am sorry to say to you in confidence however
    that he was not over popular with us – the cause you know as well as I do"
    (McDonald 1907b:265). For biographies, see Fleming 1940:434-5; Blakey Smith
    1987:720-1; and Williams 1975:198-9.
27 In a letter to the governor and committee from York Factory on 1 September
    1822, George Simpson requested their attention to "the rather authoritative
    and independent tone" used by ships' captains and "the discretionary power
    with which they appear yet to conceive themselves vested both in regard to
    Ships and Cargo" (Fleming 1940:384). These problems convinced John
    McLoughlin that the trade could be better conducted by using posts along the
    coast rather than depending on vessels. This is one of the reasons plans to
    abandon Fort Langley were reversed.
28 We can see hints of this in Archibald McDonald's comment that "a rank
    N'Wester" (James McMillan) was promoted to be superintendent of Red River,
    a colony with which McDonald had had a close association and bitter ex-
    perience (McDonald 1907a:259-60). This conflict may also have been a factor
    in McLeod's problems with the "young gentlemen" while on the Clallam
    expedition.
29 Merk 1968:91. The first Sandwich Islanders had received only food and cloth-
    ing. When they were paid the regular wage of £17, the Canadian and Euro-
    pean servants were so dissatisfied that the Sandwich Islanders' wages were
    reduced to £10.
30 In March 1828, John McLoughlin requested £100 for a number of clerks but
    kept Michel Laframboise, who was asking £50, at £37. Nevertheless he admit-
    ted to George Simpson that he "could sooner dispense with a gentleman than
    him. People only know the value of an interpreter when they have none"
    (McLoughlin 1828b:162). Years later, Laframboise complained to Charles Wilkes
    that he had not received what he considered his due (Wilkes 1845 [5]:349).
31 Of the 40 percent reserved for officers, chief traders received 1/85 share and
    chief factors 2/85.
32 In reminiscing, John Tod found it difficult to understand "the uncommon high
    proportion of ever available extraordinary men in the higher ranks of the service
    – [a] proportion not reached, as persons say who are better able than I am to

judge such a matter, in any modern industrial or commercial organization" (Sproat 1954:191).

33 Clerks aspiring to become commissioned officers could become traders, chief traders, or factors. While the increase in pay was important, the shares in the company were even more desirable. As profits declined, however, some men, many of whom raised large families – George Barnston and James McMillan are good examples – found their incomes inadequate.

34 Deciding which men to promote could not have been an easy task. When Archibald McDonald received his chief factorship, it was clearly a reward for past service. Letitia Hargrave was bitter that her husband, James, had lost out to "an old useless man," and she was convinced that favouritism was involved (McLeod 1947:116). Alexander Christie, writing to James Hargrave, expressed surprise that clerks had not been promoted to chief traderships instead of appointing a chief factor (Glazebrook 1938:411). These are small indications of the tensions that increased as the number of positions decreased.

35 Foster 1975 describes the position of Indian trader as one to which the mixed-blood children of the fur trade aspired, but Annance was not born or raised in fur trade society and had undoubtedly been given reason to believe that his superior education would provide him with the same opportunities as other clerks. James McMillan felt that either Francis Annance or Donald Manson could have taken charge of Fort Langley, and he found Annance "as usual very useful" (McMillan 1827b:17); but George Simpson chose to leave Archibald McDonald in that position.

36 For an excellent study of women in the fur trade, see Van Kirk 1980. For a discussion of fur trade families, see Brown 1980.

37 In writing to James Hargrave, James McMillan complained about "backbiting and slander" (Glazebrook 1938:85). He was undoubtedly reacting to the growth of racial prejudice with the arrival of white women (see Van Kirk 1980: chapter 9). In another letter to Hargrave (Glazebrook 1938:143), he spoke glowingly of the new school which was "doing wonders in the improvement of our Half breeds." He may well have seen his own grandchildren there. It would appear that his wife kept apart from the native-born and was commended for this by Hargrave in a letter to his fiancée (Brown 1980:132).

38 For a discussion of the conflicts, see W. Kaye Lamb's introduction to Rich 1941.

39 See Ray 1974 and Fisher 1977. These historians, among others, have disproved the once widely held notion that the Native peoples were innocents duped by wily white traders. Their thesis can be supported by evidence in the Fort Langley journals. Nevertheless a few white men, frequently terrified and surrounded by thousands of Natives every fishing season, were able to survive, impose their values, and use the Natives in many ways. They established the basis for the white dominance that overwhelmed the Natives during the settlement period.

40 Johnson 1824:54, explaining the use of points, described the comma as "denoting the smaller pause, the semicolon next, then the colon, and the full-point terminating the sentence."

JOURNAL KEPT BY GEORGE BARNSTON, 1827-8

1 Matthews left the Columbia District the year Helen was born. Kilakotah then became the country wife of James McMillan. See note 2, Journal, 1828-9, p. 249.

2 For biographies, see Dunlop and Wilson 1941:16-7; Fleming 1940:427; and Brown and Van Kirk 1982:52-3.

3 Few of the twenty-one men returned home; many became settlers as the fur trade declined. Their names appear in the *Catholic Church Records* and in various censuses and petitions. Simon Plamondon, Oliver Bouchard, Pierre Charles, François Faniant from Sorel, Dominque Faron from Montreal, and Anawiskum Macdonald retired in the Cowlitz Valley. Amable Arquoitte from Montreal, Louis Boisvert, and Joseph Cornoyer from Sorel retired in the Willamette Valley. James Baker appears on the census for Clackamas County in the 1840s. Laurent Sauvé from Vaudreuil managed a Hudson's Bay Company dairy on an island at the junction of the Willamette and Columbia rivers that still carries his name. Jean Baptiste Dubois, who was on the exploratory expedition of 1824, was drowned at Fort Nez Perces on 27 July 1828. François Xavier Tarihonga and Antoine Pierrault were killed by the Clallam, and John Kennedy, who was from Sligo, Ireland, died at Fort Langley. Abraham Vincent was probably dismissed from the service and sent out. No mention is made of Jean Baptiste Ettue, Jacques Pierrault, or Louis Satakarata dit Rabaska in the church records or later censuses. Como, born in Hawaii in 1795, started his service with the North West Company and died at Fort Vancouver in 1850 (information supplied by Bruce Watson). Peopeoh, according to Jason Allard in his *Reminiscences*, was a relative of the "Kings of the Sandwich Isles" who acted as a guardian of the Hawaiians employed by the Hudson's Bay Company. He was a central figure in the Hawaiian settlement on Kanaka Creek. See Duncan 1972; Morton 1988; and Barman 1995.

4 Donald Manson, 1796-1880, was born in Thurso, Scotland. He joined the Hudson's Bay Company in 1817 and reached Fort Vancouver late in 1825. After he left Fort Langley with Governor Simpson in October 1828, he took Felicité Lucier as his wife. One of their sons, John Donald, married Aurelia, daughter of J.M. Yale. Manson was in charge of Fort Simpson in 1831-2, constructed Fort McLoughlin in 1833, and was in charge of Kamloops in 1841, a post on the Stikine in 1843-4, and Fort St. James in 1844-57, from where he retired to a farm in the Willamette Valley. For biographies, see Rich 1938:458; 1955:222-41; Munnick 1969b:217-25; and Holmes 1972:495-6.

5 Horses were introduced into North America by the Spanish. Fur traders frequently rented or bought them from the Native peoples. James McMillan had difficulty obtaining horses from Scanewah because John McLoughlin had forced Scanewah to trade at Fort Langley instead of Fort Vancouver (McMillan 1827a:15d). This prohibition and the establishment of Fort Langley in Scanewah's hinterland were undoubtedly serious threats to his political and economic power.

6 Trade goods, supplies, and fur were bundled into "pieces" of eighty or ninety pounds.

7 Evidently the reluctant Scanewah, forced to provide horses, drove a hard bargain. When the expedition against the Clallam passed this way in June 1828, they were told that McMillan paid at the rate of five skins for each horse to cross the portage. The leaders of the expedition considered this much too high; they offered a rate of two and a half skins to cross and return and insisted that they would not pay in ammunition or blankets, but only in strouds (Dye 1907:18).

8 *Chevreux: chevreuil* is the French name for roe deer, but Canadiens used the term for mule deer, according to Leechman's *Glossary*, and for jumping deer, according to Ross Cox (Stewart and Stewart 1957:370). David

Douglas confirmed this and left a description of the jumping deer, found in great numbers in the Columbia District (Douglas 1904 [5,3]:265). At Fort Langley, the term *chevreuil* may have been used to describe the deer common to the Lower Mainland or the coast, which is the Columbian blacktail deer (*Odocoileus hemionus columbianus*), but it was also used to describe a fawn. See Archibald McDonald's journal entry for 1 June 1829, p. 114, this volume.

9   Sinoktin (also recorded as Sinoughton by the traders) was one of the guides for the McMillan expedition of 1824.

10 An entry in the log of the *Cadboro* noted that Clallam Indians visited it and offered to bring furs if the schooner would come into the bay. They warned the captain not to trust the "Cowitzan...[whom] they described as a ferocious & bad set of Indians" (A. Simpson 1827a:7d).

11 This is confirmed by an entry in the log of the *Cadboro:* "At 9 fired a light gun for our land party having learned from an Indian that they were not far distant" (A. Simpson 1827a:8).

12 One horse died, and it was feared the other would have a similar fate (A. Simpson 1827a:9).

13 Boarding nets were used "to prevent them troubling us," and at sunset a gun was fired (A. Simpson 1827a:9d).

14 Simpson recorded the site as "not sufficient in fuel" nor "a good supply of water" (A. Simpson 1827a:9d).

15 Simpson was using George Vancouver's chart, which he considered "a most valuable acquisition" (A. Simpson 1827a:9). But Vancouver had not entered the mouth of the Fraser, which may explain the concerns Simpson expressed in the ship's log (A. Simpson 1827a:10d). McMillan had come through the south arm when returning from an exploratory trip in 1824. He had sounded to a depth of four to seven fathoms (Annance 1824-5:8). In his report he warned that vessels exceeding 150 to 200 tons burthen would not have sufficient draft (Merk 1968:249), but the *Cadboro* was only seventy tons. Simpson took it into the river only because McMillan insisted.

16 Thomas Sinclair, an Orkneyman, served on various Hudson's Bay Company craft from 1824 to 1834 and was master of the *Cadboro* for a time (see Fleming 1940:456).

17 Simpson complained that no supply of fish had been obtained from the Natives, "obliging us to live upon Ship's provision" (A. Simpson 1827a:11).

18 "At 5 a canoe with Scatchit Indians came along side with Skins for sale but the...Skins considered too high none was traded" (A. Simpson 1827a:11).

19 Probably *Pseudotsuga menziesii*, a conifer of the pine family, first described by Archibald Menzies, naturalist and surgeon with the Vancouver expedition, and later named Douglas-fir after Scottish botanist David Douglas. See North Bluff on Map 2.

20 A sextant was used to calculate latitude by measuring the angle of celestial bodies above the horizon from the observer's position.

21 See Map 2 for the location of Cowichan villages, which were summer camps. Somenos in the Cowichan Valley, Penelakut on Kuper Island, and Quamichan on the Cowichan River downstream from Somenos were the winter homes of the inhabitants.

22 Named after "Pitt of the Hble Committee" (McMillan 1827b:16d).

23 This is probably the spot marked "Tree Island" on Map 2.

24 Whittlakainum was the Kwantlen chief presented with a chief's clothing by the McMillan expedition of 1824. He is also mentioned in Alexander

McKenzie's journal, kept while he was on the *William and Ann* (McKenzie 1825).

25 It is hardly surprising that Barnston is inconsistent in his spelling of McMillan's name, since McMillan was himself inconsistent. His will begins, "I, James MacMillan," but is signed McMillan, the spelling he uses for his children's names. Some of his letters in his own hand are signed MacMillan.

26 Governor Simpson planned to use the *Cadboro* to carry on coastal trade. He sent instructions that an experienced officer should be sent with Lieutenant Aemilius Simpson, newly arrived on the Pacific coast, to show him how to carry on the business of trading with the Natives (Rich 1941:43). Alexander Roderick McLeod, chief trader, being "disposable," was sent for this purpose. McMillan reported that McLeod did all he could to help with the establishment of the fort "but suffers much on board. The confinement of a vessel does not agree with his active habits" (McMillan 1827b:16). McLeod was the leader of the expedition against the Clallam in June 1828. For biographies, see Fleming 1940:448-50; Nunis 1968b:279-97; and Williams 1975:190-1; 1988:569-70. See also Appendix A in this volume.

27 McMillan had intended to build the fort at the mouth of the Salmon River, where he had reached the Fraser in 1824, because he knew that the possibilities for agriculture there were good.

28 On another occasion, William Lackey's conduct was considered "highly improper" (Barker 1948:252).

29 For other descriptions of this technique, see sketch by John Keast Lord, p. 29, this volume, and his description in Lord 1866:183-6; Work 1824:220-1; H. Stewart 1977:68-71; and Suttles, "The Ethnographic Significance of the Fort Langley Journals," pp. 182-3.

30 These rapids were named Simpson's Falls when the governor came down the Fraser in October 1828, but the name fell into disuse. In 1847 Fort Yale, named after J.M. Yale, was established at this location.

31 These saws were used by two men, one above and one below the log laid over a pit. The Sandwich Islanders or "Owhyhees," were usually assigned this difficult work of sawing planks and squaring logs.

32 The incidence of venereal disease was very high in fur trade country. "On our arrival here we discovered Vincent was suffering dreadfully from venereal, and that four others had severe Gonorrheas, to which latter number one Man more has been added since" (McMillan 1827a:14d). "We have still 5 men labouring under the 'Chinook love Fever' altho 7 were sent back," Simpson noted on his trip from the Columbia District to Norway House in 1825 (Merk 1968:10).

How was this problem brought under control at Fort Langley? Some of the affected men may have been sent out. We know that Abraham Vincent was dismissed (see note 52, Journal, 1827-8) and James Baker (see journal entry for 26 March 1828) went to Fort Vancouver with the Simpson Party, but Antoine Pierrault (see journal entry for 7 September 1827) remained. The mercury treatment may have been effective, but McDonald's insistence that no woman be allowed into the fort unless she became a wife was probably the main reason that venereal disease was eliminated at Fort Langley.

33 Pickets were four to five inches thick and fifteen feet high (McMillan 1827a:14d).

34 So plentiful did the salmon become in the following weeks that McMillan, writing to his friend John McLeod on 21 January 1828, said, "We could trade

at the door of our Fort I suppose a million of dried Salmon if we chose enough to feed all the people of Rupert's Land" (McMillan 1828b:102-4).

35 A mercury salve, though toxic, was the best-known treatment for syphilis.

36 The American-owned brig *Owhyhee* reached Juan de Fuca Strait on 15 May 1827 and was at the mouth of the Columbia River from 29 May to 14 June before it left for San Francisco (Howay 1933:324-9). McMillan was on board and was told by the mate that the captain, a man named Dominie, gave twice as much for furs as did the company and that six other American vessels were on the coast (Rich 1941:45-6).

37 According to Ross Cox, each clerk in the North West Company had to learn how to bleed (Stewart and Stewart 1957:357).

38 This was an indication of mercury poisoning. The dose was usually reduced at this point, but mercury cream would continue to be applied in the hope that the symptoms of the disease would disappear (Hunter 1810:500-55; a copy of this book was at Fort Vancouver).

39 An all-salmon diet lacked vitamin C. The men were probably suffering from scurvy; once potatoes were available, the men became healthy. By 1827 a great deal was known about remedies for scurvy and Europeans often depended on the Natives to supply cures. But the Native women in the fort who were from the Columbia District were away from their traditional food sources, and the fort people were still very fearful of their neighbours. Dr. John Naish (personal communication) suggests that a low caloric intake would also cause weakness.

40 McMillan sent two letters to McLoughlin. The letter dated 14 September was sent via the *Cadboro,* and the 15 September letter went with Scanewah. Both letters were received and are in HBCA (McMillan 1827a, 1827b).

41 For a discussion of these terms see Suttles 1987:137-51.

42 Barnston left the measurements blank in the post journal, probably intending to fill them in later; but in copying the journals he left the blanks again, perhaps because he was ill and chose not to make an effort to ascertain the dimensions.

43 McDonald was at Fort George when Governor Simpson arrived on 7 November 1824 and immediately dispatched the McMillan expedition to the Fraser. When McDonald was sent to take charge of the post at Thompson's River (Kamloops) in January 1826, plans to establish the post on the Fraser that year were still in place.

44 According to Mrs. Agnes Thorne, Shashia's eldest son was named after him. Suttles (personal communication) has pointed out that if two men shared the name, it would not have been used by both men at the same time. The son, it should be noted, predeceased his father.

45 Although Europeans had ceased to display heads on pikes, they were within living memory of the Napoleonic Wars, which witnessed a barbarity that makes Native savagery pale by comparison.

46 Many anecdotal accounts describe slavery among the Natives. For one example, see Dennis 1930. For a more analytical discussion, see Suttles, "The Ethnographic Significance of the Fort Langley Journals," pp. 205-6.

47 Five sailors from the *Cadboro* were sent for creek water on the eastern shore of Vancouver Island opposite Point Marshall at the north end of Texada Island. A group of six or seven Natives attacked them, killing Edward Driver and wounding Peter Calder (A. Simpson 1827b:19-19d; Rich 1941: 53-4).

48 The skins would have been dusted by beating them with sticks to dislodge dirt and dust.

49 All Saints' Day, a Christian holy day to honour all saints, known and unknown, was kept in fur trade country to satisfy the Canadien employees.

50 For biographies, see Binns 1967; Cline 1974; and Williams 1975:193; 1985:660-3.

51 They had probably built a "stick chimney," which was made by laying sticks crosswise and cementing the frame with clay or mud. The river cuts through clay banks at the site of the old fort.

52 This is the last reference to Abraham Vincent in the Fort Langley Journals. He was not replaced. The complement of men dropped from twenty-one to twenty. His name appears on a list of men at Fort Colville on 18 April 1828 who were going out with the express (HBCA B.45/z/1).

53 Collar wire was used to make snares, principally to catch birds.

54 Probably they were given a noggin of rum.

55 Christmas Day was usually observed very quietly at the forts, possibly reflecting the Calvinist influence of the Scotsmen who were often in charge.

56 Hogmanay, or New Year's Eve, is a time of celebration in Scotland. The Scottish influence, the fact that little work was necessary in the dead of winter, and the fact that the contracts were usually renewed at this time made New Year's Day the most important holiday in fur trade society.

57 Louis Ossin was born in Sorrel in Lower Canada about 1800. He joined the North West Company in 1820 and was employed by the Hudson's Bay Company at York Factory in the Athabasca District and at Fort Alexandria, New Caledonia, in 1825-6. From 1830 to 1836 his name appears as a trapper from Fort Vancouver. In 1841 he became a settler and a free trapper. See Rich 1955:241-3.

58 Etienne Pepin from Yamaska was still at Fort Langley in 1850. Jason Allard recalled him to be a farm overseer in 1858 (Nelson 1927:21). He is also listed on outfits in 1858-9 (HBCA B.226/g/5:13d-14 and B.226/g/6:10d-11). A biography is to found in Morton 1988 (1):263.

59 Until the eighteenth century, wood charcoal was the chief fuel used for blacksmithing and metalworking. A dome-shaped mound, or "pit," of logs was built around a wooden chimney. The mound was sealed with leaves, earth, or turf, and the chimney was filled with kindling, which was ignited. With a limited supply of air, the volatile part of the wood burned away, leaving the carbon. This charcoal, when burned, produced the high temperature needed to work iron and provided a substitute for coal at the forts. In a description of this process at Spokane in 1825, John Work referred to the construction of a "pit or furnace." Alder was used and the burning took fifteen days (Work 1825-6:116-32).

60 This refers to the exploratory trip of 1824. Work mentions elk in the Salmon River Valley (Work 1824:219), and McMillan's report mentions red deer (Merk 1968:248).

61 The spring express delivered reports and mail to headquarters. The furs were sent later in the spring or in early summer.

62 This rumour proved to be true: "It is with deep sorrow I have to inform you that Mr. Alexr McKenzie, Antoine Perrault, Chartier, Tarrhonga and Baptiste Boiseau were murdered on January last by the Clallam Tribe inhabiting Hood's Canal" (McLoughlin 1828b:34d). There was also a Chinook woman in the party who was held captive. See note 18 in the introduction to this volume, and Appendix A in this volume.

63 Probably Joseph Cornoyer, Jean Bte. Dubois, Jean Baptiste Ettue, Dominque Faron, Anawiskum McDonald, Simon Plamondon, and Pierre Charles.

64 "Packet" was a term used to describe a mail boat. The mail sent out undoubtedly included this journal, now in the Hudson's Bay Archives, and McMillan's report to the governor and council (McMillan 1828a).

JOURNAL KEPT BY
JAMES MCMILLAN AND ARCHIBALD MCDONALD, 1828-9

1 According to Diane Payment, this child was the Helene McMillan listed in Sprague and Fry 1983: table 1. Her birthdate was given as 1810, and she married a Métis named Baptiste Boyer. Her mother was Marie Letendre, probably a relative of Jean Baptiste Letendre, who travelled with David Thompson, as did James McMillan.

2 Van Kirk (1980:183) suggests that James McMillan did not sever his ties with Kilakotah until 1829, but according to Munnick (1969a:194), she became the wife of Louis Labonte only two or three years after his son from a previous country marriage was born in 1818. McMillan had been at Spokane before he left on his furlough of 1823-4. It seems likely that he "turned over" Kilakotah and her daughters, Helen Matthews and Victoria McMillan, to Labonte at that time. When Fort Colvile was established in 1826, Spokane was abandoned. Labonte brought his family to Fort Vancouver, and it was there that Barnston met and took Helen as his country wife. Victoria's first husband was Joseph McLoughlin, son of the chief factor.

3 James McMillan's father, Allan, and his father's cousin, Archibald MacMillan, brought a large group of emigrants from Lochaber to Upper Canada in 1802. The headstone in the churchyard of St. Andrew's, Williamstown, erected to the memory of Allan MacMillan, shows his date of death to be 5 January 1823; he was seventy-one years old. The headstone was erected by a son, John, and two daughters, Margaret and Helen.

4 St. Andrew's Church, Archives of Ontario, Ms 107:279. According to Heather Devine (1994:96), these were also children of Marie Letendre. It is possible that he left them with his relatives in Upper Canada. Allan was later employed by the Hudson's Bay Company, according to information obtained by Hugh MacMillan.

5 In a letter to John McLeod written from Fort Langley in January 1828, James McMillan expressed his gratitude, particularly to Charlotte, for "having my two little girls in care what to me is very dear" (McMillan 1828b:102).

6 In his retirement, James McMillan owned Alexandria House on the outskirts of Perth, in the parish of Tibbermore. Two more sons were born, which increased his white family to eight children. He wrote to George Simpson, "My only ambition is to see them well educated which in this Land of taxes is no joke" (McMillan 1843:119).

7 Williams 1975:183. According to Hugh MacMillan, the family had a tutor, an indication that no school existed in the remote Glen Pean Valley.

8 The quality of each Hudson's Bay Company blanket was indicated by small dark marks woven into the edge. Each mark, or "point," represented the value of one beaver pelt.

9 This treatment must surely have further harmed Scanewah's prestige and left him very vulnerable.

10 Until Manson returned, the people at the fort knew nothing more about the Clallam massacre than the rumours they heard from the Indians.

11   The furs gathered during the year – stretched, dried, and packed in bales – had to be sent to Fort Vancouver for shipment to London. Instead of sending a brigade, the furs were sent on the *Cadboro*, probably because of the danger of attack.

12   This word is difficult to decipher, but is probably "prog," which means food obtained by foraging; but it could be "prey," which, according to Leechman, means a portion of food or ration.

13   This letter, dated 10 May 1828, was handed to Thomas Dears on 22 June 1828, while he was on the punitive expedition against the Clallam. Although Scanewah was killed, the letter passed from tribe to tribe until it was delivered (Ermatinger 1828; Dye 1907:20).

14   Probably Francis A. Champagne, listed as a steersman in 1833 (HBCA A.15/29:26). It is difficult to identify Jacques, since the name is so common.

15   First reference to Pierre Therrien. He probably came to Fort Langley with Manson in exchange for Jean Baptiste Dubois, who was sent to Fort Nez Percés and drowned there on 17 July 1828 (HBCA B.223/d/19:7). Therrien was shot to death accidently when the *Cadboro* fired a salute on leaving the fort (McDonald 1930-1:6d). The ammunition was a wad of hard rope yarn (McDonald 1831a).

16   This may have been the same technique Daniel Harmon reported using to take sturgeon weighing about 400 pounds in nets at Fort Fraser in 1815 (Lamb 1957:181), though on 23 May 1812 they had not been able to take a 250-pound sturgeon (McLeod 1971:106). See Suttles, "The Ethnographic Significance of the Fort Langley Journals," pp. 182-3.

17   This letter has not been located.

18   It is impossible to be certain about the identity of this child. Baker, Bouchard, Cornoyer, Ettue, Perrault, and Sauve, all at Fort Langley when the child was born, were sent to Fort Vancouver. Though some of their children were later christened, there is no record of a Louis Langley. Louis Satakarata, described by George Barnston as Iroquois, was the only man still at Fort Langley in 1830 who had sons, which makes it quite possible that he was the father. It seems that McMillan used the term "whites" to describe company employees, evidently a common practice. John Tod, writing to Edward Ermatinger, told of the fever at Fort Vancouver "which carried off upwards of 300 Indians – most of the whites were attacked with it also, but none have died, excepting an Iroquois" (Tod 1831:19). All the women in the fort were, of course, Native.

19   "The smoke or fire bag with flint and steel, and usually a pipe and space for tobacco, was indispensable to every one, as life might depend on ability to start a fire" (Sproat 1954:134). Charles Wilkes, writing in 1842, described the "tobacco and fire pouch" as a bag "generally made of red or blue cloth, prettily worked with beads ... and it has usually several long tails to it, which are worked with silk of gaudy colours" (Wilkes 1845[4]:370).

20   The *Cadboro* had come directly to Fort Langley from a punitive expedition against the Clallam.

21   James Birnie, a Scot, joined the North West Company in 1818, worked for the Hudson's Bay Company until 1846, and settled at Cathlamet, Washington, where he died in 1864. See Fleming 1940:428-9 and Williams 1975:202.

22   There is little doubt that the major topic of conversation would be the action against the Clallam.

23   Shamans possessed special powers. "The Doctor" had probably proven that he had the ability to cure sickness. See Suttles, "The Ethnographic Significance of the Fort Langley Journals," p. 191.

24 Wilson Duff (1952:26) did not believe that the Squamish would be wintering in Burrard Inlet in 1828-9. He suggested that James McMillan did not know the geography of the country, which was new to him. When McMillan led the 1824 expedition from Fort George to the lower Fraser, he had Vancouver's chart with him, and was thus able to place the mouth of the Fraser, which Vancouver had missed, between Point Roberts and Point Grey (G. Simpson 1825:142d). In 1827 the founding expedition also used Vancouver's map (see note 17 to the 1827-8 journal in this volume). McMillan would have known the location of Burrard Inlet on a map, but there is no evidence that he explored it. Duff also suggested that McMillan was mistaken because he could not have communicated with the Natives. Randy Bouchard and Dorothy Kennedy (personal communication) believe that McMillan's statement is accurate not only for the above reasons, but because, according to George Simpson (1825:142), McMillan was able to communicate directly with the Natives he met in the winter of 1824. He described their language has having "some affinity to that spoken by the Picahouse tribe in the vicinity of Okanagan," where McMillan had spent considerable time. For a very different opinion about the ability of the traders to communicate with the Natives and a discussion of the same piece of evidence, see Suttles, "The Ethnographic Significance of the Fort Langley Journals," pp. 164, 173, 257-8.

25 Probably refers to the killing of two or three Kamloops horses by Babiard (McLeod 1971:35-6). The event was reported to have occurred on 30 September, so the news reached Fort Langley very quickly.

26 Pitch or resin was heated and used to fill the cracks in boats and canoes. Frequently a piece of heated charcoal was used to keep the resin molten as the cracks were filled.

27 The voyageurs heralded their approach by singing paddling songs.

28 Dr. Hamlyn was employed by the Hudson's Bay Company in 1824 and served in the Red River settlement, but in 1828 he was sent to the Columbia District, where he remained until 1830. For a biography, see Rich 1939:250-2.

29 James Murray Yale joined the Hudson's Bay Company in 1815, serving at various posts. After the amalgamation he was sent to New Caledonia, where he remained until 1827. After serving as a clerk under Archibald McDonald, he was put in charge of Fort Langley when McDonald left. He remained there until 1859, when he retired to Victoria. For a biography, see Rich 1938:473-4; Lamb 1972:719-20; and Williams 1975:230.

30 The Simpson expedition arrived with twenty-seven men and left for Fort Vancouver with thirty. Three men – Louis Delenais, Charles Charpentier, and Etienne Onaise – were left at Fort Langley, and six men from there – James Baker, Oliver Bouchard, Joseph Cornoyer, Jean Baptiste Ettue, Jacques Pierrault, and Laurent Sauvé, went to Fort Vancouver and appear on the Fort Vancouver list of servants for outfit 1828, leaving Fort Langley with seventeen men (HBCA B.223/d/19:1d).

31 A gun salute usually marked such a departure.

32 According to Daniel Harmon, "drinking and fighting" was the usual way of holidaying among Canadiens in the trade. "I would rather fifty drunken Indians in the fort, that five drunken Canadiens" (Lamb 1957:65).

33 Archibald McDonald provides a description of the fort in the last entry in McLeod 1971:38-9.

> The Fort is 135 feet by 120, with two good bastions, and a gallery of four feet wide all round. A building ___ feet long, of three compartments for

the men, a small log house of two compartments, in which the gentlemen themselves now reside, and a store of about ___ feet are now occupied, besides which there are two other buildings, one a good dwelling house, with an excellent cellar and a spacious garret, a couple of well finished chimnies [chimneys] are up, and the whole inside now ready for wainscoting and partitioning, four large windows in front, one in each end, and one with a corresponding door in the back. The other is a low building with only two square rooms and a fire place in each, and a kitchen adjoining made of slab. The out door work consists of three fields, each planted with thirty bushels of potatoes, and look well. The provision shed, exclusive of table stores, is furnished with three thousand dried salmon, sixteen tierces salted ditto, thirty-six cwt. flour, two cwt. grease, and thirty bushels salt.

34 This is an indication that James McMillan had been much less strict about allowing women into the fort than McDonald was to be. There is no record that country marriages were arranged for the single men at Fort Langley until after McDonald took charge. For three days in November 1828, less than two months after his arrival, he established a firm pattern. On 26 November he appears open to negotiating marriage; on 27 November he refused "an impudent application" by one of the men whose reason for leaving the fort was obvious; and on 28 November he sent Whitlakenum packing, along with "women for the accommodation of the Fort." His treatment of Delannais (see entries for 1 and 2 January 1829 in these journals) must finally have made clear that no dalliance was to be allowed, but country marriages with Native women would be arranged (see Maclachlan, "Introduction" to this volume).There is no record of any slaves becoming wives. Even the Hawaiians, Como and Peopeoh, at the bottom of the increasingly rigid fur trade hierarchy, took wives who strengthened the fort's trade ties (see journal entry for 7 March 1829 in this volume). What McDonald was outlawing was prostitution.

35 Although telegraphy was first invented in France by Claude Chappe in 1794, it was not widely used until about the mid-nineteenth century, after the development of the Morse code. McDonald was obviously using the earlier meaning of telegraph, "to signal."

36 Previously called the Lillooet, this river was named for Benjamin Harrison, a member of the Hudson's Bay Company committee, by the Simpson expedition of 1828 (Fleming 1940:40). For a biography of Harrison, see Fleming 1940:252–3.

37 Sumas Lake was a large, shallow body of water and was drained in the 1920s.

38 The small cannon, or "wall pieces," were mounted on swivels.

39 During the winter months the Natives would hold dancing parties, during which some people would enter a trancelike state and perform dances or sing songs that had been acquired through a guardian spirit. These spirit dances have continued to the present, although their function has changed over the years. See Duff 1964: 107; Amoss 1978, for a more recent study; and Suttles, "The Ethnographic Significance of the Fort Langley Journals," p. 191.

40 "At Christmas and New Year they are served out with flour to make cakes or puddings, each man receives half a pint of rum. This they call a *regale*, and they are particularly grateful for it" (Stewart and Stewart 1957:354).

41 Candles and tallow to make candles appear on supply orders at Vancouver, but no lanterns appear on any of the inventories that have survived. The lights provided for this dance may have been torches made at the fort.

42 John McLoughlin later noted that Delannais' wages had not been confiscated and indicated that they should not be (Barker 1948:7-8).

43 Pieces of timber bent naturally or two pieces joined to fit at an angle and used to secure parts of a ship together.

44 Homer Barnett assumed that the potlatch was a "comparatively late development reinforced by an inflationary economy resulting from white contact" (1955:253). See also Suttles, "The Ethnographic Significance of the Fort Langley Journals," pp. 192-3.

Journal Kept by Archibald McDonald, 1829-30

1 McDonald wrote to John McLoughlin on this date with the intention of sending the letter via the Okanagan. This letter, or a copy of it, was sent on 22 March 1829 with the Yale expedition (McDonald 1829a:29).

2 This is confirmation that the original were stick chimneys. See note 51 of Journal, 1827–8, in this volume.

3 Copies of the letters to the governor and council dated 11 March 1829 and letters to McLoughlin, one dated 20 February and another dated 11 March were copied into the new journal (HBCA B.113/a/3:30).

4 According to Delbert McBride (personal communication), Plamondon's wife was the daughter of Scanewah. This child must be Sophie, who was baptized on 7 June 1842 and married the same day to Michael Cotnoir. Her age was given as twelve years and three months (Munnick 1979), but this must be an error, for in McDonald's report of 1830 Plamondon was reported to be the father of one girl. These records show two other Plamondon children born to the Cowlitz wife. Therese, aged six years, and Marie Anne, aged four and a half years, were baptized on 16 December 1842. McBride is descended from Marie Anne.

5 McDonald's decision to allow some of the single men to marry and bring local women into the fort probably led to the disputes. The wives of Yale, Therrien, Ossin, Delannais, and Como, newly introduced, may have been resented by the wives already in the fort. In the report of 1830, Annance, Plamondon, Dominque Faron, Faniant, and Louis Satakarata were all listed as fathers and so probably brought wives to Fort Langley. The eleventh would have been the wife of John Kennedy.

6 This dispatch, dated 22 March 1829, is in HBCA D.4/122:38-39. It is also copied into the journal (HBCA B.113/a/3:31d-32d), and is, in effect, a copy of the journal entry for 21 March.

7 During the winter months the men have been able to venture some distance from the fort, but once the Natives begin arriving in great numbers for the fishing, the traders will stay closer to home. The stones are required to replace clay chimneys, but suitable ones were not to be found close to the fort.

8 Governor Simpson was still at Fort Vancouver and sent the letter from there.

9 The two Boston vessels were the *Convoy* and the *Owhyhee*. See Barker 1948:91 and Howay 1933:324-9.

10 St. Vincent was a Cowlitz chief. He accompanied the McLeod expedition as an assistant interpreter (Dye 1907:19).

11 McDonald was aware of Simpson's intention to extend farming operations in order to make the posts self-sufficient. Further exploration (see journal entry for 19 April 1829 in this volume) made McDonald aware of the advantages of the large prairie but also of the dangers in working so far from the fort. In 1834, when the fort people felt more secure, a large farm was established in the Salmon River Valley. After the old fort burned down, the new fort at the mouth of the Salmon river replaced it in 1840. Agriculture at the forts supplied the posts, and a surplus for export enabled Simpson to offer to supply the Russian posts with much-needed provisions – something American maritime traders had not done consistently. The treaty with the Russians gave the Hudson's Bay Company greater control over the Northwest Coast.

12 Coming down the Fraser River on 10 October 1828, the Simpson party reached the present site of Hope at 10 o'clock (McLeod 1971:38). The Chilliwack people, who inhabited the area around Chilliwack Lake and its headwaters, used the trails to reach the Fraser River (Wells 1987:217).

13 Given the difficulties the traders had in understanding Native languages (see Suttles, "The Ethnographic Significance of the Fort Langley Journals," pp. 164, 257-8), it is hard to believe that the Natives understood the oration. It may have been designed for headquarters as much as for the local audience.

14 The chinook, or spring, salmon arrive in the Fraser River in April and May. They are usually large fish, but these four may have been jacks or chinook, which mature early and return to spawn after a much shorter period than usual. See Suttles, "The Ethnographic Significance of the Fort Langley Journals," pp. 179-80.

15 "Home-guard" was a term used in the fur trade for the Natives close to the fort who became intermediaries in the trade. By attempting to contact and deal directly with as many groups as possible, McDonald tried, usually unsuccessfully, to subvert the efforts of both the Kwantlen and the Cowichan to retain control of the trade.

16 The *Convoy* and the *Owhyhee* did not leave until July 1830. The *Owhyhee* was the vessel trading in the sound at this time (Howay 1934:10-21).

17 McDonald's use of the term *chevreuille* to describe the young of an elk confirms this use of the term. See note 8 to the 1827-8 journal in this volume.

18 Etienne Oniazie was an Iroquois with the North West Company in the Columbia District. He deserted from the McKenzie party in 1819 but was on the books at Fort George in 1823, and he was on the McMillan expedition to the Fraser in 1824.

19 Annance was listed as the father of three boys in the report McDonald sent in February 1830. One son was born on 23 December 1826 (McDonald 1826:13d), and one of the three was drowned (Annance 1832).

20 The *William and Ann* was shipwrecked entering the Columbia River in March 1829; the crew and cargo were lost.

21 McDonald's wife, Jane, was on board the *Cadboro*. She brought with her McDonald's eldest son, Ranald, nearly five years old, and her own children, Angus, almost three years old, and eighteen-month-old Archibald (Cole 1979:152).

22 Two hundred skins in each of nine deal boxes and a pack of one hundred, making 1,900 skins (McDonald 1829-30:32d).

23 The letter to John McLoughlin outlining these proposals was sent out with the *Cadboro*. It is to be found in McDonald's letter book. Amable Arquoitte and Louis Boisvert were the two men who left (McDonald 1829-30:31d-32d).

24 Shashia may have been attempting to repair or maintain his alliance with the Lekwiltok.

25 McDonald has obviously acquired some knowledge of the purposes and function of the potlatch. It may be that this was easier for him to obtain because he had allowed the single men to take local women as wives and thus become attached to the fort.

26 Traders *en derouine* went to drum up business and collect debts.

27 *Oncorhynchus gorbuscha*, the pink, or humpback, salmon, spawns every second year. It still appears in the Fraser River in years ending in odd numbers. See Suttles, "The Ethnographic Significance of the Fort Langley Journals," p. 180.

28 Probably refers to Douglas-fir, which belongs to the pine family.

29 HBCA D.4/123:17. The letter was not sent at this time, but was taken to Fort Vancouver by McDonald himself. See entry for 23 October 1829 in this volume.

30 At this time of year, the river would have been full of salmon that died after spawning.

31 See note 24, Journal, 1828-9, in this volume. Since McDonald did not make this statement in the post journal, he probably got the information from reading McMillan's entry. We have no way of knowing if he confirmed it independently.

32 McDonald is probably referring to coho salmon (*Oncorhynchus kisutch*). Sockeye (*O. nerka*) and pink (*O. gorbuscha*) salmon appear in the river during the summer, and chum, or dog (*O. keta*), and coho arrive in the fall. See Suttles, "The Ethnographic Significance of the Fort Langley Journals," pp. 179-80.

33 In this letter, dated 14 November 1829, McDonald proposed arrangements to conform with the directions from Simpson. A copy is in his letter book (McDonald 1830-1:33-4).

34 The *Vancouver*, a sixty-ton schooner, was built at Fort Vancouver in 1827 (Barker 1948:112).

35 To appreciate the significance of McDonald's feat in persuading the men that he needed to renew their contracts, see McMillan 1828a.

36 Hoops were made from hazel and small vine maple, according to Mrs. Amy Cooper (Wells 1987:134).

JOURNAL KEPT BY ARCHIBALD MCDONALD, FEBRUARY-JULY 1830

1 Reproduced in Barker 1948:70-1.

2 McDonald 1830-1:1-3.

3 Joseph Klyne was Jane McDonald's nephew.

4 This child, named Eliza, the eldest of James Murray Yale's three daughters, predeceased him.

5 Anderson Lake and Seton Lake: A.C. Anderson named these lakes after himself and a relative, Colonel Seton, who was drowned when the troopship *Birkenhead* was sunk.

6 The Lillooet River and Lillooet Lake.

7 The Birkenhead River: On Captain Richard's map of 1859, the Birkenhead is shown as the Scaalux River.

8 For more information about Lolo (also known as Jean Baptiste, Leolo, and St. Paul) see Brown and Lamb 1939:115-27, which includes a picture of Captain St. Paul and his wife and two daughters.

9 This comment may provide insight into the economics of the fur trade (see Suttles, "The Ethnographic Significance of the Fort Langley Journals," p. 209, but it may also reflect the "feeling" of a fond father. McDonald had three small sons and his wife, Jane, was pregnant with Alexander, born on 8 October 1830 (Jean Cole, personal communication).

10 McDonald believed that John Kennedy died from inflammation of the lungs. This was frequently a diagnosis for tuberculosis in Victorian times. It is also possible that Kennedy suffered a heart attack.

11 The migratory birds had left.

12 Captain Thompson of the *Convoy* entered the Columbia on 24 February 1830 and traded in opposition to the Hudson's Bay Company throughout the spring (McLoughlin 1830a:31).

13 Jean Baptiste Ouvre joined the Hudson's Bay Company as a *millieux* from Montreal in 1813.

14 In Chinook Jargon, *pichak* means "bad."

15 McDonald 1830-1:3-3d. Como, Charpentier, Aniwaskin McDonald, Plamondon, Ossin, and Peopeoh were the men sent. Yale was told in written instructions from McDonald that "Should men be scarce at the depot Plamondon, Charpentier & Ossin can be left."

16 On 2 May 1830 the brig *Isabella*, under the command of Captain William Ryan, was wrecked while trying to enter the Columbia River.

17 The *Eagle* was built in England in 1824 and purchased for the Columbia trade in 1827 (see Rich 1941:55).

LETTER BOOK AND OTHER NOTES KEPT BY ARCHIBALD MCDONALD, 1830-1

1 McDonald copied this extract (dated August-September) from the journal for 1830-1 into his letter book.

2 McDonald 1830-1:7. William Ryan was retained by the Hudson's Bay Company in 1829 and was put in charge of the brig *Isabella*. The ship was wrecked at the mouth of the Columbia River. Ryan was demoted, but after several years of service he redeemed himself and was put in charge of the *Cadboro*. He retired in 1836. For a biography, see Rich 1941:355.

3 McDonald 1830-1:7d.

4 On 8 June 1830, Tolmie reported that an expedition led by Archibald McDonald from Fort Nisqually to Hood's Canal was accompanied by Shallicum, "a chief of some note & well disposed towards the whites." Shallicum, though not the murderer, possessed McKenzie's double-barrelled gun (Tolmie 1963:201).

5 McDonald 1830-1:7d.

6 McDonald's rationalizing discounts the knowledge he had that the Owhyhee, Maniso, had been subject to fits. It also ignores the information that Shashia had given him, which proved to be reliable. He was aware that company policy demanded good relations with the Native peoples. It is also true that the mischievous rumours must have carried great weight, but perhaps a more significant fact was his recollection that A.R. McLeod's reputation had been severely damaged because he was perceived as timid in taking punitive action against the Clallam. This appears to be the most logical explanation for McDonald's determination to attack the Nanaimo village even though he had no positive proof that Maniso had been murdered, and even though he realized what

terrible consequences could have followed. The notes McDonald wrote to Ryan, and the written instructions he provided to both Annance and Yale, suggest a mounting excitement and the development of a "war hysteria." This is not surprising, considering the claustrophobic atmosphere at the fort and its reduced work force, situated in the midst of a huge population of Natives.

The Ethnographic Significance of the Fort Langley Journals

1 I would like to thank Robert Boyd, Yvonne Hajda, Barbara Lane, Morag Maclachlan, and Shirley Suttles for making many useful suggestions and correcting many errors. Remaining errors are, of course, mine.

2 Horatio Hale, philologist with the U.S. Exploring Expedition, which visited the Oregon country in 1841, commented on the "extraordinary harshness" of the sounds of the languages of the Northwest Coast. The Chinook language was so difficult for Europeans to learn that after more than thirty years of "close intercourse" that the traders and settlers had maintained with the Natives, only one white man had ever become fluent in their language. This was a member of Astor's first expedition who had been nursed by the Natives during a long illness and "chose to occupy himself in acquiring a knowledge of their tongue, and by so doing obtained no little celebrity among both foreigners and Indians." Hale suggested that the "extreme difficulty" of learning the Native language was one reason for the rise of Chinook Jargon (Hale 1846:533, 562).

Other jargons or pidgins may have developed at other forts. In his report on the exploring expedition of 1824, James McMillan wrote that the Natives on the Fraser "speak a language that has such an affinity to that of the Piscahouse [Wenatchee] Tribe or Okinagan, that I was enabled to maintain a conversation with them" (Merk 1968:249). What McMillan used may have been a pidgin Wenatchee or Okanagan. Halkómelem is indeed related to the languages of the Wenatchee and the Okanagan, but the relationship is at least as distant as that between English and Swedish (M. Dale Kinkade, personal communication). Unless there was a Wenatchee or Okanagan speaker present, the conversation would have necessarily been restricted to the relatively few words with recognizable cognate forms. Two entries in the Fort Langley Journals suggest limited understanding of the Natives. First, there is a reference to "our imperfect Knowledge of the language" (22 March 1828). The context suggests that this may refer to communication with the Pilalt, who are later said (9 April 1828) to speak a different language from the Kwantlen. But in fact, the Pilalt and Kwantlen spoke dialects of the same language that differ in accent about like North American and Australian English, and a fluent speaker should have been able to accommodate to this. Second, when a party of Lillooet came to the fort, the traders got little information from them because they could not understand them (15 May 1828). But Lillooet is in fact much closer to Wenatchee and Okanagan than Halkomelem is, and thus McMillan should have been able to communicate with these visitors as well as he had done with the Kwantlen in 1824.

Chinook Jargon rather than the local Lushootseed was certainly used at Fort Nisqually, where on 25 June 1833 William Fraser Tolmie wrote in his journal (Tolmie 1963:210): "Have begun making a vocabulary of the Chenooke gibberish, by which we communicate with the indians – it is a vile compound of English, French, American & the Chenooke dialect." A bit later Tolmie began collecting a Lushootseed vocabulary, commenting "it is much more copious & also more guttural that the Gibberish" (1963:213). On another occasion (1963:221–2), after trying to explain the Creation and the Deluge and finding the Natives were not following, he wrote: "The Chinook is such a miserable medium of communication, that very few ideas can be expressed in it."

3 Quimby (1948) documents the presence of Asian, Pacific Islanders, and Africans on the outer coast during the first decade of the maritime fur trade.

4 The term "tribe" is used here simply because it is the term used in the journals and still commonly used and understood for these groups. It is not intended to imply any particular kind of organization.

5 Company officers give two sets of figures, one compiled by McDonald in 1830 and another by James Yale at Fort Langley in 1838 (dated 1 January 1839). McDonald gives an estimate of 3,250 men for the Coast Salish of the whole region including the Strait of Georgia, Juan de Fuca Strait, Puget Sound, and the lower Fraser (plus 160 for the Lillooet and 750 for the lower Thompson). We do not know whether "men" means all adult males or simply heads of families. Assuming that it means the former and adult males constituted one fourth of the population, we might estimate the total Coast Salish population of this region as around 13,000 (or 16,640, if we include the Lillooet and lower Thompson). But if we assume that "men" means family heads and use a ratio derived from Yale's figures, we get a total of 21,073. Moreover, McDonald's list seems to omit some tribes, and thus either total could be too low. However, his figures are round numbers and clearly rough estimates based on his own observations and the judgments of Native people he thought reliable, and there are serious differences between his figures and those of the Yale census.

Yale's census covers the same region as McDonald's, excluding the Clallam on Juan de Fuca Strait and the Puget Sound tribes south of the Skagit. It lists the heads of families, followed by number of wives, sons, daughters, and "followers" (presumably slaves), as well as canoes and guns, giving a total of 1,269 family heads and a total population of 9,427 (averaging 7.42 persons per family) for the region covered. Again, some tribes that we know existed at the time are omitted. Possibly they are subsumed within larger tribes, but possibly they were missed. Moreover, some individuals seem misidentified as to tribe. For example, the Lummi chief Sawhumkun, whom McKenzie and Scouler met in 1825, is listed as a Skagit, and his name is followed in the Skagit list by that of his son Chowitsut, who was identified as "head chief" of the Lummi in the treaty with the United States negotiated in 1855. Such apparent errors may simply reflect the method by which the data were collected; perhaps the two Lummi men had arrived at the fort with a party of Skagits and had been counted with them.

The most glaring discrepancy between McDonald's and Yale's figures is in the Upriver Halkomelem area. McDonald gives a total of 1,420 men for this area, a huge number compared with his 300 for the Island Halkomelem tribes and 170 for the Downriver tribes. McDonald himself was surprised at the size of the population upriver but asserted that it came from reliable sources. Harris (1994) accepts these figures as evidence of the richness of the Fraser Canyon. The canyon was indeed rich when the salmon were running, which is why people from as far away as Vancouver Island went there. But Yale's estimate of 1,401 for the total population of the Upriver Halkomelem is less than McDonald's 1,420 for the number of men. There is no evidence of any disaster that might have reduced the upriver population so greatly in the years between McDonald's estimates and Yale's head count. Yale's totals of 1,779 for the Island Halkomelem and 529 for the Downriver Halkomelem seem, at least proportionally, more in keeping with what I would expect, and I am therefore strongly inclined not to take McDonald's figures seriously.

6 In fact, the journals usually use "Cowichan" in its restricted sense. But extensions of name persisted into the twentieth century to refer to all of the speakers of Halkomelem (Boas 1887, 1894; Curtis 1913:32) or to all of the Coast Salish of British Columbia (Goddard 1934).

7 John Work reported (Elliott 1912:222) that four canoes of the "Cahotitt" tribe met the party as they were going downriver. He does not say where the meeting occurred but says, "This village was at some distance up a river which falls into the bay." In his description of the party's descent of the river he mentions two bays, one identified by his editor, T.C. Elliott, as the mouth of Pitt River, the other as the channel in front of New Westminster. Aemilius Simpson's 1827 chart of the Fraser (see Map 2) from the mouth to a point above McMillan Island shows only the Cowichan and Nanaimo villages, suggesting that the Kwantlen had no village on that stretch of the Fraser itself.

8 The site of the first fort was evidently called snák̉ʷəməł (Hill-Tout in Maud 1978:3:68; Duff 1952:27), from which snək̉ʷəmáłəł, the Semiahmoo name (hence the English) for the Nicomekl River, is derived. Hill-Tout gave as the name of the tribe what appears to be a plural of the name of the village; however, in the 1940s my Semiahmoo–Lummi consultant, Julius Charles, and in the 1950s my Katzie source, Simon Pierre (Suttles 1955:12), identified this tribe with a name that may be anglicized "Snókomish." This name must be the source of "Snugumish," which McKelvie (1991:52) implies is the Native name for the site of the first fort. There were also at least three small groups on the north bank of the Fraser above the site of the fort, at Whonnock, Stave River, and Hatzic, that were earlier or later absorbed by the Kwantlen.

9 It is likely that the Tsawwassen village at English Bluff had been abandoned at this time, to be reoccupied a generation or so later (Bouchard and Kennedy 1991). The Coquitlam were identified by Boas and by Hill-Tout as a small group subordinate to the Kwantlen. Information collected at Musqueam indicates that some Musqueams moved into Coquitlam territory in the late nineteenth century. The Burrard people, whose territory included the upper end of Burrard Inlet, reportedly once spoke Halkomelem but later, because of their small numbers and intermarriage, adopted the Squamish language.

10 The Chilliwack, Pilalt, and Tait are the tribes described by Duff under the heading "Upper Stalo." The use of "Stalo" (the "a" is pronounced as in "father"), from Upriver Halkomelem stá·ləw "river," as a collective term for the tribes of the Fraser Valley, seems to be relatively recent. In the orthography adopted by the Coqualeetza Education Training Centre it is spelled "Stó:lō," which (since the first "o" is as the "a" in "father") is still pronounced "Stalo."

11 In official usage since the 1870s, "Cowichan" has been used to refer to the people of the villages on the Cowichan River and Cowichan Bay only, while those of Stuart Channel have been designated "Chemainus."

12 There are no terms in the Native languages for cardinal directions. Terms for the northern end of the Strait of Georgia and for Puget Sound mean roughly "north" and "south," respectively, if the speaker is somewhere near the southern end of the Strait of Georgia. But the basic directional terms refer simply to water: "toward the shore," "away from the shore," "upstream," "downstream," "seaward," "landward," "this side (of the water)," "that side (of the water),"

and so on. This must have created problems when Natives and Europeans tried to communicate about geography.

13 Barnston's identification of Semiahmoo home territory, Boundary Bay (which he called "Birch Bay" on 4 October 1827), as "Sanch Bay" on 24 July 1827, suggests that the Semiahmoo were considered a part of the Saanich. They are listed as a separate tribe in McDonald's census of 1830 (as "Summuamus") and in James Yale's census of 1839 (as "Sinayamie" at "Birch Bay," with relationships with the Kwantlen and Lummi). However, in an undated census in the papers of James Douglas (1878) they are listed as the "Semiama," a division of the "Sanetch." The name of the Saanich chief who used the Salmon River also suggests this link. "Chaheinook" is probably čəx̌ínəqʷ, a name borne early in this century by a Saanich man at Patricia Bay. The name was said to have been Semiahmoo, given to him by his Semiahmoo mother.

14 The journalists knew the Lummi by name. McKenzie met a party of "Lummies" on Lummi Island in the summer of 1825, and journal entries mention "Holumma [Lummi] Country" (13 February 1828) and "the Osaak [Nooksack] or Whullumy [Lummi] river" (5 February 1830). However, in December 1828 it was simply "Two Indians from the neighbourhood of Bellingham's Bay" who came to trade and attend a "feast & dance" given by the Kwantlens (20 December 1828). These two were most likely Lummi, but because in some charts then in use "Bellingham Bay" included Samish Bay, the two may possibly have been Samish, the Northern Straits-speaking tribe south of the Lummi, or even Nuwhaha (also called "Upper Samish"), a Lushootseed-speaking tribe on the Samish River and Lake Whatcom.

15 The complex history of Lekwiltok expansion has been traced by Mauzé 1992 and Galois 1994:223-35).

16 The "Chinook" that appears in the journals is a variant spelling of the name of the Saanich chief "Chaheinook."

17 See Harper 1971, fig. 194 (p. 260) for a watercolour done while there, and fig. 192 (p. 259) for an oil painting, a composite done later from the watercolour and sketches. Kane's oils may contain elements from different places and are less reliable than his watercolours and sketches.

18 In the past the term "long-house" or "longhouse" for the Northwest Coast plank house was used by only a few writers on the Coast Salish (perhaps only Hill-Tout and Duff), but I do not believe it was used by the Native people until around the 1960s, when it and the term "elder" seem to have spread rapidly throughout the region, with the result that even the Haida, whose traditional plank houses are roughly square, have adopted the term "longhouse."

19 Another reason for seasonal movement was comfort. In early June 1830, mosquitoes were such a plague that the Natives had "mostly abandoned the vicinity either for the Falls or Sea Shore" (3 July 1830).

20 According to Duff's (1952:62) Upper Stalo sources, the main run of chinooks appeared after the middle of July and lasted through August and early September. Kew (1996, fig. 2) shows chinook present from February through November.

21 One of Duff's (1952:66) Upper Stalo sources said that formerly only "spring" (chinook) salmon were dried for food, implying that sockeyes were used only for oil; however, the huge quantities of dried and fresh fish, presumably sockeyes, brought down from "the fisheries" argues against this.

22 I use the term "chief" here for the men so designated in the journal. This usage does not imply that these men had the authority ascribed to chiefs in other

regions. See Miller and Boxberger 1994 for a critique of a recent reinterpretation of Puget Sound leaders as heads of "chiefdoms."

23 James Douglas visited the Cowichans on the Cowichan River in 1852, and reported: "They live in several villages, each having a distinct chief, or headman, who cannot be said to rule the community which acknowledges his supremacy, as there is no code of laws, nor do the chiefs possess the power or means of maintaining a regular government; but their personal influence is nevertheless very great with their followers" (1854:216).

24 For a summary of interpretations of the potlatch and sources, see Suttles and Jonaitis (1990:84-6).

25 Barnett (1955:68) suggested that the summer gathering on Lulu Island may have been partly motivated by the desire to trade. But if this had been a major activity there, it seems more likely that the journalists would have commented on it.

26 There are terms in the Native languages for "buy," "sell," "price," and so on. The term for "buy" has cognates in geographically separated Salish languages and must be old (Suttles, n.d.).

27 Codere (1950:89-97) concluded from the Kwakiutl family histories recorded by George Hunt that the Kwakiutl did not use Hudson's Bay Company blankets in potlatches until after Fort Rupert was established in 1849. If Codere's conclusion is correct, it would mean that the Coast Salish were nearly two decades ahead of the Kwakiutl in potlatching with trade blankets. But with all the traders on the coast, it seems very unlikely that the Kwakiutl were not getting trade blankets before 1849.

28 Drucker (1939) suggested that during the maritime fur trade on the outer coast the power of the traditional chiefs was weakened by the fact that lower-ranking men could acquire wealth and potlatch, something they could not have done earlier. However, Collins (1950) found that during the period of land-based fur trade in the Coast Salish region, the new means of acquiring wealth allowed Skagit leaders to achieve greater power, strengthening class distinctions. Collins is probably right for the Coast Salish, whose "chiefs" did not have as much control of resources as those of the outer coast. This is one of the questions discussed by Wike (1958).

29 James Point, a Musqueam born in 1881, recalled trapping with his father-in-law in the early years of this century. They trapped in the same area, only every other winter, and left enough beaver to ensure the survival of the population.

APPENDIX A: THE CLALLAM MASSACRES

1 One version is in Curtis (1913:24) and another is in Lambert (1972: 13-8). The accounts differ in detail, but both attribute the murders to insults and abuse suffered by Clallam guides at the hands of white men.

2 One of these journals is in BCA and a copy in a different hand is in HBCA (Ermatinger 1828). The BCA journal was published in the *Washington Historical Quarterly* (Dye 1907) and in McDonald (1980).

3 McLoughlin wished to send the 193-ton brig *Eagle*, which was on its first trip to the Columbia District. However, the captain demurred, so the 70-ton *Cadboro* was sent instead (Rich 1941:58).

4 Ermatinger was reluctant to comply and stated that Governor Simpson had a copy (Ermatinger 1830a:46d). Forced to defend himself, Ermatinger wrote to

Simpson contradicting some of Laframboise's information (Ermatinger 1830:102d).

5 A. Simpson 1828:11-11d. Aemilius Simpson's account, though more objective than Ermatinger's, reflects his disapproval of McLeod's hesitancy.

References

Amoss, Pamela. 1978. *Coast Salish Spirit Dancing*. Seattle and London: University of Washington Press

Anderson, A.C. 1878. History of the Northwest Coast. BCA M/B/27

Annance, Francis N. 1824-5. A journal of a voyage from Fort George (Columbia River) to Fraser River in the winter of 1824 and 1825. HBCA B.76/a:1-9d. See also Thompson 1991

– 1832. Annance to Yale, 13 October, Yale Family. BCA Add Mss 182, Vol. 2, Folder 2, Letter 17

Auger, Leonard A. 1959. St. Francis through 200 years. *Vermont History* 27(3):287-304

Bancroft, Hubert Howe. 1884. *History of the Northwest Coast, 1800-1846*. San Francisco: A.L. Bancroft

Barker, Burt Brown, ed. 1948. *Letters of Dr. John McLoughlin Written at Fort Vancouver, 1829-1832*. Portland, OR: Binfords & Mort

– 1959. *The McLoughlin Empire and Its Rulers*. Glendale, CA: Arthur H. Clark

Barman, Jean. 1995. New land, new lives: Hawaiian settlement in B.C. *Hawaiian Journal of History* 29:1-32

Barnett, Homer G. 1938. The nature of the potlatch. *American Anthropologist* 40:349-58

– 1955. *The Coast Salish of British Columbia*. Eugene: University of Oregon Press

Barnston, George. 1827-8. Fort Langley journal. HBCA B.113/a/1

– 1829. Letter to James Hargrave, March 22. NAC MG19 A21 Series 1:158

Barnston, George, James McMillan, and Archibald McDonald. 1827-30. Fort Langley journal. BCA A/B/20/L2

Barry, J. Wilson. 1933. Astorians who became permanent settlers. *Washington Historical Quarterly* 24(4):284-6

Binns, Archie. 1967. *Peter Skene Ogden: Fur Trader*. Portland, OR: Binfords & Mort

Blakey Smith, Dorothy. 1987. Aemilius Simpson. In *Dictionary of Canadian Biography* 6:720-1. Toronto: University of Toronto Press

Boas, Franz. 1887. Zur Ethnologie Britisch-Kolumbiens. *Petermanns Geographische Mitteilungen* 33(59):129-33. Gotha, Germany

– 1894. Indian tribes of the Lower Fraser River. In *64th Report of the British Association for the Advancement of Science for 1890*, 454-63. London

Bouchard, Randy, and Dorothy Kennedy. 1991. *Tsawwassen Ethnography and Ethnohistory*. Victoria: B.C. Indian Language Project. Also appearing as Sect. 6 of

Archaeological Investigations at Tsawwassen, B.C. Vol. 1. Coquitlam, BC: Arcas Consulting Archaeologists

Bowsfield, Hartwell, ed. 1979. *Fort Victoria Letters, 1846-51.* Vol. 31. Winnipeg: Hudson's Bay Record Society

Boyd, Robert T. 1990. Demographic history, 1774-1874. In *Handbook of North American Indians.* Vol. 7, Northwest Coast, 135-48. Washington: Smithsonian Institution

– 1994. Smallpox in the Pacific Northwest: The first epidemics. *B.C. Studies* 101:5-40

Brown, George, and W. Kaye Lamb. 1939. Captain St. Paul of Kamloops. *British Columbia Historical Quarterly* 3(2):115-26

Brown, Jennifer S.H. 1980. *Strangers in Blood: Fur Trade Company Families in Indian Country.* Vancouver: UBC Press

Brown, Jennifer, and Sylvia Van Kirk. 1982. George Barnston. In *Dictionary of Canadian Biography* 11:52-3. Toronto: University of Toronto Press

Brown, Robert. 1870. The last of the chiefs. *All the Year Round* (12 March):345-7

Carl, G. Clifford, W.A. Clemens, and C.C. Lindsey. 1959. *The Fresh-water Fishes of British Columbia.* Handbook No. 5. Victoria: Royal British Columbia Museum

Carlson, Roy L. 1994. Trade and exchange in prehistoric British Columbia. In *Prehistoric Exchange Systems in North America,* ed. T.G. Baugh and J.E. Ericson, 307-61. New York: Plenum Press

Charland, Thomas-M., O.P. 1964. *Les Abenakjs d'Odanak, 1675-1870.* Montreal: Les éditions du Levrier

Clark, R.C. 1934. Hawaiians in early Oregon. *Oregon Historical Quarterly* 35(1):22-31

Cline, Gloria G. 1974. *Peter Skene Ogden and the Hudson's Bay Company.* Norman: University of Oklahoma Press

Codere, Helen. 1950. Fighting with property: A study of Kwakiutl potlatching and warfare, 1792-1930. In *Monograms of the American Ethnological Society* 18. New York: J.J. Augustin

Cole, Jean Murray. 1979. *Exile in the Wilderness: The Life of Chief Factor Archibald McDonald, 1790-1853.* Don Mills, ON: Burns and MacEachern; Seattle: University of Washington Press

– 1985. Archibald McDonald. *Dictionary of Canadian Biography* 8:526-8. Toronto: University of Toronto Press

Collins, June M. 1950. Growth of class distinctions and political authority among the Skagit Indians during the contact period. *American Anthropologist* 52:331-42

Conn, Richard T. 1960. The Iroquois in the west. *The Pacific Northwesterner* 4(4):59-63

Connolly v. Woolrich. 1867. *Lower Canadian Jurist.* Vol. 11. Montreal: John Lovell

Coues, Elliott, ed. 1965. *New Light on the Early History of the Greater Northwest: The Manuscript Journals of Alexander Henry and of David Thompson, 1799-1814.* Minneapolis: Ross and Haines

Cryer, B.M. N.d. *Indian Legends.* Vol. 2. BCA F82/C88.1

Cullen, Mary K. 1979. *The History of Fort Langley, 1827-96.* Canadian Historic Sites: Occasional Papers in Archaeology and History No. 20. Ottawa: Parks Canada

– 1980. Outfitting New Caledonia, 1821-58. In *Old Trails and New Directions: Papers of the Third North American Fur Trade Conference,* ed. Carol M. Judd and Arthur J. Ray, 231-51. Toronto: University of Toronto Press

Curtis, Edward S. 1913. *The North American Indian.* Vol. 9. Norwood, MA: Plimpton Press

Davies, John. 1980. *Douglas of the Forests.* Seattle: University of Washington Press

Davies, K.G., ed. 1961. *Peter Skene Ogden's Snake Country Journal, 1826-7*. London: Hudson's Bay Record Society 23

Day, Gordon M. 1981. *The Identity of the Saint Francis Indians*. Canadian Ethnology Service Paper No. 71. Mercury Series. Ottawa: National Museum of Man

Dee, H.D. 1943. An Irishman in the fur trade: The life and journals of John Work. *British Columbia Historical Quarterly* 7(4):229-70

Dennis, Elsie F. 1930. Indian slavery in the Pacific Northwest. *Oregon Historical Quarterly* 31(1):69-81; (2):181-95; (3):285-90

Devine, Heather. 1994. The Indian-Metis connection: James McMillan and his descendants. In *The Lochaber Emigrants to Glengarry*, ed. Rae Fleming, 92-105. Toronto: Natural Heritage/Natural History

Donald, Leland, 1984. The slave trade on the Northwest Coast of North America. *Research in Economic Anthropology* 6:121-58

Douglas, David. 1904. Sketch of a journey to northwestern parts of the continent of North America during the years 1824-1825-1826-1827. *Oregon Historical Quarterly* 5(3):230-71 and 5(4):325-69

Douglas, James. 1852. Douglas to McKay, 20 September. Nanaimo Correspondence. BCA A/C/20.1/N15

– 1853. Douglas to McKay, 20 May. Nanaimo Correspondence. BCA A/C/20.1/N15

– 1854. Report of a canoe expedition along the east coast of Vancouver Island. *Journal of the Royal Geographical Society* 24:245-9

– 1878. Census of the Indian Population of the N.W. Coast. Transcription by Ivan Petrov. In Private Papers, 2d ser., Bancroft Library, University of California, Berkeley

Douglas, Jesse S. 1942. Matthews' adventures on the Columbia. *Oregon Historical Quarterly* 4(2):105-48

Drucker, Philip. 1939. Rank, wealth, and kinship in Northwest Coast society. *American Anthropologist* 41:55-64 (reprinted in McFeat 1966, 134-46)

Duff, Wilson. 1952. The Upper Stalo Indians of the Fraser Valley, British Columbia. In *Anthropology in British Columbia Memoirs* Vol. 1. Victoria: Provincial Museum

– 1964. The impact of the white man. In *The Indian History of British Columbia*. Vol. 1. In *Anthropology in British Columbia Memoirs* Vol. 5. Victoria: Provincial Museum

Duncan, Janice K. 1972. *Minority without a Champion: Kanakas on the Pacific Coast, 1788-1850*. Portland: Oregon Historical Society

Dunlop, George A., and C.P. Wilson. 1941. George Barnston. *The Beaver* (December):16-7

Dye, Eva Emery. 1907. Earliest expedition against Puget Sound Indians: Notes connected with the Clallam expedition kept by Francis Ermatinger. *Washington Historical Quarterly* 1(2):16-29

Elliott, T.C., ed. 1912. Journal of John Work. *Washington Historical Quarterly* 3 (October):198-228

Elmendorf, William W. 1993. *Twana Narratives*. Seattle, London, and Vancouver: University of Washington Press and UBC Press

Ermatinger, Francis. 1828. Notes connected with the Clallam expedition. HBCA D.4/123:8-15d and BCA A/B/20 V5A. See also Dye 1907 and L. McDonald 1980

– 1830a. Ermatinger to McLoughlin, 24 January. HBCA D.4/123:46d-47

– 1830b. Ermatinger to Simpson, 9 April. HBCA D.4/123:102d-104

Fisher, Robin. 1977. *Contact and Conflict: Indian-European Relations in British Columbia, 1774-1890*. Vancouver: UBC Press

– 1996. Fur trade and colonization, 1774-1871. In *The Pacific Province*, ed. Hugh J.M. Johnston, 47-67. Vancouver and Toronto: Douglas and McIntyre

Fleming, R. Harvey, ed. 1940. *Minutes of Council, Northern Department of Ruperts Land, 1821-31*. London: Champlain Society for the Hudson's Bay Record Society 3

Fogdall, Alberta Brooks. 1978. *Royal Family of the Columbia*. Fairfield, WA: Ye Galleon Press

Foster, John E. 1975. The Indian trader in the Hudson's Bay fur trade tradition. In *Proceedings of the 2d Congress, Canadian Ethnology Society* 2:571-85. Mercury Series Paper 28. Ottawa: National Museum of Man

Galbraith, John S. 1957. *The Hudson's Bay Company as an Imperial Factor, 1821-1869*. Berkeley: University of California Press

– 1976. *The Little Emperor: Governor Simpson of the Hudson's Bay Company*. Toronto: Macmillan

– 1985. Sir George Simpson. In *Dictionary of Canadian Biography* 8:812-9. Toronto: University of Toronto Press

Galois, Robert. 1994. *Kwakwaka'wakw Settlements, 1775-1920: A Geographical Analysis and Gazetteer*. Vancouver: UBC Press

Gibson, James R. 1985. *Farming the Frontier: The Agricultural Opening of the Oregon Country, 1786-1846*. Vancouver: UBC Press

– 1992. *Otter Skins, Boston Ships, and China Goods: The Maritime Fur Trade of the Northwest Coast, 1785-1841*. Montreal and Kingston: McGill-Queen's University Press

Glazebrook, G.P. de T., ed. 1938. *The Hargrave Correspondence, 1821-1843*. Toronto: Champlain Society

Goddard, Pliny Earle. 1934. *Indians of the Northwest Coast*. 2nd ed. Handbook Series 10. New York: American Museum of Natural History

Gough, Barry M. 1984. *Gunboat Frontier: British Maritime Authority and the Northwest Coast Indians, 1846-1890*. Vancouver: UBC Press

Gunther, Erna. 1972. *Indian Life on the Northwest Coast of North America as Seen by the Early Explorers and Fur Traders during the Last Decades of the Eighteenth Century*. Chicago: University of Chicago Press

Hafen, LeRoy R., ed. 1965-72. *The Mountain Men and the Fur Trade of the Far West*. 10 vols. Glendale, CA: Arthur H. Clark

Hale, Horatio. 1846. Ethnography and philology. In *United States Exploring Expedition during the Years 1838, 1839, 1840, 1841, 1842*. Vol. 6. Philadelphia: Lee and Blanchard (reprinted Ridgewood, NJ: Gregg Press 1968)

Harper, J. Russell, ed. 1971. *Paul Kane's Frontier, Including Wanderings of an Artist among the Indians of North America by Paul Kane*. Austen: University of Texas

Harris, Cole. 1994. Voices of disaster: Smallpox around the Strait of Georgia in 1782. *Ethnohistory* 41(4):591-626

Hart, J.L. 1973. *Pacific Fishes of Canada*. Bulletin 180. Ottawa: Fisheries Research Board of Canada

Hayman, John, ed. 1989. *Robert Brown and the Vancouver Island Exploring Expedition*. Vancouver: UBC Press

Holm, Bill. 1991. Historical Salish canoes. In *A Time of Gathering: Native Heritage in Washington State*, ed. Robin K. Wright, 238-47. Seattle: Burke Museum and University of Washington Press

Holmes, Kenneth L. 1971. John McLoughlin. In *The Mountain Men* 8:235-45. Glendale, CA: Arthur H. Clark

– 1972. Donald Manson. In *Dictionary of Canadian Biography* 10:495-6. Toronto: University of Toronto Press

Hopwood, Victor. 1973. David Thompson's canoes. In *Proceedings of the Seventh Annual Conference of the Association of Canadian Map Librarians* (28-30 June):44-52

– 1995. Notes on David Thompson's clinkerbuilt canoes. Unpublished paper presented at the Columbia Fur Trade Conference, 29 September-1 October

Howay, F.W. 1918. The dog's hair blankets of the Coast Salish. *Washington Historical Quarterly* 9 (2):83-92

– 1933. The brig *Owhyhee* in the Columbia, 1827. *Oregon Historical Quarterly* 34(4):324-29

– 1934. The brig *Owhyhee* in the Columbia, 1829-30. *Oregon Historical Quarterly* 35(1):10-21

HBCA. B76. Fort George Papers

– B.113. Fort Langley Papers

– B.223. Fort Vancouver Papers

– B.226. District Statements

– C.1. Log of the *Cadboro*

– D.e & D.5. G. Simpson correspondence inward

Humphreys, J.A. N.d. History of the Cowichan Indians as told by themselves. BCA F/3/H88

Hunter, John. 1810. *A Treatise on the Venereal Disease*, 3rd ed.

Jenness, Diamond. 1955. The faith of a Coast Salish Indian. In *Anthropology in British Columbia Memoirs*. Vol. 3. Victoria: Provincial Museum

Johnson, John. 1824. *Typographia*. London: Longman, Hurst, Rees, Orme, Brown & Green (republished London: Gregg Press in association with the Archive Press 1966)

Judd, Carol M. 1980. Native labour and social stratification in the Hudson's Bay Northern Department, 1770-1870. *Canadian Review of Sociology and Anthropology* 17(4):305-14

Kane, Paul. 1968. *Wanderings of an Artist Among the Indians of North America*. Edmonton: Hurtig (first published London: Longman, Brown, Green, Longmans and Roberts 1859; rev. ed. Toronto: Radisson Society of Canada 1925)

Karamanski, Theodore J. 1982. The Iroquois and the fur trade of the far West. *The Beaver* (Spring):5-13

Kennedy, Alexander. 1824-5. George Fort (Columbia River) Report. HBCA B.76/e/1:2d

Kew, Michael. 1992. Salmon availability, technology, and cultural adaptation in the Fraser River watershed. In *A Complex Culture of the British Columbia Plateau: Traditional Stl'átl'imx Resource Use*, ed. Brian Hayden, 177-221. Vancouver: UBC Press

Knight, Rolf. 1996. *Indians at Work: An Informal History of Native Indian Labour in British Columbia 1858-1930*. Vancouver: New Star Books

Koppel, Tom. 1995. *Kanaka: The Untold Story of Hawaiian Pioneers in British Columbia and the Pacific Northwest*. Vancouver and Toronto: Whitecap Books

Lamb, W. Kaye, ed. 1957. *Sixteen Years in the Indian Country: The Journal of Daniel Williams Harmon*. Toronto: Macmillan of Canada

– ed. 1960. *Simon Fraser: Letters and Journals, 1806-1808*. Toronto: Macmillan of Canada

– ed. 1969. *Journal of a Voyage to the Northwest Coast of North America during the Years 1811, 1812, 1813, and 1814 by Gabriel Franchere*. Toronto: Champlain Society

– James Murray Yale. 1972. *Dictionary of Canadian Biography* 10:719-20. Toronto: University of Toronto Press

– John McLoughlin. 1985. *Dictionary of Canadian Biography* 8:575-81. Toronto: University of Toronto Press

Lambert, Mary Ann. 1972. *Dungeness Massacre and Other Regional Tales*. Port Orchard, WA: Publisher's Printing

Landerholm, Carl, ed. 1956. *Notices & Voyages of the Famed Quebec Mission to the Pacific Northwest, 1838-1847*. Portland: Champeog Press for the Oregon Historical Society

Langemann, Gwyn, Gayel Horsfall, and William Quackenbush. 1983. Derby: A Report on the Archaeological Survey and Test Excavations at Fort Langley. Unpublished

Lavender, David. 1968. Thomas Mackay. In *The Mountain Men* 6:259-77. Glendale, CA: Arthur H. Clark

Leechman, Douglas. N.d. Glossary of Fur Trade Terms. Unpublished. BCA Add Mss 1290

Lewis, William S. 1918. Archibald McDonald. *Washington Historical Quarterly* 9(2):93

Lincoln, Leslie. 1991. *Coast Salish Canoes*. Seattle: Center for Wooden Boats

Lord, John Keast. 1866. *The Naturalist in Vancouver Island and British Columbia*. London: Bentley

McDonald, Archibald. 1826-7. Journal of Occurrences at Thompson's River. HBCA B.97/a/2

– 1828-9. Fort Langley Journal. HBCA B.113/a/2

– 1829a. McDonald to governor and council, 20 March. HBCA D.4/122:38-9

– 1829b. McDonald to McLoughlin, 14 November. HBCA D.4/233:28-8d

– 1829-30. Fort Langley Journal. HBCA B.113/a/3

– 1830. Report to Governor and Council, 25 February. HBCA D.1/123:66d-72

– 1830-1. Letter Book and Other Notes. HBCA B.113/b/1

– 1831a. McDonald to Ermatinger, 20 February. Edward Ermatinger Papers, 1828-56. BCA A/B/40/Er 62.4 (originals in NAC)

– 1831b. Report to Governor and Council, Northern Department. Fort Langley, 10 February. HBCA D.4/125:61d-63d

– 1907a. Beginning of Fraser River Fisheries. *Washington Historical Quarterly* 1(3):258-60

– 1907b. Beginning of Fort Simpson. *Washington Historical Quarterly* 1(3):264-6

McDonald, Lois, ed. 1980. *Fur Trade Letters of Francis Ermatinger*. Glendale, CA: A.H. Clark

McFeat, Tom, ed. 1966. *Indians of the North Pacific Coast*. Toronto: McClelland and Stewart (reprinted Seattle: University of Washington Press 1967)

McKay, Joseph. 1852a 18 Sept. Nanaimo Correspondence 1852-3. BCA A/C/20.1/N15

– 1852b 30 Sept. Nanaimo Correspondence 1852-3. BCA A/C/20.1/N15

– 1852c 22 Oct. Nanaimo Correspondence 1852-3. BCA A/C/20.1/N15

– 1855-7. Nanaimo Journal. BCA A/C/20.1/N15.2.

McKelvie, B.A. 1945. Jason Allard: Fur-trader, prince, and gentleman. *British Columbia Historical Quarterly* 4:243-57

– 1991. *Fort Langley: Birthplace of British Columbia*. Victoria: Porcepic Books

McKenzie, Alexander. 1825. Remarks on board the brig *William & Ann*, Henry Hanwell master from Fort George Columbia River to Observatory Inlet. 28th May 1825. HBCA B.223/a/1:2-39

Mackie, Richard Somerset. 1997. *Trading Beyond the Mountains: The British Fur Trade on the Pacific, 1793-1843*. Vancouver: UBC Press

Maclachlan, Morag. 1983. The founding of Fort Langley. In *The Company on the Coast*, ed. E. Blanche Norcross, 9-28. Nanaimo: Nanaimo Historical Society

– 1993. The case for Francis Annance. *The Beaver* 73(2):35-9

McLeod, Malcolm, ed. 1971. *Peace River: A Canoe Voyage from Hudson's Bay to the Pacific: Journal of the Late Chief Factor Archibald McDonald.* Edmonton: Hurtig (first published Ottawa: J. Durie 1872)

MacLeod, Margaret A., ed. 1947. *The Letters of Letitia Hargrave.* Toronto: Champlain Society 28

McLoughlin, John. 1827. McLoughlin to Simpson, 20 March. HBCA D.4/120

– 1828a. McLoughlin to Simpson, 20 March. HBCA D.5/3:162

– 1828b. McLoughlin to Simpson, 20 March. HBCA D.4/121:34d-35

– 1829a. McLoughlin to Governor and Council, 15 March. HBCA D.4/123:89-93

– 1829b. McLoughlin to Francis Ermatinger, 8 December. HBCA B.223/b/5

– 1830a. McLoughlin to Samuel Black, 24 February. HBCA B.223/b/5

– 1830b. McLoughlin to Simpson, 30 March. HBCA D.4/123:89-93

McMillan, James. 1821. Will. HBCA A.36:10

– 1824. Extract from Mr. chief trader MacMillan's report of his voyage and survey from the Columbia to Frazer's River. London. British Public Records Office FO5/208:161-62 (published in Merk 1968:248-50)

– 1827a. Letter to McLoughlin, 14 September. HBCA D.4/121:14-15d

– 1827b. Letter to McLoughlin, 15 September. HBCA D.4/121:16-17

– 1828a. Report to governor and council 15 February. HBCA D.4/121:23-4

– 1828b. Letter to John McLeod, 21 January. BCA A/B/40/M22K:102-5

– 1843. Letter to George Simpson, 24 February. HBCA D.5/8:119

McTaggart-Cowan, Ian. N.d. *The Mammals of British Columbia.* Handbook No. 11. Victoria: British Columbia Provincial Museum

Maranda, Lynn. 1984. *Coast Salish Gambling Games.* Canadian Ethnology Service Paper 93. Mercury Series. Ottawa: National Museum of Man

Maud, Ralph, ed. 1978. *The Salish People: The Local Contribution of Charles Hill-Tout.* Vancouver: Talon Books

Maurault, Joseph A. 1866. *Histoire des Abenakis depuis 1605 jusqu'a nos jours.* Sorel, PQ: A l'Atelier Typographie de la "Gazette de Sorel"

Mauzé, Marie. 1992. *Les fils de Wakai: Une histoire des Indiens Lekwiltoq.* Paris: Editions Recherche sur les Civilisations

Merk, Frederick, ed. 1968. *Fur Trade and Empire: George Simpson's Journal, 1824-25.* Rev. ed. Cambridge, MA: Harvard University Press

Miller, Bruce G., and Daniel L. Boxberger. 1994. Creating chiefdoms: The Puget Sound case. *Ethnohistory* 41(2):267-93

Mitchell, Donald. 1984. Predatory warfare, social status, and the North Pacific slave trade. *Ethnology* 23(1):39-48

Mitchell, Donald, and Leland Donald. 1985. Some economic aspects of Tlingit, Haida, and Tsimshian slavery. *Research in Economic Anthropology* 7:19-35

Mitchell, Elaine Allan. 1972. Sir George Simpson: The man of feeling. In *People and Pelts: Selected Papers: Second North American Fur Trade Conference,* ed. Malvina Bolus, 83-101. Winnipeg: Peguis Publishers

Moresby, John. 1909. *Two Admirals.* London: John Murray

Morton, Jamie. 1988. *Fort Langley: An Overview of the Operation of a Diversified H.B.C. post, 1848-1858, and the Physical Context in 1858.* Microfiche Report Series No. 340. Ottawa: Environment Canada

Munnick, Harriet. 1969a. Louis Labonte. In *The Mountain Men* 7:191-9. Glendale, CA: Arthur H. Clark

– 1969b. Donald Manson. In *The Mountain Men* 7:217-25. Glendale, CA: Arthur H. Clark

– 1971. The Ermatinger brothers. In *The Mountain Men* 8:156-73. Glendale, CA: Arthur H. Clark

– 1972. Simon Plamondon. In *The Mountain Men* 9:321-30. Glendale, CA: Arthur H. Clark

Munnick, Harriet, compiler, in collaboration with Mikell Warner. 1979. *Catholic Church Records of the Pacific Northwest: St. Paul, Oregon, 1839-1898.* Portland, OR: Binfords & Mort

Naughton, E. Momilani. 1983. Hawaiians in the fur trade: 1811-1875. MA thesis, Western Washington University

Nelson, Denys. 1927. *Fort Langley, 1827-1927.* Vancouver: Art, Historical and Scientific Association of Vancouver

Nicolls, M. 1988. Jane Klyne McDonald, 1810-1879. *British Columbia Historical News* 21(4):2-5

Nicks, Trudy. 1980. The Iroquois and the fur trade in western Canada. In *Old Trails and New Directions: Papers of the Third North American Fur Trade Conference*, ed. Carol M. Judd and Arthur J. Ray, 85-101. Toronto: University of Toronto Press

Nielson, Barry J. 1933. Astorians who became permanent settlers. *Washington Historical Quarterly* 24(4):282-301

Norcross, E. Blanche, ed. 1979. *Nanaimo Perspective.* Nanaimo: Nanaimo Historical Society

Nunis, Doyce B., Jr. 1968a. Michel Laframboise. In *The Mountain Men* 5:145-70. Glendale, CA: Arthur H. Clark

– 1968b. Alexander Roderick McLeod. In *The Mountain Men* 6:279-97. Glendale, CA: Arthur H. Clark

Pillsbury, Hobart. 1927. *New Hampshire: A History.* Vol. 4. New York: Lewis Historical Publishing

Plamondon, George Francis. 1961. The Plamondon family. *Cowlitz County Historical Quarterly* 3(3):1-28

Quimby, George I. Culture contact on the Northwest Coast, 1785-1795. *American Anthropologist* 50:247-55

Rathbun, Richard. 1900. A review of the fisheries in the contiguous waters of the state of Washington and British Columbia. In *Report of the Commissioner for the Year Ending June 30, 1899, U.S. Commission of Fish and Fisheries*, 251-350. Washington, DC: U.S. Government Printing Office

Ray, Arthur J. 1974. *Indians in the Fur Trade.* Toronto: University of Toronto Press

– 1996. *I Have Lived Here Since the World Began.* Toronto: Lester Publishing and Key Porter Books

Rich, E.E., ed. 1938. *George Simpson's Journal of Occurrences in the Athabaska Department and Report 1820-21.* Toronto: Champlain Society for the Hudson's Bay Record Society 1

– ed. 1939. *Simpson's 1828 Journey to the Columbia.* London: Champlain Society for the Hudson's Bay Record Society 10

– ed. 1941. *McLoughlin's Fort Vancouver Letters.* First Series 1825-38. Toronto: Champlain Society for the Hudson's Bay Record Society 4

– ed. 1955. *A Journal of a Voyage from Rocky Mountain Portage in the Peace River to the Sources of Finlays Branch and Northwestward in Summer 1824 by Samuel Black.* London: Hudson's Bay Record Society 18

– 1976. The fur traders: Their diet and drugs. *The Beaver* 307(1):42-53

Sampson, William R. 1976. John Work. In *Dictionary of Canadian Biography* 9:850-4. Toronto: University of Toronto Press

Scouler, John. 1905. John Scouler's journal of a voyage to N.W. America, F.G. Young, ed. *Oregon Historical Quarterly* 6(1):54-75, (2):159-205, (3):276-87

Simpson, Aemilius. 1827a. Log of the *Cadboro*. HBCA C.1/128

– 1827b. Letter to McLoughlin, November. HBCA D.4/121:19

– 1828. Account of the McLeod expedition to the Clallams 22 September. HBCA B.223/c/1:11-14

Simpson, George. 1825. Report from Fort George Columbia River, 10th March 1825. HBCA A.12/1

Spaulding, Kenneth A., ed. 1956. *The Fur Hunters of the Far West*. Norman: University of Oklahoma Press (first published London: Alexander Ross [the author], 1855)

Sprague, D.N., and R.P. Fry. 1983. *Genealogy of the First Metis Nation*. Winnipeg: Pemmican Publications

Sproat, Gilbert M. 1954. The career of a Scotchboy. E. Madge Wolfenden. *British Columbia Historical Quarterly* 19, nos. 3 and 4

Stewart, Edgar I., and Jane R. Stewart, eds. 1957. *Adventures on the Columbia River*. Norman: University of Oklahoma Press (first published New York: Ross Cox [the author], 1832)

Stewart, Hilary. 1977. *Indian Fishing*. Vancouver: J.J. Douglas

Suttles, Wayne. 1951. The economic life of the Coast Salish of Haro and Rosario Straits. PhD dissertation in anthropology, University of Washington (published 1974 in *Coast Salish and Western Washington Indians*. Vol. 1. New York: Garland Publishing)

– 1954. Post-contact culture change among the Lummi Indians. *British Columbia Historical Quarterly* 18(1-2):29-102

– 1955. Katzie ethnographic notes. In *Anthropology in British Columbia Memoirs*. Vol. 2. Victoria: Provincial Museum

– 1960. Affinal ties, subsistence, and prestige among the Coast Salish. *American Anthropologist* 62:296-305 (reprinted in Suttles 1987)

– 1963. The persistence of intervillage ties among the Coast Salish. *Ethnology* 2:512-25 (reprinted in Suttles 1987)

– 1987. *Coast Salish Essays*. Vancouver: Talon Books

– 1990. Central Coast Salish. In *Handbook of North American Indians*. Vol. 7, Northwest Coast, 453-75. Washington, DC: Smithsonian Institution

– N.d. Terms for economic processes in two Coast Salish languages. Manuscript in author's possession

Suttles, Wayne, and Aldona Jonaitis. 1990. History of research in ethnology. In *Handbook of North American Indians*. Vol. 7, Northwest Coast, 312-22. Washington, DC: Smithsonian Institution

Teit, James A. 1900. The Thompson Indians of British Columbia. *Memoirs of the American Museum of Natural History* 4(5):163-392

– 1906. The Lillooet Indians. *Memoirs of the American Museum of Natural History* 2(5):193-200

– 1930. The Salishan Tribes of the Western Plateaus. In *Bureau of American Ethnology, 45th Annual Report*, 1927-8. Washington, DC: Smithsonian Institution

Thomas, Gregory. 1985. James McMillan. *Dictionary of Canadian Biography* 8:583-4. Toronto: University of Toronto Press

Thompson, Laurence C., and M. Dale Kinkade. 1990. Languages. In *Handbook of North American Indians*. Vol. 7, Northwest Coast, 30-51. Washington, DC: Smithsonian Institution

Thompson, Nile. 1991. Opening the Pacific slope. *Cowlitz Historical Quarterly* 33(1):3-44

Tod, John. 1831. Tod to Ermatinger. Papers of Edward Ermatinger, 1826-43. BCA A/B/40/Er 62.3 (originals in NAC)

– 1842. Tod to Ermatinger. Papers of Edward Ermatinger, 1826-43. BCA A/B/40/Er 62.3 (originals in NAC)

Tolmie, W.F. 1963. *Physician and Fur Trader: The Journals of William Fraser Tolmie.* Vancouver: Mitchell Press

Van Kirk, Sylvia. 1980. *Many Tender Ties: Women in Fur Trade Society, 1670-1870.* Norman and London: University of Oklahoma Press

Wagner, Henry R. 1933. *Spanish Explorations in the Strait of Juan de Fuca.* Santa Ana, CA: Fine Arts Press

Wallin, Deborah. 1987. A very pretty man: The life of Simon Plamondon. MA thesis. Western Washington University, Bellingham

Wells, Oliver. 1987. *The Chilliwacks and Their Neighbors.* Ralph Maud, Brent Galloway, and Marie Weeden, eds. Vancouver: Talon Books

West, Oswald. 1942. Oregon's first white settlers on French Prairie. *Oregon Historical Quarterly* 43:198-209

Wike, Joyce. 1958. Problems in fur trade analysis: The Northwest Coast. *American Anthropologist* 60:1086-101

Wilkes, Charles. 1845. *Narrative of the United States Exploring Expedition, 1838-42.* Vols. 4 & 5. Philadelphia: Lea and Blanchard

Williams, Glyndwr, ed. 1975. *Hudson's Bay Miscellany, 1670-1870.* Winnipeg: Hudson's Bay Record Society 30

– 1985. Peter Skene Ogden. In *Dictionary of Canadian Biography* 8:660-3. Toronto: University of Toronto Press

– 1988. Alexander Roderick McLeod. In *Dictionary of Canadian Biography* 7:569-70. Toronto: University of Toronto Press

Work, John. 1824. Journal of a voyage from Fort George to the northward, winter 1824. BCA A/B/40/W89.2. See also Elliott 1912

– 1825-6. Journal, 21 June 1825 to 12 June 1826. BCA A/B/40/W89.4

– 1829. Work to Ermatinger, 28 March. Ermatinger Papers: Inward Correspondence, 1828-56. BCA A/B/40/Er 62.4 (originals in NAC)

Yale, James. 1839. Census of Indian population [from Fort Langley] crossing over to Vancouver's Island and coasting at about latitude 50' from there returning southward along the mainland and up Frasers River to Simpson Falls. HBCA B.223/2/1:30-53

INDEX

THE PIONEERS OF BRITISH COLUMBIA